KNITWEAR
design
WORKSHOP

KNITWEAR
design
WORKSHOP

A Comprehensive Guide to Handknits

SHIRLEY PADEN

INTERWEAVE.
interweavestore.com

Photographer, Joe Hancock (unless otherwise noted)
Photo stylist, Carol Beaver
Makeup, Cathy McKay
Art director, Liz Quan
Cover and interior designer, Anne Shannon
Production, Katherine Jackson

Interweave Press LLC
201 East Fourth Street
Loveland, CO 80537-5655 USA
interweavestore.com

Printed in China by Asia Pacific Offset Ltd.

Library of Congress Cataloging-in-Publication Data

Paden, Shirley.
    Knitwear design workshop : the comprehensive guide to handknits / Shirley Paden, author.
       p. cm.
    Includes bibliographical references and index.
    ISBN 978-1-59668-086-9 (hardcover with concealed wire-o)
    1. Knitting. 2. Women's clothing. 3. Clothing and dress measurements. I. Title.
TT825.P34 2009
746.43'2--dc22
                     2009010989

10 9 8 7 6 5 4 3 2 1

Acknowledgments

This book is dedicated *to my mother* whose words and wisdom will continue to guide and inspire me for the rest of my life.

AND

To my husband whose encouragement, support, devotion, and patience have made this project possible.

SPECIAL THANKS

to the following editors at Interweave:

Tricia Waddell for her wonderful support and direction throughout the project.

Ann Budd who worked ceaselessly on this project as she gently guided me through navigating the choppy waters of editing.

Thanks to the best project team I could ever have hoped for:

Diana Berardino and Suzanne K. Wakamoto (a.k.a. "the girl genius"). As project managers they figuratively roped themselves to me and climbed this project mountain at my side. Diana managed the first half and Suzanne the second. Theirs were the hands I could reach out and hold onto day or night throughout this book journey.

Joan Forgione who worked tirelessly to make certain that the first draft of the manuscript was correct and who was always available to lend a helping hand on any part of the project.

Mari Tobita who worked diligently as both the in-house technical editor and an invaluable member of the knitting team.

Rafael De Peña whose hard work and dedication to perfection in creating both the fashion and technical illustrations has brought a feeling of freshness and elegance to the book.

Karin Thomas and her unwavering artist's eye that she applied constantly as she worked diligently to make the charts and schematics both consistent in their appearance and visually appealing.

Alice Schwartz and Yvette Walton who came out of retirement to lend their expert knitting hands to an old friend.

Lisa Hoffman, Veronica Manno, and Michele Wang who worked so hard on perfecting and professionally finishing the knitting projects.

Megumi Hirai for her willingness to make so many of the swatches and to be the all around back-up hands for the project.

Diane Claster for the many hours spent on overflow typing.

FOREWORD

*"I shall be telling this with a sigh
somewhere ages and ages hence:
Two roads diverged in a wood, and I –
I took the one less traveled by,
and that has made all the difference."*

—Robert Frost

I am often asked why and how I selected hand-knitwear design as a profession. With tongue-in-cheek I begin the story of my adventure in a time-honored way. "A long time ago in a far-off land . . ." while working in the information technologies industry, a coworker asked me if I knew how to bind off. She had just learned to knit but had not learned what to do at the end. Even though I had not knit for years, I remembered. As I worked the bind-off, I experienced an epiphany that unbeknownst to me would change my life forever.

That evening, I visited a yarn shop and bought some yarn, needles, and a pattern book. Here I would like to say "and the rest is history," but I wasn't quite ready for "happily every after."

I began knitting every chance I got. Shortly thereafter, fate took the reins, and I fell ill. With major surgery imminent, I prepared for my hospital stay packing only my knitting needles as nonessentials. While in the hospital, my company was sold. Suddenly, I was unexpectedly unemployed.

There I stood at one of life's many crossroads (still hooked to the IV pole) free to "follow my own bliss." In the following weeks, I decided to take "the road less traveled" and become a knitwear designer. Let's examine that logic. I only knew how to knit and sort of purl and could barely follow a pattern without a visit to the yarn shop for help. To any astute observer, this was not my "calling." When I announced my future direction, most of my friends thought that my post-surgery drugs had not yet cleared my system. Nevertheless, spurred on by the thought of truly "following my own bliss" I picked up my knitting needles and measuring tape, took a "vow of poverty," and soldiered on undaunted by the reality that I did not have a clue as to how to proceed.

I was happy with my newfound freedom and had a burning desire to work in hand-knitwear design, but, I knew that I needed a clear, concise plan.

I laid out my business direction by asking myself several key questions that ended up forming my business plan. First, why do I want to make clothing out of string and two sticks when I could easily buy commercially knitted garments? The logic escaped everyone else; sometimes even me. I realized that what captivated me was the way handknitted clothing continues to survive and how it ignites a creative spirit in every culture on earth.

Now, how do I narrow my focus to a manageable few facets of handknitting? I have always been fascinated by clothing construction, therefore it was logical for me to focus on garments. I narrowed the stitch pattern options to lace, cables, and colorwork and organized them into the themes: Lovely in Lace, Covered in Cables, and Creative Colorwork. While very manageable, these categories were broad enough to allow lots of room for experimentation.

What type of garments should I focus on? I did not want to lock myself into a single category of garment. I decided on three categories: Country, which is primarily sweaters, Town & Country, which includes jackets, suits, dresses, etc., and Evening, which includes formalwear.

My final challenge was more philosophical: How do I both honor this antique art form and design clothing that reflects the time that I am living in? I decided on the "2T" approach for my designs—"trend with tradition." I would overlay very traditional stitch patterns onto trendy shapes. I had my business plan.

The next year I worked hard to learn as much about handknitted garment construction as possible. Finally, I designed and knit my first sample line. Customers would try on the samples and have their measurements taken for a custom fit. I would then knit the garments.

Every designer has a different approach, mine is architectural. Precise measurements are at the foundation. I begin with a picture or a sketch that conveys the "feeling" of the garment—elegant, casual, etc., then match it with a pattern stitch. I then transfer those ideas to a formal schematic. I use the schematic measurements to create the building blocks for the design construction.

Remember, a clothing designer is an artist. As Michelangelo explained that he could see David inside the block of marble, we see the garment in the ball of yarn. It is the same creative process. Enjoy the journey!

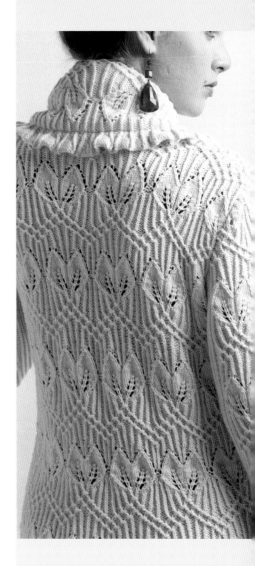

"Remember, a clothing designer is an artist."
—Shirley Paden

Table of Contents

INTRODUCTION

There are few more rewarding experiences in life than making, giving, or receiving a handknitted garment. These garments are worn with pride, diligently cared for, then passed down to succeeding generations as symbols of all that is good in humankind. Every handknitter has connected with this energy and, at the end of the garment-construction journey, has made something special and unique.

A review of what has been achieved in handknitting over the last millennium is no less than astounding. We find beautifully made brocade garments, beaded handbags, fine lace wedding veils, and shawls, all worn by the European aristocracy and royalty. We also find wonderfully textured Aran patterns and color knits that are artistic masterpieces. In fact, in the rich history of handknitting, we find the most unexpected range of seemingly infinite possibilities for self-expression.

This wonderful series of accomplishments notwithstanding, most knitters, no matter how experienced, will quite willingly volunteer that many of the finished garments they have spent countless hours making have turned out differently than they had anticipated. The most concentrated area of dissatisfaction is in garment fit. The root of this problem seems to be threefold. It begins with an insufficient understanding of commercial pattern instructions followed by a lack of attention to the details of making a meaningful gauge swatch. These two problems are compounded by a lack of knowledge about how to take proper body and/or garment measurements.

The purpose of this book is to explore the various techniques involved in designing handknited garments with a perfect individual fit. It is for handknitters at any level who want to free themselves of commercial patterns and design their own, from traditional garments to stunning works of wearable art. It is for those who want to experiment with garment shaping, those who want to write commercial patterns, and those who simply want to understand or make minor modifications to commercial patterns. The only prerequisites are to be able to add, subtract, multiply, and divide!

You will soon discover that garment design is far easier than you may have thought. The chapters in this book will take you step by step from an initial idea to taking measurements, selecting a pattern stitch, drawing a sketch and schematic, writing knitting instructions, and finishing a garment professionally. Sample step-by-step instructions are given for creating shapes for many silhouette possibilities.

HOW TO USE THIS BOOK

This book follows the approach of my design classes—teaching through example. This is not a theoretical design book, but rather one that explains the step-by-step process of using measurements, calculations, and schematics to create knitted designs. Chapters 1 and 2 discuss the planning process. Chapters 3 and 4 provide the foundation for the rest of the book; using pullover examples, I illustrate the basic design techniques and silhouettes that are used throughout the book. Chapters 5 through 11 explore different types of garments, design alternatives, and finishing techniques. Some of you will want to immediately jump to a specific chapter where your interest lies. I urge you to read Chapters 3 and 4 before doing so, as the other chapters are built upon the basic information discussed there.

Throughout the book, you will see the following headings:

> **Key Measurements** is a list of the important body measurements needed to construct the garment or garment piece discussed.
>
> **Conversion of Measurements to Numbers of Stitches and Rows** takes the key schematic measurements and translates them into the necessary numbers of stitches and rows.
>
> **Notes** provide assumptions that are used in a particular example.
>
> *For our sample garment* summarizes what has been detailed in the preceding steps and provides instructions as you would find in a formal written pattern.
>
> **Tip boxes** provide important information about the technique under discussion.

My objective is not to teach you how to be a professional designer. Instead, I want to help you acquire the skills necessary to design your own original knitwear with a perfect fit and a professional finish. I hope that you'll find stimulation for your creative abilities and the confidence to let your ideas take shape. Pick up your needles and create a masterpiece.

chapter one
Planning Your Design

RESEARCHING AND REFINING AN IDEA

Every design begins with an inspiring thought, whether fueled by a desire to satisfy a creative drive or in response to a favorite garment or other visual stimuli. There are innumerable reasons for wanting to design or replicate a garment, but the journey to a successful end begins with the same first step. That is, to carefully think about the item you plan to construct. What is its purpose—everyday wear, special occasion, gift? What do you want the design to convey— comfort, elegance, utility? What key elements are important to the look of your design—body shape and length, neck shape and depth ("V", round, square, boat, etc.), sleeve shape and length (bell or turn-back cuffs, short or full length, etc.), type of sleeve cap (raglan, set-in, dropped shoulder, etc.), and edgings, collar, buttons, and so on. Take the time to let your design ideas take shape. Draw sketches, visit your yarn shop, browse through books of stitch patterns, and envision your garment.

When you have a clear picture in your mind, you're ready to lay out a design profile. Fill out as much of the Design Profile Outline on page 13 as you can. (Photocopy this page and fill it out for every garment you make.) This will help you solidify your design ideas in preparation for generating knitting instructions.

DESIGN PROFILE OUTLINE

Designer Name

GARMENT DESCRIPTION

Designer Overall Objectives *(summarize the purpose the garment will serve for the wearer at its completion)*

Describe the feeling(s) to be projected through the garment *(use two to four adjectives)*

Type of garment *(cardigan, pullover, etc.)*

Projected wearer *(male, female, child, etc.)*

Yarn name, fiber content, and size

Needle size

Name and source of the stitch pattern

Finished dimensions of the gauge swatch *(including number of stitches and rows)*

CONSTRUCTION ELEMENTS:

Length *(cropped, waist, hip, knee, etc.)*

Structure/shape *(tapered, kimono, blouson, etc.)*

Sleeve/armhole type *(dropped, set-in, raglan, etc.)*

Sleeve length *(short, bracelet, wrist, thumb)*

Neckline type *("V", shawl, round, scooped, square, etc.)*

Other elements *(buttons, zipper, etc.)*

Special ornaments *(embroidery, crochet, beads, etc.)*

Other important elements or designer notes

There are five key garment silhouettes, but for now you need only determine the general properties—will the garment be cropped or long; boxy or hug the curves of the body? To a large extent, the garment shape will determine the fabric selection. For example, a thick yarn and a bulky stitch pattern worked in a silhouette that stops at the hips and follows the body curves may make you look heavier, something you may or may not want.

Next, return to the yarn shop to narrow down your yarn choices and choose the pattern stitches that are best suited for your garment silhouette. Consider the "3-Fs": form, fabric, and function. Simply put, the end use of the garment (function) must be taken into consideration when selecting the yarn/stitch pattern combination (fabric), and both function and fabric must be considered together with the shape of the garment (form). The 3-Fs will help steer you toward the practical, which is easily overlooked when creativity flows.

Test a few stitch patterns with a few different yarns so that you'll be able to select the combination that best conveys the "feeling"—sophisticated, trendy, sporty, conservative—that you want to achieve in your design.

LAYOUT OF THE DESIGN IDEA

You're now ready to generate a sketch of your idea, take measurements, knit a swatch of the fabric, make a chart of the stitch pattern, and draw a schematic.

Using a pencil, draw a full-page sketch of your design (place tracing paper over a photo if you're uncomfortable sketching freehand). Capture all of the design elements that appeal to you, such as an unusual cuff or neckline, an off-center front closure, collar, etc. Sketch, erase, and resketch until you're satisfied with the overall look.

Draw a sketch of your design idea.

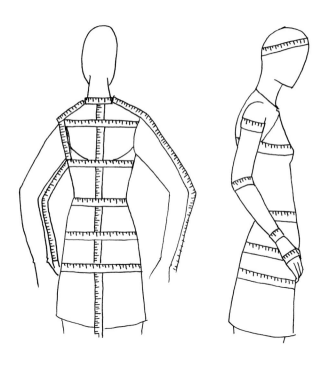

Accurate body measurements are key to a perfect fit.

TAKING MEASUREMENTS

In designing a knitted garment, there are two important sets of measurements—body measurements and finished garment measurements. Accurate body measurements are key to a well-fitting garment. You may also need to take measurements from a garment (called a "comfort" garment) that fits the way that you want your sweater to fit. Compare these measurements to the body measurements to determine the amount of ease—the difference between the garment measurements and the actual body measurements—that you want to add.

Body Measurements

You'll get the most accurate body measurements if you wear just your undergarments, a body suit, or a form-fitting tunic. Stand in front of a mirror to make sure you're standing straight and holding the tape measure in the correct place. Ideally, another person should take the measurements as you observe in the mirror. Measure all of the parts of the body listed in the Individual Measurements Worksheet on page 19. If you want to work to a general size instead of taking your own measurements, refer to the Standard Body Measurements Charts on pages 328 to 331.

Shoulder Width: Measure across the back between the shoulder bones, where a set-in sleeve seam would end. Round the shoulders so that the tops of the shoulder bones are easier to feel, then stand up straight with good posture and measure across the top of the back from the outside top of one shoulder bone to the other.

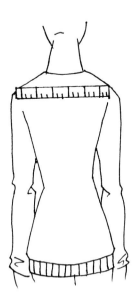

shoulder width

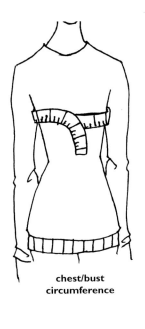

chest/bust circumference

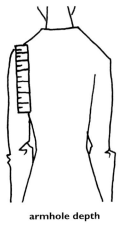

armhole depth

Chest/Bust Circumference: Measure around the fullest area. Standing erect, take a deep breath to fully expand your chest.

Armhole Depth: Measure in the back from the top of the shoulder bone to the underarm, then add ¹/₂" to 2" (1.3 to 5 cm) for ease at the underarm. The amount of extra length will depend on how snug you like your sleeves to fit against your underarm.

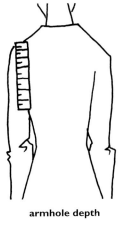

raglan depth

Raglan Depth: Measure in the back from 1" (2.5 cm) below the neck bone to the underarm. Add ¹/₂" to 2" (1.3 to 5 cm) depending on how snug you like a sleeve to fit against your underarm.

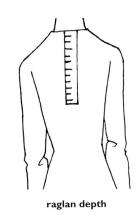

waist circumference

Waist Circumference: Measure around the narrowest area. Add ¹/₂" (1.3 cm) for ease.

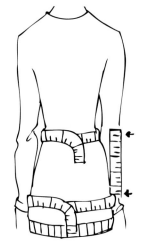

hip circumference

length from waist to hip

Hip Circumference: Measure around the fullest area. If your garment will stop before the fullest area, measure that part of your hip.

Length from Waist to Hip: Measure from the base of the waist indentation to the fullest area of the hip. The length used in commercial patterns is 5" to 7" (12.5 to 18 cm).

Neck Width: Measure the back of the neck only. Standing erect, slide both hands simultaneously along each side of your neck toward your shoulders until they stop at the indentation between the end of the neck and the beginning of the shoulder. The neck width is the point where the neck slope stops. Measure between where your hands stopped.

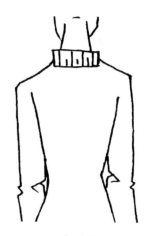

neck width

Back Neck Depth: Tie a string around your waist, making sure it follows a horizontal path. In back, measure from the base of the neck, 1" (2.5 cm) below the neck bone to the top of the string and note the length.

Front Neck Depth: Tie a string around your waist, making sure that it follows a horizontal path. In front, measure from the center of the clavicle to the top of the string and note the length. Subtract this number from the back neck depth to get the front neck depth for a high round neck shaping.

back neck depth

front neck depth

Body Length at Back: Measure from the top of the shoulder to the lower edge of the garment back. Measure from 1" (2.5 cm) below the base of the neck bone if you plan to include shoulder shaping. Note: Most sweaters end 3" to 5" (7.5 to 12.5 cm) below the waist; outer jackets end at the hips. Tie a string or second tape measure around the body where the garment will end, then measure to the string or to the top of the second tape measure.

Body Length at Front: Measure from the top of the shoulder to the lower edge of the garment front. This measurement will only be needed if the back and front will have different lengths.

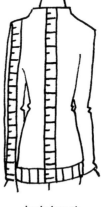

body length at back

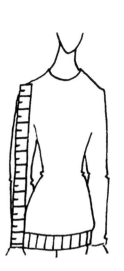

body length at front

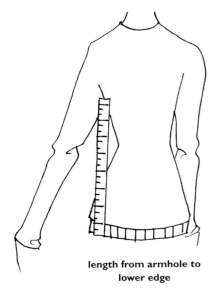

**length from armhole to
lower edge**

Length from Armhole to Lower Edge: Measure from
the underarm to the desired length. Subtract between
$1/2$" and 2" (1.3 and 5 cm) to allow for length ease in
the armhole. See armhole depth.

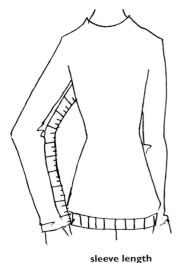

sleeve length

Sleeve Length: With the arm held away from the body
and slightly bent at the elbow, measure along the
inside of the arm from the underarm to the desired cuff
position at the wrist bone.

Upper Arm Width: Measure around the fullest
area in the middle of the upper arm. Let the
arm hang in a natural position.

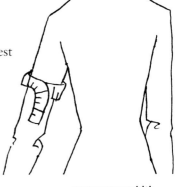

upper arm width

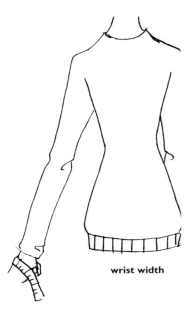

wrist width

Wrist or Base of Sleeve Width:
Measure around the arm where the
sleeve will end. To ensure that the cuff will pass over
the hand, tuck the thumb under and measure around the
hand at the thumb knuckle, just above the knuckles of the
four fingers.

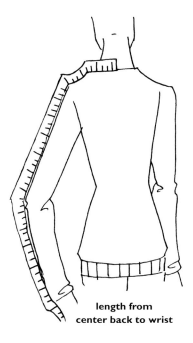

length from center back to wrist

Length from Center Back to Wrist:
(for dropped-shoulder garments, kimonos, dolmans, etc.) With the arm held out away from the body and the elbow slightly bent, measure from the base of the back neck bone, across the top of the shoulder, and down the outside of the arm to the wrist bone.

Name

Type of Garment

Date

	Body	Garment	Ease
Shoulder Width			
Chest/Bust			
Armhole Depth			
Raglan Depth			
Waist			
Hips			
Length from Waist-to-Hip			
Neck Width			
Front Neck Depth			
Back Neck Depth			
Body Length at Back			
Body Length at Front			
Length from Armhole to Lower Edge			
Sleeve Length			
Upper Arm Width			
Wrist/Base of Sleeve			
Length from Center Back to Wrist			
Other			

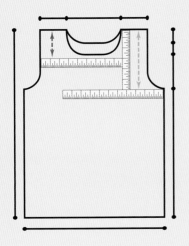
"Comfort" Garment Measurements

Your body measurements alone will be of little use since a garment made to those measurements would be tight and uncomfortable if you could, in fact, get into it. Therefore, you'll want to also take measurements from various garments that you feel comfortable wearing to determine the amount of ease that's comfortable for you. For the best results, measure a knitted garment that's made of a similar weight to the fabric you plan to knit and that fits the way you like. Be aware that a garment made with bulky or hairy yarn will have both an inside and an outside measurement. The outside of the garment will be puffier, thus wider. If you use the outside measurement of a bulky garment for a garment that you plan to knit out of fine yarn, your garment may end up a little looser than you expected. In this case, it would be better to use the inside measurement.

If you don't have a knitted garment to measure for fit, take measurements of a woven one. But because woven fabrics do not have the stretch of knitted fabrics, they are generally 1" to 2" (2.5 to 5 cm) larger than their knitted counterparts. Keep in mind that cable and twist-stitch patterns will make dense, narrow fabrics while openwork and lace patterns will make very stretchy fabrics. If you use the measurements of a dress made of a tightly woven fabric such as denim for a dress you plan to knit in a lace fabric, you'll have to allow for the differences in stretch. A knitted lace garment can match your body measurements more closely. Conversely, an unlined close-fitting stockinette-stitch dress will cling to the body's curves more than a close-fitting dress made of woven fabric. Typically, you'll want to add $1/2$" to 1" (1.3 to 2.5 cm) of ease to the knitted fabric to attain a similar drape to the woven dress.

 tip A knitted garment is constructed to fit the body as the fabric is knitted, rather than cut to shape. Therefore, if the fabric construction, size, or shape is incorrect, your only recourse is to ravel all or part of the garment, undoing many hours of work.

For now, all of your working numbers will be based on measurements taken from your selected garment(s). These will later be translated to numbers of stitches and rows based on your gauge swatch (more on that on page 63). Take your time and double check all measurements following the guidelines that follow. The measurements given are for a double-taper silhouette, which includes waist and bust shaping. Classic silhouettes are the same width from the lower edge to the armholes.

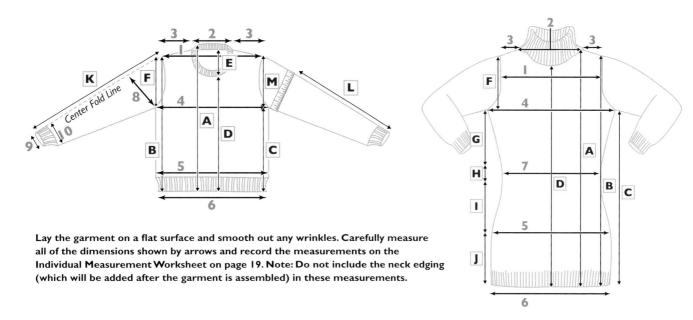

Lay the garment on a flat surface and smooth out any wrinkles. Carefully measure all of the dimensions shown by arrows and record the measurements on the Individual Measurement Worksheet on page 19. Note: Do not include the neck edging (which will be added after the garment is assembled) in these measurements.

WIDTH MEASUREMENTS

1. Cross-Back Width: Measure across the body from the top of one armhole to the top of the other (where shoulders are joined to the tops of sleeves).

2. Back Neck Width: Measure across the back of the neck between the outer edges of the neck that meet the inside edges of the shoulders. (Do not include the neck edging in this measurement.)

3. Shoulder Width: Measure straight across from the top of the sleeve seam (where the shoulders are joined to the top of the sleeves) to the outer edge of the neck. (Do not include the neck edging in this measurement.)

4. Chest/Bust Width: Measure across the widest area from underarm to underarm. (Multiply this number by two to get the circumference.)

5. Bottom Body (Hip) Width: Measure across the lower edge of the body. If the garment has ribbing that pulls in the bottom edge, stretch the ribbing by gently pulling outward at each edge until the piece lays flat. Have someone else hold it out for you or pin it at several places around the bottom in the stretched position. Measure straight across the bottom above any ribbing or edging. (Multiply this number by two to get the circumference.)

6. Bottom Ribbing Width: Stretch the ribbing as wide as necessary to give a tapered line (do not stretch to the fully expanded width) between the ribbing and the bottom body edge, then measure across. Release the ribbing to a totally relaxed state, then measure across. (Multiply each of these numbers by two to get the relaxed and expanded circumferences.)

7. Waist Width: Measure straight across the narrowest part of the waist. (Multiply this number by two to get the circumference.)

8. Upper Arm Width: Measure across the folded sleeve just below the underarm. Multiply this number by two.

9. Cuff Ribbing Width: Stretch the ribbing as wide as necessary to give a tapered line between the ribbing and bottom sleeve edge (do not stretch to the fully expanded width), then measure across. Release the ribbing to a totally relaxed state, then measure across. Multiply these numbers by two.

10. Wrist Width: Measure across the lower edge of the sleeve just above the ribbing. (Stretch and pin the ribbing as for measuring the bottom body width.)

LENGTH MEASUREMENTS

To prepare for the length measurements, place upholstery pins horizontally in the side edge of garment at the key points—the point where the hips begin to slope toward the waist, the base of the waist indentation, and the top of the waist indentation. When measuring, measure straight between the pins; do not follow the curves of the garment.

A. Total Garment Length: (back neck bone to bottom edge) Measure down from the top of the shoulder (where the neck and shoulder come together) to the bottom edge of the garment.

B. Length to Shoulder: (top of shoulder to bottom edge) Measure down from the top of the armhole (where the shoulder and sleeve seam meet) to the bottom edge of the garment.

C. Length to Armhole: Measure down from the underarm (where the body and sleeve are seamed together) to the bottom edge of the garment.

D. Length to Front Neck: Measure down from the base of the front neck to the bottom edge of the garment. (Do not include the neck edging in this measurement.)

E. Front Neck Depth: Measure down from the top of the back neck to the base of the front neck.

F. Armhole Depth: Measure straight down from the top of the armhole to the underarm. Note: The sleeve cap shaping will cause a curve along the armhole edge between the underarm and the shoulder. Make sure the tape measure goes straight down from the shoulder to the sleeve seam at the underarm. Do not follow the curve.

G. Armhole-to-Waist Length: Measure straight down from the underarm to the top of the waist.

H. Waist Length: Measure the total length of the waist indentation.

I. Waist-to-Hips Length: Measure straight down from the bottom of the waist to the widest area of the hips.

J. Hip-to-Bottom Edge Length: Measure straight down from the hip to the lower edge.

K. Total Sleeve Length: Measure along the edge of the center crease from the shoulder down to the bottom edge of the sleeve (including ribbing).

L. Sleeve Length to Armhole: Place a rigid ruler straight across the sleeve horizontally from the armhole to the center crease. Measure along the center crease from the top of the ruler to the bottom of the sleeve. Note: It will be difficult to measure this width on the inside edge of the seam because the tapered increases are made along this edge, therefore this part of the sleeve will slant on a diagonal; the line of the center crease is straight.

M. Sleeve Cap Length: Leaving the ruler in place, measure down from the top of the shoulder (where the sleeve and shoulder are seamed) to the top of the ruler. This number should match the difference between the total sleeve length (K) and the sleeve length to armhole (L).

UNDERSTANDING EASE

In order to move comfortably in a garment, there has to be some ease, or extra width. Most designers allow about 2" (5 cm) of ease for a garment that will be worn over undergarments. This means that the garment measures about 2" (5 cm) more in circumference than the actual body measurements, or 1" (2.5 cm) wider across the front and back. Usually, an additional 1" to 2" (2.5 to 5 cm) are added to the standard ease amount for outerwear that is worn over clothing, for a total of 3" to 4" (7.5 to 10 cm) of ease. See the Ease Allowance Chart on page 24 for typical ease amounts for different sizes.

Keep in mind that these are standards, and they may not correspond to the way you like your clothing to fit. The amount of ease is a personal choice. Compare your body measurements to a garment that fits well to get an idea of the amount of ease that's comfortable for you. Try on and measure several garments to determine your ease preferences. You may like the way one garment fits in the bust, the way another fits in the sleeve and armhole, and the way a third fits at the neck. In each case, lay the garment out flat on a hard surface (a table or measuring board), measure the parts that you like, then compare those measurements to your recorded body measurements to determine the desired amount of ease.

Ease is also used as a design element. Additional ease is added to produce the billowing sleeves on a poet's coat or the roominess in the bust and armhole of a drop-shoulder pullover designed to have an unstructured, oversized fit. Negative ease is used in the body of a garment designed to be form fitting (the sleeves usually include ease to allow for arm movement). When designing with negative ease, be mindful of the elastic properties in the yarn and stitch pattern you select. Wool is more resilient and therefore more elastic than nonresilient fibers such as cotton or ramie (more on this in Chapter Two).

EASE ALLOWANCE CHART

Ease: Amount of room allowed between body measurements and garment measurements for movement.

Chest Size (actual body measurement)	Standard	Roomy	Tight	Form Fitting (negative ease)
32" (81.5 cm)	34" (86.5 cm)	36" (91.5 cm)	33" (84 cm)	30" (76 cm)
34" (86.5 cm)	36" (91.5 cm)	38" (96.5 cm)	35" (89 cm)	32" (81.5 cm)
36" (91.5 cm)	38" (96.5 cm)	40" (101.5 cm)	37" (94 cm)	34" (86.5 cm)
38" (96.5 cm)	40" (101.5 cm)	42" (106.5 cm)	39" (99 cm)	36" (91.5 cm)
40" (101.5 cm)	42" (106.5 cm)	44" (112 cm)	41" (104 cm)	38" (96.5 cm)
42" (106.5 cm)	44" (112 cm)	46" (117 cm)	43" (109 cm)	40" (101.5 cm)
44" (112 cm)	46" (117 cm)	48" (122 cm)	45" (114.5 cm)	42" (106.5 cm)
46" (117 cm)	48" (122 cm)	50" (127 cm)	47" (119.5 cm)	44" (112 cm)
48" (122 cm)	50" (127 cm)	52" (132 cm)	49" (124.5 cm)	46" (117 cm)

SELECTING A BODY SHAPE
AND DRAWING A SCHEMATIC

Select the silhouette on the following pages that most closely matches your sketch. Using a pencil and tracing paper, trace the shape over a photocopy of your sketch. Next, use colored pencils, pens, or markers to outline each additional design element you'd like to add—shoulder shaping, collar, bell sleeves, etc. This photocopy will be used as the basis for your schematic, as well as a place to make notes or comments about the design. Drawing directly on the photocopy will give you a good visual representation of how your sketched design ideas will translate to a real garment. Make additional photocopies if you want to sketch other ideas—do not draw on the original sketch so that you can use it again later, if desired.

Draw both width and length measurement lines on each part of your photocopied sketch to generate a rough schematic. Finally, draw a schematic on graph paper. Or simply use the blank schematic provided here that matches your garment shape.

Sketch of a garment as worn.

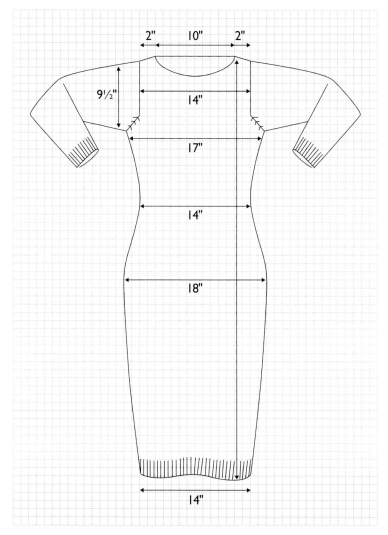

**Schematic of garment
showing measurements.**

CLASSIC SILHOUETTE WORKSHEET

The classic silhouette is the most common body shape for a sweater. The body measurement is based on the bust/chest measurement, plus the desired amount of ease. The body is worked straight from the bottom edge to the base of the armholes, then the armholes are shaped over 1" to 3" (2.5 to 7.5 cm) by decreasing to the desired cross-back width.

A classic silhouette is worked in two parts. The first part is worked from the bottom edge to the beginning of the armhole; the second is worked from the beginning of the armhole to the top of the shoulder and includes the armhole, neck, and shoulder shaping. If the neck is deeper than the armhole (as in a deep V-neck shaping), the neck shaping may begin in the first part.

Name

Date

Yarn

Color/Dye Lot

Needle Size   Gauge

BODY MEASUREMENTS

Hips   +   ease =

Waist   +   ease =

Bust   +   ease =

Shoulder Width

Length

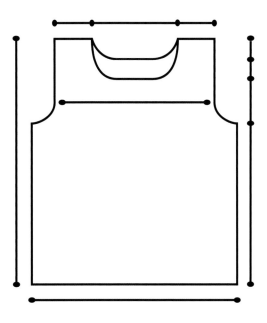

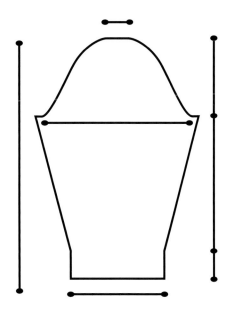

The body of a dropped-shoulder garment resembles a wide scarf with a neck opening and sleeves. In its purest form, a dropped-shoulder garment is constructed as a rectangle with no armhole or shoulder shaping and is therefore an ideal first garment project. The body measurement is based on the bust measurement, plus the desired amount of ease. The body is worked in two parts—the first part is worked even from the bottom edge of the garment to the beginning of the neck shaping; the second part is worked from the beginning of the neck to the top of the shoulders. For a more tailored fit, the back neck and shoulders can be shaped.

Name _____

Date _____

Yarn _____

Color/Dye Lot _____

Needle Size _____ Gauge _____

BODY MEASUREMENTS

Hips _____ + _____ ease = _____

Waist _____ + _____ ease = _____

Bust _____ + _____ ease = _____

Shoulder Width _____

Length _____

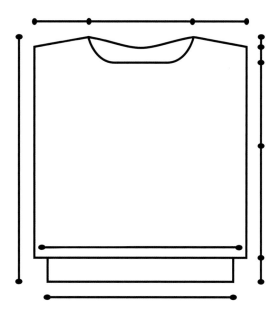

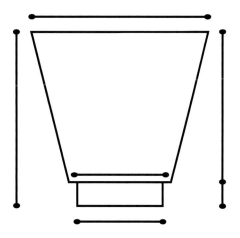

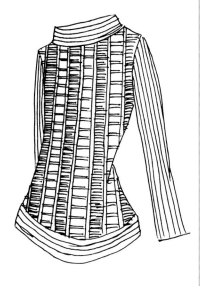

A double-taper silhouette has an hourglass shape that follows the outline of the body from the hips to the bust. Proper fit depends on accurate placement of the hip, waist, and bust shaping. Therefore, it's imperative that each part of the body and "comfort" garment is carefully measured both in width and length.

A double-taper silhouette is worked in four parts. The first part is worked from the bottom edge to the hips. The second part is worked from the hips to the base of the waist, during which time the width is tapered from the hip measurement to the waist measurement, then the garment is worked even at the waist for 1½" (3.8 cm). The third part is worked from the top of the waist to the beginning of the armhole, during which time the width is tapered from the waist width to the bust width, ending about 3" (7.5 cm) below the beginning of the armhole. The fourth part is worked from the beginning of the armhole to the top of the shoulder and includes the neck shaping unless the neck is deeper than the armhole (as in a deep V-neck shaping). The armholes are shaped by decreasing from the bust width to the cross-back width.

Name
_____

Date
_____

Yarn
_____

Color/Dye Lot
_____

Needle Size _____ Gauge _____

BODY MEASUREMENTS

Hips _____ + _____ ease = _____

Waist _____ + _____ ease = _____

Bust _____ + _____ ease = _____

Shoulder Width
_____

Length
_____

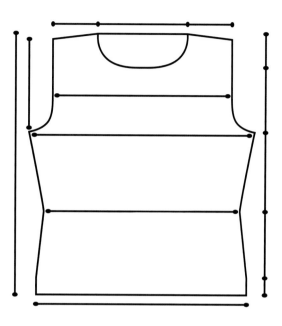

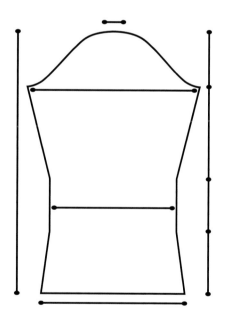

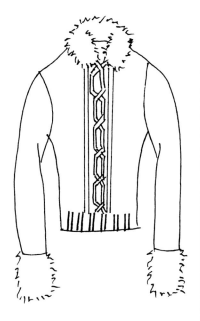

A single-taper garment has the same shape as the top half of the double taper and can end at the hips or waist. The waist-length version forms a lovely tailored line that follows the outline of the upper body. This shape is often used for cropped bolero jackets and for less boxy alternatives to the classic silhouette. The hip-length version has a cocoon-like shape that follows the format of an inverted trapezoid—narrower at the hem and wider at the chest/bust area. This is a flattering silhouette for body shapes with narrow hips and broad chests or large busts.

Both versions are worked in two parts—the hip-length version begins with the hip measurement; the waist length version begins with the waist measurement. In the first part, the body width is tapered from the bottom edge, ending about 2" to 3" (5 to 7.5 cm) below the beginning of the armhole. The second part is worked from the beginning of the armhole to the top of shoulder and includes the armhole, neck, and shoulder shaping. As with the previous silhouettes, deep necklines may begin in the first part. The armholes are shaped by decreasing from the bust width to the cross-back width.

Name
_____

Date
_____

Yarn
_____

Color/Dye Lot
_____

Needle Size   Gauge
_____

BODY MEASUREMENTS

Hips   +   ease =
_____

Waist   +   ease =
_____

Bust   +   ease =
_____

Shoulder Width
_____

Length
_____

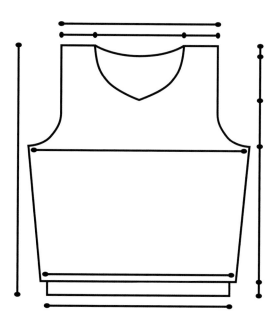

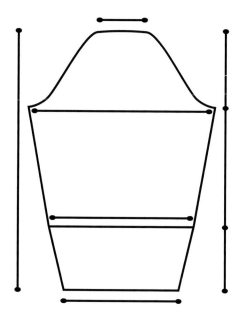

A reverse taper forms a true trapezoid—it is wider at the bottom and narrower at the top. Depending on the length of the garment, the bottom width is based on the hip or waist measurement, plus ample ease; the top width is based on the bust measurement. This shape is often used to provide ease of movement in coats and other garments that are worn over clothing or when extra ease is desired at the base of a garment. This shape is flattering on bodies with wide hips and narrow chests or small busts.

A reverse taper is worked in two parts. The first part is worked from the bottom edge to the beginning of the armhole, during which time the extra width is tapered to the chest/bust width, ending about 2" to 3" (5 to 7.5 cm) before the beginning of the armhole. The second part is worked from the beginning of the armhole to the top of the shoulder and includes the armhole, neck, and shoulder shaping. As with the previous silhouettes, a deep neckline may begin in the first part. The armholes are shaped by decreasing from the bust width to the cross-back width.

Name

Date

Yarn

Color/Dye Lot

Needle Size   Gauge

BODY MEASUREMENTS

Hips   +   ease =

Waist   +   ease =

Bust   +   ease =

Shoulder Width

Length

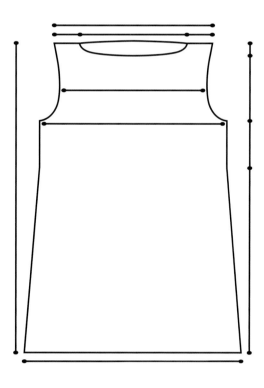

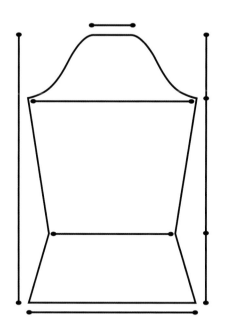

chapter two

Selecting the Fabric

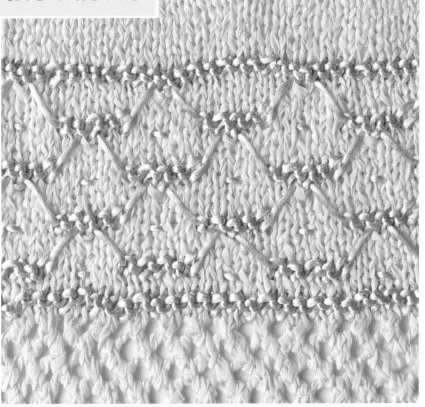

CHOOSING THE YARN

The fabric of your garment, that is, the combination of yarn and stitch pattern, is a key component of the design process. The qualities you envision in your garment will be brought to life by the inherent qualities of the yarn and how it is knitted.

When choosing yarns, read the information on yarn labels and ball bands to learn the fiber content, care instructions, and any special processing that the yarn has undergone (moth proofing, mercerization, etc.), as well as the approximate length of yarn in each ball, the recommended stockinette-stitch gauge and needle size, and the color name or number and dye lot. There is often a subtle, but nonetheless noticeable, difference in dye lots of the same color. Always use yarn from the same dye lot throughout a garment.

All photos in this chapter: Ann Swanson.

FIBER CONTENT

Yarns are composed of natural or synthetic fibers. Natural fibers are derived from protein (animal) or cellulose (vegetable) sources. Protein fibers include wool, alpaca, cashmere, mohair, llama, camel, vicuña, angora, qiviut, buffalo, and silk. Vegetable fibers include cotton, ramie, flax (linen), bamboo, sisal, and hemp. Man-made fibers are chemically engineered and include rayon, lyocell, nylon, polyester, polypropylene, and acrylic.

Animal (Protein) Fibers

Wool has been spun from the fleece of sheep all over the world. There are hundreds of breeds of sheep, each with its own properties. Wool is therefore available in such a diverse range of sizes and textures as to be unparalleled in the realm of natural fibers. Wool is gathered in different ways depending on the breed of sheep. For some of the more primitive breeds (such as Shetland and Icelandic), there is a break in growth in late spring or early summer. At this time, the fleece peels away from the body and is hand plucked (called rooing). For other breeds, there is no seasonal break in wool growth. These breeds are typically shorn in the spring (or twice a year in hot climates). The yield varies between breeds, but most sheering produces about seven pounds of wool per animal (before cleaning).

The structure of the individual fibers makes wool insulating, which enables it to maintain an even temperature. Wool has historically been worn in some of the hottest, driest climates, as well as the coldest regions of the planet. The fibers can absorb up to 30% of their own weight in moisture and still feel dry—it's no wonder that wool is a favorite for the sweaters worn by Aran fisherman who spend a good part of their lives working in the harsh damp climate of the North Atlantic. Wool's absorbent properties make it easy to dye; therefore it is available in a broad range of colors. Because it is a form of animal protein, wool is a favorite food source for clothes moths and carpet beetles.

There are two broad categories of wool yarn, based on the spinning process: worsted and woolen. In general, higher quality and longer fibers are processed into fine worsted yarn; shorter fibers are processed into woolen yarn. All wool is prepared by cleaning and carding to straighten the fibers. If the fiber is coarse with a staple length of less than 3" (7.5 cm), it is twisted into roving (continuous strands of washed fiber) and wound into balls for spinning into woolen yarn. If the fiber is finer with a staple length of more than 3" (7.5 cm), it is combed and drawn through a narrow opening in preparation for spinning into worsted yarn.

The best-known wool comes from Merino sheep, which are renowned for their fine fleece. Merino accounts for about 40% of the world's wool production. With staple lengths of 2" to 4" (5 to 10 cm), merino can be spun into very fine to thick yarns. It is used for a range of projects, from rugged outdoor wear to fragile dressy garments. Over the past two centuries, Merino sheep have been crossbred with many other varieties, most notably the Rambouillet sheep of France. Another popular wool comes from Shetland sheep, indigenous to the Shetland Islands that neighbor Great Britain.

Shetland wool is typically spun into a 2-ply loosely spun worsted yarn. Because it is lightly spun, it is not a good choice for clothing requiring hard wear.

In 1939, congress passed the Wool Products Labeling Act that mandated that products containing wool be labeled according to specific categories. **New** or **Virgin Wool** has never been used in manufacture. **Reprocessed** or **Reclaimed Wool** is reclaimed from woven scraps on the cutting room table or floor and from mill ends that are reprocessed into manufactured products. **Lambswool** is wool from a young sheep (any breed) that is less than seven months old. **Reused Wool** is fiber recovered from items used by consumers that has been respun or rewoven.

Cashmere comes from the fleece of Kashmir goats, indigenous to the mountains of China and Tibet. Rather than being sheared, the fiber is gathered every spring by combing the winter undercoat of the goats. Cashmere yarn is very fine and soft (but subject to pilling). It is truly a luxurious fiber. Cashmere is not as strong as wool and should not be used for clothing that will get hard wear. Like wool, cashmere is a resilient fiber that absorbs dyes well. It is expensive because each goat provides little more than 4 ounces (110 grams) of fiber a year—it may take the fleece of several goats to produce enough yarn to make a single pullover.

Mohair comes from the fleece of Angora goats, indigenous to the Ankara region of Turkey, but today, most of the goats raised for fiber live in Texas. The goats are shorn twice a year. Mohair has many of the qualities of wool—it is a durable fiber with good insulating properties and it absorbs dyes well. However, it is less resilient than wool, it can be hot and uncomfortable to wear, and it sheds. Mohair is usually blended with nylon or wool to strengthen it. Kid mohair is spun from the first shearing of a baby Angora goat (up to eighteen months old). It is soft and fine, but it breaks easily in its pure state.

Alpaca (also spelled Alpaga) and llama come from distant relatives of the camel. Most alpaca and llama fiber comes from domesticated animals that live at elevations of 12,000 to 16,000 feet (3,658 to 4,877 meters) in South America, primarily in Bolivia and Peru. Alpaca is fine and lustrous and extremely well insulating. There are two breeds of alpaca—huacaya and suri. Huacaya fiber is stronger and more crimped than that of the suri and reacts to dyeing and processing much the same as wool. Suri fiber is straight to slightly wavy, less lustrous, and sensitive to processing chemicals. Therefore, most dyed alpaca comes from the huacaya breed. Because huacaya fibers have more crimp than suri, huacaya yarns are lighter and loftier than suri yarns of the same weight. All alpaca fiber is lightweight and has great insulation properties, which makes it a good choice for clothing. However, alpaca lacks the elasticity of wool and tends to stretch if knitted into a heavy garment.

Llama fiber is coarser than alpaca but warmer, lighter, and stronger than wool. It is also hypoallergenic. Historically, llama was used for carpets and rugged outer clothing. Today, however, dehairing (removal of the coarse hairs to leave just the soft undercoat) results in fiber that rivals cashmere in softness. Llama yarn is available in weights ranging from fingering to bulky and in a broad range of natural colors as well as dyed colors (the hair absorbs dye easily). It is available pure or blended with a variety of other fibers, including wool, kid mohair, angora, and silk.

Vicuña and guanaco are two wild members of the same camelid family that includes the llama and alpaca. Vicuña live in extremely high altitudes where the temperatures are warm during the day and drop to freezing at night. Their insulating hair traps the warm air during the day close to their bodies so they can withstand freezing temperatures for extended periods. The fiber is softer and warmer than any other animal, but it is sensitive to chemical treatment and is therefore mostly available in natural colors. Vicuña have been raised for wool from the time of the Incas, but due to unrestricted hunting, their numbers were reduced to near extinction in the 1960s, and they were declared endangered in 1974. Since then, their numbers have increased and government-sponsored shearing roundups help prevent poaching. Because vicuña can be shorn only every three years, the annual production is small, which makes it very expensive.

Guanaco, which live in the same mountainous regions as the vicuña, are more abundant and are classified as "threatened" rather than "endangered." Like the vicuña and llama, guanaco coats contain both coarse guard hairs and a soft undercoat. The dehaired undercoat is long and soft and thinner than even the best cashmere.

Camel hair comes from the winter undercoat of the Asian or Bactrian camel. As with the Kashmir goat, the hair is gathered as it is shed; it is not shorn. Because camel fiber does not absorb dye easily, most camel yarns are available only in natural colors. Camel hair is very soft and fine and is considered a luxury yarn. It is expensive because the annual yield is low.

Angora comes from hair that is combed or shorn from Angora rabbits. Because the hairs are relatively short, angora is commonly combined with other fibers to facilitate spinning. Angora is a soft, luxurious fiber, but it sheds and is expensive due to the low annual yield per animal. The highest quality angora yarn is spun from fibers that are combed, which sheds less than yarn spun from shorn fibers.

Qiviut comes from the winter coat of the Arctic musk ox. It is gathered from shed hair, which makes it a luxury fiber with limited availability. Because it is lightweight and extremely warm, it is practical for very cold climates.

Silk comes from the filaments spun by silkworms to form their cocoons. Each cocoon is formed by a single continuous filament that can be up to 1 mile (1.6 kilometers) long. The cocoons are carefully unwound so that the filaments can be spun together to make yarn. Cultivated silkworms are fed only mulberry leaves and prepare their cocoons in a controlled environment to produce the highest-quality filament (bombyx silk). This fiber has the most beautiful feel and luster. Wild silkworms produce a coarser filament (tussah silk).

Silk has great insulation properties, and, like wool, it breathes and is comfortable next to the skin. Silk is very strong and can be spun into very fine yarns. Silk is nonresilient and can stretch. The careful cultivation and processing required for manufacture makes silk an expensive yarn. It is often blended with other fibers.

Vegetable (Cellulose) Fibers

Cotton comes from the bolls of cotton plants. It is grown throughout the world and processed into many different grades. At the high end are Egyptian, Sea Island, and Pima grades, which have long staples that produce fine, lustrous yarns. At the lower end is matte cotton, which resembles string.

Cotton is a popular choice for clothing in warm climates because it absorbs moisture and dries quickly, therefore producing a cooling effect on the body. It is nonallergenic and easy to care for—it's actually stronger wet than dry, which facilitates laundering. But, because cotton is a nonresilient fiber, it will stretch. Cables or other dense pattern stitches that add weight may not be suitable choices for cotton yarns. Cotton is moth resistant, but may mildew in wet climates.

Mercerizing, invented by John Mercer during the nineteenth century, is a process of treating cotton with sodium hydroxide (lye) and then stretching it. This makes the cotton smoother, less fuzzy, more lustrous, and less likely to shrink than untreated cotton.

Linen (Flax), one of the oldest known textile fibers, is derived from the stem of the flax plant. Linen is sturdy and durable, and like cotton, is comfortable to wear in hot climates because it draws moisture away from the body. It is also easily laundered and moth and perspiration resistant. But linen is also a heavy and nonresilient fiber that can feel stiff (although it softens with repeated washing). It is usually spun into very fine yarns to compensate for its weight. Unlike cotton, linen is weaker when wet and prone to abrasion. Linen is usually blended with other fibers to offset these drawbacks.

Ramie is a linen-like fiber made from the stem of a nettle called China grass. It has a long history in Asia, especially in China. Like linen, ramie is a strong, durable fiber. It is easy to wash, but stiff and nonresilient. It is usually blended with other fibers. Ramie is mildew resistant.

Allo, hemp, jute, and sisal are vegetable fibers that are heavier and coarser than linen and ramie. They have been traditionally used for twine, rope, netting, and burlap. Today, all of these fibers can be found either alone or blended with other fibers in knitting yarns. Allo comes from the bark of the girardinia plant grown in Nepal at the foot of the Himalayas. It is naturally antibacterial and mold resistant. Historically, it has been used to make rope. Today, it is dyed with natural dyes and knitted into vests and fine shawls.

Hemp comes from the outer fibers of the hemp plant. It is considered the strongest natural fiber and is softer, more insulating, more absorbent, and more breathable than cotton. Fabrics made of hemp last longer than their cotton counterparts. It is used alone or blended with silk, cotton, rayon, or allo.

Jute comes from the stem of the jute plant and was historically used for rope twine and burlap bags. It can be mixed with other fibers, both natural and synthetic. Jute is fire and heat resistant, but it loses its strength when wet and is also prone to microbial attack.

Sisal comes from the stem of the *Agave sisalana* cactus plant. Because it is strong, durable, stretchable, and resistant to deterioration in salt water, it has been traditionally used for agricultural twine. Today it is also used for handknitted massage gloves and washing mitts. It is blended with wool or acrylic to produce a softer yarn.

Bamboo comes from a group of woody evergreen plants that comprise the largest member of the grass family. There are about 1,000 species of bamboo that grow in diverse climates, from the cold mountains to the hot tropics. Bamboo is notable for its soft feel and natural antibacterial properties. It is highly absorbent and is therefore available in a broad color range. Pure bamboo is nonresilient and has a greater tendency to stretch than other plant fibers and is therefore often mixed with wool to add resiliency. Pattern stitches that contract lengthwise, such as slip-stitch patterns, are a good choice for this type of yarn. Open and stretchy stitches, such as lace, may stretch lengthwise.

Man-Made Vegetable Fibers

Rayon, first manufactured in 1910, is spun from the regenerated cellulose of wood chips or cotton lint. Rayon has similar properties to cotton, but it is softer and more lustrous. It absorbs dye well and can be found in a broad range of colors. There are two types of rayon—viscose and cuprammonium. They have the same properties, but are manufactured differently. Rayon blends well with other fibers. Unlike other synthetics, it will scorch (like cotton), rather than melt, when pressed at a high temperature. Rayon is a nonresilient fiber that tends to stretch, especially if knitted in a dense or heavy stitch pattern.

Lyocell (trademarked Tencel) was introduced in 1990 as a type of rayon. It was reclassified in 1996 and became the first new generic fiber group to be approved by the Federal Trade Commission in thirty years. Like rayon, lyocell is produced from wood pulp, but it is more durable than rayon and stronger when wet. Lyocell more closely resembles cotton than any other regenerated cellulosic fiber. It is stronger than cotton both dry and wet (which makes it machine washable), breathable, resistant to abrasion, absorbent (even more than cotton), and colorfast. It has a good drape and moderate wrinkle resistance. Like cotton and other cellulose fibers, lyocell will scorch (not melt) when burned. Like rayon, it absorbs dye well. However, lyocell has poor elasticity and may be damaged by mildew and silverfish. It is typically blended with other fibers in handknitting yarns.

Modal is a cellulosic fiber made from beech-wood chips. It combines the benefits of natural fibers with the soft feel of some of the synthetics. It has the water-absorbing properties of cotton and the luster and feel of silk. Modal retains its luster even after a number of washings.

Resiliency (Elasticity) is the ability of a fiber to return to its original shape after it has been stretched. Resilient fibers can bend without breaking, and this characteristic will help prevent a garment from creasing and wrinkling. The elbows and knees of a garment made from a fiber with high resiliency, for example, can withstand heavy wear. Most fibers made of animal fiber are resilient. Nonresilient fibers, such as silk and plant fibers, tend to stretch.

Loft is the air space within and between individual fibers and gives fibers insulating properties. The natural crimp in wool, for example, produces a lofty open structure that can trap heat. Fibers with high loft also have high elasticity, which prevents the fabrics from becoming flat during wear. To test loft, squeeze the yarn widthwise as you would a slice of bread. If it springs back, it has loft. Most animal fibers have loft.

Pilling or **Abrasion** is a problem most commonly associated with softly spun yarns, particularly those spun from short fibers. It occurs when friction causes fibers to break away from the yarn structure and clump into little balls. To test for pilling or abrasion, hold your hand as if to snap your fingers. Place two strands of yarn between the snapping fingers and quickly roll them back and forth several times. If the yarn begins to separate or peel apart, it will likely pill under normal body abrasion in a garment, such as where the arms rub against the body.

Felting is a property unique to animal fibers, particularly wool. It occurs when the fibers are repeatedly compressed and relaxed while wet. Felting causes the fibers to lock together, reducing the loft and resiliency and resulting in shrinkage. You must be careful not to inadvertently felt fibers when washing wool.

Static Electricity is created by an accumulation of motionless electrical charges. It occurs primarily in synthetic fibers that lack the ability to absorb moisture.

Synthetic Fibers

Synthetic fibers are chemically derived from coal and petroleum byproducts. Nylon was the first synthetic to appear in 1938, followed by many others, including acrylic and polyester. Many synthetics are referred to by their brand names, which are trademarks owned by their manufacturers, although several corporations manufacture the same chemical compositions. All synthetic yarns are manufactured as long filaments. When made into knitting yarns, the filaments are cut to the staple lengths of natural fibers, then spun into yarn. They are strong and abrasion resistant, yet resilient. However, synthetics do not absorb moisture, so they tend to feel hot, pill, hold static charges (which makes them more easily soiled), and are more difficult to clean than natural fibers.

Nylon (Polyamide) was originally named for the first polyamide fiber introduced by the DuPont Corporation, but has come to be used as a generic term. Nylon is lightweight, strong, and elastic, but it holds static charges and can melt when pressed at a high temperature. Because nylon is so strong, it is often combined with weaker fibers.

Polyester, trademarked Dacron or Vycron, is often combined with other fibers to add strength, stability, and wrinkle resistance. A bit of polyester will help a garment hold its shape.

Polypropylene contains several key qualities found in natural fibers—it is insulating, absorbent, and less likely to hold static charges than other synthetic fibers. Polypropylene is commonly spun into yarn that resembles wool.

Acrylic is manufactured to imitate wool and is available in many weights and a broad range of colors. However, it does not contain wool's insulating properties, nor does it contain the elasticity of other synthetic fibers, so it can stretch. Acrylic is often combined with natural fibers to counteract these drawbacks. Acrylic is more flammable than nylon or polyester.

YARN CONSTRUCTION

In addition to fiber content, you must also take into account the process by which the fiber is spun to make yarn. Fibers are classified as filament or staple, based on the length of a continuous strand. Yarns spun from long filaments have a smoother, shinier finish than those spun from shorter staples. All synthetic yarns are filament yarns, while silk is the only natural filament yarn. Filaments must be cut to staple lengths to be spun into yarns. Nonetheless they retain lustrous qualities. All other fibers are classified by their staple lengths (the length to which the fiber grows naturally). Staple lengths vary from $1^{1}/_{2}$" to $6^{1}/_{2}$" (3.8 to 16.5 cm) for wool and mohair; linen can be even longer.

Twist

The amount of twist added to the fibers as they are spun into yarn affects a yarn's performance. In general, the longer the individual fibers, the less twist needed to hold them together, although fibers of any length can be twisted tightly or loosely to form yarn. Loosely spun yarns tend to pill, and garments made from them may stretch. Wool yarns that are spun from long fibers are called worsted-spun yarns. Worsted-spun yarns will withstand heavy use and abrasion without pilling.

Wool yarns that are spun from shorter fibers are called woolen-spun yarns. Woolen-spun yarns have a fuzzier surface (and therefore are prone to pilling) and are not as strong as their worsted-spun counterparts. They are best used for garments that receive gentle wear.

Plies

The number of plies—strands of spun yarn twisted around each other—also affects yarn strength and durability. A single strand of spun yarn is called a "single" or "singles." Singles are plied together to add thickness and strength. For example, a 4-ply yarn is made up of four singles twisted together. The number of plies does not dictate the diameter of the yarn. A 4-ply yarn, for example, may be very fine or very thick, depending on the diameter of each individual strand. The number of plies works with the amount of twist to determine a yarn's strength—a thin, tightly twisted 4-ply yarn will withstand heavy wear better than a thick, lightly twisted singles yarn.

YARN WEIGHT CLASSIFICATION

Yarns are classified according to their diameter (thickness)—commonly referred to as the yarn weight. In general, yarn weights are categorized according to the number of stitches that comprise 4" (10 cm) of stockinette stitch. The categories indicate how fine or bulky a fabric produced by a particular yarn will be. This knowledge is critical if you want to substitute yarns for a project.

Specific yarn weight categories have changed over the past few decades, but the basic categories have remained essentially the same. For years, the groups were based on the size of needles used to knit them, with "fingering" or "fine weight" indicating the thinnest type of yarn to "extra bulky," indicating the thickest type of yarn. In the 1980s, the groups were renamed based on gauge—the number of stitches that comprise 4" (10 cm) of stockinette stitch.

The Craft Yarn Council of America has drawn up guidelines for a standard yarn weight system to bring uniformity to yarn labels and published patterns. Yarns are classified by number, according to the weight of the yarn and the manufacturer's recommendations for gauge and needle size.

STANDARD YARN WEIGHT SYSTEM

Yarn Weight Symbol & Category Name	0 LACE	1 SUPER FINE	2 FINE	3 LIGHT	4 MEDIUM	5 BULKY	6 SUPER BULKY
Type of Yarns in Category	Fingering, 10-count, Crochet Thread	Sock, Fingering, Baby	Sport, Baby, Aran	DK, Light Worsted, Rug	Worsted, Afghan,	Chunky Craft,	Bulky, Roving
Knitted Gauge* Range in Stockinette Stitch to 4" (10 cm)	33–40 sts	27–32 sts	23–26 sts	21–24 sts	16–20 sts	12–15 sts	6–11 sts
Recommended Needle in Metric Size Range	1.25–2.25 mm	2.25–3.25 mm	3.25–3.75 mm	3.75–4.5 mm	4.5–5.5 mm	5.5–8 mm	8 mm and larger
Recommended Needle in U.S. Size Range	000–1	1–3	3–5	5–7	7–9	9–11	11 and larger

*Guidelines Only: The above reflect the most commonly used gauges and needles for specific yarn categories.

CHOOSING A PATTERN STITCH

One of the advantages of knitting is that you get to design the structure (weight, drape, movement, etc.) of your fabric. The first step is to choose a pattern stitch. All pattern stitches are made up of the same two building blocks: knit and purl stitches. Look through the many stitch-pattern books available on the market to find patterns that will produce the qualities you want to convey. Take time to knit samples of various patterns with various yarns and needle sizes. Some of the qualities of the major pattern stitch groups are outlined below to help you understand how they might behave in a garment.

Knitted fabrics have elasticity in two directions: vertical and horizontal. The amount of elasticity in a particular pattern stitch will affect how a finished garment will drape and hang.

The right side of stockinette stitch appears as all knit stitches.

STOCKINETTE STITCH

Stockinette stitch, formed by alternating right-side rows of knit stitches and wrong-side rows of purl stitches, is the foundation for nearly all other stitch patterns. The wrong side of a knit stitch is identical to the right side of a purl stitch and vice versa.

The knit (right) side of stockinette stitch has a structure of smooth interlacing loops that form vertical lines as the fabric is constructed. This side has widthwise elasticity—it tends to pull in widthwise to become narrower, and it tends to stretch lengthwise to become longer.

The purl (wrong) side has a structure of interlacing loops that form horizontal ridges. This side has lengthwise elasticity and widthwise expansion—it tends to expand widthwise to become wider, and it tends to pull in lengthwise to become shorter. The purl side will therefore be shorter and wider than the knit side. That is why stockinette-stitch fabrics tend to curl at the edges. Put on a knitted dress inside out and you'll find that it has magically become shorter and wider. In this way, stockinette fabric is brilliantly constructed as two fabrics in one.

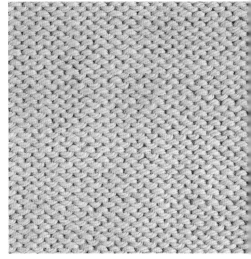

The wrong side of stockinette stitch appears as all purl stitches.

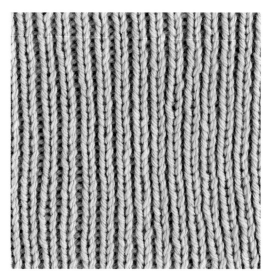

Ribbing forms vertical lines; single (k1, p1) ribbing is shown here.

RIBBING
. . . .

Ribbing is formed when knit and purl stitches alternate horizontally, but are aligned vertically. In k1, p1 ribbing (also referred to as single or 1/1 ribbing), one knit stitch alternates with one purl stitch. Because a ribbed fabric lies flat, ribbing is commonly used as a border for stockinette-stitch garments. When a rib pattern contains the same number of alternating knit and purl stitches, the ribbing is completely reversible—both sides show the same alternation of knit and purl stitches, and the fabric has an accordion look. The knit stitches will dominate the look of the fabric, and the purl stitches will recede to push the knit side of the stitch forward on the other side. Turn the fabric over and you'll see knit stitches where there were purl stitches.

When knit stitches dominate, they will determine the elasticity of the fabric. In k1, p1 ribbing, the fabric will form vertical lines along the face of the fabric and produce widthwise elasticity—the fabric will pull in and become narrow. If you make a garment with this stitch pattern, you must include sufficient ease and average the width (see page 69) to prevent unwanted cling. However, you can use this property to your advantage as a simple way to produce waistline shaping without having to introduce increases or decreases.

Many patterns grow out of the ribbing format, including cable and twist-stitch patterns. All are arranged so that the knit stitches emboss the front of the fabric as the purls recede into the background. All have widthwise elasticity and will be narrower than the same number of stitches worked in stockinette.

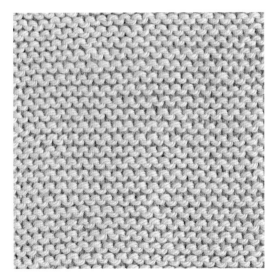

Garter stitch forms horizontal lines of purl stitches.

GARTER STITCH

Garter stitch is the simplest of all stitches. Every stitch of every row is knitted. (When worked circularly, rounds of knitted stitches alternate with rounds of purled stitches.) Because the wrong side of a knit stitch forms a purl stitch, you can also produce garter stitch by purling every stitch of every row. Although the stitches are knitted on every row, the knitting alternates between right- and wrong-side rows, so that the surface looks like alternating rows of knit and purl stitches. This is the horizontal equivalent of k1, p1 ribbing. In this case, horizontal lines of purl stitches sweep across both sides of the fabric. Purl stitches dominate garter stitch while the knit stitches recede and the fabric behaves like a sideways accordion—it contracts lengthwise and expands widthwise to become shorter and wider.

Because the knit stitches recede in garter stitch, the fabric grows slowly in length. Garter stitch produces a denser fabric and takes longer to knit than the same length of stockinette stitch. If you work the two pattern stitches side by side (as in a stockinette body worked simultaneously with garter-stitch buttonbands), you will have to work short-rows in the garter pattern every 4 or 6 rows to accommodate for the differences in lengthwise contraction between the two stitch patterns.

Broken ribs involve pairs of rib stitches that alternate position across the fabric.

BROKEN RIBS

In broken-rib patterns, pairs of rib patterns (such as k1, p1 or k2, p2) alternate positions as they travel vertically up the fabric. For a specific number of rows (usually 4 or 6), the stitch pattern is worked on right-side rows with one member of the 2- or 4-stitch pair followed by the other member (for example, k1 or k2 followed by p1 or p2). On wrong-side rows, the stitches are worked as they appear when they face the knitter. Then, the same number of rows is worked similarly, only this time beginning with the second member of the pair (for example, p1 or p2 followed by k1 or k2). The two sequences are repeated at regular intervals. In this structure, the k1, p1 or k2, p2 sequence changes from the classic accordion type ribbing (where knit stitches push outward and the purl sts seem to disappear) to a patterned fabric that lacks the elasticity of ribbing. The fabric will be more flat and, because the knit and purl stitches do remain vertically aligned throughout, the fabric will be wider than ordinary ribbed fabrics.

Seed stitch alternates one knit stitch and one purl stitch both horizontally and vertically.

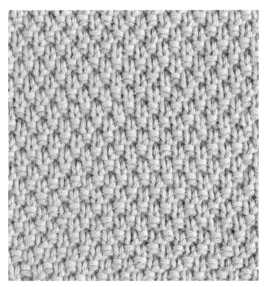

Moss stitch alternates one knit stitch and one purl stitch horizontally and offsets them every second row.

CHECK PATTERNS

Check patterns are stitch patterns in which alternating groups of knit and purl stitches travel across the fabric as a unit to form a geometric pattern with an equal number of knit and purl stitches. These patterns usually have the same number of rows as stitches for a given measurement. The two smallest units of these groupings are seed stitch (1/1 check) and double moss stitch (2/2 check). In these patterns, the knit and purl stitches align side by side and the stitches push away from each other to create a very flat fabric and a stitch gauge that is wider than it is tall. Because these patterns have fewer stitches and more rows for every inch of knitting, they will pull up vertically to become denser row-wise.

In twisted stockinette, every stitch of every row is worked through the back loop.

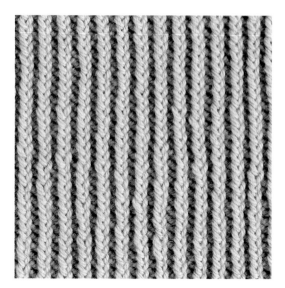

In twisted rib, every stitch that appears as a knit stitch on the right side is worked through the back loop.

TWISTED STITCHES

Twisted-stitch patterns are made by knitting or purling through the back loop of the stitches (i.e., the leg of the stitch that lies on the back of the needle instead of the leg that lies on the front, as is usual). The most basic of these types of stitch patterns is twisted stockinette, in which every stitch (knit stitches on right-side rows and purl stitches on wrong-side rows) is worked through the back loop. Probably the most popular of these is twisted k1, p1 ribbing, in which every stitch that appears as a knit stitch on right-side rows is worked through the back loop. Twisted rib is often used as the edging for cabled sweaters.

It's no surprise that the widthwise elasticity is compromised in patterns that include twisted stitches. The twisted stitches cause these fabrics to be narrower than stockinette fabric knitted with the same number of stitches. Twisting stitches on both right- and wrong-side rows also makes the fabric denser and will restrict its stretch both widthwise and lengthwise. This type of ribbing will help prevent sagging of nonresilient fibers.

The twist adds wonderful textural dimension, both in vertical and horizontal arrangements. But be aware that this type of pattern stitch requires more yarn than stockinette stitch to achieve the same width.

In twist-stitch patterns, one stitch crosses over the adjacent stitch.

TWIST STITCHES

Twist-stitch patterns are ones in which one stitch crosses over another stitch—in effect, the stitches exchange places horizontally. In the simplest format, one stitch crosses over its neighbor; in the most complex format, a stitch crosses over neighboring stitches on subsequent rows to create an embossed fabric of elaborate latticework. These embossed patterns are typically formed by knit stitches traveling across a background of purl stitches to form beautiful high-relief designs.

As with twisted stitches, twist-stitch patterns result in widthwise contraction and will consume more yarn than for the same width of stockinette stitch. The overall stretch of the fabric will also be restrained, so this type of pattern should be worked in a resilient fiber with a high loft (such as wool) to prevent the fabric from becoming overly dense and heavy and therefore prone to stretching. Worked with a resilient fiber, these types of patterns are good choices for outerwear. They restrict the width and prevent lengthwise sagging, which prevents the stretching that normally occurs in outerwear knitted with heavier yarns.

CABLES

Like twist-stitch patterns, cable patterns are formed by exchanging the positions of two or more stitches. Cable stitches are named for the total number of stitches involved and for the direction that the overlapping stitches lean. There are a number of ways to describe the same stitch pattern. For example, C6F ("cable 6 front"), C6L ("cable 6 left"), and 3/3LC ("3 over 3 left cross") all describe the same thing. Six stitches are involved, the first three stitches are held in the front as the next three stitches are worked, then the first three stitches are worked so that the three top stitches lean to the left. To make the top stitches lean to the right, the first set of stitches is held in the back of the work while the second set is worked, which may be denoted as C6B, C6R, or 3/3RC.

The most common cables are made with knitted stitches against a purled background. However, knitted cables can be worked against a knitted background, or purled cables can be worked against a knitted or purled background. There are no rules specifying how wide a cable can be or how many rows are worked between crossings. Cables can be worked as panels or as overall patterns. They can be used in combination with ribs, lace, or twist stitches to create a variety of effects.

As with twisted stitches and twist-stitch patterns, cable patterns have less widthwise elasticity. A cable fabric will be narrower than a stockinette-stitch fabric worked on the same number of stitches. If you want to include a panel of cable stitches surrounded by another stitch pattern, you will have to take into account the reduced elasticity of the cables when determining the total width.

SLIP-STITCH PATTERNS

Slip-stitch patterns are worked by slipping individual stitches from the left needle to the right needle without knitting or purling them to create a variety of interesting texture and color patterns. Slip-stitch patterns are surprisingly easy to work, but the overall effect is visually complex.

Slip-stitch fabrics are dense and firm. The slipped stitches skip a row of knitting, thereby packing the rows closer together than normal. This reduces the depth of the stitches and shortens the fabric. It takes more rows to knit a specific length of slip-stitch fabric because two or more rows are needed to work all of the stitches in a row. This type of dense fabric is ideal for outerwear.

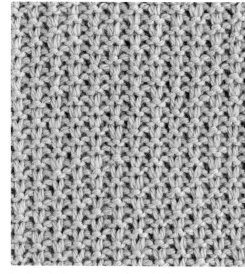

In slip-stitch patterns, selected stitches are slipped from the left needle to the right needle without being knitted.

STRANDED KNITTING

Stranded knitting involves working two or more colors in the same row. This type of colorwork is often called "Fair Isle" after the technique used in the Shetland Isles where there is a traditional adherence to using only two colors in a given row. When these patterns are worked, the unused color is carried (stranded) across the back of the work. To prevent long strands from floating across the wrong side of the fabric, the stranded yarn is caught by the working yarn at regular intervals. Stranded-colorwork patterns are typically worked in stockinette stitch. Even tension between the knitted stitches and stranded yarn is essential for a smooth, uniform fabric. If the stranded yarn is pulled too tightly between the knitted stitches, or if it doesn't extend all the way to the edges of the knitting, the fabric will pucker.

The stranded yarns add an insulating second layer to these types of fabrics. However, if the yarn is thick, the fabric can be quite heavy. It is therefore a good idea to use thinner yarns composed of resilient fibers to keep the project light weight. Nonresilient fibers (such as cotton) will exaggerate any tension variations.

In stranded knitting, two or more colors are worked in the same row to form a double-thick fabric.

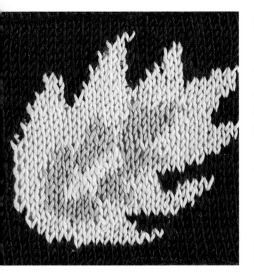

In intarsia patterns, a separate ball or length of yarn is used for each block of color.

INTARSIA

Intarsia is a method used to create areas of colors in pictorial or graphic designs. Each area of color is worked with a separate ball or length of yarn so that the colors are not stranded across one another on the back of the work. Unlike stranded patterns, intarsia patterns result in a single thickness. The key to success is tightening the stitches and twisting the yarns around each other at color changes. As with stranded patterns, resilient fibers (such as wool) are best for this type of colorwork because they minimize tension variations.

LACE PATTERNS

Lace patterns are constructed with a combination of yarnovers that create holes and decreases that cause the fabric to slant at different angles. For the overall width of the fabric to remain constant, the number of increases must equal the number of decreases. There are two types of lace—those in which yarnovers and decreases are worked on every row and those in which a plain row (knitted or purled) alternates with a row of yarnovers and decreases.

As lace patterns are knitted, the fabric contracts and appears deceptively narrow. Lace patterns must be stretched and blocked to their full width to reveal their beauty. It's important to measure the gauge on a good-sized swatch that has been properly blocked. Lace is commonly used for scarves and shawls knitted out of fine yarn on small needles. But it is also lovely worked in heavier yarns, on larger needles, or combined with other stitch patterns.

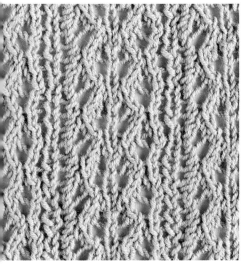

Lace patterns are produced by a combination of yarnover increases and directional decreases.

UNDERSTANDING PATTERN-STITCH INSTRUCTIONS

Each pattern stitch is based on repeating numbers of stitches and rows that make up a single "motif." Technically, the number of stitches is called a "multiple," and the number of rows is called a "repeat." A pattern that repeats over 10 stitches in width and 12 rows in length is described as having a multiple of 10 and a repeat of 12. However, most pattern books describe the structure of a pattern based on its multiple, but will use the term "repeat" to describe both the number of stitches in a multiple and the number of rows in a repeat.

For the pattern to be balanced across the knitting, you will want to center the multiples across the width. Often, this will require an odd number of repeating stitch multiples, with one placed in the center, and half repeats at each edge. You will also want an even number of repeats along the length. However, depending on the number of rows in a pattern repeat and its affect on the overall length of your project, you can usually end with half of a repeat. The row that you end on will depend on how the pattern will flow top-to-bottom when the pieces are seamed.

In written instructions, the stitch multiple is commonly designated by asterisks; the instructions will say to "repeat from * to *" or "repeat from *" to indicate repeating multiples. Some stitch patterns require extra stitches to make the motif appear symmetrical or balanced across the width. These extra balancing stitches are called "plus" stitches. Such pattern multiples are described in terms of the number of stitches per multiple plus the number of balancing stitches, for example, a "multiple of 10 + 3." "Plus" stitches can be added at the beginning of the row or at the end of the row, or split between the two.

Single (k1, p1) ribbing is an example of a pattern with a multiple of 2 and repeat of 2. To make the pattern symmetrical (so that it begins and ends with a knit stitch), you'll want to add 1 stitch at the end of the row. The balanced pattern is therefore written as a multiple of 2 + 1 and would appear as follows:
Right-side rows: *K1, p1; repeat from * to last stitch, end k1.
Wrong-side rows: P1, *k1, p1; repeat from * to end.

In addition to "plus" stitches, I recommend adding a selvedge stitch at each end of a row of knitting. Selvedge stitches are extra stitches that will be worked into seams and are not technically part of the fabric width. They are included in the stitch counts, but they are not included when figuring the stitch multiple or the finished garment width (because they are taken up in the seams). This becomes an important distinction when working with thick yarns—in a garment body worked at a gauge of four stitches to an inch (2.5 cm), an entire inch of width could be lost in the two side seams if no seaming stitches (selvedges) are added. To facilitate seaming and for a neat side edge of the fabric, all increases and decreases used to shape a piece should be worked inside the selvedge stitches.

CHARTS

Although row-by-row instructions can be written for any pattern stitch, they can be cumbersome to follow, especially for long and complicated patterns. Therefore, pattern stitches are commonly represented graphically in a chart. A chart is a grid of symbols that indicate how to work every stitch of every row. Charts are shorthand representations of the right side of the knitted fabric. You can glance at a chart and immediately see how the stitches relate to each other horizontally and vertically. A chart will show at least one complete multiple and repeat, as well as "plus" stitches required for balancing. Charts may or may not show selvedge stitches, so be sure to read the instructions concerning these stitches.

Each row of a chart represents a row of knitting, and each box represents one stitch, with the bottom row of the chart representing the first row of knitting. Right-side rows (RSR) are read from right to left, just the same as a right-side row is knitted, and wrong-side rows (WSR) are read from left to right. Unless otherwise specified, the bottom row of a chart (Row 1) is considered a right-side row and all subsequent odd-numbered rows are right-side rows. The even-numbered rows represent wrong-side rows. Right-side rows are typically called odd rows and wrong-side rows are typically called even rows. Keep in mind that the symbols on most charts show what will appear on the right-side of the fabric. Therefore when you encounter a symbol for a knit stitch while working a wrong-side row, you'll want to purl that stitch (so that a knit stitch will appear on the right side).

Be aware that some patterns begin with a wrong-side row as Row 1. In this case, odd-numbered rows of the chart will represent wrong-side rows and even-numbered rows of the chart will represent right-side rows. Sometimes, stitch patterns will begin with a wrong-side "foundation" or "set-up" row that must be worked in preparation for the first right-side row. Set-up rows typically aren't numbered so that Row 1 will be a right-side row. Set-up rows are not considered part of the pattern repeat. Most often they are the same as the last wrong-side row of the pattern repeat, which is reused to provide a foundation for the first right-side row in the repeat.

When the knitting is worked circularly in rounds, there are no wrong-side rows. Because the right side is always facing you as you knit, every row of the chart is treated as a right-side row and is read from right to left. There is no need for balancing stitches when a pattern stitch is worked in rounds—simply work a full number of multiples. The last stitch of one motif multiple will always be adjacent to the first stitch of the next multiple.

There may be times when it will be more practical to work a project circularly than back and forth in rows, such as knitting a skirt. In most cases, converting a stitch pattern from flat to circular requires little more than eliminating the "plus" stitches. Be sure to read wrong-side rows as right-side rows—stitches that are purled on the wrong side will be knitted on the right side and vice versa.

 tip Knitted stitches tend to be more wide than tall, so that a knitted swatch will appear somewhat squat and wide compared to the proportions of a pattern charted on square graph paper.

One of the advantages of working from a chart versus written instructions is that the "knit speak," with all its abbreviations, is eliminated. However, many beautiful pattern stitches, especially ones from older books, may be presented in a row-by-row format only. To translate row-by-row written instructions to a chart format, refer to the photo of the stitch pattern to help you understand the structure.

INTERNATIONAL SYMBOLS

Many stitch dictionaries provide only charted representations of the stitch patterns. The symbols used in the charts will be explained with each chart, or there will be a comprehensive key at the beginning or end of the book. While there are no true universal standards for charting knitting symbols, there are many that have widespread international usage and are referred to as "international symbols." These symbols visually represent the movement of the stitches and can help you use a broad variety of charts for patterns written in different languages. If a chart uses symbols that do not represent the movement of the stitches, rechart it using international symbols. Doing so will help you learn the meaning of the symbols and help you become familiar with the true movement of the stitch pattern that must be balanced and centered on a garment. The smiling diamonds charts and swatch illustrate this relationship.

Swatch of the expanded smiling diamonds pattern.

```
20  X * O Z * O Z * O O O O O O * S O * S O *
    V Z * O Z * O Z * O O O O O * S O * S O * S   19
18  V ~ ~ Z * O Z * O Z * O O O * S O * S O * S ~
    V ~ ~ Z * O Z * O Z * O * S O * S O * S ~ ~   17
16  V ~ ~ V Z * O Z * O O O O O * S O * S V ~ ~
    V ~ ~ V ~ Z * O Z * O O O O * S O * S ~ V ~ ~ 15
14  V ~ ~ V ~ ~ Z * O Z * O * S O * S ~ ~ V ~ ~
    V ~ ~ V ~ ~ V Z * O O O O O * S V ~ ~ V ~ ~   13
12  V ~ ~ V ~ ~ V ~ Z * O O O * S ~ V ~ ~ V ~ ~
    V ~ ~ V ~ ~ V ~ ~ Z * O * S ~ ~ V ~ ~ V ~ ~   11
10  O O O O * S O * S O * X * O Z * O Z * O O O
    O O O * S O * S O * S V Z * O Z * O Z * O O    9
8   O O * S O * S O * S ~ V ~ Z * O Z * O Z * O
    O * S O * S O * S ~ ~ V ~ ~ Z * O Z * O Z *    7
6   O O O * S O * S V ~ ~ V ~ ~ V Z * O Z * O O
    O O * S O * S V ~ ~ V ~ ~ V ~ Z * O Z * O      5
4   O * S O * S ~ V ~ ~ V ~ ~ V ~ ~ Z * O Z *
    O O O * S V ~ ~ V ~ ~ V ~ ~ V Z * O O          3
2   O O * S ~ V ~ ~ V ~ ~ V ~ ~ V ~ Z * O
    O * S ~ ~ V ~ ~ V ~ ~ V ~ ~ V ~ Z *            1

    22 21 20 19 18 17 16 15 14 13 12 11 10 9 8 7 6 5 4 3 2 1
```

O	k on RS; p on WS
*	yarnover
S	k2tog WS; p2tog WS
~	p on RS; k on WS
V	k1tbl RS; p1tbl WS
Z	k2tog tbl RS; p2tog tbl WS
X	p3tog tbl WS

Chart for the expanded smiling diamonds pattern, plotted with German symbols.

beg first rep
p2tog tbl

end last
rep p1

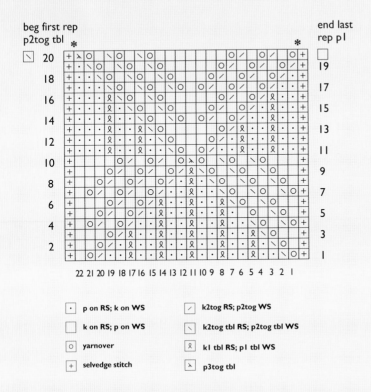

·	p on RS; k on WS
(blank)	k on RS; p on WS
o	yarnover
+	selvedge stitch
/	k2tog RS; p2tog WS
\	k2tog tbl RS; p2tog tbl WS
ℓ	k1 tbl RS; p1 tbl WS
λ	p3tog tbl

Chart plotted with international symbols.

COMBINING PATTERN STITCHES

Many sweater designs combine textures produced by different pattern stitches for practical and esthetic purposes. For example, ribbing is often used as an edging for a garment knitted in stockinette stitch. By itself, a fabric knitted in stockinette stitch will curl at the edges. Ribbing, which is a balanced, flat pattern, will prevent the fabric from curling. In addition, the elasticity of ribbing will help hold the shape of the cuff and neck edges. Worked in a fancy yarn or incorporating cables or twisted stitches for added texture, ribbing becomes a key structural component of a garment as well as a lovely decorative accent.

Pattern stitches can be combined in vertical or horizontal arrangements to add texture, structure, and visual appeal. When combining pattern stitches horizontally, be sure to swatch them together to get a true understanding of how they work as a single fabric in terms of drape, elasticity, total width as a unit, weight, visual appeal, etc. When combining pattern stitches vertically, swatch each one separately to accurately measure the width and length of each. Then combine them in another swatch to see how they work as a single fabric in terms of drape, etc.

THE GAUGE SWATCH

Once you have selected yarn, evaluated its fiber properties, researched and selected the pattern stitch options, you're ready to knit a swatch. Swatches allow you to see exactly how the yarn works as a fabric and to determine the best needle size. They also can be used to estimate the total amount of yarn needed for the entire garment (see page 261). Do not rush this important step. The first time you work with a particular yarn, begin by working a preliminary swatch in stockinette stitch, regardless of the stitch pattern you plan to use in the garment. This will provide a pure, uninterrupted example of how the yarn will feel as fabric. Using the needle size recommended by the manufacturer (listed on the ball band), knit a swatch that measures 6" to 8" (15 to 20.5 cm) square. Block the swatch as you plan to block the sweater (see page 261). When dry, evaluate how the fabric feels (the "hand" of the fabric). If the swatch feels too dense, try again with larger needles; if it feels too loose, try again with smaller needles. Repeat the swatching process until you're happy with the results. You are then ready to knit a gauge swatch in your chosen pattern stitch.

The accuracy in fit of the finished garment depends on a representative swatch and accurate gauge measurement. Although a 4" (10 cm) square will tell you if the needle size is appropriate, it is not large enough to indicate how the stitches and fabric will behave as a garment. As you knit and the yarn flows through your fingers, you will fall into a rhythm. This rhythm will affect your gauge. The rhythm at which you'll knit across 4" (10 cm) is not the same as the rhythm at which you'll knit across 20" (51 cm). You'll want the swatch to be large enough so that you'll hold and manipulate it the same way you'll manipulate the garment pieces. For best results, this swatch should measure about 8" (20.5 cm) square and include two or three horizontal multiples and at least one and a half vertical repeats to give you plenty of time to become accustomed to the pattern stitch. Knit the swatch under the same conditions you plan to knit the garment. The more relaxed and at ease you are when working the pattern, the more even and consistent your tension will be. The bigger the difference between the number of stitches in the swatch and garment, the greater the chances that the gauge measured in the swatch will not match the gauge measurement for the garment. You are going to base every number on your schematic and the project's yarn needs on your swatch measurements. It's important to be accurate.

As you work, make notes of anything that might affect your knitting of the actual garment. Does the pattern stitch make for slow progress? Is it much wider than you thought? Thicker? Does the project consume enormous amounts of yarn? This is the time to ponder and make changes. Swatch a variety of yarns and stitch patterns to give yourself lots of possibilities. Choose your favorites, then wash or block them as you plan to wash or block the finished garment.

MEASURING GAUGE

When knitting a garment vertically (from hem to neck or from neck to hem), the width is represented by stitches that run horizontally across the row. Length is represented by rows that run vertically along the fabric. Your schematic tells you how many inches, horizontally and vertically, are needed for each part of the garment. Your gauge will tell you how many stitches and how many rows it will take to make those inches of fabric. Gauge is based on the diameter of the yarn (bulky, fine, etc.), the size of the needles, and the pattern stitch.

 tip **MEASURING GAUGE**

- A separate gauge measurement must be taken for each pattern stitch using the yarn and needles you plan to use for the garment.

- Each swatch must be knitted by the same person who will knit the garment. Even when working with the same yarn, needles, and stitch pattern, two different knitters are likely to get slightly different gauges.

- Measure across the entire width and length of the swatch (excluding selvedge stitches), not just 4" (10 cm) of an 8" (20.5 cm) swatch. If you do not, you are likely to miss fractions of stitches or fractions of rows that could add up to significant width or length differences when translated into a full-size garment.

Stitch Gauge

This is the most important element in sweater planning because the garment width will be determined by your stitch-gauge calculations. If those numbers are incorrect, the sweater will not fit properly. Lay the swatch flat on a hard surface. Do not stretch it. Use a tape measure to measure across the entire width (excluding selvedge stitches, if there are any). Make note of the width to the nearest ⅛" (3 mm). Divide the number of stitches in the swatch (excluding selvedge stitches) by the number of inches measured. For example, if your swatch has 45 stitches and measures 7⅝" (19.4 cm) wide, your stitch gauge is 5.90 stitches to the inch (2.5 cm).

45 stitches ÷ 7.625" (19.4 cm) = 5.902 stitches per inch (2.5 cm)

For the most accurate results, work with numbers to two decimal places, without rounding up or down. In our example, 5.902 would become 5.90. Use the conversion table at left to convert fractions of inches to decimals for your calculations.

Row Gauge

Row gauge is often overlooked in garment planning based on the philosophy that you can take out your tape measure to check length or make adjustments by knitting fewer or more rows in each section. This approach does work if you're using stockinette stitch. However, if your stitch pattern involves stitch and row pattern repeats, the row-gauge calculations are quite important when planning the total garment length as well as the pattern breaks at the armholes, neck, and shoulders. You will want the pattern to break at appropriate rows in these areas for a garment to look its best.

Use the tape measure to measure along the entire length, excluding the cast-on and bind-off rows, again making note of the length to the nearest ⅛" (3 mm). Divide the number of rows in the swatch (excluding the cast-on and bind-off rows) by the number of inches measured. For example, if your swatch has 66 rows and measures 10⅜" (26.4 cm) long, your row gauge is 6.41 rows to the inch (2.5 cm).

66 rows ÷ 10.375" (26.4 cm) = 6.36 rows per inch (2.5 cm)

CONVERTING FRACTIONS AND DECIMALS

Fraction	Decimal
⅛	.125
¼	.25
⅜	.375
½	.5
⅝	.625
¾	.75
⅞	.875

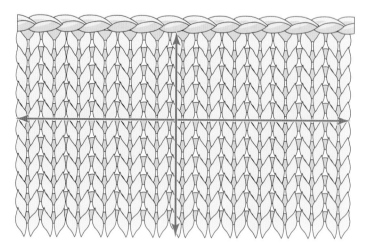

Measure the swatch widthwise and lengthwise.

TRANSLATING MEASUREMENTS TO NUMBERS OF STITCHES AND ROWS

Now that you know how many stitches and rows make up 1" (2.5 cm) of our knitted fabric, it's an easy matter to translate the measurements on your schematic to knitting instructions. All you do is multiply each width measurement by the stitch gauge to determine the number of stitches and multiply each length measurement by the row gauge to get the number of rows to work.

For example, let's consider a drop-shoulder, boat-neck pullover without any edging treatment that measures 38" (96.5 cm) in circumference. In this example, the front is identical to the back, and the two sleeves are worked alike. Let's plan to knit our sweater at a stockinette-stitch gauge of 5.9 stitches and 6.4 rows to the inch (2.5 cm).

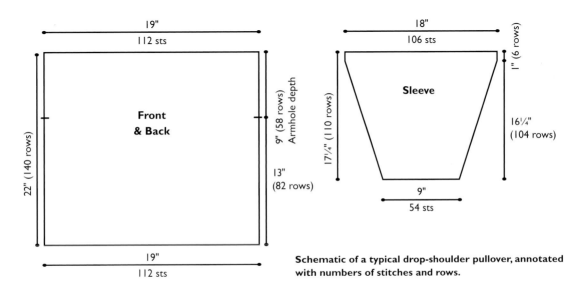

Schematic of a typical drop-shoulder pullover, annotated with numbers of stitches and rows.

BODY

Our sample sweater is worked straight from the cast-on at the lower hem to the bind-off at the shoulders in two pieces—one for the back and one for the front. To determine the number of stitches to cast on for the back, multiply the width by the stitch gauge.

> 19" (48.5 cm) × 5.9 stitches/inch = 112.1 stitches

Because we can't knit partial (112.1) stitches, we need to round this to a whole number. For this example, we'll round to 112 stitches.

Our schematic tells us that we want the total body length to be 22" (56 cm). To determine the number of rows to work, multiply the length by the row gauge.

> 22" (56 cm) × 6.4 rows/inch = 140.8 rows

We can't knit partial rows either, so we need to round this up to 141 rows or down to 140 rows. It's always a good idea to work an even numbers of rows so there will be the same number of right-side rows as wrong-side rows. Therefore, round down to 140 rows. Knit the 112 stitches for 140 rows, then bind off all the stitches. Knit an identical piece for the front.

SLEEVES

The sleeves are worked with an even taper from the cuff to the armhole edge. To determine the number of stitches to cast on, multiply the cuff width by the stitch gauge.

9" (23 cm) × 5.9 stitches/inch = 53.1 stitches

We can round this number up to 54 stitches or down to 53 stitches. For our example, maintain an even number of stitches and round up to 54 stitches.

Based on our schematic, we know that we want to knit for a total of 17$\frac{1}{4}$" (44 cm). To determine the number of rows to work, multiply the length by the row gauge.

17$\frac{1}{4}$" (44 cm) × 6.4 rows/inch = 110.4 rows

To maintain an even number of rows, round to the nearest even number and work for 110 rows.

But notice that the upper sleeve is wider than the cuff. During these 110 rows, we'll need to increase stitches to achieve the desired top width of 18" (45.5 cm). To determine the number of stitches needed at the top of the sleeve, multiply the upper sleeve width by the stitch gauge.

18" (45.5 cm) × 5.9 stitches/inch = 106.2 stitches

Again, we can't knit partial stitches, so we need to round to a whole number. Because we started with an even number of stitches for the cuff, we want an even number of stitches for the upper sleeve, so we round down to 106 stitches.

To determine the number of stitches that are needed to increase between the cuff and upper sleeve, subtract the number of cuff stitches from the number of upper sleeve stitches.

106 stitches at upper sleeve – 54 stitches at cuff = 52 stitches to be increased

To maintain symmetry, the increases are worked in pairs—one increase at each edge of the sleeve—so we will need to add 26 (half of 52) stitches at each side.

$$26 \overline{)110} \quad \begin{array}{r} 4 \\ \hline -104 \\ \hline 6 \end{array}$$

To determine a simple estimate of how often to work the increase rows (this will be discussed in detail in Chapter 3), divide the total number of rows by the number of increase stitches for each side.

110 rows ÷ 26 increase stitches = increase on each side of every 4.23 rows

In Chapter 3, we'll learn how to refine the increase spacing, but for now it's sufficient to work an increase at each edge of every 4th row 26 times for a total of 104 rows, then work the remaining 6 rows even to end with 110 rows total.

We now know that we will cast on 54 stitches for the cuff, increase 1 stitch at each edge of the piece on every 4th row 26 times to get 106 stitches for the upper arm. This will take a total of 104 rows. Work 6 rows after the last increase for the desired total of 110 rows, then bind off all the stitches.

CALCULATING YARN REQUIREMENTS

Few things can create more anxiety during a project than the fear of running out of yarn. It is important to purchase a sufficient quantity of yarn at the beginning of your project so that you're sure to have enough yarn from the same dye lot to complete that project. In fact, it is always a good idea to purchase an extra ball or two for insurance.

Although there are charts that provide yardage estimates for garments knitted at different sizes and gauges, most are based on a classic garment body shape knitted in stockinette stitch. If your garment has a different shape or is worked in a different stitch pattern, these yardages may not apply. But you can easily calculate the yardage for yourself if you know three things: the number of yards (meters) used in your gauge swatch, the anticipated square inches in your garment, and the number of yards in each ball or skein of yarn.

To begin, make note of the number of yards (or meters) that are in a full ball of yarn. If this information isn't included on the yarn label, run the yarn through a commercial yarn counter or measure the number of yards against a yardstick. Knit your swatch from a full ball, then count the number of yards that remain. Subtract the number of yards remaining from the number you began with to get the number of yards used in the swatch. For example, if the yarn we used contained 150 yards per ball and 33 yards remained after knitting the swatch, we'd calculate:

> 150 yards (137 meters) per ball – 33 yards (30 meters) remaining after knitting the swatch
> = 117 yards (107 meters) in the swatch

Next, calculate the area of the swatch, then calculate the area of the projected garment. Divide the area of the garment by the area of the swatch to determine the number of swatches that would be required to make up the garment. Finally, multiply the number of yards (meters) in the swatch by the number of swatches that would equal the desired garment area to get the total number of yards (meters) required for the garment. Let's walk through these steps for our sample drop-shoulder pullover.

Step 1: Calculate the Area of the Gauge Swatch
Our gauge swatch measures 7¼" (18.5 cm) wide and 8¼" (21 cm) long. To determine the area of the swatch, multiply the width by the length.

7.25" (18.5 cm) × 8.25" (21 cm)
= 59.8 square inches (388.5 square cm)

Step 2: Calculate the Area of the Garment
Using the schematic as a reference, multiply the widest part of each piece by the total length to determine the number of square inches (square cm) in each piece. Because it's always a good idea to err on the side of caution, pretend that each piece is a rectangle defined by its largest width and length dimensions.

Back: 19" (48.5 cm) wide × 22" (56 cm) long
= 418 square inches (2,716 square cm)

Front: 19" (48.5 cm) wide × 22" (56 cm) long
= 418 square inches (2,716 square cm)

Sleeves: 18" (45.5 cm) wide × 17¼" (44 cm) long
= 310.5 square inches (2,002 square cm)

Total: (back + front + 2 sleeves) 418 + 418 + 310.5 + 310.5 = 1,457 square inches (9,436 square cm)

Step 3: Determine the Number of Swatches in the Garment
Divide the total number of square inches (square cm) in the garment by the number of square inches in the swatch to determine the number of swatches in the entire garment.

1,457 square inches (9,463 square cm) in garment ÷ about 60 square inches (389 square cm) in swatch = about 24.3 swatches in garment

Step 4: Determine the Number of Yards of Yarn Needed in the Garment
Multiply the number of swatches in the garment by the number of yards in each swatch to determine the number of yards in the garment.

24.3 swatches in garment x 117 yards (107 meters) per swatch = 2,843 yards (2,600 meters) in garment

Step 5: Determine the Number of Balls of Yarn Needed
The yarn we want to use has 135 yards (123 meters) in each ball. To determine the number of balls needed, divide the total yards of yarn required by the number of yards in each ball or skein of yarn to determine the number of balls required in the garment.

2,843 yards (2,600 meters) ÷ 135 yards (123 meters)/ball = 21.06 balls

Rounding up to the next whole number tells us that we need 22 balls of this yarn for this project. Because this doesn't leave much extra yarn in case something goes wrong, I'd recommend purchasing an extra ball so you're sure to have enough of the same dye lot.

chapter three

Classic Silhouette Pullover

In this chapter, we'll go through the construction process and introduce important design techniques that will be used throughout the book. We will create step-by-step instructions from a working schematic that has the widthwise and lengthwise measurements translated into numbers of stitches and rows based on the gauge measurements. To illustrate these steps, we'll build the most common shape—a pullover with a classic body silhouette worked in four pieces (a front, a back, and two identical sleeves) all worked upward from the lower edge.

The "blueprint" for your garment is really a series of worksheets and charts. The first shows all the essential numbers and measurements necessary for shaping your garment translated into stitches and rows. These numbers annotate the working schematic—a drawing of the garment pieces that includes all measurements, corresponding stitch or row numbers, gauge numbers, pattern repeats, and other pertinent information. The final worksheet creates the step-by-step calculations and instructions needed to construct your garment—increases, decreases, pick-up layouts, and shaping. If you plan to write a formal pattern, add a list of every technique you plan to use. This will become the "notes" section of your written pattern.

For garments planned with stitch patterns other than stockinette, you will need an additional worksheet to plan the flow of the stitch pattern so that it is centered both widthwise and lengthwise on the body and sleeves. Always chart several stitch and row pattern repeats to ensure a clear picture of the stitch pattern flow. Make a series of small charts to examine how the pattern will flow across the side seams of a pullover, between body and sleeves, and across the front opening of a cardigan.

Designing handknits is not a complicated process; it is simply a matter of following a series of logical steps. If you have followed the instructions for selecting yarn, making a gauge swatch, drawing a sketch, and taking body and garment measurements, you have gathered all of the necessary "tools" for laying out your garment. The balance of the process is the equivalent of assembling the pieces.

In a classic silhouette, the width of the front and back is the same from the cast-on edge to the base of the armholes. Our example pullover measures 36" (91.5 cm) at the bust (18" [45.5 cm] width) and includes set-in sleeves, a high round neck, and shaped shoulders. The body and sleeves are worked in stockinette stitch and edged with k1, p1 ribbing.

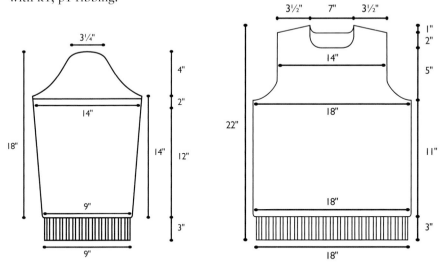

Classic silhouette schematic.

Conversion of Measurements to Numbers of Stitches and Rows

WIDTHS

Number of stitches in border (hip width × border stitch gauge)
   18" (45.5 cm) × 6.5 stitches/inch = 117 stitches

Number of stitches at base of body (hip width × body stitch gauge + 2 selvedge stitches)
   18" (45.5 cm) × 5.5 stitches/inch + 2 selvedge stitches = 101 stitches

Number of stitches in bust width (bust width × body stitch gauge + 2 selvedge stitches)
   18" (45.5 cm) × 5.5 stitches/inch + 2 selvedge stitches = 101 stitches

Number of stitches in cross-back (shoulder-to-shoulder width × body stitch gauge + 2 selvedge stitches)
   14" (35.5 cm) × 5.5 stitches/inch + 2 selvedge stitches = 79 stitches

Number of stitches in neck width (neck width × body stitch gauge)
   7" (18 cm) × 5.5 stitches/inch = 38.5 stitches; round up to nearest odd number = 39

Number of stitches in each shoulder (shoulder width × body stitch gauge + 1 selvedge stitch)
   3½" (9 cm) × 5.5 stitches/inch + 1 selvedge stitch = 20.25 stitches; round down to nearest even number = 20 stitches

LENGTHS

Number of rows in border (border length × border row gauge)
   3" (7.5 cm) × 9 rows/inch = 27 rows; round up to nearest even number = 28 rows

Number of rows from beginning of body to base of armhole (length × body row gauge)
   11" (28 cm) × 7.5 rows/inch = 82.5 rows; round down to nearest even number = 82 rows

NEEDLES
Border: Size U.S. 4 (3.5 mm)
Body: Size U.S. 6 (4 mm)

SWATCH MEASUREMENTS
Border (k1, p1 ribbing): 52 stitches = 8" (20.5 cm) wide; 54 rows = 6" (15 cm) long (Note: measurements are averaged between the relaxed and stretched states; see page 69).
Body (stockinette stitch): 44 sts = 8" (20.5 cm) wide; 60 rows = 8" (20.5 cm) long

GAUGE
Border (k1, p1 ribbing): 6.5 stitches and 9 rows = 1" (2.5 cm)
Body (stockinette stitch): 5.5 stitches and 7.5 rows = 1" (2.5 cm)

KEY MEASUREMENTS
Bust circumference: 34" (86.5 cm) + 2" (5 cm) ease = 36" (91.5 cm)
Bust width: 18" (45.5 cm)
Cross-back width: 14" (35.5 cm) + 0" ease = 14" (35.5 cm)
Neck width: 7" (18 cm)
Shoulder width: 3½" (9 cm)
Length from bottom to base of armholes: 3" (7.5 cm) for lower ribbing + 11" (28 cm) for lower body = 14" (35.5 cm)
Armhole depth: 5" (12.5 cm) + 2" (5 cm) ease = 7" (18 cm)
Length from base of armholes to base of front neck: 5" (12.5 cm)
Length from base of front neck to base of shoulder: 2" (5 cm)
Shoulder slope: 1" (2.5 cm)

Notes

- A garter-stitch selvedge (knit every row) is added to each end of all rows in the stockinette-stitch portions to facilitate seaming.
- Rows are worked in pairs (a right-side row followed by a wrong-side row) so all row numbers are rounded to even numbers.
- Measurements include ease allowance.
- The front and back are worked identically to the beginning of the neck shaping; the front neck is shaped differently than the back neck.
- Both sleeves are worked identically.

PATTERN SYMMETRY

Pattern symmetry is important for balancing the pattern at the edge and is critical for a professional finished look along the seams. In the same way that selvedges are used as seaming stitches for the body of the garment, seaming stitches are also used for cuffs and borders. Seams are worked just inside these edge stitches. Seaming a knit stitch to a purl stitch can create a less-than-professional look if the k1, p1 stitch pattern is left unaltered. Therefore, another stitch should be added to the multiple so that there will be a knit stitch at each end of the needle. This will make the pattern a multiple of 2 stitches plus 1 balancing stitch so that there will be a knit stitch at each edge, which will curl to the wrong side. When seaming, reach across the knitted edge stitches and seam the first purl stitches on each side together for the side seams to look invisible as the seamed purl stitches appear as a single stitch.

Number of rows from base of armhole to base of front neck (length × body row gauge)
    5" (12.5 cm) × 7.5 rows/inch = 37.5 rows; round up to nearest even number
    = 38 rows

Number of rows from base of front neck to base of shoulder (length × body row gauge)
    2" (5 cm) × 7.5 rows/inch = 15 rows; round down to nearest even number = 14 rows

Number of rows in armhole (armhole length × body row gauge)
    7" (18 cm) × 7.5 rows/inch = 52.5 rows; round down to nearest even number = 52 rows

Number of rows in shoulder slope (length × body row gauge)
    1" (2.5 cm) × 7.5 rows/inch = 7.5 rows; round up to nearest even number = 8 rows

Number of rows from base of armhole to base of back neck (length × body row gauge)
    7¼" (18.5 cm) × 7.5 rows/inch = 54.5 rows; round to the nearest even number
    = 54 rows

Number of rows from base of back neck to top of shoulder (length × body row gauge)
    ¾" (2 cm) × 7.5 rows/inch = 5.6 rows; round up to the nearest even number = 6 rows

MATH CHECK!

The total number of rows worked should add up to the desired total length.

Total rows: 28 + 82 + 38 + 14 + 8 = 170 rows

Length in ribbing: 3" (7.5 cm) × 9 rows/inch = 28 rows

Length in stockinette stitch: 11" (28 cm) + 5" (12.5 cm) + 2" (5 cm) + 1" (2.5 cm) × 7.5 rows/inch = 142 rows

Total length in ribbing and stockinette stitch: 28 rows + 142 rows = 170 rows

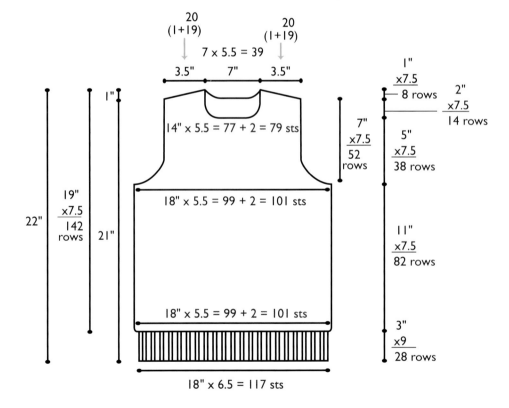

Schematic of the example classic body silhouette annotated with numbers of stitches and rows.

I always recommend knitting the back first so that any unanticipated problems can be worked out where they will be less noticeable. This also allows you to become familiar with your stitch pattern and establish a smooth tension before beginning the front. However, for figuring out the knitting instructions, we'll begin with the front, which typically has more steps than the back.

Step 1: Cast-On and Ribbing/Border

The front begins with stitches cast on for the lower edge, which are worked in k1, p1 ribbing on the smaller needles. We therefore need to calculate the number of stitches to cast on based on the gauge of the ribbing.

To allow for the stretch in ribbing, calculate the gauge based on the average between its relaxed and expanded states as described below. For our example, the ribbing swatch contains 40 stitches and measures 5" (12.5 cm) wide when relaxed and 8" (20.5 cm) wide when stretched. Divide the number of stitches by the width to get the gauge for each:

> Relaxed: 40 stitches ÷ 5" (12.5 cm) = 8 stitches/inch
> Stretched: 40 stitches ÷ 8" (20.5 cm) = 5 stitches/inch
> Average: (8 stitches/inch + 5 stitches/inch) ÷ 2 = 6.5 stitches/inch

We know that we want the lower edge of our sweater to measure 18" (45.5 cm) wide. Multiply this width by the averaged gauge to determine the number of stitches for the ribbing.

> 18" (45.5 cm) × 6.5 stitches/inch = 117 stitches

The row gauge for the ribbing is 9 rows = 1" (2.5 cm), and the pattern is planned for 3" (7.5 cm).

> 9 rows × 3" (7.5 cm) = 27 rows

AVERAGING RIBBING GAUGE

To allow for the stretch in ribbing, calculate the gauge based on the average between its relaxed and expanded states (so that it will be neither too baggy nor too tight). To do this, knit a swatch that measures about 6" (15 cm) wide and 3" (7.5 cm) long. Measure the width of the swatch with the ribbing relaxed, then measure it again while stretching it as much as you feel necessary to give the desired cling. Do not stretch the ribbing as far as it will go unless that's the way you want the border to fit around your body. The measurements will give the "relaxed" and "stretched" gauges.

Ribbing looks "baggy" when it is too close to the desired width when relaxed. Remember that in ribbing the purl stitches tend to recede on the front and push out as knit stitches on the reverse side of the fabric. In effect, they visually disappear when the ribbing is relaxed, but they do add width when the ribbing is stretched to any degree. Therefore, there will be far too much fabric in the ribbing if it isn't stretched when the gauge is determined. This will cause the border to be heavy and wobble out of shape.

To begin, divide the number of stitches in the swatch by the relaxed width to get the relaxed gauge (in stitches/inch), then divide the number of stitches by the stretched width to get the stretched gauge (in stitches/inch). To get the averaged gauge, add the two gauges together, then divide the sum by two.

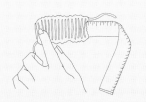

Measure the width of the ribbing in its relaxed state.

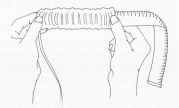

Measure the width of the ribbing stretched the desired amount.

SHAPING FORMULA FOR CALCULATING DECREASE AND INCREASE RATES

Written instructions generally say to decrease (or increase) a certain number of stitches "evenly spaced" across a row of knitting, leaving it up to the reader to figure out exactly how to space those decreases (or increases). In simple cases, the number of decreases (or increases) fits evenly into the number of stitches on the needle. For example, if there are 110 stitches that need to be decreased to 100 stitches (10 stitches decreased), work the decreases at 11-stitch intervals. Divide the total number of stitches by the number of stitches to be decreased to determine how often to work the decreases: 110 ÷ 10 = 11. In this case, work the decreases every 11 stitches.

But what if there are 117 stitches in the ribbing, and we want to decrease 16 stitches to 101 stitches for the body? In this case, dividing the total number of stitches by the number of stitches to be decreased, gives an answer that involves partial stitches: 117 ÷ 16 = 7 with a remainder of 5. To figure out how to distribute these remaining 5 stitches, we can thank Cheryl Brunette for introducing the "more-or-less" shaping formula in her book *Sweater 101*. Cheryl's method uses simple long division to determine how to evenly space any number of decreases or increases.

To begin, let's review the components of long division.

Divisor: The number by which another number is divided. This is the number of decreases (or increases) we want to make (16 in our example).

Dividend: The number to be divided. This is the number of stitches on the needle before any decreases (or increases) have been worked (117 in our example).

Quotient: The whole number of times the divisor fits into the dividend. In rare cases, the quotient times the divisor will equal the dividend. More often, the quotient times the divisor is less than the dividend. In our example the quotient is 7.

$7 \times 16 = 112$ **(which is the closest number to 117 that is divisible by 16)**

This is the number of stitches in the first decrease (or increase) interval.

Remainder: The number left over after the divisor fits into the dividend a whole number of times. In our example, the remainder is 5.

$117 - 112 = 5$

This is the number of stitches in the second decrease (or increase) interval. Note that if the long-division formula has a remainder, the increases or decreases will have to be worked over two different intervals if they are to be evenly distributed across the row.

For our example, first divide 117 by 16 to get a quotient of 7 and a remainder of 5. In other words, 16 can go into 117 a total of 7 times with 5 remaining:

$(16 \times 7) + 5 = 117$

$112 + 5 = 117$

MATH CHECK
$7 \times 11 = 77$
$8 \times 5 = 40$
$\overline{16 \quad 117}$

Use long division to determine the increase or decrease interval.

To use this formula to figure out the decrease intervals, first subtract the remainder (5 in our example) from the divisor (16 in our example) to get what we call the "expanded remainder" (11 in our example).

$$16 - 5 = 11$$

Both the remainder and the expanded remainder are shown at the bottom of the long-division calculation.

Next, add 1 to the quotient (7 in our example) to get the "expanded quotient" (8 in our example:

$$7 + 1 = 8$$

Both the quotient and the expanded quotient are shown at the top of the long-division calculation. The quotient represents the first decrease/increase intervals; the expanded quotient represents the second decrease/increase interval. (If there were no remainder, there would be no expanded remainder or expanded quotient.)

Here's the "magic" part. There is a diagonal relationship between the two quotients and the two remainders. Draw diagonal lines from the upper left (the quotient) to the lower right (the expanded remainder) and from the upper right (the expanded quotient) to the lower left (the remainder) to see which numbers pair up. In our example, the quotient (7) pairs with the expanded remainder (11) and the expanded quotient (8) pairs with the remainder (5). This tells us to decrease every 7th stitch 11 times, then decrease every 8th stitch 5 times for a total of 16 decreases spread out over 117 stitches.

You might notice that this equation will space the decreases slightly farther apart in the last half of the row than at the beginning. For truly evenly spaced decreases (or increases), alternate the two intervals across the row. For example, instead of working all eleven 7-stitch intervals followed by all five 8-stitch intervals, alternate two 7-stitch intervals with one 8-stitch interval five times, then end with a 7-stitch interval.

Also notice that this calculation places the last decrease (or increase) on the very last stitch of the row. One way to avoid this is to divide the first interval in half, then work that number of stitches before the first decrease (or increase) and the remaining half after the last decrease (or increase). In our example, we'd divide one of the 8-stitch intervals in half so that 4 of these stitches are worked at the beginning of the row and 4 of these stitches are worked at the end of the row. The first decrease would therefore occur on the 3rd and 4th stitches, then the 7-stitch interval would be worked 11 times, then the 8-stitch interval would be worked 4 times (not 5 because we're splitting one interval between the two ends of the needle), then the remaining 4 stitches would be worked.

K2, k2tog, [k5, k2tog] 11 times, [k6, k2tog] 4 times, k4

We could also alternate the two intervals to achieve a more uniform placement of the decreases.

K2, k2tog, [k5, k2tog] 2 times, [k6, k2tog] 1 time, [k5, k2tog] 2 times, [k6, k2tog] 1 time, [k5, k2tog] 2 times, [k6, k2tog] 1 time, [k5, k2tog] 2 times, [k6, k2tog] 1 time, [k5, k2tog] 3 times, k4.

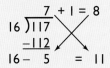

The diagonal relationship between the quotient (7) and the expanded remainder (11) tells us to work 7 stitches between each decrease for the first 11 decreases. The diagonal relationship between the expanded quotient (8) and the remainder (5) tells us to work 8 stitches between each decrease for the remaining 5 decreases.

To check the math, we see that we work the 7-stitch interval 11 times (11 stitches decreased over 77 stitches), we work the 8-stitch interval 4 times (4 stitches decreased over 32 stitches), we work an additional 4 stitches at the beginning of the row (1 stitch decreased over 4 stitches), and we work an additional 4 stitches at the end of the row (no stitches decreased over 4 stitches). The total number of stitches worked should equal the number of stitches we began with (117) and the total number of decreases worked should equal the number we wanted to decrease (16).

Total stitches: 77 + 32 + 4 + 4 = 117 stitches

Total decreases: 11 + 4 + 1 = 16 stitches

 MATH CHECK!

Just like in elementary-school math, it's always a good idea to check your calculations. Multiply the bottom number by the top number in each diagonal partnership. The sum of the two results should equal the number of stitches that were originally on the needles (the dividend).

7 × 11 = 77 (the number of stitches worked in the 7-stitch intervals)

8 × 5 = 40 (the number of stitches in the 8-stitch intervals)

77 + 40 = 117 (the number of stitches we began with)

Add the two remainder numbers (the numbers at the bottom) to double check the number of stitches that need to be decreased or increased (the divisor).

5 + 11 = 16

✳ *tip*   **CONDENSED FORMULA**

$$\begin{array}{r} 7 \\ 16\overline{)117} \\ -\underline{112} \\ 5 \end{array}$$

Omit the expanded quotient and expanded remainder in the "condensed formula."

A simplified alternative, which I call the "condensed formula" method, is to simply work the remainder at the end of the row after all of the increases and decreases have been worked. This version is used in situations where the difference between the quotient and remainder is 2 stitches or less. In this case, the number of stitches at the beginning and end will automatically be balanced in the normal long-division formula. In our example, we would work the 7-stitch interval 16 times, then end by working the remaining 5 stitches: [K5, k2tog] 16 times, k5. In this example, a 7-stitch interval requires that 5 stitches are worked before the first decrease, which matches the number of remaining stitches (5). Therefore, we would have 5 stitches worked before the first decrease as well as 5 stitches worked after the last decrease.

Keep in mind that 2 stitches are involved in a decrease (k2tog, for example). In our example, the first decrease interval is 7 stitches. Therefore, work the interval by knitting the first 5 stitches, then knitting the next 2 together (the 6th and 7th stitches). Work this k5-k2tog sequence 11 times. The second decrease interval is 8 stitches. Therefore, knit the first 6 stitches, then knit the next 2 together (the 7th and 8th stitches). Work this k6-k2tog sequence 5 times.

If we were working increases instead of decreases, the placement of the increases would depend on the type of increase used. For example, if the make-one (M1) method, which involves picking up the running strand between two stitches, is used, the increases would be worked after the 7th stitch in the first interval and after the 8th stitch in the second interval. If, on the other hand, a type of increase that involves working into a stitch (such as working into the front and back of a stitch; k1f&b) is used, then the increases would be worked in the 7th stitch in the first interval and in the 8th stitch in the second interval.

> Increase after the last stitch of the interval if using the make-one (M1; lift the running thread between two stitches and knit it through its back loop) method; increase in the last stitch of the interval if using the bar method (knit into the front and back of the same stitch).

For another example, let's say we have 52 stitches on our needles and we need to increase 5 stitches evenly spaced to result in 57 stitches. The diagonal relationship between the quotients and remainders in the long-division calculation at right tells us to increase every 10th stitch 3 times, then every 11th stitch 2 times. The first three intervals involve 30 original stitches and add 3 stitches; the second two intervals involve 22 original stitches and add 2 stitches. A total of 52 original stitches have been worked and a total of 5 stitches have been increased to give the desired 57 stitches now on the needles.

For a simpler example, let's say we have 120 stitches worked in k1, p1 ribbing, and we want to decrease 20 stitches as we transition to stockinette stitch. The long-division calculation at right shows that 20 fits into 120 evenly 6 times (with no stitches remaining). To balance the number of stitches at the beginning and the end of the row, subtract the first interval from the interval schedule, divide it in half, and place half (3 stitches) at the beginning of the row and half (3 stitches) at the end. In this case, begin with k1, k2tog, then work (k4, k2tog) 19 times, then end with k3. Or simply work as follows: *K4, k2tog; rep from * 19 more times, for a total of 20 times.

> The sum of the remainder and the expanded remainder equals the divisor.

> See page 332 for details on the many ways the shaping formula can be used in knitwear design.

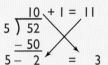

The diagonal relationship between the quotient (10) and expanded remainder (3) tells us to work 10 stitches between each increase for the first 3 increases. The diagonal relationship between the expanded quotient (11) and the remainder (2) tells us to also work 11 stitches between each increase for the remaining 2 increases. The stitch count on the needles will have increased from 52 to 57 stitches.

$$20\overline{)120}$$
$$\underline{-120}$$
$$0$$

A single diagonal partnership is worked when there is no remainder. Our example tells us to work a decrease every 6 stitches 20 times. The stitch count on the needles will have decreased from 120 to 100 stitches.

Because rows are worked in pairs—one wrong-side row for every right-side row—this must be tweaked to be an even number, either by rounding down to 26 or rounding up to 28. In this case, round up to 28 to add a bit more length.

For our sample front, use the smaller needles to cast on 117 stitches. Work these 117 stitches in ribbing as [k1, p1] 58 times, k1. For this pattern, the first and the last stitch are knit stitches on right-side rows. Because these edge stitches are worked in stockinette (knit right-side rows; purl wrong-side rows), they roll inward (to the wrong side) and virtually disappear. They are used as selvedge stitches so that the k1, p1 ribbing will appear continuous at the side seams.

Divide 117 beginning stitches by 16 decreases to determine an even distribution of decreases. In this example, decrease every 7th stitch 16 times, then work the last 5 stitches.

Step 2: Transition from Ribbing/Border to Body

In this step, the knitting changes from ribbing to stockinette stitch. To achieve the desired 18" (45.5 cm) width in the stockinette-stitch gauge, decrease 16 stitches across the first row of stockinette stitch to end up with the necessary 101 stitches. Using the condensed version of the shaping formula described on page 72, divide 117 original stitches by 16 increase stitches to find that we should decrease every 7th stitch 16 times, then work the last 5 stitches.

For our sample front, work this right-side row as [k5, k2tog] 16 times, k5.

Step 3: Lower Body

The lower body of a classic silhouette is worked the same width from the top of the ribbing to the armholes.

A garter-stitch selvedge stitch helps prevent the edges from curling and facilitates seaming.

SELVEDGE STITCHES

For garments worked in pieces that will be seamed, it's a good idea to add an extra "selvedge stitch" at each edge—one at the beginning of the row and one at the end of the row. These edge stitches will be taken up in the seams and will not contribute to the width of the garment. If these selvedge stitches are not added, the circumference of the finished sweater will be somewhat smaller than calculated.

I like to work selvedge stitches in garter stitch (knit every row) so that they help prevent the stockinette-stitch fabric from curling, which makes it easier to measure and seam the pieces together. It also makes it easy to count rows—the purl "bumps" appear on every other row.

Always work increases and decreases inside the selvedge stitches. Note that selvedge stitches are the first stitches bound off during shaping and that they need to be reestablished after binding off for an armhole or neck.

BEWARE OF LENGTHWISE STRETCH

If you knit a long garment such as an outerwear sweater, jacket, or coat, or if the yarn you use is heavy or nonresilient, it's possible that the weight of the fabric will cause the piece to stretch. To determine if this is the case, work the front until it measures about 2" (5 cm) less than the desired length to the beginning of the armhole, making sure that you have worked all of the waist-to-bust increases, if there are any. Place the stitches on a length of yarn and clamp the held stitches in a skirt hanger or ask a friend to hold it up while you measure the length as it hangs freely. Next, measure the length with the piece lying on a flat surface. If the piece feels heavy and the difference between the two measurements is more than 2" (5 cm), you can be fairly certain that the garment will have a "drip" length—the garment will gain length when it is worn. To account for this drip, you may need to alter the number of rows worked in each piece. But, before you do, knit the back to the same length, baste the body pieces together at the sides, and try it on, holding it on your body 2" (5 cm) below where the base of the planned armhole will be. You may find that the lengthwise stretch is not as severe when the pieces are seamed and stretched widthwise on your body and that no row adjustments will be necessary. However, if the piece does drip, work fewer rows accordingly. To check the sleeve drip, work the sleeve until it measures about 2" (5 cm) less than the length to the beginning of the cap shaping, baste the inner arm seam, and pull it up to the proper place on your arm.

For our sample front, change to the larger needles and work the selvedge stitches in garter stitch (knit every row) and the center 99 stitches in stockinette stitch until the stockinette section of the piece measures 11" (28 cm)—82 stockinette rows worked. It's a good idea to stop knitting after about 5" (12.5 cm) to check the gauge as described at right. Once you've verified that you're knitting to the specified gauge, continue working even until the piece reaches the desired length and number of rows.

Step 4: Armhole Shaping

At the armholes, the body changes from the width at the bust to the cross-back measurement above the armholes. This shaping is typically worked over 1½" to 3" (3.8 to 7.5 cm) in length. It usually begins with an initial bind-off that measures ½" to 1" (1.3 to 2.5 cm) in width at each side, followed by successively fewer stitches bound off and ending with one or more single-stitch bind-off(s). The first stitch bound off at each side is the selvedge stitch (it will be reestablished after all armhole bind-offs have been worked).

In our example, decrease a total of 22 stitches at the armholes.

101 stitches in bust − 79 stitches in cross-back = 22 stitches to decrease

For symmetrical shaping, decrease 11 stitches at each side. It's a good idea to plot the decreases on graph paper to ensure a smooth slope, as shown below.

The schematic on page 68 shows that the upper body (the beginning of the armhole shaping to the beginning of the shoulder shaping) is worked over 52 rows. During these 52 rows, the armhole is shaped over the first 10 rows and the front neck is shaped over the last 14 rows. Therefore, there are 28 rows between the end of the armhole shaping and the beginning of the neck shaping.

52 rows total − 10 armhole shaping rows − 14 neck shaping rows = 28 rows between last row of armhole shaping and first row of neck shaping

For our sample front, use the sloped method described on page 77 to bind off 4 stitches at the beginning of the first 2 rows, bind off 3 stitches at the beginning of the next 2 rows, bind off 2 stitches at the beginning of the next 2 rows, then bind off 1 stitch at the beginning of the next 4 rows for a total of 11 stitches bound off at each side over 10 rows. Reestablish the selvedge stitches at each side and continue even until the armholes measure 5" (12.5 cm)—38 rows total.

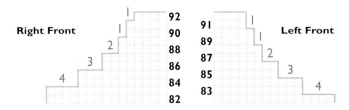

Plot of the armhole decreases for the right and left front.

GAUGE CHECK

After you've worked about 5" (12.5 cm), check to make sure that you're getting the gauge you used in your calculations. Slip all of the stitches onto a length of yarn, block the piece as you plan to block the garment, then measure the stitch and row gauges. If these gauges are the same as initially calculated, place the stitches back on the needles and continue knitting. If the gauges are different, record the new gauges, then rip out the knitting and begin again, making the necessary adjustment by increasing or decreasing stitches and planning to knit more or fewer rows.

ARMHOLE-SHAPING SCHEDULE

Odd-numbered rows are right-side (RS) rows; even-numbered rows are wrong-side (WS) rows.

Garment Row	Shaping Row	Stitches Bound Off
83 (RS)	1	4
84 (WS)	2	4
85	3	3
86	4	3
87	5	2
88	6	2
89	7	1
90	8	1
91	9	1
92	10	1

Total: 22 stitches (11 stitches each side) bound off over 10 rows.

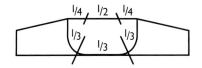

The neck is divided in three sections—the center bind-off and decreases worked along each side. Typically, one-half or one-third of the stitches are bound off initially, then the rest are divided between the two sides.

Step 5: Front Neck Shaping

The most important part of planning the neck shaping is to allow for a width big enough (including neckband edging) to accommodate the head but not so big that the garment falls off the shoulders. A 1" (2.5 cm) ribbed border will reduce the total circumference of the finished neck opening by 1" (2.5 cm). The shallower the neck depth, the wider the width must be, and vice versa. For a close-fitting neck opening on a pullover, plan on adding a zipper or button placket to allow the opening to fit over the head. For a very deep "V" neckline, the neck opening must be narrower to keep it from falling off the shoulders. In general, the neck comprises between 40% and 50% of the cross-back measurement.

In our example, the high round neck is 7" (18 cm) wide, which translates to 39 stitches, and 2" (5 cm) deep before the beginning of the shoulder shaping, which translates to 14 rows. The 8 rows of shoulder shaping will contribute another 1" (2.5 cm) for a total neck depth of 3" (7.5 cm), or 22 rows. There are two conventions for shaping the front neck based on the number of center neck stitches bound off in the first row of shaping—one-third (which produces a slightly narrower neckline) or one-half (which produces a slightly wider neckline). Both methods involve decreasing the same number of total stitches over the same number of total rows, but the distributions of the decreases differ. In both cases, the neck shaping is divided in three sections—the center bind-off and an identical set of decreases worked at each edge.

ONE-THIRD INITIAL BIND-OFF

In this scenario, one-third of the stitches are bound off on the first row of shaping, one-third are bound off on the right side of the neck in a series of steps, and one-third are bound off on the left side of the neck in a similar series of steps. In our example, we begin with 39 neck stitches.

39 neck stitches ÷ 3 sections = 13 stitches/section

Although 39 can be divided evenly by 3, this type of calculation often results in fractions of stitches. In these cases, adjust the three sections so that there are whole numbers of stitches in each, working more stitches in the initial bind-off, if necessary. Chart the neck stitches and rows to help you distribute the side decreases to create a nice, even curve.

For our sample front, bind off the center 13 stitches on the first row, then work the right and left sides separately, using the sloped bind-off method described at right. Begin the shaping for the left neck edge (as worn) on the second row and begin the shaping for the right neck edge (as worn) on the third row. On each side, bind off 4 stitches once, then bind off 3 stitches once, then bind off 2 stitches 2 times, then bind off 1 stitch 2 times, for a total of 13 stitches bound off on each side.

SLOPED BIND-OFF

The sloped bind off forms a smooth curve and prevents "stair steps" from forming between subsequent bind-off rows. This is achieved by not working the last stitch of the previous row, then slipping the first stitch on the bind-off row purlwise to the right-hand needle, then binding off the unworked stitch by lifting it over the slipped stitch and off the needle. These unworked stitches pull the rows closer together to form the curved edge. This technique is ideal when shaping armholes, necks, and shoulders.

On the first row, bind off as usual to define the initial part of the bind-off slope. Work the next row to the last stitch but do not work the last stitch. Instead, turn the work so that the unworked stitch becomes the first stitch on the right-hand needle. Keeping the yarn in back of the work, slip the first stitch on the left-hand needle purlwise, then bind off the unworked stitch by lifting it over the slipped stitch and off the needle (as for a regular bind-off).

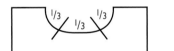
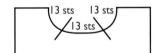

Divide the neck stitches in thirds; in our example, there are 13 stitches in each third.

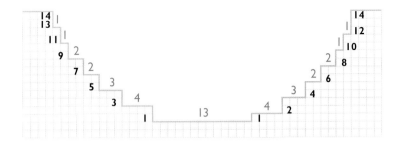

Plot of the front neck bind-offs. Bind-off stitches are shown in red; row numbers are shown in black.

In this scenario, one-half of the stitches are bound off on the first row of shaping and the other half are evenly divided between the left and right sides of the neck (one-quarter each). The stitches are bound off on the two sides in a series of steps. In this example, we have 39 neck stitches.

39 neck stitches ÷ 2 = 19.5 stitches

Because 39 cannot be evenly divided in half, adjust the numbers so that there is a whole number of stitches in each of the three sections. If 20 stitches are included in the center bind-off, 19 stitches will remain to be divided between the two sides. But 19 can't be evenly divided by 2. If, however, 21 stitches are included in the center bind-off, 18 stitches will remain to be divided between the two sides, leaving 9 stitches at each side.

39 neck stitches – 21 center bind-off stitches = 18 stitches for the two sides combined
18 stitches ÷ 2 sections = 9 stitches at each side

In this case, we added 2 stitches to the center bind-off, but we could have just as easily subtracted 2 stitches to give us 10 stitches at each side. Whether to add or subtract stitches from the center bind-off section is a matter of personal choice, adding stitches will make the base of the neckline slightly wider; subtracting stitches will make it slightly narrower.

Divide the neck stitches in half, designate half of the stitches for the initial bind-off, and divide the other half of the stitches equally between the two sides (one-quarter at each side). In this example, there are 21 stitches in the center and 9 stitches at each side.

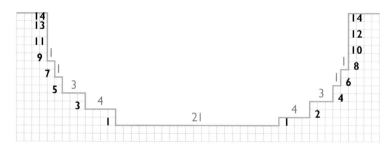

Plot of the neck decreases. Bind-off stitches are shown in red; row numbers are shown in black.

For our sample front, bind off the center 21 stitches on the first row, then work the right and left sides separately, using the sloped bind-off method described on page 77. Begin the shaping for the left neck edge (as worn) on the second row and begin the shaping for the right neck edge (as worn) on the third row. On each side, bind off 4 stitches once, then bind off 3 stitches once, then bind off 1 stitch 2 times, for a total of 9 stitches bound off each side.

Step 6: Shoulder Shaping

In our example, the shoulder shaping, or slope, is worked over the final 1" (2.5 cm) of the body, which translates to 8 rows. Because the bind-offs can only be worked at the beginning of rows, divide the number of rows in half to determine the number of rows available for binding off on each side.

8 rows total ÷ 2 = 4 bind-off rows on each side.

Next, divide the number of stitches in each shoulder by the number of bind-off rows in the shoulder slope. In our example, we have 20 stitches at each shoulder after the neck shaping is complete.

20 shoulder stitches ÷ 4 bind-off rows = 5 stitches to bind off on each bind-off row

For our sample front, use the sloped technique (see page 77) to bind off 5 stitches at each armhole edge (beginning of right-side rows for the left armhole edge of the garment; beginning of wrong-side rows for the right armhole edge of the garment) 4 times.

Step 7: Back

The back is worked exactly as the front through the 10 armhole shaping rows. In our example, the back neck begins when the armholes measure 7¼" (18.5 cm), which translates to 54 rows. The back neck shaping begins after the first 2 rows of the shoulder shaping have been completed.

For our sample back, repeat Step 1 through Step 4, but continue working the upper body even until a total of 52 rows have been worked from the beginning of the armhole.

Step 8: Back Neck and Shoulder Shaping

In the remaining 1" (2.5 cm), or 8 rows, both the shoulders and back neck are shaped. The back neck shaping creates a slight curve below the back neck bone and typically involves just ½" to 1" (1.3 to 2.5 cm) of length. The initial bind-off removes 50% to 75% of the neck stitches. The remaining stitches are then evenly distributed between the two sides and are bound off in one, two, or three segments. Fewer steps are used to shape the back neck than the front neck because the back shaping is typically much shallower.

 tip For the shoulder seams to match, the back shoulders must be shaped the same way as the front shoulders.

Plot of the back neck and shoulder shaping. Bind-off stitches are shown in red; row numbers are shown in black.

ROW-BY-ROW INSTRUCTIONS FOR BACK NECK AND SHOULDER SHAPING

Use the sloped method to bind off stitches for the back neck and shoulders. Note that odd-numbered rows are right-side (RS) rows and even-numbered rows are wrong-side (WS) rows.

Row 1:
(RS) Bind off 5 shoulder stitches at the beginning of the row, then knit to the end of the row.

Row 2:
(WS) Bind off 5 shoulder stitches at the beginning of the row, then purl to the end of the row.

Row 3:
Bind off 5 stitches at the beginning of the row, knit until there are 19 stitches on the needle after the bind-off gap (10 right shoulder stitches plus 9 right side neck stitches), bind off the center 21 back neck stitches, knit remaining 24 stitches (9 left side neck stitches plus 15 left shoulder stitches). From here on, the two sides of the neck will be worked separately.

Row 4:
Bind off 5 stitches at the beginning of left-hand side, purl to the gap formed by the neck bind-offs; join a second ball of yarn to the beginning of the right-hand side, bind off the first 5 stitches, purl to the end of the row.

Row 5:
Bind off 5 stitches at the beginning of the right-hand side, knit to the gap formed by the neck bind-offs; bind off 5 stitches at the beginning of the left-hand side, knit to the end of the row.

Row 6:
Bind off 5 stitches at the beginning of the left-hand side, purl to the gap formed by the neck bind-offs; bind off 4 stitches at the beginning of the right-hand side, purl to the end of the row.

Row 7:
Knit all stitches on the right-hand side; bind off 4 stitches at the beginning of the left-hand side, knit to the end of the row.

Row 8:
Bind off the remaining stitches on each side.

For our sample back, shape the back neck over ¾" (2 cm), using the one-half initial bind-off method (see page 78). Therefore, shape the neck over 6 rows by binding off 21 stitches on the first row of neck shaping, then binding off 9 stitches at each neck edge in two segments (5 stitches in the first segment and 4 stitches in the second segment). Note that this happens at the same time as the shoulders are shaped over 8 rows by binding off 5 stitches at each armhole edge 4 times. Plot the neck and shoulder decreases on graph paper to help visualize the different decrease rates.

 tip

The back neck of a garment does not have to be formally shaped. In truth, the back neck needs to be only a tiny bit lower than the top of the shoulder. If you use a three-needle bind-off (see page 263) to join the shoulders, the single extra row worked on the shoulders creates enough contour for a good fit. If you plan to add a collar, a higher back neck is preferable because it prevents the garment from dipping down in the back.

MATH CHECK!

The number of rows from the beginning of the armhole to the beginning of shoulder shaping plus the number of rows in the shoulder shaping should equal the total number of rows in the upper body, and there should be the same number of rows in the front as in the back.

In our example, there are 52 rows from the beginning of the armhole to the beginning of the shoulder and 8 rows in the shoulder shaping.

> 52 rows in armhole + 8 rows in shoulder
> = 60 rows total in upper body

For the front, there are 38 rows from the armhole to the beginning of the neck, 14 rows in the front neck shaping, and 8 rows in the shoulder shaping.

> 38 rows in armhole + 14 rows in neck shaping + 8 rows in shoulder
> = 60 rows total in upper body

SLEEVES

The sleeve for our sample sweater is worked from the cuff to the shoulder. The cuff is worked in the desired pattern for the desired length, then a transition row is worked to add or subtract stitches as necessary so that the desired width is maintained when the pattern changes from the cuff pattern to the sleeve pattern. The sleeve is tapered to the desired upper arm width, ending a couple of inches below the beginning of the armhole, then worked even before the "set-in" cap is shaped to fit the armhole of the body.

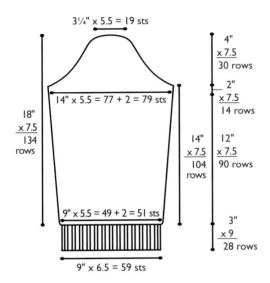

Set-in sleeve schematic annotated with numbers of stitches and rows.

GAUGE

Body (stockinette stitch): 5.5 stitches and 7.5 rows = 1" (2.5 cm)

Rounded body gauge: 6 stitches and 8 rows = 1" (2.5 cm)

KEY MEASUREMENTS

Cuff width: 8" (20.5 cm) + 1" (2.5 cm) ease = 9" (23 cm)

Upper arm width: 12" (30.5 cm) + 2" (5 cm) ease = 14" (35.5 cm)

Cap length: 4" (10 cm), based on calculations we'll perform later.

Final bind-off width: 3¼" (8.5 cm)

Cuff-to-cuff measurement (length from wrist to armpit + length from armpit to the shoulder + cross-back width + shoulder to other armpit + armpit to other wrist) 56" (142 cm)

Cuff length: 3" (7.5 cm)

Sleeve length from top of cuff to armhole: 14" (35.5 cm)

Armhole depth: 7" (18 cm)

Conversion of Measurements to Number of Stitches and Rows

WIDTHS

Number of stitches in cuff (cuff width × border stitch gauge)

    9" (23 cm) × 6.5 stitches/inch = 58.5; round up to 59 stitches for an odd number of stitches to balance the ribbing pattern

Number of stitches at base of sleeve (cuff width × body stitch gauge + 2 selvedge stitches)

    9" (23 cm) × 5.5 stitches/inch + 2 selvedge stitches = 51.5 stitches; round down to the nearest odd number = 51 stitches

Number of stitches at upper arm (upper arm width × body stitch gauge + 2 selvedge stitches)

    14" (35.5 cm) × 5.5 stitches/inch + 2 selvedge stitches = 79 stitches

Number of stitches in final cap bind-off (final bind-off width × body stitch gauge)

    3¼" (8.5 cm) × 5.5 stitches/inch = 17.9 stitches; round up to the next odd number = 19 stitches

LENGTHS

Number of rows in cuff (border length × border row gauge)

    3" (7.5 cm) × 9 rows/inch = 27 rows; round up to the nearest even number = 28 rows

Number of rows from top of cuff to beginning of cap (sleeve length × body stitch gauge)

    14" (35.5 cm) × 7.5 rows/inch = 105 rows; round down to the nearest even number = 104 rows

Number of rows in cap (cap length × sleeve row gauge)

4" (10 cm) × 7.5 rows/inch = 30 rows

Number of rows in body armhole (length × body row gauge)

7" (18 cm) × 7.5 rows/inch = 52.5 rows;
round down to nearest even number = 52 rows

Step 9: Cast-On and Ribbing/Border

The sleeve begins with stitches cast on for the border or cuff, which are worked in k1, p1 ribbing on the smaller needles. We therefore need to calculate the number of stitches to cast on based on the averaged stitch gauge of the ribbing (see page 69) by multiplying the cuff measurement by the averaged cuff stitch gauge.

9" (23 cm) × 6.5 stitches/inch = 58.5 stitches

Round this number up to 59 stitches to give an odd number of stitches to balance the k1, p1 ribbing (see page 68), beginning and ending with a knit stitch: [k1, p1] 29 times, k1.

The row gauge for the ribbing is 9 rows = 1" (2.5 cm) and the pattern calls for 3" (7.5 cm) of ribbing.

9 rows × 3" (7.5 cm) = 27 rows; round up to 28 rows to maintain an even number of rows

For our sample sleeve, use the smaller needles to cast on 59 stitches, then work in ribbing for 28 rows.

Step 10: Transition from Ribbing/Border to Sleeve

We now change from ribbing to stockinette stitch. To achieve the desired 9" (23 cm) width in the stockinette-stitch gauge, 8 stitches must be decreased across the first row to end up with the necessary 51 stitches. The diagonal relationship between the quotient (7) and the expanded remainder (5) in the shaping formula tells us to decrease every 7th stitch 5 times. The diagonal relationship between the expanded quotient (8) and the remainder (3) tells us to also decrease every 8th stitch 3 times. Because decreases involve 2 stitches, work the first series of decreases as [k5, k2tog] 5 times, and the second series of decreases as [k6, k2tog] 3 times. To prevent the final decrease from falling on the last stitch, work the first decrease midway through the first interval, then work the remaining 7 intervals, and end by working the remaining stitches of the first interval.

For our sample sleeve, balance the edges by dividing 7 in half and placing 4 stitches at the beginning and 3 stitches at the end of the row. Work this row as k2, k2tog, [k5, k2tog] 4 times, [k6, k2tog] 3 times, k3.

Use the shaping formula to determine an even distribution of decreases. In this example, decrease every 7th stitch 5 times and every 8th stitch 3 times. To prevent the final decrease from falling on the last stitch, work the first decrease midway through the first interval and work the balance of that interval at the end.

To plan for an equal number of increases along each side of the sleeve, the difference between the number of stitches in the upper arm and the cuff should be divisible by 2. In most cases, this means that if there is an even number stitches in the cuff, there should be an even number of upper arm stitches; if there is an odd number of stitches in the cuff, there should be an odd number of stitches in the upper arm. (This rule doesn't apply if you use a combination of stitch patterns, some of which involve an odd number of stitches and some of which involve an even number of stitches.)

Step 11: Sleeve Taper to Upper Arm

In this step, work to the armhole while at the same time increasing stitches to create a smooth taper from the cuff to the upper arm width. To determine how many stitches to increase during the taper, subtract the number of stitches in the first row after the cuff transition from the number of stitches in the upper sleeve.

> 79 stitches in upper arm − 51 stitches at top of cuff = 28 stitches to be increased

Because the increases are worked as pairs (1 stitch increased at each end of the needle), there will be 14 increase rows.

> 28 stitches to be increased ÷ 2 stitches increased per increase row = 14 increase rows

The sleeve taper typically begins at the top of the cuff and ends 2" to 3" (5 to 7.5 cm) below the beginning of the armhole to allow sufficient length of the full width for comfort and ease of movement. In our example, the length from the cuff to the armhole measures 14" (35.5 cm) and the taper will end 2" (5 cm) before the beginning of the armhole, which means the taper is calculated over 12" (30.5 cm) of sleeve length.

> 12" (30.5 cm) of shaping × 7.5 rows/inch = 90 rows of shaping

To determine how to space these increases evenly, use the shaping formula to divide the number of shaping rows (90) by the number of increase rows to be worked (14). The diagonal relationship between the quotient (6) and the expanded remainder (8) tells us that we'll increase every 6th row 8 times. The diagonal relationship between the expanded quotient (7) and the remainder (6) tells us to also increase every 7th row 6 times.

For our sample sleeve, change to larger needles, then increase 1 stitch at each end of the needle every 6th row 8 times, then every 7th row 6 times—79 stitches. Work 14 rows (2" [5 cm]) even for a total of 104 rows to the desired length of 14" (35.5 cm) from the transition row.

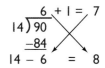

Use the shaping formula to determine an even distribution of increase rows. In this example, increase every 6th row 8 times and every 7th row 6 times.

Step 12: Cap Shaping

For the upper body to fit properly, the sleeve cap must fit easily into the armhole opening, and there must be sufficient ease in the upper torso to allow for unrestrained movement of the shoulders and arms. When the front, back, and sleeves are sewn together, the sleeve seams should emerge from the underarm, extend along the outer edge of the top of the arm between the underarm and the shoulder, and across the outer edges of the shoulder bones.

The cross-back and armhole depth are key measurements in calculating a proper-fitting cap. If the cross-back is too wide, extra fabric at the underarm will give the appearance of a modified drop-shoulder silhouette. If the cross-back is too narrow, the sleeves will be too short. If the armhole depth is too shallow, the cap will pull up past the shoulder bone and restrict the ease of your upper-body movements. If the armhole depth is too long, the extra depth in the cap will bunch up in the underarm area.

When calculating the sleeve cap, you'll use the actual stitch and row gauges as well as those gauges rounded to the nearest even number. This is because the same shaping is worked in pairs of stitches (the same decreases are worked at each end of the needle to produce a symmetrical cap) and pairs of rows (an equal number of right-side and wrong-side rows). Other key measurements are the armhole depth (as measured on the body), the width of the upper sleeve, and the length from the cuff of one sleeve to the cuff of the other sleeve (the entire length of one sleeve, the width of one shoulder, the neck width, the width of the other shoulder, and the entire length of the other sleeve). The total knitted length of both sleeves (including the caps) plus the cross-back (shoulder-to-shoulder) width should add up to the wrist-to-wrist measurement.

For a proper fit when the pieces are seamed, the cap must be a few inches shorter than the armhole depth (underarm to shoulder). In general, the difference between the length of the sleeve cap and the length of the armhole is based on the bust/chest circumference. Typically, for bust/chest circumferences up to 30" (76 cm), the difference is 2" (5 cm); for circumferences between 30" and 48" (76 and 122 cm), the difference is 3" (7.5 cm); for circumferences over 48" (122 cm), the difference is 4" (10 cm). Use these numbers as a general guide, but always work out custom calculations for each project.

A set-in sleeve cap is worked in four sections.

A set-in sleeve cap is shaped like a narrow bell curve that extends from the base of the underarm to the shoulder, across the top of the shoulder, and back down to the base of the underarm. It is worked in four sections. In Section 1, stitches are bound off to match the armhole bind-offs of the body. In Section 2, the center portion of the cap is shaped by tapering the sides to the last ½" (1.3 cm) of cap length. In Section 3, the top slope is formed by binding off 2" (5 cm) in width (1" [2.5 cm] at each side) in the last ½" (1.3 cm) of the cap. In Section 4, the remaining stitches are bound off all at once. Although the sections are worked in order, we will work the calculations for Section 1 first, followed by Section 4, Section 3, then Section 2. This is because we have enough information to calculate the numbers for Sections 1, 3, and 4. Section 2 is determined by the numbers calculated for the other sections.

Sleeve caps are planned to fit into the armhole of a garment. Therefore, the cap calculations are based on the armhole depth and the bind-off sequence used to the shape the armholes on the body. The armholes are typically shaped over 1½" to 3" (3.8 to 7.5 cm) of rows. The first bind-off increment usually removes between ½" and 1" (1.3 and 2.5 cm) of stitches at each side. You can plan your cap shaping to match the body armhole shaping exactly or match as few as the first two bind-off rows (one on each side), depending on the width and length of the cap. In the following example, only the first two body bind-offs are matched.

There is also some leeway in the how the center cap decreases are worked, and it's a good idea to plot the cap on graph paper after planning the decrease schedule based on the instructions given here. Keep in mind that if the total cap length is correct, the final bind-off width is correct, and the initial cap bind-off matches the initial armhole bind-off, your sleeve will fit.

Section 1: Armhole Bind-Off Match

The cap shaping begins with the same set of bind-offs (usually ½" to 1" [1.3 to 2.5 cm] in width) worked at the base of the armhole of the sweater body so that the base of the sleeve exactly matches the base of the armhole. In our example, we bound off 4 stitches at each armhole edge for a total of 8 stitches bound off over 2 rows.

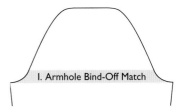

I. Armhole Bind-Off Match

Section 4: Final Bind-Off

For a smooth fit, the bind-off row at the top of the cap should measure a little less than one-quarter of the upper arm width. First divide the upper arm width by 4, then subtract ¼" (6 mm) from this number.

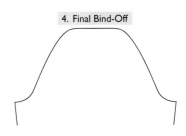

4. Final Bind-Off

> Upper arm width ÷ 4 − ¼" (6 mm) = final bind-off width
> 14" (35.5 cm) ÷ 4 = 3½" (9 cm)
> 3½" − ¼" (6 mm) = 3¼" (8.5 cm)

To determine the number of stitches in this width, multiply this number by the stitch gauge.

> Final bind-off width × stitch gauge = number of stitches in final bind-off
> 3¼" (8.5 cm) × 5.5 = 17.875; round up to odd number to match upper arm
> = 19 stitches

In our example, bind off 19 stitches on the last row of the cap.

tip If the upper arm stitch count is an even number, the final cap bind-off must also be an even number (and vice versa) because the same number of stitches is decreased at each side of the cap.

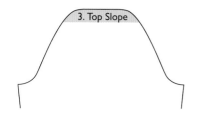

Section 3: Top Slope

This is the steeper slope worked over the last ½" (1.3 cm) of the cap shaping to round out the top of the bell-shaped curve of the cap. In this section, 2" (5 cm) of stitches (1" [2.5 cm] on each side) are bound off over this final ½" (1.3 cm) of rows. Use the rounded stitch and row gauges in these calculations (because the same number of stitches must be bound off at each side and the bind-offs must occur over an even number of rows). First, multiply the rounded stitch gauge by 2 to determine the number of stitches to be bound off in this section.

6 stitches/inch × 2 = 12 stitches

Next, divide the rounded row gauge by 2 to determine the number of rows to work the final bind-offs.

8 rows/inch ÷ 2 = 4 rows

Divide the number of stitches by the number of rows to determine how many stitches to bind off on each row of this section.

12 stitches ÷ 4 rows = 3 stitches bound off on each of 4 rows

In our example, bind off 3 stitches at the beginning of each of 4 rows.

Section 2: Center Cap

To begin, we need to determine the total number of rows in the cap. This number is based on the width of the final bind-off, the estimated cap length based on the chest/bust circumference given in the table below left, and the armhole depth. To begin, divide the final bind-off in half (because half of the final bind-off falls on the front of the shoulder and half on the back of the shoulder).

Final bind-off ÷ 2 = half of final bind-off width
3¼" (8.5 cm) ÷ 2 = 1⅝" (4 cm)

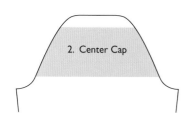

ESTIMATED CAP LENGTH (DIFFERENCE BETWEEN CAP LENGTH AND ARMHOLE DEPTH BASED ON CIRCUMFERENCE)

Bust/Chest Circumference	Difference Between Length and Armhole Depth
Less than 30" (76 cm)	2" (5 cm)
30" to 48" (76 to 122 cm)	3" (7.5 cm)
More than 48" (122 cm)	4" (10 cm)

Next, subtract half of the estimated cap length (see box at left) and half of the final bind-off from the armhole depth to get the total cap length.

armhole depth − half estimated cap length − half final bind-off = total cap length
7" (18 cm) − 1½" (3.8 cm) − 1⅝" (4 cm) = 3⅞" (9.8 cm);
we'll round up to an even 4" (10 cm)

Finally, multiply this number by the row gauge to get the total number of rows in the cap.

4" (10 cm) × 7.5 rows/inch = 30 rows

In our example, the cap length is 4" (10 cm), which is 3" (7.5 cm) shorter than the armhole depth of 7" (18 cm).

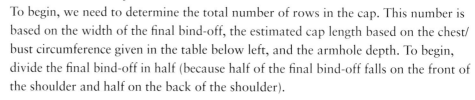

MATH CHECK!

Armhole depth − cap length = amount cap is shorter than armhole
7" (18 cm) − 4" (10 cm) = 3" (7.5 cm)

The number of stitches to decrease in this section is determined by subtracting the number of stitches in the armhole bind-off match (Section 1), top slope (Section 3), and final bind-off (Section 4) from the number of stitches in the upper arm.

> Stitches in upper arm − stitches decreased in armhole match − stitches decreased in top slope − stitches in final bind-off = total number of stitches to decrease in center taper
>
> 79 upper arm stitches − 8 stitches bound off in Section 1 − 12 stitches bound off in Section 3 − 19 stitches bound off in Section 4 = 40 stitches

Because we want these 40 stitches evenly divided between the two sides of the cap, we'll decrease 20 stitches at each edge.

The number of rows over which to decrease these 40 stitches is determined by subtracting the number of rows in the armhole bind-off match (Section 1) and top slope (Section 3) from the total number of rows in the cap.

> Total rows in cap − rows in armhole match − rows in top slope
> = number of rows in center cap
>
> 30 rows total − 2 rows in armhole bind-off match − 4 rows in top slope = 24 rows

We now know that we need to decrease 20 stitches on each side of the needle (40 stitches total) over 24 rows of knitting. Use the shaping formula to plan the sequence of these decreases.

SHAPING ELEMENTS

The decreases used in shaping the sleeve cap can be worked in a series of single decreases that can be made to slant to the right, slant to the left, or they can be worked in a series of bind-offs, using the sloped method (see page 77) to produce smooth edges. When single decreases are stacked one on top of another in adjacent rows, a "decorative" line of stitches results. These types of decreases, called shaping elements, are commonly used along raglan shaping. The decreases are typically made at the beginning and end of right-side rows; wrong-side rows are worked even. If you do not want visible shaping elements along the edge of your cap, use the sloped bind-off technique. In this case, the shaping is worked at the beginning of every row.

Begin by dividing the number of stitches to bind off (40) by the number of rows in this section (24).

The diagonal relationship between the quotient (1) and the expanded remainder (8) in the shaping formula tells us to bind off 1 stitch at the beginning of 8 rows. The diagonal relationship between the expanded quotient (2) and the remainder (16) tells us to also bind off 2 stitches at the beginning of 16 rows.

Divide the larger number (16) by the smaller number (8) to determine the number of 2-stitch bind-offs worked for every 1-stitch bind-off.

> 16 (2-stitch bind-offs) ÷ 8 (1-stitch bind-offs) = 2

$$\begin{array}{r} 1 \quad +1 = 2 \\ 24\overline{)\,40} \\ \underline{-24} \\ 24 - 16 \quad = \quad 8 \end{array}$$

Use the shaping formula to determine an even distribution of 40 bind-off stitches over 24 rows. In this example, bind off 1 stitch 8 times and bind off 2 stitches 16 times.

SLEEVE-CAP SHAPING SEQUENCE

SECTION 1

Cap Row #	Section 1 Row #	Stitches Bound Off
1	1	4
2	2	4

A total of 8 stitches are bound off over 2 rows in Section 1.

79 upper arm stitches – 8 stitches bound off = 71 stitches remain in cap

SECTION 2

Cap Row #	Section 2 Row #	Stitches Bound Off
3	1	2
4	2	2
5	3	2
6	4	2
7	5	1
8	6	1
9	7	2
10	8	2
11	9	2
12	10	2
13	11	1
14	12	1
15	13	2
16	14	2
17	15	2
18	16	2
19	17	1
20	18	1
21	19	2
22	20	2
23	21	2
24	22	2
25	23	1
26	24	1

A total of 40 stitches are bound off over 24 rows in Section 2.

71 stitches in cap – 40 stitches bound off = 31 stitches remain in cap

SECTION 3

Cap Row #	Section 3 Row #	Stitches Bound Off
27	1	3
28	2	3
29	3	3
30	4	3

A total of 12 stitches are bound off over 4 rows in Section 3.

31 stitches in cap – 12 stitches bound off in Section 3 = 19 stitches remain in cap.

SECTION 4

Cap Row #	Section 4 Row #	Stitches Bound Off
31	1	19

The remaining 19 stitches are bound off in a single row in Section 4.

In other words, work a 2-to-1 ratio: two 2-stitch bind-offs for every 1-stitch bind-off. Keep in mind that rows need to be worked in pairs—a right-side row followed by a wrong-side row so that identical bind-offs are worked on each side of the cap. Therefore, each 2-to-1 ratio will consist of 6 rows: 2 stitches bound off at the beginning of 4 rows (2 stitches bound off at each side 2 times) followed by 1 stitch bound off at the beginning of 2 rows (1 stitch bound off at each side 1 time).

To determine the number of times to work this 6-row sequence, divide the number of rows in this section of the cap (24) by the number of rows in the sequence (6).

24 rows ÷ 6 rows per section = 4 sections of the 6-row sequence.

Whether you begin with binding off 2 stitches at the beginning of 4 rows or binding off 1 stitch at the beginning of the next 2 rows is up to you. For our example, let's choose to begin by binding off 2 stitches 4 times. *Bind off 2 stitches at the beginning of the next 4 rows, then bind off 1 stitch at the beginning of the following 2 rows; repeat from * 3 more times.

For our sample sleeve, bind off 4 stitches at the beginning of the next 2 rows (Section 1), then use the sloped method (see page 77) to [bind off 2 stitches at the beginning of the next 4 rows, then bind off 1 stitch at the beginning of the following 2 rows] 4 times (Section 2), then bind off 3 stitches at the beginning of the next 4 rows (Section 3), then bind off the remaining 19 stitches (Section 4).

MATH CHECK!

The sum of the number of stitches decreased in Sections 1, 2, 3, and 4 should equal the number of stitches in the upper arm of the sleeve (79 stitches).

Section 1: 8 stitches

Section 2: 40 stitches

Section 3: 12 stitches

Section 4: 19 stitches

Total: 8 stitches + 40 stitches + 12 stitches + 19 stitches = 79 stitches

It's always a good idea to plot the cap decreases on graph paper to ensure that the cap follows a bell-shaped curve. If the charted outline does not have a rounded shape, use more of the armhole bind-off rows for the beginning bind-offs, then shorten and re-calculate the center cap rows. Be aware that if you stack too many of the same bind-offs in succession (such as 2-stitch bind-offs for more than three consecutive bind-off rows at each edge of the cap), the bell-shaped curve of the cap will be replaced by straight diagonal lines that will more closely resemble a raglan than a set-in sleeve.

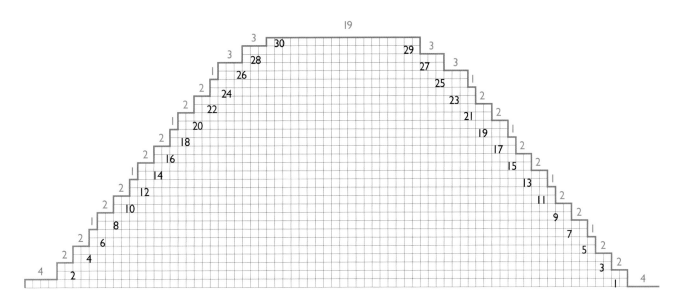

Plot of the sleeve-cap shaping. Bind-off stitches are shown in red; row numbers are shown in black.

CLASSIC BODY WORKSHEET

NEEDLE SIZE

Border   Body

_____

SWATCH MEASUREMENTS

Border   Stitch pattern

_____

Body   Stitch pattern

_____

GAUGE   For ribbing, measure the averaged gauge (see page 69).

Border stitch gauge

_____

Border row gauge

_____

Body stitch gauge

_____

Body row gauge

_____

KEY MEASUREMENTS (INCLUDING EASE)

Bust circumference

_____

Bust width

_____

Cross-back width

_____

Neck width

_____

Shoulder width

_____

Length from bottom of garment to base of armholes

_____

Notch width _(modified-drop shoulder)_

_____

Armhole depth _(set-in sleeve)_

_____

Length from base of armholes to base of front neck

_____

_____

Length from beginning of front neck to base of shoulders

_____

_____

Shoulder slope

_____

Neck-to-wrist measurement

_____

Percentage of stitches in initial front-neck bind-off

_____

_____

Percentage of stitches in initial back-neck bind-off

_____

_____

Fill out the information on this page and use it in conjunction with your schematic to create step-by-step knitting instructions.

CALCULATIONS FOR NUMBERS OF STITCHES AND ROWS

Number of stitches in border (hip width × border stitch gauge)

Number of stitches at base of body
(hip width × body stitch gauge + 2 selvedge stitches)

Number of stitches in bust width
(bust width × body stitch gauge + 2 selvedge stitches)

Number of stitches in notch (modified drop-shoulder only)
(notch width × body stitch gauge)

Number of stitches in cross-back
(shoulder-to-shoulder width × body stitch gauge + 2 selvedge stitches)

Number of stitches in neck width
(neck width × body stitch gauge)

Number of stitches in each shoulder
(shoulder width × body stitch gauge + 1 selvedge stitch)

Number of rows in border
(border length × border row gauge)

Number of rows from beginning of body to base of armhole
(length × body row gauge)

Number of rows from beginning of body to base of front neck
(length × body row gauge)

Number of rows from beginning of body to base of back neck
(length × body row gauge)

Number of rows from beginning of body to base of shoulder
(length × body row gauge)

Number of rows from base of armhole to base of front neck
(length × body row gauge)

Number of rows from base of front neck to base of shoulder
(length × body row gauge)

Number of rows in notch (modified-drop shoulder)
(notch depth × body row gauge)

Number of rows in armhole (armhole length × body row gauge)

Number of rows in shoulder slope (length × body row gauge)

Number of rows from base of armhole to base of back neck
(length × body row gauge)

Number of rows from base of back neck to base of shoulder
(length × body row gauge)

Fill out the information on this page and use it in conjunction with your schematic to create step-by-step knitting instructions.

SLEEVE WORKSHEET

NEEDLE SIZE

Border _____ Body _____

SWATCH MEASUREMENTS

Border _____ Stitch pattern _____

Body _____ Stitch pattern _____

KEY MEASUREMENTS

Cuff width _____

Upper arm width _____

Cap length _____

Cuff-to-cuff measurement _____
(*twice the length from center Back-to-Wrist*)

GAUGE   For ribbing, measure the averaged gauge (see page 69).

Border stitch gauge _____   Border row gauge _____

Body stitch gauge _____   Body row gauge _____

Rounded stitch gauge _____

Rounded row gauge _____

Fill out the information on this page and use it in conjunction with your schematic to create step-by-step knitting instructions.

CALCULATIONS FOR NUMBERS OF STITCHES AND ROWS

Number of stitches in cuff
(knuckle measurement × border stitch gauge)

Number of stitches at base of sleeve
(knuckle measurement × sleeve stitch gauge
+ 2 selvedge stitches)

Number of stitches at upper arm
(upper arm measurement × sleeve stitch gauge
+ 2 selvedge stitches)

Number of stitches increased during taper
(number of stitches at upper arm − number of
stitches at base of sleeve; divide this number by two
to get the number of increases worked at each side)

Number of stitches in final cap bind-off
(final bind-off width × sleeve stitch gauge)

Number of rows in cuff
(border length × border row gauge)

Number of rows for taper (taper length ×
sleeve row gauge − work even section at top)

**Number of rows from top of cuff to beginning
of cap** (sleeve length × sleeve row gauge)

Number of rows in cap
(cap length × sleeve row gauge)

ADDITIONAL MEASUREMENTS FOR SET-IN SLEEVE CAP

Cap Section 1: Armhole Bind-Off Match
Repeat the first 2 rows of armhole shaping on body

Cap Section 2: Center Cap
Final bind-off ÷ 2 = half of final bind-off width

armhole depth − half estimated cap length (see box
on page 86) − half final bind off = total cap length

total cap length × row gauge = number of rows in cap

Stitches in upper arm − stitches decreased in
armhole match − stitches decreased in top slope
− stitches in final bind-off = total number of stitches
to decrease in center cap taper

Total rows in cap − rows in armhole match
− rows in top slope = number of rows in center cap

Cap Section 3: Top Slope
2" (5 cm) × rounded stitch gauge = number of stitches bound off

½" (1.3 cm) × rounded row gauge
= number of rows to work the bind-offs

Number of stitches bound off ÷ number of rows to work
the bind-offs = number of stitches to bind off on each row

Cap Section 4: Final bind-off
Upper arm width ÷ 4 − ¼" (.6 cm) = final bind-off width

Final bind-off width × stitch gauge = number of stitches
in final bind off

Fill out the information on this page and use it in conjunction with your schematic to create step-by-step knitting instructions.

chapter four
Alternate Pullover Silhouettes

Although the classic silhouette described in the previous chapter is the most common, a number of other silhouettes are also important in knitwear design. The first two alternatives—dropped shoulder and modified dropped-shoulder silhouettes—involve armhole variations. The remaining three—double-taper, single-taper, and reverse-taper silhouettes—involve body shaping. Each of the following examples will be for a pullover worked in four pieces—a front, a back, and two identical sleeves—all worked upward from the lower edge. However, these techniques can be used in many different kinds of garments or sections of garments.

DROPPED SHOULDER

A drop-shoulder silhouette is an unshaped rectangle that produces a T-shaped garment. This style is often chosen for sporty or outdoor clothing because the unstructured silhouette allows for comfortable ease of movement. However, the unstructured fit results in excess fabric in the underarm area.

In a dropped-shoulder silhouette, the lower body is worked the same as the classic body silhouette described in Chapter 3, but the upper body lacks armhole shaping. The body width is based on the bust width (with ease) unless the garment is very long, in which case, the lower body width is based on the hip width (with ease) and is tapered to the bust width about 3" (7.5 cm) below the bust. The body continues even at the bust width to the shoulders, with the neck shaped along the way. The neck width is generally 35% to 45% of the cross-back measurement, but can be as wide as 55% of that measurement, depending on the neck style (see Chapter 9). The average neck width is 47% of the cross-back measurement for a standard high round (crew) neck. The depth for this type of neck is usually between 2" and 3" (5 and 7.5 cm). Because the bust width is wider than the cross-back width, a neck width based on the bust width will range between 35% and 45% of the bust measurement, with an average of 40%.

Blocks & Cables, first published in the Fall 2002 issue of *Knitter's Magazine,* is an example of a dropped-shoulder pullover.

Photo: Alexis Xenakis

Because there is no armhole shaping in a dropped-shoulder silhouette, there is no specific armhole depth—it can be as deep as you want. But keep in mind that the excess fabric above the bust will hang down past the shoulders and along the upper arms. The wider the garment, the lower this excess fabric will extend down the arms and the shorter the sleeves will need to be. For this reason, the sleeve length is determined by subtracting half of the planned garment width at the bust from the center-neck-to-wrist measurement.

For a more fitted drop-shoulder sweater, use less ease in the bust area. For example, for a "roomy" fit in a coat, use 3" (7.5 cm) of ease in the bust instead of 5" (12.5 cm). Base the top of your sleeve on your upper arm measurement plus 2" (5 cm) of ease. Trimming the excess fabric in this manner will make the upper body of the garment closer to the actual body measurements, which will maintain the comfortable fit, but add more structure.

Our example pullover will have a 40" (101.5 cm) bust circumference (20" [51 cm] width) and a high round neck and shaped shoulders. The body and sleeves are worked in stockinette stitch and edged with knit 1, purl 1 ribbing that is worked on smaller needles.

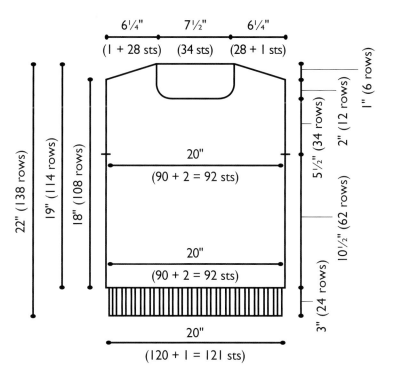

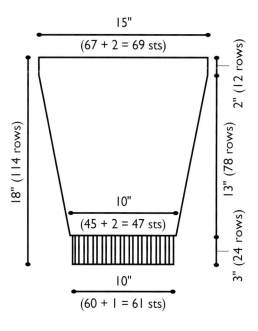

Schematic of the example dropped-shoulder silhouette, annotated with numbers of stitches and rows.

NEEDLES

Border: Size U.S. 5 (3.75 mm)
Body: Size U.S. 7 (4.5 mm)

GAUGE

Border (k1, p1 ribbing) 6 stitches and 8 rows = 1" (2.5 cm)
Body (stockinette stitch) 4.5 stitches and 6 rows = 1" (2.5 cm)

KEY MEASUREMENTS

Bust circumference: 40" (101.5 cm), includes 2" (5 cm) ease
Bust width: 20" (51 cm)
Neck width: 7½" (19 cm)
Length from bottom to base of front neck: 19" (48.5 cm)
Length from bottom to base of shoulders: 21" (53.5 cm)
Shoulder slope: 1" (2.5 cm)
Neck-to-wrist measurement: 28" (71 cm)
Sleeve length: (neck-to-wrist measurement – half of bust width) 18" (45.5 cm)

Conversion of Measurements to Numbers of Stitches and Rows

WIDTHS

Number of stitches in border (hip width × border stitch gauge + 1 balancing stitch)
20" (51 cm) × 6 stitches/inch + 1 balancing stitch = 121 stitches

Number of stitches at base of body (hip width × body stitch gauge + 2 selvedge stitches)
20" (51 cm) × 4.5 stitches/inch + 2 selvedge stitches = 92 stitches

Number of stitches in bust width (bust width × body stitch gauge + 2 selvedge stitches)
20" (51 cm) × 4.5 stitches/inch + 2 selvedge stitches = 92 stitches

Number of stitches in neck width (neck width × body stitch gauge)
7½" (19 cm) × 4.5 stitches/inch = 33.75 stitches;
round up to nearest whole number = 34 stitches

Number of stitches in each shoulder (shoulder width × body stitch gauge + 1 selvedge stitch)
6¼" (16 cm) × 4.5 stitches/inch + 1 selvedge stitch = 29.125 stitches;
round down to nearest whole number = 29 stitches

Number of stitches in the cuff (cuff measurement × border stitch gauge + 1 balancing stitch)
10" (25.5 cm) × 6 stitches/inch + 1 balancing stitch = 61 stitches

Number of stitches at base of sleeve (cuff measurement × sleeve stitch gauge + 2 selvedge stitches)
10" (25.5 cm) × 4.5 stitches/inch + 2 selvedge stitches = 47 stitches

Number of stitches at upper arm (upper arm measurement × sleeve stitch gauge + 2 selvedge stitches)

15" (38 cm) × 4.5 stitches/inch + 2 selvedge stitches = 69.5 stitches;
round down to nearest odd number = 69 stitches

LENGTHS

Number of rows in border (border length × border row gauge)
3" (7.5 cm) × 8 rows/inch = 24 rows

Number of rows from beginning of body to base of shoulder (length × body row gauge)
18" (45.5 cm) × 6 rows/inch = 108 rows

Number of rows from beginning of body to back neck (length × body row gauge)
19" (48.5 cm) × 6 rows/inch = 114 rows

Number of rows from base of front neck to base of shoulder (length × body row gauge)
2" (5 cm) × 6 rows/inch = 12 rows

Number of rows from beginning of body to base of front neck (length × body row gauge)
16" (40.5 cm) × 6 rows/inch = 96 rows

Number of rows in shoulder slope (length × body row gauge)
1" (2.5 cm) × 6 rows/inch = 6 rows

Number of rows in cuff (border length × border row gauge)
3" (7.5 cm) × 8 rows/inch = 24 rows

Number of rows in sleeve above top of cuff (sleeve length × sleeve row gauge)
15" (38 cm) × 6 rows/inch = 90 rows

 tip

For a more fitted drop-shoulder silhouette, use less ease in the bust area. For a pullover, for example, use 3" (7.5 cm) of ease instead of 5" (12.5 cm) and base the top of the sleeve on the upper arm measurement plus 2" (5 cm) of ease. The upper body garment will measure closer to the actual body measurements and will maintain the comfortable fit that is the hallmark of this design style.

The total number of rows worked in the body should add up to the desired total body length.

Total rows: 24 + 62 + 34 + 12 + 6 = 138 rows

Length in border: 3" (7.5 cm) × 8 rows/inch = 24 rows

Length in body: 10½" (26.5 cm) + 5½" (14 cm) + 2" (5 cm) + 1" (2.5 cm) = 19" (48.5 cm)
       19" (48.5 cm) × 6 rows/inch = 114 rows

Total body length: 24 rows + 114 rows = 138 rows

The total number of rows worked in the sleeve should add up to the desired total sleeve length.

Total rows: 24 + 90 = 114 rows

Length in border: 3" (7.5 cm) × 8 rows/inch = 24 rows

Length in sleeve: 15" (38 cm) × 6 rows/inch = 90 rows

Total sleeve length: 24 rows + 90 rows = 114 rows

Step 1: Front Cast-On and Ribbing/Border

Cast on with smaller needles and, beginning and ending with a knit stitch on right-side rows, work k1, p1 ribbing for 3" (7.5 cm).

For our sample front, use the smaller needles to cast on 121 stitches. Work right-side rows of the ribbing as [k1, p1] 60 times, k1 until a total of 24 rows have been worked.

Step 2: Transition from Ribbing/Border to Body

To maintain the desired 20" (51 cm) width in the stockinette-stitch gauge, decrease 29 stitches across the first row of stockinette to end up with the necessary 92 stitches. The diagonal relationships in the shaping formula tell us to decrease every 4th stitch 24 times and every 5th stitch 5 times. Because decreases involve 2 stitches (k2tog), work a decrease on every 3rd and 4th stitches (i.e., k2, k2tog) 24 times, then on every 4th and 5th stitches (i.e., k3, k2tog) 5 times. To make the last 4 stitches of the row mirror the first 4 stitches, work the second shaping interval just 4 times, then work the last 5 stitches as k1, k2tog, k2.

For our sample front, work this row as [k2, k2tog] 24 times, [k3, k2tog] 4 times, k1, k2tog, k2—92 stitches.

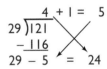

Use the shaping formula to determine an even distribution of decreases. In this example, decrease every 4th stitch 24 times and every 5th stitch 5 times.

Step 3: Lower Body

The lower body is worked straight to the base of the front neck.

For our sample front, change to the larger needles and work even in stockinette stitch on these 92 stitches for 16" (40.5 cm) to the base of the front neck—96 stockinette rows worked.

Step 4: Armhole Shaping

There is no armhole shaping for a drop-shoulder sweater; skip this step.

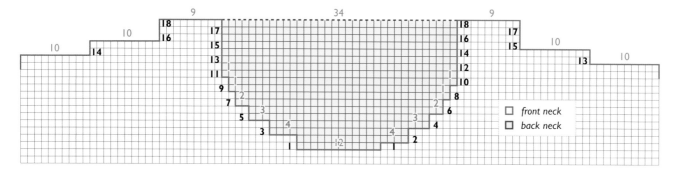

Plot of the neck and shoulder. Bind-off stitches are shown in red; row numbers are shown in black.

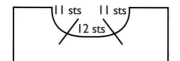

Divide the neck stitches in thirds; in this example, there are 12 stitches in the center section and 11 stitches at each side.

Step 5: Front Neck Shaping

For our example, shape the neck with the one-third initial bind-off (see page 77). Therefore, bind off the center 12 stitches on the first row, then work the remaining 11 stitches of neck shaping on each side over 2" (5 cm), or 12 rows, which includes the final wrong-side row. Plot the shaping on graph paper to ensure a smooth even slope.

For our sample front, bind off the center 12 stitches on the first row. Using the sloped method (see page 77), at each neck edge, bind off 4 stitches 1 time, then bind off 3 stitches 1 time, then bind off 2 stitches 1 time, then bind off 1 stitch 2 times—29 stitches remain at each side. Work even on the remaining stitches until a total of 108 rows of stockinette stitch have been completed.

Step 6: Shoulder Shaping

For our example, we'll begin with 29 stitches at each side and shape the shoulders over 6 rows. For a tailored fit, shape the shoulders in three steps (6 rows ÷ 2 sides = 3 rows/side).

29 stitches ÷ 3 rows = 9 with a remainder of 2

This tells us that on each armhole side we bind off 10 stitches 2 times, then bind off the remaining 9 stitches. For a smooth slope, use the sloped bind-off method described on page 77.

For our sample front, at each armhole edge, bind off 10 stitches 2 times, then bind off the remaining 9 stitches.

Step 7: Back

Work the back exactly as the front to the beginning of the shoulder shaping, omitting the front neck shaping. In our example, the shoulders begin when the body measures 18" (45.5 cm) above the ribbed lower border, or a total of 108 rows of stockinette stitch have been worked.

For our sample back, cast on and work as for the front until a total of 108 rows of stockinette stitch have been completed.

Step 8: Back Neck and Shoulder Shaping

The shoulders will be shaped in three levels exactly as the front shoulders were shaped.

For our sample back, bind off 10 stitches at the beginning of the next 4 rows, then bind off the remaining 52 back neck stitches on the following wrong-side row.

Step 9: Sleeve Cast-On and Ribbing/Border

In our example, use the smaller needles to cast on 61 stitches. Balance the ribbing pattern as for the body, beginning and ending with a knit stitch, and work right-side rows of ribbing as: [k1, p1] 30 times, k1.

For our sample sleeve, use the smaller needles to cast on 61 stitches. Beginning and ending with a knit stitch on right-side rows, work k1, p1 ribbing for 3" (7.5 cm), or 24 rows.

Step 10: Transition from Ribbing to Sleeve

To maintain the desired 10" (25.5 cm) width in stockinette stitch, decrease 14 stitches to the necessary 47 stitches. The diagonal relationships in the shaping formula tell us to decrease every 4th stitch 9 times and every 5th stitch 5 times. Because decreases involve 2 stitches (k2tog), work a decrease on every 3rd and 4th stitch (i.e., k2, k2tog) 9 times, then on every 4th and 5th stitch (i.e., k3, k2tog) 5 times.

For our sample sleeve, balance the stitches at each end of the needle by working the decreases as follows: [k2, k2tog] 9 times, [k3, k2tog] 4 times, k1, k2tog, k2—47 stitches remain.

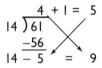

Use the shaping formula to determine an even distribution of decreases. In this example, decrease every 4th stitch 9 times and every 5th stitch 5 times.

Step 11: Sleeve Taper to Upper Arm

At this point change to the larger needles and stockinette stitch. To achieve the desired 69 stitches at the upper arm, increase 22 stitches (11 stitches at each side) over the length of the sleeve, ending 2" (5 cm) before the top of the sleeve. Therefore, space the increases evenly over 13" (33 cm), or 78 rows. The diagonal relationships in the shaping formula tell us to increase every 7th row 10 times and every 8th row 1 time.

For our sample sleeve, change to larger needles, then increase 1 stitch at each end of the needle every 7th row 10 times, then every 8th row 1 time—69 stitches. Work 12 rows even for a total of 90 rows, or until the piece measures 15" (38 cm) from the transition row.

Use the shaping formula to determine an even distribution of increases. In this example, increase 1 stitch at each edge every 7th row 10 times and every 8th row 1 time.

Step 12: Cap Shaping

There is no cap shaping in a drop-shoulder sweater. After knitting to the desired total length of 15" (38 cm), simply bind off all the stitches.

MODIFIED DROP SHOULDER

A modified drop shoulder is one of the most popular silhouettes. It gives a little more shaping than a drop-shoulder silhouette and yet is less structured than a garment with a set-in sleeve. Because it is roomy in the underarm area, it is ideal for women with large busts. The slight armhole shaping reduces some of the excess fabric that occurs at the armholes of drop-shoulder sweaters. Typically 1" to 2" (2.5 to 5 cm) in width is bound off at the base of the armhole in a series of steps to form a slant (or all at once for a horizontal notch). The upper 1" to 2" (2.5 to 5 cm) of the sleeves are shaped the same way to form a shallow sleeve cap.

In this style of garment, the sleeve calculations are worked somewhat in reverse—the upper arm width and cap shaping are determined by the armhole depth and the width of the armhole shaping in the body (the upper arm width must equal the sum of the front and back armhole depth).

Our example pullover has a 40" (101.5 cm) bust circumference (20" [51 cm] width) and is worked in a cable pattern with no special border treatment, has a one-half initial bind-off at the front neck, no shoulder shaping, and no back neck shaping.

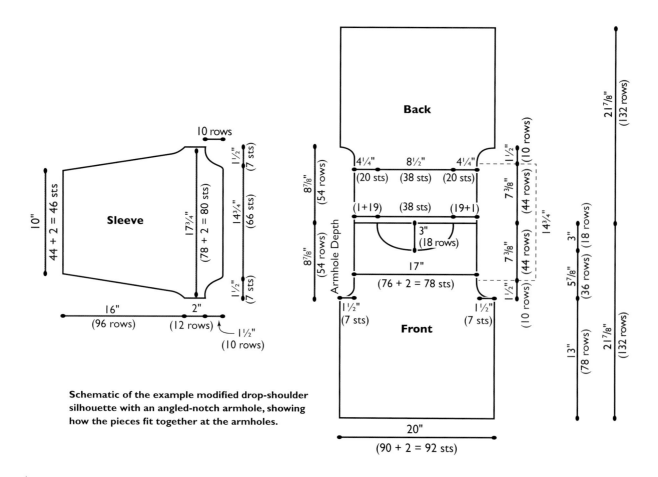

Schematic of the example modified drop-shoulder silhouette with an angled-notch armhole, showing how the pieces fit together at the armholes.

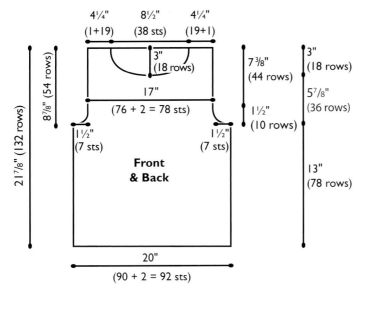

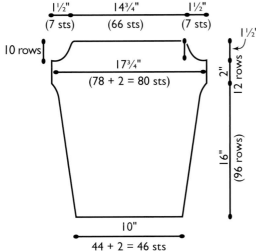

Schematic of the example modified drop-shoulder silhouette with an angled-notch armhole, annotated with numbers of stitches and rows.

GAUGE

4.5 stitches and 6 rows = 1" (2.5 cm).

KEY MEASUREMENTS

Bust circumference: 40" (101.5 cm), includes 2" (5 cm) ease

Bust width: 20" (51 cm)

Neck width: 8½" (21.5 cm)

Length from bottom to base of armholes: 13" (33 cm)

Armhole depth: 8⅞" (22.5 cm)

Notch width: 1½" (3.8 cm)

Notch length: 1½" (3.8 cm)

Length from base of armhole to base of front neck: 5⅞" (15 cm)

Length from base of front neck to base of shoulder: 3" (7.5 cm)

Shoulder slope: 0" (0 cm)

Neck-to-wrist measurement: 28" (71 cm)

Cuff width: 10" (25.5 cm)

Upper arm width: 17¾" (45 cm)

Sleeve length: (neck-to-wrist measurement – half of cross-back width) 28" (71 cm) – 8½" (21.5 cm) = 19½" (49.5 cm)

Conversion of Measurements to Numbers of Stitches and Rows

WIDTHS

Number of stitches at base of body (hip width × stitch gauge + 2 selvedge stitches)

20" (51 cm) × 4.5 stitches/inch + 2 selvedge stitches = 92 stitches

Number of stitches in bust width (bust width × stitch gauge + 2 selvedge stitches)

20" (51 cm) × 4.5 stitches/inch + 2 selvedge stitches = 92 stitches

Number of stitches in cross-back (shoulder-to-shoulder width × stitch gauge + 2 selvedge stitches)

17" (43 cm) × 4.5 stitches/inch + 2 selvedge stitches = 78.5 stitches; round down to nearest even number = 78 stitches

Number of stitches bound off at armholes (bust stitches − cross-back stitches)

92 stitches − 78 stitches = 14 stitches; 7 stitches bound off at each side

Number of stitches in neck width (neck width × stitch gauge)

8½" (21.5 cm) × 4.5 stitches/inch = 38.25 stitches;

round down to nearest even number = 38 stitches

Number of stitches in each shoulder (shoulder width × stitch gauge + 1 selvedge stitch)

4¼" (11 cm) × 4.5 stitches/inch + 1 selvedge stitch = 20.125 stitches;

round down to nearest even number = 20 stitches

Number of stitches at base of sleeve (knuckle measurement × stitch gauge + 2 selvedge stitches)

10" (25.5 cm) × 4.5 stitches/inch + 2 selvedge stitches = 47 stitches;

round down to nearest even number = 46 stitches

Number of stitches at upper arm (final bind-off stitches + 1 set of notch stitches at each side)

66 stitches + 7 stitches + 7 stitches = 80 stitches

Number of stitches in sleeve notch (notch width × stitch gauge)

1½" (3.8 cm) × 4.5 stitches/inch = 6.75 stitches;

round up to nearest whole number = 7 stitches

Number of stitches in final sleeve bind-off (stitches in upper arm − 2 sets of notch stitches)

80 stitches − 14 stitches = 66 stitches

Note: This width must equal the total length of the front and back armholes above the notch shaping.

LENGTHS

Number of rows in armhole (armhole depth × row gauge)

8⅞" (22.5 cm) × 6 rows/inch = 53.25 rows;

round up to nearest even number = 54 rows

Number of rows in armhole notch (notch length × row gauge)

1½" (3.8 cm) × 6 rows/inch = 9 rows; round up to an even number = 10 rows

Number of rows in armhole after notch (number of rows in armhole − number of rows in notch)

54 rows − 10 rows = 44 rows

Number of rows from beginning of body to base of armhole (length × row gauge)

13" (33 cm) × 6 rows/inch = 78 rows

Number of rows from beginning of body to base of front neck (length × row gauge)

18⅞" (48 cm) × 6 rows/inch = 113.25 rows; round up to nearest even number = 114 rows

Number of rows in sleeve below sleeve notch (sleeve length × row gauge)

16" (40.5 cm) × 6 rows/inch = 96 rows

Number of rows in sleeve notch (and cap) (notch length × stitch gauge)

1½" (3.8 cm) × 6 rows/inch = 9 rows; round up to nearest even number = 10 rows

HORIZONTAL-NOTCH VERSION

For a drop-shoulder pullover with a horizontal notch, add a notch width of 1½" (3.8 cm) and an armhole depth measurement of 7½" (19 cm). For most garment styles, the armhole depth generally measures to 1" (2.5 cm) to 1½" (3.8 cm) below the armpit. For a perfect fit at the armhole of a modified drop-shoulder silhouette, the width of the top of the sleeve must be double the armhole depth.

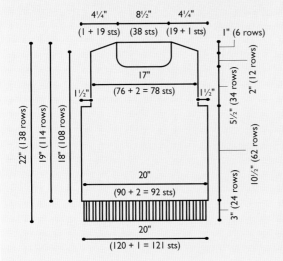
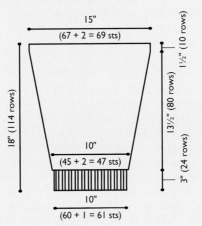
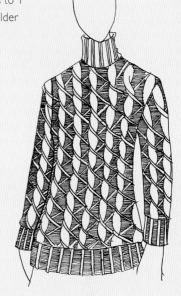

Step 1: Front Cast-On and Ribbing/Border

For our sample front, cast on 92 stitches. There is no ribbing or border in this example.

Step 2: Transition from Ribbing/Border to Body

Skip this step.

Step 3: Lower Body

For our sample front, work 92 stitches even for 78 rows, or 13" (33 cm), to the base of the armhole.

Step 4: Armhole Shaping

In this step, shape the armholes as for the classic silhouette described on page 75. Begin by binding off ½" (1.3 cm) of stitches at each edge, then bind off the remaining armhole stitches gradually over the remaining 8 rows as outlined at right.

For our sample front, use the sloped method (see page 77) to bind off 2 stitches at the beginning of the next 4 rows, then bind off 1 stitch at the beginning of the next 6 rows—78 stitches remain. Work even on 78 stitches until the armholes measure 5⅞" (15 cm), or a total of 36 rows have been worked from the initial armhole bind-off— piece measures 18⅞" (48.5 cm) from beginning.

ARMHOLE-SHAPING SCHEDULE

Odd-numbered rows are right-side (RS) rows; even-numbered rows are wrong-side (WS) rows.

Shaping Row	Stitches Bound Off
1 (RS)	2
2 (WS)	2
3	2
4	2
5	1
6	1
7	1
8	1
9	1
10	1

Total: 14 stitches (7 stitches each side) bound off over 10 rows.

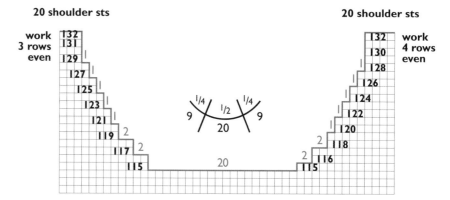

Plot of the neck shaping. Bind-off stitches are shown in red; row numbers are shown in black.

Step 5: Front Neck Shaping

For our example, use the one-half initial bind-off (see page 78). Place any extra stitches in the center and bind off the center 20 stitches on the first row, then bind off 9 stitches on each side over the remaining 3" (7.5 cm), or 18 rows, of the front. The distribution of the bind-offs is plotted on the graph above. Note that the shaping is worked through Row 128 on the right-hand side of the neck and through Row 129 on the left-hand side, but the same number of rows will be worked on each side as we work even through Row 132 on each side.

For our sample front, bind off the center 20 stitches on the first row. Work the right and left sides separately and use the sloped method (see page 77) along each neck edge to bind off 2 stitches 2 times, then bind off 1 stitch 5 times—20 stitches remain each side. Work even until 132 pattern rows have been completed.

Step 6: Shoulder Shaping

There is no shoulder shaping in this example; simply bind off all of the remaining 20 stitches on each side.

Step 7: Back

The back is worked exactly as the front to the shoulders, omitting the front neck shaping. In our example, work 78 rows to the armholes, 10 rows of armhole shaping (during which the stitch count is reduced from 92 stitches to 78 stitches), then 44 rows to the shoulders for a total of 132 rows—the piece will measure the same length as the front to the shoulders.

For our sample back, cast on 92 stitches and work in the pattern stitch for 78 rows. Shape the armholes over the next 10 rows—78 stitches remain. Work 44 rows to the shoulder for a total of 132 rows—armhole measures 8⅞" (22.5 cm).

Step 8: Back Neck and Shoulder Shaping

In our example, there is no back neck or shoulder shaping; simply bind off all 78 stitches on the same row.

Step 9: Sleeve Cast-On and Ribbing/Border

For our sample sleeve, cast on 46 stitches. There is no ribbing or border in this example.

Step 10: Transition from Ribbing/Border to Sleeve

Skip this step.

Step 11: Sleeve Taper to Upper Arm

To achieve the desired 80 stitches at the upper arm, 34 stitches (17 stitches at each side) must be increased over the length of the sleeve, ending 2" (5 cm) before the top of the sleeve. Therefore, we want to space the increases evenly over 16" (40.5 cm), or 96 rows. The diagonal relationships in the shaping formula tell us to increase every 5th row 6 times and every 6th row 11 times.

$$
\begin{array}{r}
5 \ + 1 = 6 \\
17\,\overline{)\,96} \\
-85 \\
\hline
17\ \ -11\ \ = \ 6
\end{array}
$$

Use the shaping formula to determine an even distribution of increases. In this example, increase every 5th row 6 times and every 6th row 11 times.

Odd-numbered rows are right-side (RS) rows; even-numbered rows are wrong-side (WS) rows.

Shaping Row	Stitches Bound Off
1 (RS)	2
2 (WS)	2
3	2
4	2
5	1
6	1
7	1
8	1
9	1
10	1

Total: 14 stitches (7 stitches each side) are decreased over 10 rows.

For our sample sleeve, increase 1 stitch each end of the needle every 5th row 6 times, then every 6th row 11 times. Work even on 80 stitches for 2" (5 cm), or 12 rows—sleeve measures 18" (45.5 cm) from the beginning.

Step 12: Cap Shaping

The cap is formed by binding off over the same number of inches used to shape the armhole edges on the sides of the body. In our example, the armhole notch was worked over 1½" (3.8 cm), or 10 rows. Therefore, the sleeve-cap shaping must also be worked over 1½" (3.8 cm), or 7 stitches.

For our sample sleeve, bind off 2 stitches (½" [1.3 cm]) at the beginning of the first 4 rows, then bind off 1 stitch at the beginning of each of the following 6 rows for a total of 14 stitches (7 stitches each side) bound off over 10 rows—66 stitches remain; sleeve measures 19½" (49.5 cm) from the beginning. Bind off the remaining 66 stitches on the final row.

 MATH CHECK!

The width of the stitches on the final bind-off should equal the length of the notched part of the front and back armholes.

Width of sleeve final bind-off
  66 stitches ÷ 4.5 stitches/inch = 14.66" (37.2 cm)

Length of armhole after shaping
  44 rows ÷ 6 rows/inch = 7.33" (18.6 cm) each for front and back

Total length of notched portion of front and back armholes
  7.33" (18.6 cm) for front armhole + 7.33" (18.6 cm) for back armhole
  = 14.66" (37.2 cm)

We have rounded up to the next ¼" (6 mm) on the schematic to bring this length to 14¾" (37.5 cm).

DOUBLE-TAPERED BODY

A double-tapered body silhouette follows the natural curves of the body from the hips to the bust. This involves working decreases and increases as the width changes to accommodate the hips, waist, and bust measurements and the desired amount of ease in each.

This garment silhouette is planned and worked in four sections and makes use of the shaping formula described on page 70. The waist-to-bust shaping is similar to the cuff-to-upper arm shaping of a tapered sleeve. The hip-to-waist shaping is the reverse—it's the same as if the sleeve were worked downward from the upper arm to the cuff. The waist is worked even, then the upper body is worked the same as the classic body silhouette.

Our example pullover has a 36½" (92.5 cm) hip circumference (18¼" [46.5 cm] width), 30½" (77.5 cm) waist circumference (15¼" [38.5 cm] width), and 34" (86.5 cm) bust circumference (17" [43 cm] width). It has a high round neck and straight shoulders.

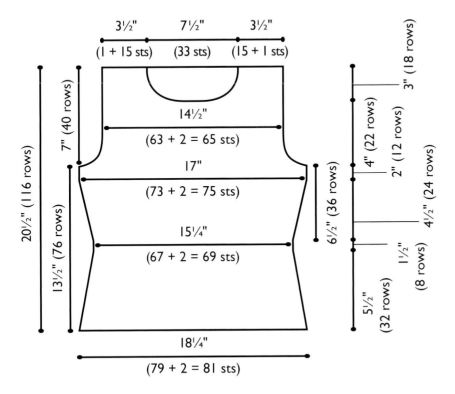

Schematic of the example double-tapered body silhouette, annotated with numbers of stitches and rows.

GAUGE

Body (lacy stripes pattern): 4.34 stitches and 5.64 rows = 1" (2.5 cm)

KEY MEASUREMENTS

Hip circumference: 36½" (92.5 cm); includes 2" (5 cm) ease, 1" (2.5 cm) each for front and back

Hip width: 18¼" (46.5 cm)

Waist circumference: 30½" (77.5 cm); includes 1" (5 cm) ease, ½" (1.3 cm) each for front and back

Waist width: 15¼" (38.5 cm)

Bust circumference: 34" (86.5 cm); includes 2" (5 cm) ease, 1" (2.5 cm) each for front and back

Bust width: 17" (43 cm)

Cross-back width: 14½" (37 cm)

Neck width: 7½" (19 cm)

Shoulder width: 3½" (9 cm)

Length from hips (lower edge) to beginning of waist: 5½" (14 cm)

Length of waist: 1½" (3.8 cm)

Length from top of waist to bust: 6½" (16.5 cm)

Length from beginning to base of armholes: 13½" (34.5 cm)

Armhole depth: 7" (18 cm); includes 1" (2.5 cm) ease each for front and back

Neck depth: 3" (7.5 cm)

Total length: 20½" (52 cm)

Classic-body shaping lines

Double-taper shaping lines

A double-tapered body follows the curves of the hips, waist, and bust.

Conversion of Measurements to Numbers of Stitches and Rows

WIDTHS

Number of stitches in hip width (hip width × body stitch gauge + 2 selvedge stitches)

18¼" (46.5 cm) × 4.34 stitches/inch + 2 selvedge stitches = 81.2 stitches; round down to nearest odd number = 81 stitches

Number of stitches in waist width (waist width × body stitch gauge + 2 selvedge stitches)

15¼" (38.5 cm) × 4.34 stitches/inch + 2 selvedge stitches = 68.2 stitches; round up to nearest odd number = 69 stitches

Number of stitches in bust width (bust width × body stitch gauge + 2 selvedge stitches)

17" (43 cm) × 4.34 stitches/inch + 2 selvedge stitches = 75.78 stitches; round down to the nearest odd number = 75 stitches

Number of stitches in cross-back (cross-back width × body stitch gauge + 2 selvedge stitches)

14½" (37 cm) × 4.34 stitches/inch + 2 selvedge stitches = 64.93 stitches; round up to nearest odd number = 65 stitches

Number of stitches in neck width (neck width × body stitch gauge)

7½" (19 cm) × 4.34 stitches/inch = 32.55 stitches; round up to nearest odd number = 33 stitches

Number of stitches in each shoulder (shoulder width × body stitch gauge + 1 selvedge stitch)

3½" (9 cm) × 4.34 stitches/inch + 1 selvedge stitch = 16.19 stitches; round down to nearest even number = 16 stitches

LENGTHS

Number of rows from beginning to beginning of waist (length × body stitch gauge)

5½" (14 cm) × 5.64 rows/inch = 31.02 rows; round up to nearest even number = 32 rows

Number of rows in waist (length × body stitch gauge)

1½" (3.8 cm) × 5.64 rows/inch = 8.46 rows; round down to nearest even number = 8 rows

Number of rows from top of waist to beginning of armhole (length × body stitch gauge)

6½" (16.5 cm) × 5.64 rows/inch = 36.66 rows; round down to nearest even number = 36 rows

Number of rows from beginning of armhole to beginning of neck (length × body stitch gauge)

4" (10 cm) × 5.64 rows/inch = 22.56 rows; round down to nearest even number = 22 rows

Number of rows from beginning of neck to top of shoulders (length × body stitch gauge)

3" (7.5 cm) × 5.64 rows/inch = 16.92 rows; round up to next even number = 18 rows

✳ *tip* If there is an odd number of stitches for the hips, there must also be an odd number of stitches for the waist and vice versa.

> The total number of rows worked in the body should add up to the total body length.
>
> **Total rows:** 32 + 8 + 36 + 22 + 18 = 116 rows
>
> **Total length:** 5½" (14 cm) + 1½" (3.8 cm) + 6½" (16.5 cm)
>   + 4" (10 cm) + 3" (7.5 cm) = 20½" (52 cm)
>
>   20½" (52 cm) × 5.64 rows/inch = 116 rows

Step 1: Front Cast-On and Ribbing/Border

For our sample front, cast on 81 stitches. There is no ribbing or border in this example.

Step 2: Transition from Ribbing/Border to Body

Skip this step.

Step 3: Lower Body

The lower body of a double-tapered silhouette is broken into four sections—the first section tapers from the hips to the waist, the second section is worked straight for the waist, the third section tapers from the waist to the bust, and the fourth section is worked straight to the armhole.

Section 1: Hips-to-Waist Taper

In this section, we decrease 12 stitches from 81 stitches at the hips to 69 stitches at the waist over the course of 5½" (14 cm), or 32 rows. Work these decreases in pairs—1 stitch at each edge of the piece—so decrease 6 stitches on each side.

The diagonal relationships in the shaping formula tell us to decrease every 5th row 4 times and every 6th row 2 times. We can choose which series (decrease every 5th row 4 times or decrease every 6th row 2 times) to work first or alternate between the two series.

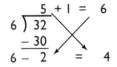

Use the shaping formula to determine an even distribution of decreases. In this example, decrease every 5th row 4 times and every 6th row 2 times.

The decreases in this section should begin at least 1" (2.5 cm) above the cast-on edge to prevent the sides from drooping, and they should end at the beginning of the waist. In most cases, including our sample garment, there is a 1" (2.5 cm) "work-even" section at the lower edge. For our example, the shaping formula tells us that the first decrease would be on either the 5th or 6th row. Because our row gauge is 5.64 rows/inch, we will automatically work even for the first 1" (2.5 cm) of the body before working the first decrease.

If the shaping formula doesn't allow for 1" (2.5 cm) to be worked even or if we were working a long sweater or dress, we'd need to plan for this initial work-even length. To do this, we'd modify the shaping formula to calculate the decrease sequence on 1 less row and 1 less stitch. This will allow us to work a decrease on the very first row of the tapered section. Otherwise, the first decrease would be worked a number of rows above the desired work-even section.

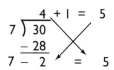

$$7\overline{)30} \quad \frac{4 \;\; +1 \;\; = \;\; 5}{}$$
$$\underline{-28}$$
$$7 - 2 \quad = \quad 5$$

Use the shaping formula to determine an even distribution of the decreases. In this example, decrease every 4th row 5 times and every 5th row 2 times.

PREVENT DROOPING HEMS

To prevent the sides of the hem from drooping on a garment with body shaping, plan to work the first 1" (2.5 cm) to 2" (5 cm) straight before beginning the shaping. For a jacket, coat, or long pullover that extends below the hips or is made of a bulky fabric, work the first 2" (5 cm) to 4" (10 cm) before beginning the taper.

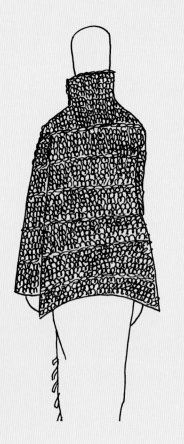

For an example of this technique, let's say we're working on 84 stitches at a row gauge of 6 rows/inch and we want to work the lower edge even for 3" (7.5 cm)—18 rows—before beginning the taper from the hip to the waist. The taper is worked over 5" (12.5 cm)—30 rows—during which time 14 stitches are decreased to end up with 70 stitches. Divide these 14 stitches evenly between the two sides—7 stitches at each side.

Using the shaping formula, divide the number of rows by the number of stitches to decrease on each side. The formula tells us to decrease every 4th row 5 times and every 5th row 2 times for a total of 7 stitches decreased over 30 rows. Note that this schedule begins the tapered section by working 4 rows, which translates to ¾" (2 cm). Doing so will extend the work-even section from the desired 3" (7.5 cm) to 3¾" (9.5 cm).

To make a decrease row the first row of the tapered section, recalculate the intervals after subtracting 1 stitch from the divisor (7 − 1 = 6) and 1 stitch from the dividend (30 − 1 = 29).

$$6\overline{)29} \quad \frac{4 \;\; +1 \;\; = \;\; 5}{}$$
$$\underline{-24}$$
$$6 - 5 \quad = \quad 1$$

Subtract 1 stitch and 1 row from the decrease/increase shaping formula to make the first row a shaping row.

The diagonal relationships in this revised calculation tell us that we'd decrease every 4th row once and every 5th row 5 times for a total of 6 stitches decreased over 29 rows. But remember that we want to decrease a total of 7 stitches over 30 rows. The missing decrease stitch and the missing row will be worked at the beginning of this tapered section.

For this example with the lower edge worked even for 3" (7.5 cm), work even on 84 stitches until the piece measures 3" (7.5 cm) from the beginning, ending with a wrong-side row. Then decrease 1 stitch at each edge on the next row, then again at each edge of the following 4th row, then again at each edge of every following 5th row 5 times—70 stitches remain.

Section 2: Waist
In this section, work even for the waist length of 1½" (3.8 cm).

For our sample front, work even on 69 stitches for 1½" (3.8 cm), or 8 rows.

Section 3: Waist-to-Bust Taper

In this section, increase from 69 stitches at the waist to 75 stitches at the bust.

> **75** stitches at bust – **69** stitches at waist = **6** stitches to increase

To work these increases in pairs (1 stitch at each edge of the piece), increase 3 stitches on each side. To ensure ease of movement at the armholes, work the last increase about 2" (5 cm) below the start of the armholes. Therefore, calculate the increases over 4½" (11.5 cm)—rounded down to 24 rows—instead of the full 36 rows, or 6½" (16.5 cm), in this section. After the increases, work the final 12 rows, or 2" (5 cm), even to the armholes.

Because this section follows the work-even section of the waist, the first row should be an increase row (as described on page 110). Therefore, calculate the shaping intervals for the remaining 2 increases over 23 rows. The modified shaping formula tells us to increase every 11th row 1 time and every 12th row 1 time.

For our sample front, increase 1 stitch at each edge of the first row of this section, then on the following 11th row once, then on the following 12th row once—75 stitches.

Section 4: Bust to Armhole

This section is typically worked even for about 2" (5 cm) to ensure ease of movement in the bust and armhole area.

For our sample front, work even on these stitches for 2" (5 cm), or 12 rows—piece should measure 13½" (34.5 cm) from the beginning.

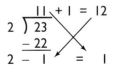

Use the modified shaping formula to determine an even distribution of increases. In this example, increase on the first row, then every 11th row 1 time and every 12th row 1 time.

 MATH CHECK!

> The sum of the lengths in each section from the beginning to the armhole should equal the total length to the armhole.
>
> Length to armhole: 13½" (34.5 cm)
>
> Hips to waist: 5½" (14 cm)
>
> Waist: 1½" (3.8 cm)
>
> Waist to bust: 6½" (16.5 cm)
>
> Total: 5½" (14 cm) + 1½" (3.8 cm) + 6½" (16.5 cm) = 13½" (34.5 cm)

ARMHOLE-SHAPING SCHEDULE

Odd-numbered rows are right-side (RS) rows; even-numbered rows are wrong-side (WS) rows.

Shaping Row	Stitches Bound Off
1 (RS)	2
2 (WS)	2
3	1
4	1
5	1
6	1
7	1
8	1

Total: 10 stitches (5 stitches each side) are decreased over 8 rows.

Step 4: Armhole Shaping

In this step, decrease 10 stitches from 75 stitches at the bust to 65 stitches at the cross-back. Again, work these decreases in pairs (one at each side), decreasing 5 stitches at each side. Work these decreases over the first 1½" (1.3 cm)—8 rows—of the 4" (10 cm) distance from the armhole to the neck (22 rows total). The decrease sequence is determined the same way as described on page 75 for the classic silhouette and is shown at left. Then work even on the remaining 65 stitches for 14 rows until the armhole measures 4" (10 cm).

For our sample front, bind off 2 stitches at the beginning of the next 2 rows, then bind off 1 stitch at the beginning of the next 6 rows—65 stitches remain. Work even on these 65 stitches until the armhole measures 4" (10 cm), or a total of 22 rows have been worked in the armhole.

Step 5: Front Neck Shaping

For our example, the center neck is 7½" (19 cm), or 33 stitches, wide and is shaped over a depth of 3" (7.5 cm), or 18 rows. Using the one-third initial bind-off method (see page 77), bind off the center 11 stitches on the first row of shaping, then bind off 11 stitches at each side in a series of steps to produce a rounded shape. The decrease sequence is shown on the graph below.

For our sample front, bind off the center 11 stitches on the first row. Work the right and left sides separately and use the sloped method (see page 77) along each neck edge to bind off 3 stitches once, then bind off 2 stitches 2 times, then bind off 1 stitch 4 times—16 stitches remain each side. Work even until 40 armhole rows and 116 total pattern rows have been completed.

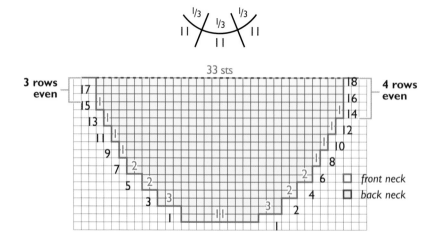

Plot of neck shaping. Bind-off stitches are shown in red; row numbers are shown in black.

Step 6: Shoulder Shaping

There is no formal shoulder shaping in this example, but we can join the shoulders with a three-needle bind-off. In preparation for doing so, place the remaining 16 stitches at each side on holders.

Step 7: Back

Work the back exactly as the front to the shoulders, omitting the front neck shaping.

For our sample back, cast on 81 stitches and work in the pattern stitch with waist and bust shaping as for front for 76 rows to the armholes. Shape the armholes over the next 8 rows—65 stitches remain. Work 32 more rows to the shoulder for a total of 116 rows—armhole measures 7" (18 cm).

Step 8: Back Neck and Shoulder Shaping

In our example, the back neck stitches are bound off and the shoulder stitches are joined to the front shoulder stitches with the three-needle bind-off.

For our sample back, work across 16 shoulder stitches, bind off the 33 center neck stitches, then work across the 16 remaining shoulder stitches. Use the three-needle bind-off (see page 263) to join the front and back together at the shoulders.

Step 9–Step 12

The sleeves are worked as described for the classic silhouette on page 81, following the desired dimensions and using the gauge of 4.34 stitches and 5.64 rows = 1" (2.5 cm).

SINGLE-TAPERED BODY

A single-tapered body silhouette follows the shaping for just the portion between the waist and bust of a double-tapered silhouette. The body is wider at the top (bust) than at the border (waist).

Our example pullover has a 32" (81.5 cm) waist circumference (16" [40.5 cm)] width) and 36" (91.5 cm) bust circumference (18" [45.5 cm] width). The pullover is worked in stockinette stitch, edged with knit 1, purl 1 ribbing that is worked on smaller needles, and has a high round neck and straight shoulders. Single increases are worked along the side edges to taper the body.

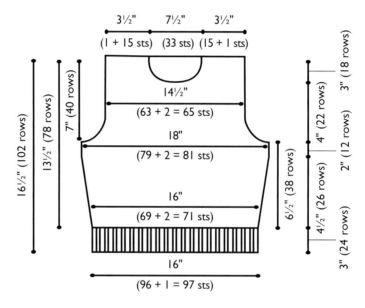

Schematic of the example single-tapered body silhouette, annotated with numbers of stitches and rows.

GAUGE

Border (k1, p1 ribbing): 6 stitches and 8 rows = 1" (2.5 cm)

Body (stockinette stitch): 4.34 stitches and 5.64 rows = 1" (2.5 cm)

KEY MEASUREMENTS

Border circumference: 32" (81.5 cm); includes 2" (5 cm) ease, 1" (2.5 cm) each for front and back

Border width: 16" (40.5 cm)

Waist circumference: 32" (81.5 cm); includes 1" (2.5 cm) ease, ½" (1.3) each for front and back

Waist width: 16" (40.5 cm)

Bust circumference: 36" (91.5 cm); includes 2" (5 cm) ease, 1" (2.5 cm) each for front and back

Bust width: 18" (45.5 cm)

Cross-back width: 14½" (37 cm)

Neck width: 7½" (19 cm)

Shoulder width: 3½" (9 cm)

Length of border: 3" (7.5 cm)

Length from waist to bust: 6½" (16.5 cm)

Length from base of armhole to base of neck: 4" (10 cm)

Neck depth: 3" (7.5 cm)

Total length: 16½" (42 cm)

Conversion of Measurements to Numbers of Stitches and Rows

WIDTHS

Number of stitches in border (waist width × border stitch gauge + 1 balancing stitch)
16" (40.5 cm) × 6 stitches/inch + 1 balancing stitch = 97 stitches

Number of stitches in waist width (waist width × body stitch gauge + 2 selvedge stitches)
16" (40.5 cm) × 4.34 stitches/inch + 2 selvedge stitches = 71.44 stitches; round down to nearest odd number = 71 stitches

Number of stitches in bust width (bust width × body stitch gauge + 2 selvedge stitches)
18" (45.5 cm) × 4.34 stitches/inch + 2 selvedge stitches = 80.12 stitches; round up to an odd number = 81 stitches

Number of stitches in cross-back (cross-back width × body stitch gauge + 2 selvedge stitches)
14½" (37 cm) × 4.34 stitches/inch + 2 selvedge stitches = 64.93 stitches; round up to an odd number = 65 stitches

Number of stitches in neck width (neck width × body stitch gauge)

      7½" (19 cm) × 4.34 stitches/inch = 32.55 stitches;

      round up to nearest odd number = 33 stitches

Number of stitches in each shoulder (shoulder width × body stitch gauge + 1 selvedge stitch)

      3½" (9 cm) × 4.34 stitches/inch + 1 selvedge stitch = 16.19 stitches;

      round down to nearest even number = 16 stitches

LENGTHS

Number of rows in border (length × border row gauge)

      3" (7.5 cm) × 8 rows/inch = 24 rows

Number of rows from waist to top of bust shaping (length × body row gauge)

      4½" (11.5 cm) × 5.64 rows/inch = 25.38 rows;

      round up to nearest even number = 26 rows

Number of rows from top of bust shaping to beginning of armhole (length × body row gauge)

      2" (5 cm) × 5.64 rows/inch = 11.28 rows; round up to nearest even number = 12 rows

Number of rows from beginning of armhole to beginning of neck (length × body stitch gauge)

      4" (10 cm) × 5.64 rows/inch = 22.56 rows; round down to nearest even number = 22 rows

Number of rows from beginning of neck to top of shoulders (length × body stitch gauge)

      3" (7.5 cm) × 5.64 rows/inch = 16.92 rows; round up to nearest even number = 18 rows

Step 1: Front Cast-On and Ribbing/Border

For our sample sweater, cast on 97 stitches using the smaller needles. Beginning and ending with a knit stitch, work right-side rows of ribbing as: [k1, p1] 48 times, k1 for 24 rows, or until the piece measures 3" (7.5 cm).

Step 2: Transition from Ribbing/Border to Body

In this row, decrease 26 stitches from 97 stitches in the border to 71 stitches in the body. The shaping formula tells us to decrease every 3rd stitch 7 times and every 4th stitch 19 times. Divide one of the 4-stitch intervals between the beginning and the end of the row so that a decrease isn't worked on the last stitch.

For our sample sweater, work this row as: [k1, k2tog] 7 times, [k2, k2tog] 18 times, k1, k2tog, k1—71 stitches remain.

Step 3: Lower Body

In this section, we change to larger needles and stockinette stitch. We also increase 10 stitches from 71 stitches at the waist to 81 stitches at the bust. Work these increases in pairs—1 stitch at each edge of the piece—so increase 5 stitches on each side. Space these increases over 4½" (11.5 cm) to end the lower body by working 2" (5 cm) straight to the base of the armhole. There are therefore 26 rows in which to space these increases. The shaping formula tells us to increase every 5th row 4 times and every 6th row 1 time.

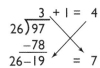

$$26\overline{)97} \quad \frac{3}{}+1=4$$
$$\frac{-78}{26-19}\quad = 7$$

In this example, decrease every 3rd stitch 7 times and every 4th stitch 19 times.

$$5\overline{)26}\quad\frac{5}{}+1=6$$
$$\frac{-25}{5-1}\quad = 4$$

Use the shaping formula to determine an even distribution of increases. In this example, increase every 5th row 4 times and every 6th row once.

For our sample sweater, increase 1 stitch at each edge of every 5th row 4 times, then on the following 6th row 1 time—81 stitches. Then work even on these 81 stitches for 2" (5 cm), or 12 rows, to the base of the armhole.

Step 4–Step 12

Work the upper body, back, and sleeves as for the classic body silhouette on page 75, using the desired measurements and a gauge of 4.34 stitches and 5.64 rows = 1" (2.5 cm).

GAUGE

Body (stockinette stitch): 7.44 stitches and 8.6 rows = 1" (2.5 cm)

KEY MEASUREMENTS

Hip circumference: 50" (127 cm); includes 12" (30.5 cm) ease, 6" (15 cm) each for front and back

Hip width: 25" (63.5 cm)

Bust circumference: 38" (96.5 cm); includes 2" (5 cm) ease, 1" (2.5 cm) each for front and back

Bust width: 19" (48.5 cm)

Cross-back width: 15" (38 cm)

Neck width: 8" (20.5 cm)

Shoulder width: 3½" (9 cm)

Length from lower edge to base of armholes: 18" (45.5 cm)

Armhole depth: 8" (20.5 cm)

Neck depth: 3" (7.5 cm)

Total length: 26" (66 cm)

REVERSE-TAPERED BODY

A reverse-tapered body silhouette follows the shaping between the hips and the bust. The body is wider at the border (hips) than at the top (bust). This silhouette produces "swing" in the lower body.

Our example pullover has a 50" (127 cm) hip circumference (25" [63.5 cm] width) and 38" (96.5 cm) bust circumference (19" [48.5 cm] width). The hip width tapers evenly from the bottom to 3" (7.5 cm) below the armhole with single decreases worked along the side edges. The armholes and body are shaped as for the classic body silhouette with a high round neck and straight shoulders.

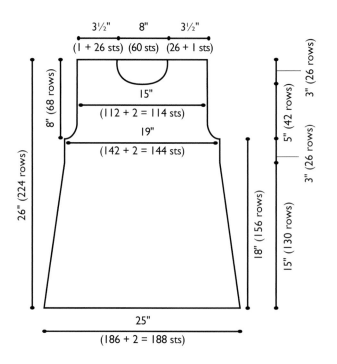

Schematic of the example reverse-tapered body silhouette, annotated with numbers of stitches and rows.

Conversion of Measurements to Number of Stitches and Rows

WIDTHS

Number of stitches in hip width (hip width × stitch gauge + 2 selvedge stitches)

25" (63.5 cm) × 7.44 stitches/inch + 2 selvedge stitches = 188 stitches

Number of stitches in bust width (bust width × stitch gauge + 2 selvedge stitches)

19" (48.5 cm) × 7.44 stitches/inch + 2 selvedge stitches = 143.36 stitches;
round up to nearest even number = 144 stitches

Number of stitches in cross-back (cross-back width × stitch gauge + 2 selvedge stitches)

15" (38 cm) × 7.44 stitches/inch + 2 selvedge stitches = 113.6 stitches;
round up to nearest even number = 114 stitches

Number of stitches in neck width (neck width × stitch gauge)

8" (20.5 cm) × 7.44 stitches/inch = 59.52 stitches;
round up to nearest even number = 60 stitches

Number of stitches in each shoulder (shoulder width × stitch gauge + 1 selvedge stitch)

3½" (9 cm) × 7.44 stitches/inch + 1 selvedge stitch = 27.04 stitches;
round down to nearest whole number = 27 stitches

LENGTHS

Number of rows from beginning to end of bust shaping (length × stitch gauge)

15" (38 cm) × 8.6 rows/inch = 129 rows; round up to nearest even number = 130 rows

Number of rows from beginning to base of armhole (length × stitch gauge)

18" (45.5 cm) × 8.6 rows/inch = 154.8 rows; round up to next even number = 156 rows

Number of rows to work even after bust shaping and before armhole (length × stitch gauge)

3" (7.5 cm) × 8.6 rows/inch = 25.8 rows; round up to nearest even number = 26 rows

Number of rows from beginning of armhole to beginning of neck (length × stitch gauge)

5" (12.5 cm) × 8.6 rows/inch = 43 rows; round down to nearest even number = 42 rows

Number of rows from beginning of neck to shoulder (length × stitch gauge)

3" (7.5 cm) × 8.6 rows/inch = 25.8 rows; round up to nearest even number = 26 rows

🌀 MATH CHECK!

The total number of rows worked should add up to the total body length.

Total rows: 156 + 42 + 26 = 224 rows

Total length: 18" (45.5 cm) + 5" (12.5 cm) + 3" (7.5 cm) = 26"
26" (66 cm) × 8.6 rows/inch = 223.6 rows;
round up to nearest even number = 224 rows

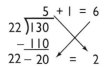

Use the shaping formula to determine an even distribution of decreases. In this example, decrease every 5th stitch 2 times and every 6th stitch 20 times.

Step 1: Front Cast-On and Ribbing/Border

For our sample sweater, cast on 188 stitches. There is no ribbing or border in this example.

Step 2: Transition from Ribbing/Border to Body

Skip this step.

Step 3: Lower Body

In this section we want to decrease 44 stitches from 188 stitches at the hips to 144 stitches at the bust. Work these decreases in pairs—1 stitch at each edge of the piece—so decrease 22 stitches on each side. Space these decreases so that the last decrease falls 3" (7.5 cm) below the beginning of the armhole. In other words, work the decreases over 15" (38 cm)—130 rows. The shaping formula tells us to decrease 1 stitch at each end of every 5th row 2 times and every 6th row 20 times.

For our sample front, decrease 1 stitch at each edge every 5th row 2 times, then decrease 1 stitch at each edge every following 6th row 20 times—144 stitches remain. Work even on these 144 stitches for 3" (7.5 cm), or 26 rows, to the beginning of the armhole.

Step 4: Armhole Shaping

In this step, use the sloped bind-off method to decrease 30 stitches from 144 stitches at the bust to 114 stitches at the cross-back. Again, work these bind-offs in pairs (1 stitch at each side), binding off 15 stitches at each side. Work these bind-offs over the first 1¾" (2 cm), or 16 rows, of the 5" (12.5 cm) distance from the armhole to the neck (42 rows total). The bind-off sequence is determined the same way as described on page 75 for the classic silhouette, and is shown at left. Work even on the remaining 114 stitches for 26 rows until the armhole measures 5" (12.5 cm).

For our sample front, bind off 4 stitches at the beginning of the next 2 rows, then bind off 3 stitches at the beginning of the next 2 rows, then bind off 2 stitches at the beginning of the next 4 rows, then bind off 1 stitch at the beginning of the next 8 rows—114 stitches remain. Work even on the remaining 114 stitches until the armhole measures 5" (12.5 cm), or 42 rows have been worked from the initial armhole bind-off.

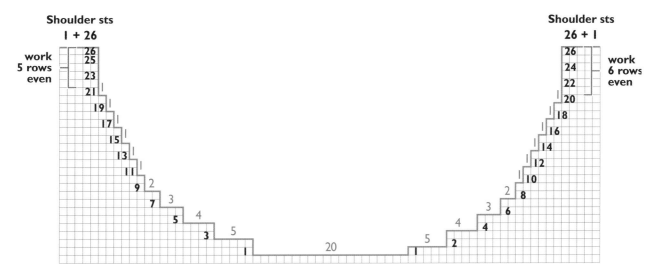

Plot of the neck shaping. Bind-off stitches are shown in red; row numbers are shown in black.

Step 5: Front Neck Shaping

For our example, the neck is 8" (20.5 cm), or 60 stitches, wide and is shaped over 3" (7.5 cm), or 26 rows. Using the one-third initial bind-off method (see page 77), bind off the center 20 stitches on the first row of shaping, then bind off 20 stitches at each side is a series of steps to produce a rounded shape. The decrease sequence is shown on the chart above.

For our sample front, bind off the center 20 stitches on the first row. Work the right and left sides separately and use the sloped method (see page 77) along each neck edge to bind off 5 stitches once, then bind off 4 stitches once, then bind off 3 stitches once, then bind off 2 stitches once, then bind off 1 stitch 6 times—27 stitches remain each side. Work even until 68 armhole rows have been completed and the armhole measures 8" (20.5 cm).

Step 6: Shoulder Shaping

There is no formal shoulder shaping in this example. Simply bind off all the stitches or place the stitches on holders in preparation for joining the shoulder with a three-needle bind-off.

Step 7– Step 12

The back and sleeves would be worked as described for the classic silhouette beginning on page 79, following the desired dimensions and using the gauge of 7.44 stitches and 8.6 rows = 1" (2.5 cm).

chapter five
Cardigans

The cardigan takes its name from the knitted waistcoat reportedly worn by the 7th Earl of Cardigan James Thomas Brudenell (1797–1868) during the famous 1854 battle of Balaclava (Ukraine) when the British fought against Russian forces. The battle was memorialized in Alfred Lord Tennyson's poem, *The Charge of the Light Brigade*. The Earl initially returned home to a hero's welcome, and the style of waistcoat he wore bore his name and became very popular. Today, his name is given to all sweaters in which the front is divided into two pieces.

The front of a cardigan is worked just like the front of a pullover, only in two pieces. When the cardigan is fastened, the two fronts measure the same width as the front of a pullover. The back and sleeves are worked the same as the back and sleeves of a pullover. Just like pullovers, cardigans can feature any type of body shape— classic, dropped shoulder, double taper, reverse taper, etc.

In this chapter, we'll discuss styles that close at the center front, have overlapping fronts, rounded lower front edges, and styles that are worked in a single piece to the underarms.

The My Fair Isle Lady cardigan, from the Fall 2006 issue of *Vogue Knitting*, has a classic silhouette with overlapping front bands.
Photo: Rose Callahan

tip

When planning for the ease in a cardigan, think about its intended use. A cardigan worn over clothing has to be roomier than a garment worn against the body. It's also important to plan ahead for the shape of the neckline, the type of buttonholes or closures, and the type of collar. These techniques are detailed in subsequent chapters; for now, just decide on the type of closure and details that are important to your design.

CENTER CLOSURE

In a cardigan with center closure, each front measures exactly half (50%) of the back width, or one-quarter (25%) of the total body circumference, including ease. The fronts meet at the center and are edged with some type of border treatment or zipper. If knitting the cardigan in a stitch pattern, plan the pattern to be continuous across the front when it is fastened. It's a good idea to add a selvedge stitch at each center front edge.

For this type of cardigan, simply draw a vertical line from the top of the front neck to the lower edge along the center of the body schematic to break the front into two halves. To make things easy, our example is worked in stockinette stitch (so there's no need to add extra stitches to balance another stitch pattern). There will be one selvedge stitch at the center front edge; otherwise, the stitch counts will be exactly half of those for the back. For our example, use the same needles, yarn, gauge, and measurements as for the classic silhouette pullover on page 66, shown on the schematic on page 122.

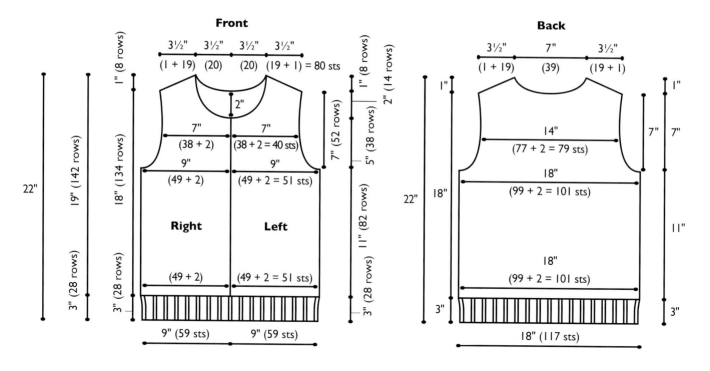

Schematic of fronts and back of the example classic-silhouette cardigan, annotated with numbers of stitches and rows.

NEEDLES

Border: Size U.S. 4 (3.5 mm)
Body: Size U.S. 6 (4 mm)

GAUGE

Border gauge (k1, p1 ribbing): 6.5 stitches
and 9 rows = 1" (2.5 cm)
Body gauge (stockinette stitch): 5.5 stitches
and 7.5 rows = 1" (2.5 cm)

KEY MEASUREMENTS

Front bust width: 18" (45.5 cm) back width
÷ 2 = 9" (23 cm)
Front width above armhole: 14" (35.5 cm)
cross-back width ÷ 2 = 7" (18 cm)
Front neck width: 7" (18 cm) back neck
width ÷ 2 = 3½" (9 cm)

Notes

• One symmetry stitch is added to the
ribbed border (see page 68).
• A garter-stitch selvedge stitch (knit
every row) is added to each end of
the row of the stockinette-stitch
portions to facilitate seaming.
• The body is worked on an odd
number of stitches, just like the
pullover on page 66.
• Rows are worked in pairs so all
row numbers are rounded to
even numbers.

Conversion of Measurements to Numbers of Stitches and Rows

FRONT WIDTHS

Number of stitches in border (half of hip width × border stitch gauge + 1 symmetry stitch)
    9" (23 cm) × 6.5 stitches/inch + 1 symmetry stitch = 59.5 stitches;
    round down to nearest odd number = 59 stitches

Number of stitches at base of body (half of hip width × body stitch gauge + 2 selvedge stitches)
    9" (23 cm) × 5.5 stitches/inch + 2 selvedge stitches = 51.5 stitches;
    round down to nearest odd number = 51 stitches

Number of stitches in front at bust (half bust width × body stitch gauge + 2 selvedge stitches)
    9" (23 cm) × 5.5 stitches/inch + 2 selvedge stitches = 51.5 stitches;
    round down to nearest odd number = 51 stitches

Number of stitches in front above armhole (half of shoulder-to-shoulder width × body stitch
gauge + 2 selvedge stitches)
    7" (18 cm) × 5.5 stitches/inch + 2 selvedge stitches = 40.5;
    round down to nearest even number = 40 stitches

Number of stitches in neck width (half of total neck width × body stitch gauge)
    3½" (9 cm) × 5.5 stitches/inch = 19.25 stitches;
    round up to nearest even number = 20 stitches

Number of stitches in shoulder (shoulder width × body stitch gauge + 1 selvedge stitch)
    3½" (9 cm) × 5.5 stitches/inch + 1 selvedge stitch = 20.25 stitches;
    round down to nearest even number = 20 stitches

LENGTHS

Number of rows in border (border length × border row gauge)

3" (7.5 cm) × 9 rows/inch = 27 rows; round up to nearest even number = 28 rows

Number of rows from beginning of body to base of armhole (length × body row gauge)

11" (28 cm) × 7.5 rows/inch = 82.5 rows; round down to nearest even number = 82 rows

Number of rows from base of armhole to base of front neck (length × body row gauge)

5" (12.5 cm) × 7.5 rows/inch = 37.5 rows; round up to nearest even number = 38 rows

Number of rows from base of front neck to base of shoulder (length × body row gauge)

2" (5 cm) × 7.5 rows/inch = 15 rows; round down to nearest even number = 14 rows

Number of rows in armhole (armhole length × body row gauge)

7" (18 cm) × 7.5 rows/inch = 52.5 rows; round down to nearest even number = 52 rows

Number of rows in shoulder slope (length × body row gauge)

1" (2.5 cm) × 7.5 rows/inch = 7.5 rows; round up to nearest even number = 8 rows

When working a cardigan in a stitch pattern, divide the pattern symmetrically around the center front opening and add a selvedge stitch so that the pattern will appear continuous when the garment is fastened.

 MATH CHECK!

The total number of rows worked in stockinette stitch should add up to the desired total length.

Total rows: 82 + 38 + 14 + 8 = 142 rows

Length in stockinette stitch portion:

11" (28 cm) + 5" (12.5 cm) + 2" (5 cm) + 1" (2.5 cm) = 19" (48.5 cm)

19" (48.5 cm) × 7.5 rows/inch = 142 rows.

The Pewter Coat, from the Winter 2006 issue of *Interweave Knits,* **is an example of a cardigan with a classic silhouette and center closure fastened with a single button.**

Photo: Chris Hartlove

Except for the shoulders, the fronts added together have one more stitch than the back.

Bust width: 51 stitches each front (102 stitches total); 101 stitches in back: 1 extra stitch in fronts

Cross-back width: 40 stitches each front (80 stitches total); 79 stitches in back: 1 extra stitch in fronts

Neck width: 20 stitches each front (40 stitches total); 39 stitches in back: 1 extra stitch in fronts

Shoulder width: 20 stitches each front; 20 stitches each back shoulder: no difference

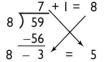

Use the shaping formula to determine an even distribution of decreases. In this example, decrease every 7th stitch 5 times and every 8th stitch 3 times.

RIGHT FRONT

For this example, begin with the right front.

Step 1: Cast-On and Ribbing/Border

The front begins with stitches cast on for the lower edge, which are worked in k1, p1 ribbing on the smaller needles.

For our sample right front, use the smaller needles to cast on 59 stitches. Work k1, p1 ribbing until the piece measures 3" (7.5 cm), or 28 rows, from the beginning.

Step 2: Transition from Ribbing to Body

To achieve the desired 9" (23 cm) width in the stockinette-stitch gauge, decrease 8 stitches across the first row of stockinette stitch to end up with the desired 51 stitches. The shaping formula tells us to decrease every 7th stitch (i.e., k5, k2tog) 5 times and every 8th stitch (i.e., k6, k2tog) 3 times. To prevent working a decrease at the end of the row, divide one of the 8-stitch intervals between the beginning of the row and the end of the row.

For our sample right front, work this row as k2, k2tog, [k5, k2tog] 5 times, [k6, k2tog] 2 times, k4—51 stitches remain.

Step 3: Lower Body

For our sample right front, change to the larger needles and work even in stockinette stitch on these 51 stitches for 11" (28 cm), or 82 rows, ending with a right-side row.

Step 4: Armhole Shaping

Beginning with a wrong-side row, follow the armhole shaping schedule for the right half of the upper body (just the shaping worked on wrong-side rows; see page 75) to decrease a total of 11 stitches over 10 rows.

For our sample right front, end with a right-side row so that shaping can begin on a wrong-side row, then bind off 4 stitches at the beginning of the first wrong-side row, then use the sloped method (see page 77) to bind off 3 stitches at the beginning of the next wrong-side row, then bind off 2 stitches at the beginning of the next wrong-side row, then bind off 1 stitch at the beginning of the next 2 wrong-side rows—40 stitches remain. Work even on these 40 stitches until there are 38 rows total to the beginning of the neck shaping.

Step 5: Front Neck Shaping

For our example, use the one-third initial bind-off method (see page 77) to shape the neck over 2" (5 cm), which translates to 14 rows when rounded to an even number of rows. When planning the shaping for a cardigan, remember that there should be the same number of stitches in each front shoulder as in each back shoulder. Therefore, to determine the number of stitches in the initial neck bind-off, work the upper body calculations in reverse. First, determine the number of stitches involved in the neck shaping by subtracting the number of shoulder stitches from the number of body stitches that remain after the armhole has been shaped.

40 body stitches – 20 shoulder stitches = 20 neck stitches

Following the one-third initial bind-off schedule used for the classic pullover on page 77, we know that we'll decrease 13 of those neck stitches along the edge of the neck. Therefore, the remaining 7 stitches must be bound off in the initial bind-off row.

20 neck stitches – 13 stitches bound off along neck slope = 7 stitches for initial bind-off

For our sample right front, begin by binding off 7 stitches at the center front edge (the beginning of right-side rows). Then use the sloped method (see page 77) to bind off 4 stitches at the beginning of the next right-side row, then bind off 3 stitches at the beginning of the next right-side row, then bind off 2 stitches at the beginning of the next 2 right-side rows, then bind off 1 stitch at the beginning of the next 2 right-side rows—20 stitches remain for the shoulder.

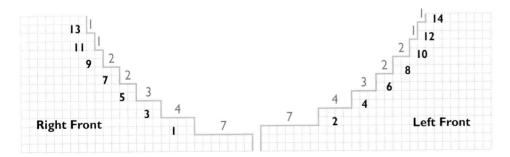

Plot of front neck shaping. Bind-off stitches are shown in red; row numbers are shown in black.

tip The number of stitches in each front shoulder must match the number of stitches in each back shoulder.

Step 6: Shoulder Shaping

The shoulder slope is worked over the final 1" (2.5 cm), which translates to 8 rows. Shape the shoulder just as the left back shoulder was shaped (see page 79). Note that this corresponds to the shaping worked on wrong-side rows only of the back shaping.

For our sample right front, use the sloped method to bind off 5 stitches at the beginning of the next 3 wrong-side rows. Bind off the remaining stitches on the following right-side row.

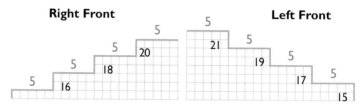

Plot of the shoulder shaping. Bind-off stitches are shown in red; row numbers are shown in black.

LEFT FRONT

The left front is worked exactly as the right front, but the shaping is reversed so that the two fronts are mirror images. To reverse the shaping, simply work the armhole and shoulder shaping at the beginning of right-side rows and work the neck shaping at the beginning of wrong-side rows.

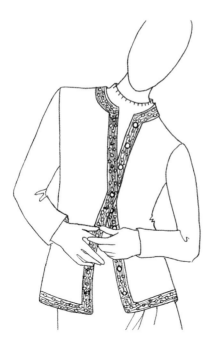

OVERLAPPING FRONT BANDS

One of the most common cardigan styles has front bands that overlap to accommodate buttons and buttonholes. The bands can be worked together with the cardigan body or worked separately and sewn into place. The overlap is planned so that, when fastened, the front measures exactly the same width as the back and the fit is the same as that of a pullover.

To begin, determine the width of the overlapping bands. In general, the bands should be about twice the width of the buttons. For our example, the buttons are ½" (1.3 cm) and the bands are 1" (2.5 cm) wide. The bands overlap their entire width so that the sum of the two front widths without the bands is 1" (2.5 cm) less than the back width; each front measures ½" (1.3 cm) less than half of the back width. The two bands will fill in the remaining 1" (2.5 cm). The front bands are worked simultaneously with the fronts on the same-size needles. Both the stockinette-stitch body gauge and the seed-stitch border gauge are factored into the stitch counts. This example uses the same measurements as for the classic pullover (see page 66). However, this cardigan will be bordered with seed stitch worked on the same needles as the body. Begin with the left front, which doesn't include buttonholes, then use the left front to calculate placement of buttonholes on the right front.

NEEDLES

Border: Size U.S. 6 (4 mm)
Body: Size U.S. 6 (4 mm)

GAUGE

Border gauge (seed stitch):
    4 stitches and 7.5 rows = 1" (2.5 cm)
Body gauge (stockinette stitch):
    5.5 stitches and 7.5 rows = 1" (2.5 cm)

KEY MEASUREMENTS

Band width: 1" (2.5 cm)

Front bust width without band:
    18" (45.5 cm) back width − 1" (2.5 cm)
    band overlap ÷ 2 = 8½" (21.5 cm)

Front width with band (width at border): 18" (45.5 cm) back width
    + 1" (2.5 cm) band overlap ÷ 2
    = 9½" (24 cm)

Front width above armhole without band: 14" (35.5 cm) cross-back
    width − 1" (2.5 cm) band overlap ÷ 2
    = 6½" (16.5 cm)

Front neck width without band:
    7" (18 cm) back neck width − 1" (2.5 cm)
    band width ÷ 2 = 3" (7.5 cm)

Notes

- The front bands are worked simultaneously with the front on the same-size needles, even though the width gauges are different.
- The buttons will be on the left front; the buttonholes will be on the right front. (For a man's sweater or for buttons on the back of woman's sweater, the buttons would be on the right and the buttonholes on the left.)

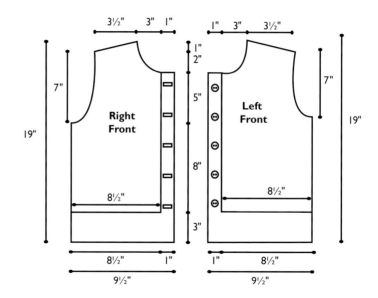

Schematic of the fronts of the example cardigan with a classic silhouette.

CALCULATE FRONT WIDTHS WITHOUT BANDS

There are two ways to calculate the width of a front without the overlapping band.

Method 1:
Subtract the width of the band from the back width and divide by two.

18" (45.5 cm) back width − 1" (2.5 cm) band width = 17" (43 cm) adjusted width

17" (43 cm) adjusted width ÷ 2 = 8½" (21.5 cm) for each front, without band

Method 2:
Divide the back width in half, then subtract half of the overlap width

18" (45.5 cm) back width ÷ 2 = 9" (23 cm) front width including band overlap

9" (23 cm) front width − ½" (1.3 cm) of overlap = 8½" (21.5 cm) for each front, without band

CALCULATE FRONT WIDTHS WITH BANDS

To calculate the width of a front including the overlapping band, divide the back width in half, then add half the band width.

18" (45.5 cm) back width ÷ 2 = 9" (23 cm)

9" (23 cm) + ½" (1.3 cm) = 9½" (24 cm) for each front, with band

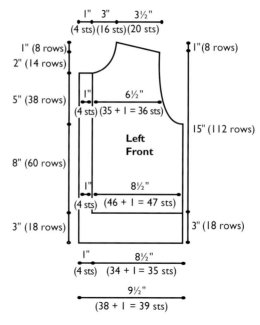

Schematic of the left front annotated with numbers of stitches and rows.

Conversion of Measurements to Numbers of Stitches

WIDTHS

Number of stitches in band (width × border stitch gauge)
   1" (2.5 cm) × 4 stitches/inch = 4 stitches

Number of stitches at border (width of front with border × border stitch gauge + 1 selvedge stitch)
   9½" (24 cm) × 4 stitches/inch + 1 selvedge stitch = 39 stitches

Number of stitches in border excluding band (width of front without band × border stitch gauge + 1 selvedge stitch)
   8½" (21.5 cm) × 4 stitches/inch + 1 selvedge stitch = 35 stitches

Number of stitches in body excluding band (width × body stitch gauge + 1 selvedge stitch)

8½" (21.5 cm) × 5.5 stitches/inch + 1 selvedge stitch = 47.75 stitches;

round down to nearest odd number = 47 stitches

Number of stitches above armhole excluding band (width × body stitch gauge + 1 selvedge stitch)

6½" (16.5 cm) × 5.5 stitches/inch + 1 selvedge stitch = 36.75 stitches;

round down to nearest even number = 36 stitches

Number of stitches in front neck excluding band (width × body stitch gauge)

3" × 5.5 stitch/inch = 16.5 stitches; round down to nearest even number = 16 stitches

LEFT FRONT

Step 1: Cast-On and Ribbing/Border

The front begins with stitches cast on for the lower edge and the buttonhole band. All of these stitches will be worked in seed stitch at a gauge of 4 stitches = 1" (2.5 cm).

For our sample left front, cast on 39 stitches. Work in seed stitch until the piece measures 3" (7.5 cm), or 22 rows.

Step 2: Transition from Border to Body

At this point, continue to work the 4 band stitches along the center front in seed stitch (it's a good idea to separate these stitches with a stitch marker). Work a selvedge stitch at the side in garter stitch and the remaining 8½" (21.5 cm) width in stockinette-stitch. To end up with the desired 47 stitches in the body width, increase 12 stitches across the first row of stockinette stitch. The shaping formula tells us to increase on or after every 2 stitches 1 time and every 3 stitches 11 times. To balance the placement of the increases at each end of the row, divide the 2-stitch interval between the beginning of the row and the end of the row, and work the 3-stitch intervals in between.

For our sample left front, work this right-side row as k1, M1, [k3, M1] 11 times, k1, place marker, then work the remaining 4 band stitches in seed stitch as established— 46 stitches in stockinette-stitch body; 1 stitch in garter-stitch side selvedge; 4 stitches in seed-stitch band; 51 stitches total.

Step 3: Lower Body

For our sample left front, continue to work the 4 band stitches in seed stitch as established, 1 selvedge stitch in garter stitch, and the remaining 46 stitches in stockinette stitch for 8" (20.5 cm), or 60 rows, ending with a wrong-side row.

Step 4: Armhole Shaping

Beginning with a right-side row, follow the armhole-shaping schedule for the left half of the pullover (just the shaping worked on right-side rows; see page 75) to decrease a total of 11 stitches over 10 rows.

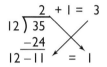

Use the shaping formula to determine an even distribution of increases. In this example, increase every 2 stitches 1 time and every 3 stitches 11 times.

For our sample left front, bind off 4 stitches at the beginning of the first right-side row, then use the sloped method (see page 77) to bind off 3 stitches at the beginning of the next right-side row, then bind off 2 stitches at the beginning of the next right-side row, then bind off 1 stitch at the beginning of the next 2 right-side rows—40 stitches remain; 35 stockinette stitches, 1 selvedge stitch, 4 border stitches. Work even on these 40 stitches until the piece measures 16" (40.5 cm) from the beginning and the armhole measures 5" (12.5 cm), ending with a right-side row.

Step 5: Front Neck Shaping

When the cardigan is buttoned, the front neck is the same as the back neck width, which is 7" (18 cm) in our example. Because the bands overlap 1" (2.5 cm) at the center front, subtract 1" (2.5 cm) from the back neck width, then divide by 2 to determine the width of the body (stockinette stitch) portion of each front neck.

7" (18 cm) total neck width – 1" (2.5 cm) band width
= 6" (15 cm) combined neck width for stockinette portions of both fronts

6" (15 cm) combined width ÷ 2 fronts
= 3" (7.5 cm) neck width in stockinette portion of each front neck

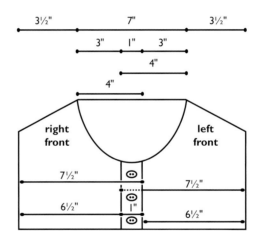

The front neck width is equal to half of the back neck width plus ½" (1.3 cm) for the portion of the band that extends beyond the exact center front.

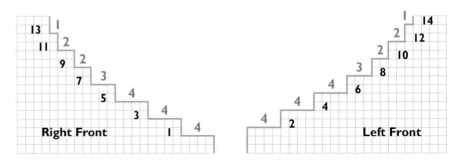

Plot of the front neck shaping. Bind-off stitches are shown in red; row numbers are shown in black.

Next, we have to add the 1" (2.5 cm) band to each front to determine the total neck width for each.

3" (7.5 cm) neck width in stockinette portion + 1" (2.5 cm) band width
= 4" (10 cm) total neck width for each front

This tells us to bind off 4" (10 cm) in width during the neck shaping. To determine the number of stitches to bind off, multiply the 3" (7.5 cm) body width by the stitch gauge and add the number of stitches in the band.

3" (7.5 cm) body width × 5.5 stitches/inch = 16 body stitches
16 body stitches + 4 band stitches = 20 stitches total bound off for each front neck

For our sample left front, shaping will begin on a wrong-side row. Bind off 4 stitches (4 band stitches) at the center front edge (the beginning of wrong-side rows). Then use the sloped method to bind off 4 stitches at the beginning of the next 2 wrong-side rows, then bind off 3 stitches on the next wrong-side row, then bind off 2 stitches on the next 2 wrong-side rows, then bind off 1 stitch on the next wrong-side row for a total of 20 stitches bound off over 14 rows—20 stitches remain for the shoulder.

Step 6: Shoulder Shaping

The shoulder slope is worked over the final 1" (2.5 cm), or 8 rows. Shape the shoulder just as the right back shoulder of the pullover was shaped (see page 79). Note that this corresponds to the shaping worked on right-side rows only of a pullover.

For our sample left front, use the sloped method to bind off 5 stitches at the beginning of the next 4 right-side rows.

RIGHT FRONT

The right front is worked as the left front, but the shaping is reversed so that the two fronts are mirror images and buttonholes are worked on the front band stitches. To reverse the shaping, simply work the armhole and shoulder shaping at the beginning of wrong-side rows and work the neck shaping at the beginning of right-side rows. To plan for the buttonholes, mark placement for the desired number of buttons evenly spaced on the left front button band, then work buttonholes on the right-front band (see Chapter 11 for buttonhole instructions) at those positions.

The Cruising Blues cardigan, from the Summer 1997 issue of *Knitter's Magazine,* is an example of a classic silhouette with overlapping front bands that are worked separately from the body.

Photo: Alexis Xenakis

INDEPENDENT OVERLAPPING BANDS

In some cases, particularly if different needles are needed for the band stitches and the body stitches, you'll want to add the band after the body portions of the fronts have been knitted. In these cases, the bands are knitted separately and sewn in place. For our example, the cardigan follows the same schematic and measurements as for the previous example of overlapping front bands (see page 127). However, this cardigan is bordered with k1, p1 ribbing (worked on smaller needles) as for the classic silhouette pullover on page 66, and the body is worked in stockinette stitch on smaller needles.

For this type of front opening, the combined width of the two fronts is less than the width of the back. Therefore, when the two fronts are placed against the back, there is a gap in the center that is filled by the front bands. For our example, the back measures 18" (45.5 cm) wide and each front measures 8½" (21.5 cm) wide. When the bands are added, each front measures 9½" (24 cm) wide. When buttoned, the bands overlap 1" (2.5 cm), and the total width of the two fronts equals the width of the back.

> 8½" (21.5 cm) right front width + 1" (2.5 cm) overlapping bands
> + 8½" (21.5 cm) left front width = 18" (45.5 cm)

Because the lower border of this cardigan is worked in the same k1, p1 rib pattern worked in the bands, the bands can be worked simultaneously with the front borders. In this case, the band stitches are cast on along with the body stitches. At the top of border, the band stitches are placed on holders and the body is worked separately to the neck. The band stitches are then returned to needles and worked separately to the neck, sewn in place, then the border stitches are bound off along with the body stitches for the neck shaping. Alternately, you can choose to cast on the band stitches separately and sew the bands to the entire length of the center fronts (see box on page 133).

Conversion of Measurements to Numbers of Stitches

Number of stitches in bands (width × border stitch gauge)
> 1" (2.5 cm) × 7 stitches/inch = 7 stitches

Number of stitches at border (width of front with border × border stitch gauge)
> 9½" (24 cm) × 7 stitches/inch = 66.5 stitches;
> round up to nearest odd number = 67 stitches

Number of stitches in front at bust excluding band (width × body stitch gauge + 1 selvedge stitch)
> 8½" (21.5 cm) × 5.5 stitches/inch + 1 selvedge stitch = 47.75 stitches;
> round up to nearest even number = 48 stitches

Number of stitches in front above armhole excluding band (width × body stitch gauge + 1 selvedge stitch)

6½" (16.5 cm) × 5.5 stitches/inch + 1 selvedge stitch = 36.75 stitches;
round down to nearest even number = 36 stitches

Number of stitches in neck width (width × body stitch gauge)

3" (7.5 cm) × 5.5 stitches/inch = 16.5 stitches;
round down to nearest even number = 16 stitches

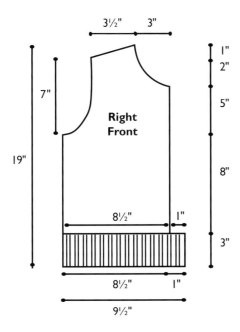

Schematic of the example right front of a cardigan with a classic silhouette and overlapping front bands

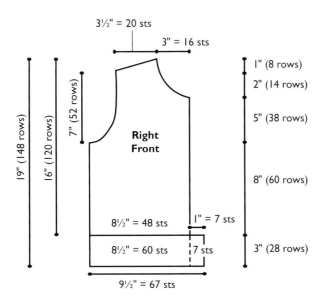

Schematic of the example right front, annotated with numbers of stitches and rows.

NEEDLES

Border: Size U.S. 4 (3.5 mm)
Body: Size U.S. 6 (4 mm)

GAUGE

Border (k1, p1 ribbing): 7 stitches and 9 rows = 1" (2.5 cm)

Body (stockinette stitch): 5.5 stitches and 7.5 rows = 1" (2.5 cm)

KEY MEASUREMENTS

Band width: 1" (2.5 cm)

Front bust width without band:
18" (45.5 cm) back width − 1" (2.5 cm) band width ÷ 2 = 8½" (21.5 cm)

Front width with band: 18" (45.5 cm) back width + 1" (2.5 cm) band width ÷ 2 = 9½" (24 cm)

Front width above armhole without band:
14" (35.5 cm) cross-back width − 1" (2.5 cm) band width ÷ 2 = 6½" (16.5 cm)

Front neck width: 7" (18 cm) back neck width − 1" (2.5 cm) band width ÷ 2 = 3" (7.5 cm)

Notes

- The front band is worked simultaneously with the front border, then the band stitches are placed on a holder while the front is worked to the beginning of the neck shaping. The band is worked separately to the neck, then sewn to the front, and the band stitches are bound off along with the initial bind-off for the front neck.

- The buttons will be on the left front; the buttonholes will be on the right front.

INDEPENDENT FRONT BANDS

To work the front bands independent of the body, omit the 7 band stitches from the initial cast-on, then work the front as described to the beginning of the neck shaping, omitting the band stitches throughout. Cast on the 7 band stitches separately, adding 1 stitch for a seaming stitch, and work in the border stitch pattern until the band measures 1" (2.5 cm) shorter than the front to the beginning of the neck shaping. Sew the band to the front, stretching it to fit, then bind off the band stitches when working the initial bind-off of the front neck, and complete the front as described.

LEFT FRONT

For this example, begin with the left front, which doesn't include buttonholes. The left front is a mirror image of the right front.

Step 1: Cast-On and Ribbing/Border

The front begins with stitches cast on for the lower edge and the buttonband. All of these stitches are worked in k1, p1 ribbing at a gauge of 7 stitches = 1" (2.5 cm).

For our sample left front, use the smaller needles to cast on 67 stitches. Work k1, p1 ribbing until the piece measures 3" (7.5 cm), or 28 rows.

$$12 \overline{)60} ^{5}$$

Use the shaping formula to determine an even distribution of decreases. In this example, decrease every 5th stitch 12 times.

Step 2: Transition from Border to Body

At this point, place the 7 band stitches on a holder, leaving 60 body stitches. To maintain the desired 8½" (21.5 cm) width in stockinette stitch, decrease 12 stitches across the first row of stockinette stitch to end up with 48 stitches. Based on the shaping formula, decrease every 5th stitch 12 times. To prevent a decrease from being worked at the end of the row, divide one 5-stitch interval between the beginning of the row and the end of the row.

For our sample left front, with the right side facing, work this row as k1, k2tog, [k3, k2tog] 11 times, k2, then place the 7 band stitches on a holder—48 stitches remain.

Step 3: Lower Body

For our sample left front, change to the larger needles and work even in stockinette stitch on these 48 stitches for 8" (20.5 cm), or 60 rows, ending with a wrong-side row.

Step 4: Armhole Shaping

Beginning with a right-side row, follow the armhole-shaping schedule for the right half of the classic pullover (see page 75). Note that this corresponds to the shaping worked on right-side rows only of a pullover.

For our sample left front, bind off 4 stitches at the beginning of this right-side row, then use the sloped method (see page 77) to bind off 3 stitches at the beginning of the next right-side row, then bind off 2 stitches at the beginning of the next 2 right-side rows, then bind off 1 stitch at the beginning of the next right-side row—36 stitches remain. Work even on 36 stitches for 30 more rows after the last bind-off row for 39 rows total to the beginning of the neck shaping, ending with a right-side row.

Step 5: Front Neck Shaping

Before binding off for the front neck, work the band stitches to 1" (2.5 cm) below the neck, adding a seaming stitch to the band stitches. Then seam the band to the front, stretching it to fit, so that the band stitches can be included in the initial bind-off of the front neck.

For our sample left front, return the 7 held band stitches onto smaller needles, rejoin yarn with the right side facing, increase 1 stitch at the body edge for seaming, then work in pattern to the end—8 stitches total. Work these 8 stitches in the established rib pattern for 12" (30.5 cm). Then stretch the band slightly so that it lays flat and pin it to the front edge of the body. With yarn threaded on a tapestry needle, sew the band in place (see Chapter 11 for seaming techniques), adding or subtracting band length as necessary for a uniform fit, and fasten off the seaming stitch—7 band stitches remain.

To shape the front neck, bind off the band stitches as part of the initial bind-off, then shape the side of the neck as for a cardigan with attached overlapping bands (see page 130).

For our sample left front, begin by binding off the 7 band stitches at the beginning of the next wrong-side row, then use the sloped method to bind off 5 stitches once, then bind off 4 stitches once, then bind off 3 stitches once, then bind off 2 stitches once, then bind off 1 stitch 2 times—20 stitches remain.

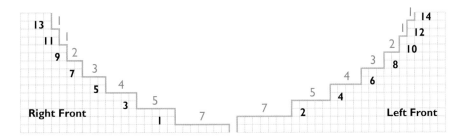

Plot of the neck and shoulder shaping. Bind-off stitches are shown in red; row numbers are shown in black.

Step 6: Shoulder Shaping

The shoulder slope is worked by binding off the remaining 20 stitches over the final 1" (2.5 cm), or 8 rows. Shape the shoulder just as the right back shoulder of the pullover was shaped (see page 79). Note that this corresponds to the shaping worked on right-side rows only of a pullover.

For our sample left front, use the sloped method to bind off 5 stitches at the beginning of the next 4 right-side rows.

RIGHT FRONT

The right front is worked exactly as the left front, but the shaping is reversed so that the two fronts are mirror images. To reverse the shaping, simply work the armhole and shoulder shaping at the beginning of wrong-side rows and work the neck shaping at the beginning of right-side rows. To plan for the buttonholes, mark placement for the desired number of buttons evenly spaced on the left front buttonband, then work buttonholes on the right-front band (see Chapter 11 for buttonhole instructions) at those positions.

OVERLAPPING FRONTS

In this style of cardigan, each front measures considerably more than half of the back width and the fronts overlap at the center. The amount of overlap can range from just a couple of inches to the entire back width, in which case, the overlap ends at the side seam. For our example, the fronts overlap 5" (12.5 cm). The border is worked in a lacy eyelet pattern that extends from the cast-on edge to a few inches below the armhole, then changes to stockinette stitch through the shoulder shaping. For simplicity, both patterns are worked on the same needles. The fronts fasten with a decorative pin.

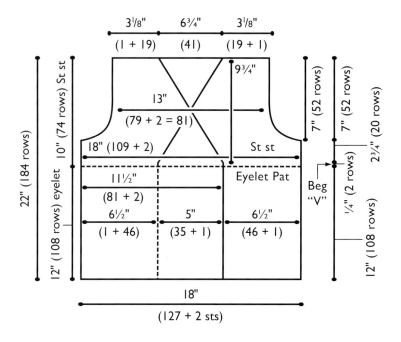

Schematic of the example body of a classic cardigan with overlapping fronts, annotated with numbers of stitches and rows. When overlapped, the combined width of the fronts measures the same as the width of the back.

Conversion of Measurements to Numbers of Stitches and Rows

WIDTHS

Number of stitches in back border width (width × pattern stitch gauge + 2 selvedge stitches)

18" (45.5 cm) × 7.06 stitches/inch + 2 selvedge stitches = 129 stitches

Number of stitches in back body width (width × pattern stitch gauge + 2 selvedge stitches)

18" (45.5 cm) × 6.06 stitches/inch + 2 selvedge stitches = 111 stitches

The Belted Wrap Jacket, from the Winter 2005 issue of *Interweave Knits*, is an example of a classic silhouette with overlapping fronts and bell sleeves.
Photo: Chris Hartlove

GAUGE

Border (eyelet pattern): 7.06 stitches and 9 rows = 1" (2.5 cm)
Body (stockinette stitch): 6.06 stitches and 7.5 rows = 1" (2.5 cm)

KEY MEASUREMENTS

Overlap width: 5" (12.5 cm)
Front width with overlap: 18" (45.5 cm) back width ÷ 2 + 2½" (6.5 cm) of overlap = 11½" (29 cm)

Front width without overlap: 18" (45.5 cm) back width − 5" (12.5 cm) overlap ÷ 2 = 6½" (16.5 cm)

Front with garment fastened: 6½" (16.5 cm) right front side width + 5" (12.5 cm) overlap portion + 6½" (16.5 cm) left front side width = 18" (45.5 cm)

Front neck width with overlap: 6¾" (17 cm)

Shoulder width: 3⅛" (8 cm)

Front neck depth: 9¾" (25 cm)

Notes

- The fronts overlap 5" (12.5 cm).
- The base of the V-neck begins before the armholes.
- The V-neck is held with a fashion pin; no buttonholes are necessary.

Number of stitches in front border width including overlap (width × pattern stitch gauge + 2 selvedge stitches)

11½" (29 cm) × 7.06 stitches/inch + 2 selvedge stitches = 83 stitches

Number of stitches in front body width including overlap (width × pattern stitch gauge + 2 selvedge stitches)

11½" (29 cm) × 6.06 stitches/inch + 2 selvedge stitches = 71.69 stitches; round down to odd number = 71 stitches

LENGTHS

Number of rows before beginning V-neck (length × body row gauge)
¼" (6 mm) × 7.5 rows/inch = 2 rows

Number of rows in front neck shaping (length × body row gauge)
9¾" (25 cm) × 7.5 rows/inch = 73.1 rows; round down to even number = 72 rows

Number of rows in armhole (length × body row gauge)
7" (18 cm) × 7.5 rows/inch = 52.5 rows; round down to even number = 52 rows

Number of rows from beginning of neck shaping to base of armhole (length × body row gauge)
2¾" (7 cm) × 7.5 rows/inch = 20.6 rows; round down to even number = 20 rows

RIGHT FRONT

For this example, begin with the right front.

Step 1: Cast-On and Ribbing/Border

The right front begins with stitches cast on for the front width plus overlap. The eyelet section is considered the border.

For our sample right front, cast on 83 stitches—46 side stitches plus 35 overlap stitches plus 2 selvedge stitches. Work the first and last stitch in garter stitch for the selvedges and work the center 81 stitches in eyelet pattern until the piece measures 12" (30.5 cm), or 108 rows, from the beginning.

Step 2: Transition from Border to Body

To maintain the desired 11½" (29 cm) width in stockinette stitch, decrease 12 stitches across the first row of stockinette stitch to end up with 71 stitches. The shaping formula tells us to decrease every 6th stitch (i.e., k4, k2tog) 1 time and every 7th stitch (i.e., k5, k2tog) 11 times. To prevent a decrease from being worked at the end of the row, divide a 7-stitch interval between the beginning of the row and the end of the row, leaving just ten 7-stitch intervals with 4 stitches worked at the beginning and 3 stitches worked at the end of the row.

For our sample right front, work this right-side row as k2, k2tog, k4, k2tog, [k5, k2tog] 10 times, k3—71 stitches remain.

Step 3: Lower Body

Because the eyelet pattern extends for 12" (30.5 cm), there are only 3" (7.5 cm) remaining of the lower body. Maintaining 1 selvedge stitch at each edge, work these 3" (7.5 cm), or 22 rows, in stockinette stitch to the armhole, including the transition row. At the same time, begin the deep V-neck shaping on the third row of this section (the first right-side row after the transition row). There are 20 rows of neck shaping in this section.

For our sample right front, purl 1 wrong-side row after the transition row.

Steps 4 and 5: Neck and Armhole Shaping

Beginning with the next right-side row (the third row of stockinette stitch), use the sloped method to bind off stitches for the neck shaping as shown on page 139. Work the neck shaping for 2¾" (7 cm), or 20 rows, to the base of the armhole, work 1 more right-side row, then beginning with the 24th row of the neck shaping, shape the armhole by binding off at the beginning of wrong-side rows 15 stitches over the next 16 rows as shown at left.

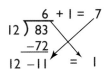

$$12 \overline{)83} \quad \frac{6 + 1 = 7}{}$$
$$\underline{-72}$$
$$12 - 11 = 1$$

Use the shaping formula to determine an even distribution of decreases. In this example, decrease every 6th stitch 1 time and every 7th stitch 11 times.

ARMHOLE-SHAPING SCHEDULE

Note: The right front follows the shaping of the wrong-side rows; the left front follows the shaping of the right-side rows. For a smooth bind-off edge, use the sloped method as described on page 77.

Shaping Row	Stitches Bound Off
1 (RS; left front)	4
2 (WS; right front)	4
3	3
4	3
5	2
6	2
7	2
8	2
9	1
10	1
11	1
12	1
13	1
14	1
15	1
16	1

V-NECK SHAPING SUMMARY

To determine how many stitches to bind off for the V-neck, subtract the number of stitches in the armhole shaping and the number of stitches in the shoulder from the number of stitches in the bust width.

71 stitches at bust – 15 stitches bound off for armhole – 20 stitches for shoulder = 36 stitches to decrease

There are 72 rows from the beginning of the V-neck shaping to the top of the shoulder. If the last 4 rows are worked even, there will be 68 rows over which to decrease these 36 stitches.

72 rows total – 4 rows worked straight = 68 rows for neck shaping

If 1 stitch is bound off on every shaping row, 34 stitches can be decreased over these 68 rows (remember that stitches can only be bound off at the beginning of a row on each side, so we have half the number of shaping rows as there are total rows). However, we need to decrease 36 stitches, or 2 more stitches than is possible by decreasing 1 stitch every decrease row. Therefore, on two of these shaping rows, 2 stitches will have to be bound off. The shaping formula tells us to bind off 2 stitches on every 17th bind-off row 2 times. This will place one 2-stitch bind-off on the 17th decrease row (the center row of the V shaping) and the second on the 34th decrease row (the final decrease row). However, to leave the line unchanged in the decrease flow along the neckline, we'll place the first 2-stitch decrease on the first row instead of following the shaping formula exactly. When all V-neck bind-offs have been worked and all 15 armhole decrease stitches have been worked, 20 shoulder stitches will remain.

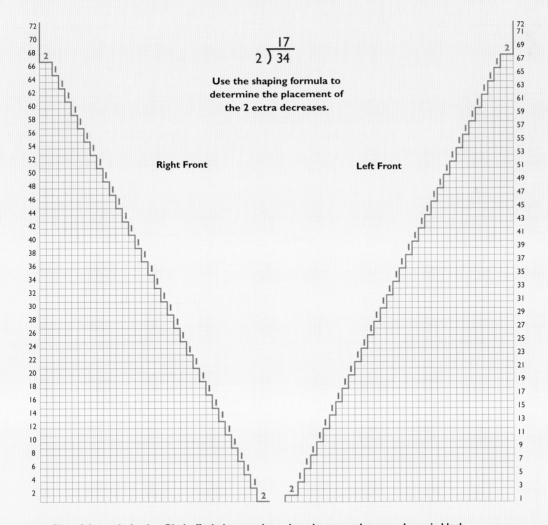

$$2 \overline{)34} ^{17}$$

Use the shaping formula to determine the placement of the 2 extra decreases.

Right Front

Left Front

Plot of the neck shaping. Bind-off stitches are shown in red; row numbers are shown in black. It's a good idea to include the shoulder stitches on the same plot.

For our sample right front, continue working the neck shaping as established and at the same time, work one right-side row even, then bind off 4 stitches at the beginning of the next wrong-side row, then bind off 3 stitches at the beginning of the next wrong-side row, then bind off 2 stitches at the beginning of the next 2 wrong-side rows, then bind off 1 stitch at the beginning of the next 4 wrong-side rows—20 stitches remain. Work even on these 20 stitches until the armhole measures 7" (18 cm), or 72 rows have been worked from the beginning of the neck shaping.

Step 6: Shoulder Shaping

There is no shoulder slope for this design.

For our sample right front, bind off all 20 remaining shoulder stitches at once.

LEFT FRONT

The left front is worked exactly as the right front, but the shaping is reversed so that the two fronts are mirror images. To reverse the shaping, simply work the armhole shaping at the beginning of right-side rows and work the neck shaping at the beginning of wrong-side rows.

ROUNDED FRONT EDGES

A rounded lower edge can soften the look of a cardigan or provide the bold style of a bolero. To create this shape, a few stitches are cast on at the beginning of the front, then additional stitches are gradually added to achieve the desired width. This is similar to how the curve of a classic armhole is shaped, only in this case the curve is convex and is created by adding stitches rather than subtracting them.

As with other types of cardigans, work out the back schematic first, then plan the full width of the fronts based on the back so that the bottom curve can be based on increasing from a percentage of the total front width to the full front width. Begin by deciding how much of the front you want to include in the curve. The front can begin with anywhere between 20% and 90% of the total number of stitches. The remaining stitches can be added over anywhere from the cast-on to 1" to 3" (2.5 to 7.5 cm) below the beginning of the armhole.

The Box Stitch Jacket, from the Winter 2007/2008 issue of *Vogue Knitting*, features rounded front edges. The body is knitted in a boxy check pattern; the edging, worked in ribbing, is added after the body is seamed.
Photo: Rose Callahan

For a very shallow curve that simply rounds the bottom edges, begin by casting on 85% to 90% of the total front stitches, then build out the curve to the full width over the next 1" to 1½" (2.5 to 3.8 cm) of rows. For example, if there are 50 stitches in the full front width and you want to begin with 85% of these stitches, begin by casting on 42 stitches.

50 total stitches × 85% = 42.5 stitches;
round down to an even number = 42 stitches

If the row gauge is 7.5 rows/inch, gradually cast on the remaining 8 stitches over the next 8 to 12 rows.

1" (2.5 cm) × 7.5 rows/inch = 7.5 rows; round up to an even number = 8 rows
1½" (3.8 cm) × 7.5 rows/inch = 11.25 rows; round up an even number = 12 rows

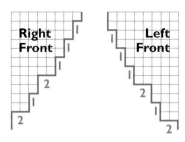

**Lower front shaping
for a shallow curve.**

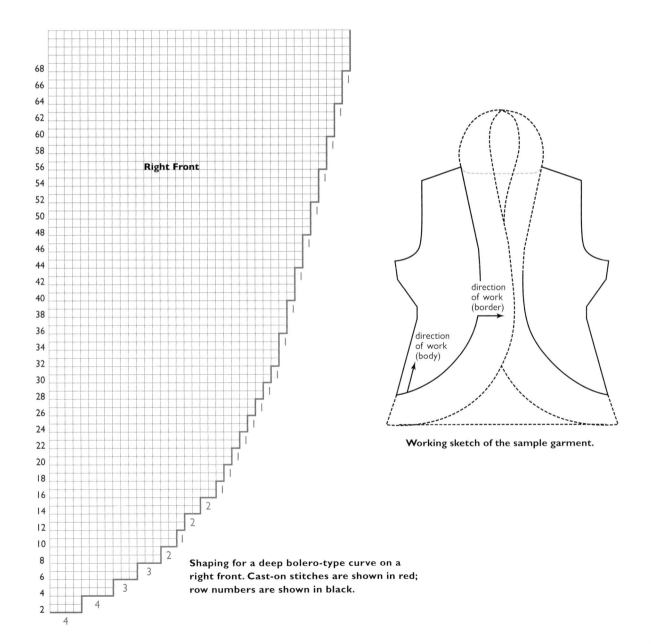

**Shaping for a deep bolero-type curve on a
right front. Cast-on stitches are shown in red;
row numbers are shown in black.**

Working sketch of the sample garment.

For a deep bolero-type front curve, begin by casting on 20% to 25% of the total front stitches, then build out the curve to the full width, ending about 3" (7.5 cm) below the beginning of the armhole. For example, if there are 50 stitches in the full front width and you want to begin with 25% of these stitches, begin by casting on 12 stitches.

50 stitches × 25% = 12.5 stitches; round down to an even number = 12 stitches

If the garment measures 12" (30.5 cm) to the beginning of the armhole, gradually cast on the remaining 38 stitches by the time the piece measures 3" (7.5 cm) before the armhole, or 9" (23 cm) from the beginning. Assuming a row gauge of 7.5 rows/inch, distribute these cast-ons over 68 rows.

9" (23 cm) × 7.5 rows/inch = 67.5 rows; round up to an even number = 68 rows

To ensure a smooth rounded edge, plot the curve on graph paper, increasing 38 stitches over 68 rows. Because stitches are cast on at the beginning of rows, there will be 34 rows available for working these cast-ons. The shaping does not typically involve every row; in this example, only 25 of the rows involved shaping.

 tip   To create a convex curve, cast on more stitches at first, then cast on progressively fewer stitches and work more rows between cast-ons. Remember that cast-ons are worked only at the beginning of rows, therefore they cannot be worked closer than every other row.

For an example, let's review the process I used to design the Box Stitch Jacket (shown on page 140), a double-taper cardigan with bolero-type front edges. This cardigan has a 2½" (6.5 cm) border around all edges that is picked up and knitted sideways (horizontally) after the pieces have been seamed together. Because this cardigan has a double-tapered silhouette, the side hip-to-waist shaping is worked at the same time as the center front shaping. To demonstrate how these shapings are worked simultaneously, we'll focus on planning the back and right front from the initial cast-on to the beginning of the armhole shaping.

 tip   When planning the dimensions of a garment, be sure to factor in the width and length of any border or edging that will be added after the pieces are seamed together. Use dotted lines to represent these borders and edgings on the schematic.

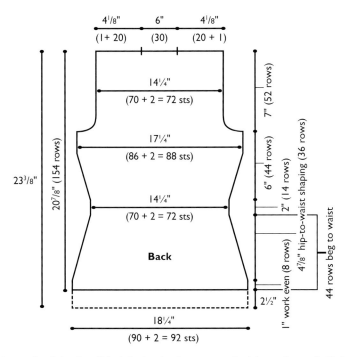

Schematic of the Box Stitch Jacket back, annotated with numbers of stitches and rows.

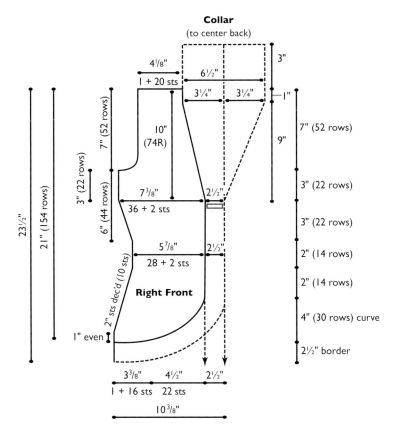

Schematic of the Box Stitch Jacket right front, annotated with numbers of stitches and rows.

GAUGE

Body (boxy check pattern):
4.88 stitches and 7.4 rows
= 1" (2.5 cm)

KEY MEASUREMENTS

Back hip width: 18¼" (46.5 cm)

Back waist width: 14¼" (36 cm)

Back width at armholes: 17¼" (44 cm)

Front width at cast-on (without border):
3⅜" (8.5 cm)

Front waist width (without border):
5⅞" (14.5 cm)

Front width at armhole (without border):
7⅜" (18.5 cm)

Border width: 2½" (6.5 cm)

Length of hip work-even section:
1" (2.5 cm)

Length from hips to beginning of waist:
5⅞" (14.5 cm)

Length of waist: 2" (5 cm)

Length from top of waist to bust:
3" (7.5 cm)

Length of bust work-even section:
3" (7.5 cm)

Length of front curve (without border):
4" (10 cm)

Length from cast-on to beginning
of V-neck (without border):
11" (28 cm)

Notes

- The base of the V-neck begins before the armholes are shaped.

- The center front is shaped at the same time as the side edge is tapered.

- The boxy check-stitch pattern is a multiple of 4 stitches + 2 balancing stitches. All stitch counts are based on this multiple, plus 2 selvedge stitches.

Conversion of Measurements to Numbers of Stitches and Rows

WIDTHS

Number of stitches in back hip width (hip width × stitch gauge + 2 selvedge stitches)
18¼" (46.5 cm) × 4.88 stitches/inch + 2 selvedge stitches = 91.06 stitches;
round up to even number to accommodate pattern multiple
= 92 stitches

Number of stitches in back waist width (waist width × stitch gauge + 2 selvedge stitches)
14¼" (36 cm) × 4.88 stitches/inch + 2 selvedge stitches = 71.54 stitches;
round up to even number to accommodate pattern multiple = 72 stitches

Number of stitches in back at armholes (bust width × stitch gauge + 2 selvedge stitches)
17¼" (44 cm) × 4.88 stitches/inch + 2 selvedge stitches = 86.18 stitches;
round up to 88 stitches to accommodate pattern multiple flow

Number of stitches in front cast-on (width × stitch gauge + 1 selvedge stitch)
3⅜" (8.5 cm) × 4.88 stitches/inch + 1 selvedge stitch = 16.47 stitches;
round up to odd number = 17 stitches

Number of stitches in front waist without border (width × stitch gauge + 2 selvedge stitches)
5⅞" (14.5 cm) × 4.88 stitches/inch + 2 selvedge stitches = 30.67 stitches;
round down to even number = 30 stitches

Number of stitches in front bust without border (width × stitch gauge + 2 selvedge stitches)
7⅜" (18.5 cm) × 4.88 stitches/inch + 2 selvedge stitches = 37.99 stitches;
round up to even number = 38 stitches

Number of stitches to increase in center front curve (width × stitch gauge + 1 selvedge stitch)
4½" (11.5 cm) × 4.88 stitches/inch + 1 selvedge stitch = 22.96 stitches;
round up to odd number = 23 stitches

LENGTHS

Number of rows in work-even section of lower body (length × row gauge)
1" (2.5 cm) × 7.4 rows/inch = 7.4 rows; round up to even number = 8 rows

Number of rows in taper from hips to waist (length × row gauge)
4⅞" (12 cm) × 7.4 rows/inch = 36 rows

Number of rows in waist (length × row gauge)
2" (5 cm) × 7.4 rows/inch = 14.8 rows; round down to even number = 14 rows

Number of rows in taper from waist to bust (length × row gauge)
3" (7.5 cm) × 7.4 rows/inch = 22.2 rows; round down to even number = 22 rows

Number of rows in center front curve (length × row gauge)
4" (10 cm) × 7.4 rows/inch = 29.6 rows; round up to nearest even number = 30 rows

BACK

Begin with the back so it can be used to calculate the shaping of the fronts.

Step 1: Cast-On and Ribbing/Border

The work-even area at the lower edge of this sweater is considered the border.

For our sample back, cast on 92 stitches; 90 stitches plus 2 selvedge stitches. Work the first and last stitch in garter stitch for selvedges and work the center 90 stitches in the stitch pattern until the piece measures 1" (2.5 cm), or 8 rows, ending with a wront-side row.

Step 2: Transition from Ribbing/Border to Body

The same stitch pattern is worked throughout; skip this step.

Step 3: Lower Body

Section 1: Hips-to-waist Taper
In this section, decrease from 92 stitches at the hips to 72 stitches at the waist over 5" (12.5 cm), or 36 rows.

92 stitches at hips – 72 stitches at waist = 20 stitches to decrease

Work these decreases in pairs (1 stitch at each edge) for 10 decrease rows. Work the first pair of decreases on the first row of this section, then divide the remaining 9 pairs over the remaining 35 rows. The shaping formula tells us to decrease every 4th row 8 times and every 3rd row 1 time. To facilitate seaming, work these decreases 1 stitch in from the edges.

Section 2: Waist
The waist is worked even for 2" (5 cm), or 14 rows.

Use the shaping formula to determine an even distribution of decrease rows. In this example, decrease on each edge of every 4th row 8 times and every 3rd row 1 time.

Section 3: Waist-to-Bust Taper

In this section, increase from 72 stitches at the waist to 88 stitches at the bust over the course of 3" (7.5 cm), or 22 rows.

88 stitches at bust – 72 stitches at waist = 16 stitches to increase

Again, work these increases in pairs so there will be 8 increase rows. Work the first pair of increases on the first row of this section, then divide the remaining 7 pairs over the remaining 21 rows. Based on the shaping formula, increase every 3rd row 7 times.

Section 4: Bust to Armholes

In this section, work even on 88 stitches for 3" (7.5 cm), or 22 rows.

$$7 \overline{)\, 21} \;\; \frac{3}{}$$

Use the shaping formula to determine the spacing of the increase rows. In this example, increase every 3rd row 7 times.

RIGHT FRONT

The right front duplicates the shaping on the left-hand side of the back—the decreases are worked at the beginning of wrong-side rows and the curve along the lower center front is shaped at the beginning of right-side rows. The front begins with 3⅜" (8.5 cm), or 17 stitches, cast on.

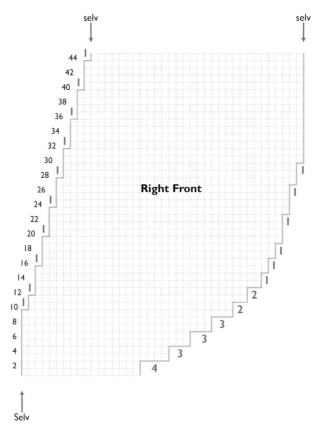

Shaping for the center front curve of the right front. Cast-on and bind-off stitches are shown in red; row numbers are shown in black.

Step 1: Cast On and Shape Center Front Curve

To begin, cast on 17 stitches (1 selvedge stitch + 16 body stitches). The curve is shaped by increasing 4½" (11.5 cm) in width over 4" (10 cm) in length. Based on the stitch and row gauge, cast on an additional 22 body stitches + 1 front selvedge stitch over 30 rows. To ensure a smooth, even curve, plot these cast-ons on graph paper.

For our sample right front, cast on 4 stitches at the beginning of the next right-side row, then cast on 3 stitches at the beginning of the next 3 right-side rows, then cast on 2 stitches at the beginning of the next 2 right-side rows, then cast on 1 stitch at the beginning of the next 3 right-side rows, then cast on 1 stitch at the beginning of every 2nd right-side (i.e., every 4th) row 3 times for a total of 23 stitches cast on over 30 rows. Designate the last stitch cast-on as the selvedge stitch and work even along this edge to the base of the neck shaping. At the same time, shape the left-hand side-seam edge of the piece on wrong-side rows as for the left-hand edge of the back.

LEFT FRONT

Work the left front as the right front but in mirror image. Reverse the shaping by working the side increases and decreases at the beginning of right-side rows and working the center front shaping at the beginning of wrong-side rows.

The Fair Isle Vest, from the Winter 2005/2006 issue of *Vogue Knitting*, is an example of a cardigan worked in a single piece so that the Fair Isle pattern is continuous around the body.
Photo: Paul Amato

ONE-PIECE CONSTRUCTION

There are times when you'll want a pattern stitch to flow continuously around the body without interruption by side seams. In these cases, work the right front, back, and left front in a single piece to the armholes, then work the fronts and back separately to the shoulders to create the armhole openings. Plan the right front, back, and left front separately as for a cardigan body worked in three pieces that are seamed together, but work the three pieces side by side on the needles. Keep in mind that the center front, armholes, and shoulders will interrupt the pattern flow and plan the placement of the pattern multiples and repeats accordingly before you begin knitting.

To begin, cast on the stitches for the right front, then the back, then the left front. Note that a selvedge stitch is added to both edges, which become the center front edges when the piece is finished. Work all of these stitches to the base of the armholes, at which point the fronts and back are divided and worked separately to the shoulders. This dividing row is typically a right-side row. Work across the right front stitches, then place these stitches on a holder. If the garment has armhole shaping, work the first armhole bind-off row as you work across the back. After working the back stitches, place the left front stitches on another holder. Continue working the back through the shoulders. If the garment has no armhole shaping, simply divide the work, placing the two front sections on holders, then begin by working even on the back.

After completing the back, rejoin the yarn at the armhole edge of the wrong side of the right front. Beginning with the first row of armhole bind-offs, work the front to the shoulders as usual. Finally, return the left front stitches to the needles, rejoin the yarn at the armhole edge of the right side (these stitches were not worked on the dividing row), and beginning with the first row of the armhole bind-offs, work to the shoulder as usual.

It's a good idea to add selvedge stitches at each armhole edge after the dividing row. Plan for these stitches in the anticipated stitch count after the pieces are divided. Then, after working the armhole bind-offs, establish the selvedge stitches by simply working the first and the last stitch of every row in garter stitch.

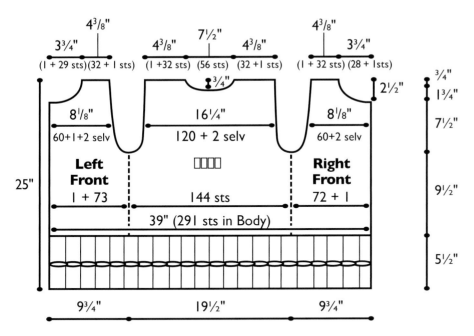

Schematic of the example vest worked in one piece, annotated with numbers of stitches.

 tip

If your pattern stitch includes a balancing stitch or stitches for symmetry, those extra stitches will most likely be located at the front edges and will be included in the neck width. Work the pattern with the established balancing stitches. They will be the first stitches decreased in the front neck shaping. It is possible that there may be balancing stitches on just one front. If this is the case, you will bind off more stitches on one front than the other when shaping the front neck. It is important to include these details in the schematic so that you can be assured that the front and back shoulders will have the same number of stitches and that the stitch pattern matches when the shoulders are seamed.

GAUGE

Body (Fair Isle pattern):
7.44 stitches and 7.2 rows = 1" (2.5 cm)

KEY MEASUREMENTS

Bust circumference: 39" (99 cm)
Back width below armhole: 19½" (49.5 cm)
Back width above armhole: 16¼" (41.5 cm)
Front width below armhole: 9¾" (25 cm)
Front width above armhole: 8⅛" (20.5 cm)
Neck width: 7½" (19 cm)
Shoulder width: 4⅜" (11 cm)
Length of ribbing: 5½" (14 cm)
Length from top of ribbing to bottom of armhole: 9½" (24 cm)
Length from beginning of armhole to beginning of back neck: 9¼" (23.5 cm)
Length from beginning of armhole to beginning of front neck: 7½" (19 cm)
Length of armhole: 10" (25.5 cm)
Front neck depth: 2½" (6.5 cm)

Notes

• The body is worked in one piece to the armholes.
• One selvedge stitch is added to each center front edge.
• Body measurements include 2" (5 cm) ease.
• The stitch pattern is a multiple of 12 stitches + 1 balancing stitch.

For an example, let's review the process I used to design the Fair Isle Vest shown on page 148. When planning this type of construction, focus on centering the pattern repeat before and after the armhole break. The calculations must take into account the bust circumference and the number of multiples of the pattern stitch.

Conversion of Measurements to Numbers of Stitches

Number of stitches in back (width × stitch gauge)
    19½" (49.5 cm) × 7.44 stitches/inch= 145.08 stitches;
    round down to even number = 144 stitches

Number of stitches in right front (width × stitch gauge + 1 selvedge stitch)
    9¾" (25 cm) × 7.44 stitches/inch + 1 selvedge stitch = 73.54 stitches;
    round down to nearest odd number = 73 stitches

Number of stitches in left front (width × stitch gauge + 1 balancing stitch + 1 selvedge stitch)
    9¾" (25 cm) × 7.44 stitches/inch + 1 balancing stitch + 1 selvedge stitch = 74.54 stitches;
    round down to nearest even number = 74 stitches

Total number of body stitches (circumference × stitch gauge + 2 selvedge stitches)
    39" (99 cm) × 7.44 stitches/inch + 2 selvedge stitches = 292.16 stitches;
    round down to an odd number = 291 stitches

To begin, determine the number of stitch pattern multiples that are in the body by dividing the body stitches (without selvedge stitches) by the number of stitches in a pattern multiple.

    288 body stitches ÷ 12 stitches/multiple = 24 pattern multiples + 1 balancing stitch

To balance the twenty-four 12-stitch multiples across the entire circumference, begin by centering the 12 multiples at the center back. They will be flanked on the right-hand side by a selvedge stitch and the 6 multiples of the right front and they will be flanked on the left-hand side by the 6 multiples of the left front, along with a balancing stitch and a selvedge stitch.

 tip When the back and fronts are worked together and there is a balancing stitch during the initial pattern layout, plan how that stitch will be worked as the garment is shaped.

At the armholes, the body is separated into three separate pieces—right front, back, and left front—that are worked separately to the shoulders. Because the left front contains the balancing stitch, 1 more stitch will have to be bound off in the neck shaping on that side so that there will be the same number of stitches in the left front shoulder as the left back shoulder. In addition, in order to include selvedge stitches along the armhole edges of the fronts and back, decrease 2 fewer stitches in the back (1 at each edge) armhole shaping and 1 less stitch on each front armhole shaping. After the armhole shaping is complete, the first stitch at each armhole edge will be worked as a selvedge stitch.

For our example, shape the armhole by decreasing from 144 stitches in the lower back to 122 stitches in the upper back.

144 lower back stitches – 122 cross-back stitches

= 22 stitches to decrease; 11 stitches to decrease at each side

At the armholes, one 12-stitch pattern repeat is removed at each edge, leaving ten 12-stitch pattern repeats in the back and five 12-stitch pattern repeats on each front. But the calculations are for decreasing only 11 stitches at each edge. The additional stitch at each armhole edge is the selvedge stitch.

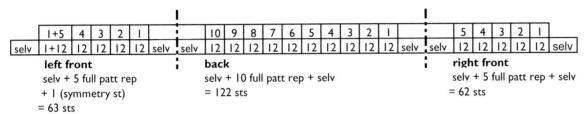

left front
selv + 5 full patt rep
+ 1 (symmetry st)
= 63 sts

back
selv + 10 full patt rep + selv
= 122 sts

right front
selv + 5 full patt rep + selv
= 62 sts

Distribution of the pattern multiples above the armholes.

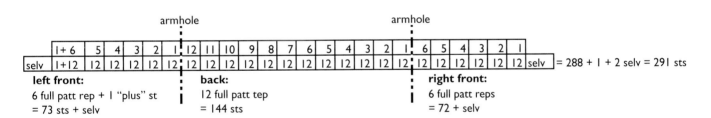

left front:
6 full patt rep + 1 "plus" st
= 73 sts + selv

back:
12 full patt tep
= 144 sts

right front:
6 full patt reps
= 72 + selv

Distribution of the pattern multiples around the body.

The right front began with six 12-stitch multiples + 1 selvedge stitch, for a total of 73 stitches. After eliminating one 12-stitch multiple during the armhole shaping and adding a second selvedge stitch after separating the front and back at the beginning of the armhole shaping, 62 stitches remain (five 12-stitch repeats + 2 selvedge stitches).

> 73 lower front stitches – 62 cross-back stitches
> = 11 stitches to decrease in the armhole shaping

The left front began with six 12-stitch multiples + 1 balancing stitch + 1 selvedge stitch, for a total of 74 stitches. After eliminating one 12-stitch multiple during the armhole shaping and adding a second selvedge stitch after separating the front and back, 63 stitches remain (five 12-stitch multiples + 1 balancing stitch + 2 selvedge stitches).

> 74 lower front stitches – 63 cross-back stitches
> = 11 stitches to decrease in the armhole shaping

On the armhole dividing row, which is a right-side row, work across the 73 right front stitches and place these stitches on a holder. Next, work across the 144 back stitches, including the first (right-side) row of armhole shaping. Place the remaining 74 left front stitches on another holder, leaving just the back stitches on the needles. Turn the work around and work the second (wrong-side) row of the armhole shaping on the back. Continue working the back through the shoulder shaping as usual.

Rejoin yarn to the armhole edge of the right front, and beginning with the first (wrong-side) row of the armhole shaping, work the right front through the shoulder shaping as usual. Finally, rejoin yarn to the armhole edge of the left front, and beginning with the first (right-side) row of the armhole shaping for this front, work to the top of the shoulder shaping as usual. When all of the shaping (including the neck shaping) has been worked, 33 stitches will remain for each shoulder.

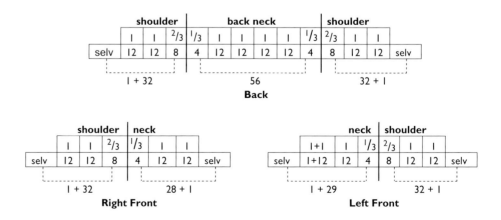

Distribution of the pattern multiples for the front and back shoulders and necks.

STITCH-PATTERN FLOW

Plan the stitch pattern to be continuous at the center front and center the pattern multiple across the fronts and back. To do this, the left front should end with the first half of the pattern multiple and the right front should begin with the second half of the multiple. The right front side edge should end with the beginning half of the pattern while the right side of the back should begin with the last half of the stitch pattern.

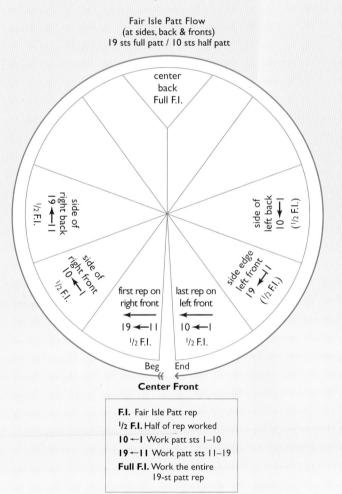

Fair Isle Patt Flow
(at sides, back & fronts)
19 sts full patt / 10 sts half patt

center back Full F.I.

side of right back 19 ←11 1/2 F.I.

side of left back 10 ←1 (1/2 F.I.)

side of right front 10 ←1 1/2 F.I.

side edge left front 19 ←11 (1/2 F.I.)

first rep on right front ← 19 ←11 1/2 F.I.

last rep on left front ← 10 ←1 1/2 F.I.

Beg | End

Center Front

F.I.	Fair Isle Patt rep
1/2 F.I.	Half of rep worked
10 ←1	Work patt sts 1–10
19 ←11	Work patt sts 11–19
Full F.I.	Work the entire 19-st patt rep

The stitch pattern should flow unbroken from the center edge of the right front to the center edge of the left front. The last half of the pattern multiple is worked at the beginning of the right front and the first half is worked at the end of the left front.

My Fair Isle Lady, from the Fall 2006 issue of *Vogue Knitting*, is an example of a stitch pattern that flows continuously around the body. The pattern flow is shown at left.
Photo: Rose Callahan

chapter six

Skirts and Dresses

Skirts follow the same construction principles as a reverse-taper body silhouette or a bell-cuff taper. The key areas to fit are the waist and hips. Dresses combine techniques for a skirt and a sweater. Typically, skirts are worked from the hem to the waist; dresses are worked from the hem to the shoulders. The taper from hem to waist (for a skirt) or from hem to shoulders (for a dress) is calculated the same as tapers in pullovers. The taper can be worked along the sides or in specifically planned areas across the entire width of the body.

To begin, take your body measurements as described on page 15, then measure a skirt or dress that fits comfortably to determine the ease amounts at the hip and waist. Be sure to plan for sufficient ease at the hemline for an unrestrained walking step. In most cases, the front and back of a skirt are identical.

The skirt in the Peek Through Skirt & Midriff Tank, from the Summer 2003 issue of *Interweave Knits,* is an example of a straight skirt.

Photo: Chris Hartlove

SKIRT MEASUREMENT GUIDELINES

- The hip-to-waist shaping typically occurs over 5" to 7" (12.5 to 18 cm) of length.
- The lower edge of a straight skirt is typically 2" to 4" (5 to 10 cm) larger than the hip measurement.
- The lower edge of an A-line skirt is typically 4" to 8" (10 to 20.5 cm) larger than the hip measurement.
- Skirt length can vary from 16" (40.5 cm) for a mini to 30" (76 cm) for a mid-calf length, and averages about 22" to 23" (56 to 58.5 cm) for an adult of average height.

The Almost Serious Suit, from the Fall 2001 issue of *Interweave Knits*, includes a straight skirt.
Photo: Chris Hartlove

NEEDLES

Facing: Size U.S. 6 (4 mm)
Body: Size U.S. 7 (4.5 mm)

GAUGE

Facing (stockinette stitch): 4.57 stitches and 6.78 rows = 1" (2.5 cm)
Body (stockinette stitch): 4.4 stitches and 6.58 rows = 1" (2.5 cm)

KEY MEASUREMENTS

Waist circumference: 30" (76 cm) + 2" (5 cm) ease = 32" (81.5 cm)
Hip circumference: 38" (96.5 cm) + 4" (10 cm) ease = 42" (106.5 cm)
Hem circumference: 42" (106.5 cm)
Length of hem facing: ¾" (2 cm)
Length from top of hem facing to hipline: 14" (35.5 cm)
Length from hips to waist: 7" (18 cm)
Waistband height: 1½" (3.8 cm)

Notes

- The front and back are identical; make two pieces the same.
- A garter-stitch selvedge (knit every row) is added to each end of all rows to facilitate seaming.
- Rows are worked in pairs (a right-side row followed by a wrong-side row) so all row numbers are rounded to even numbers.
- Measurements include ease allowance.
- All shaping decreases are worked one stitch in from the edge (i.e., inside the selvedge stitches).

STRAIGHT SKIRT

In a straight skirt, the lower edge (the hem) width is typically 2" to 4" (5 to 10 cm) wider than the hips. The width tapers from the widest part at the hips to the narrowest part at the waist. The taper can be worked along the side seams or circularly stacked around the full circumference of the skirt. Note that the same circular-shaping techniques can be applied in sleeves, cuffs, or yokes of sweaters worked in rounds.

SIDE-SEAM SHAPING

Let's begin by looking at a straight skirt worked in two pieces—an identical front and back—and shaped along the side seams. Our example skirt measures 21" (53.5 cm) wide at the hips and 16" (40.5 cm) wide at the waist. It is knitted in stockinette stitch and has a ¾" (2 cm) folded hem (worked on smaller needles), a 1½" (3.8 cm) waistband with elastic (also worked on smaller needles), and a 7" (18 cm) taper from the hips to the waist.

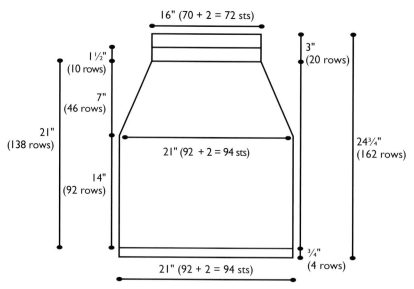

16" (70 + 2 = 72 sts)

1½" (10 rows)

3" (20 rows)

7" (46 rows)

21" (138 rows)

21" (92 + 2 = 94 sts)

24¾" (162 rows)

14" (92 rows)

¾" (4 rows)

21" (92 + 2 = 94 sts)

Schematic of the sample straight skirt annotated with numbers of stitches and rows.

Conversion of Measurements to Numbers of Stitches and Rows

WIDTHS

Number of stitches at hem (hem width × stitch gauge + 2 selvedge stitches)
> 21" (53.5 cm) × 4.40 stitches/inch + 2 selvedge stitches = 94.4 stitches;
> round down to even number = 94 stitches

Number of stitches at hips (hip width × stitch gauge + 2 selvedge stitches)
> 21" (53.5 cm) × 4.40 stitches/inch + 2 selvedge stitches = 94.4 stitches;
> round down to even number = 94 stitches

Number of stitches at waist (waist width × stitch gauge + 2 selvedge stitches)
> 16" (40.5 cm) × 4.40 stitches/inch + 2 selvedge stitches = 72.4 stitches;
> round down to even number = 72 stitches

LENGTHS

Number of rows in hem facing (facing length × facing row gauge)
> ¾" (2 cm) × 6.78 rows/inch = 5.08 rows;
> round down to nearest even number = 4 rows

Number of rows from top of hem facing to hipline (length × row gauge)
> 14" (35.5 cm) × 6.58 rows/inch = 92.12 rows;
> round to nearest even number = 92 rows

Number of rows from hipline to waist (length × row gauge)
> 7" (18 cm) × 6.58 rows/inch = 46.06 rows;
> round down to nearest even number = 46 rows

Number of rows in waistband (waistband length × facing row gauge)
> 1½" (3.8 cm) × 6.78 rows/inch = 10.17 rows;
> round down to nearest even number = 10 rows

Number of rows in waistband facing (facing length × facing row gauge)
> 1½" (3.8 cm) × 6.78 rows/inch = 10.17 rows;
> round down to nearest even number = 10 rows

FRONT OR BACK

The front and back are worked the same.

Step 1: Cast-On and Hem Facing

Begin by casting on stitches for the hem facing. To reduce bulk and facilitate seaming, cast on and work the facing with smaller needles. The facing is worked in stockinette stitch for about ¾" (2 cm), then a turning ridge is worked.

For our sample skirt, use smaller needles and a provisional method (see box at right) to cast on 94 stitches. Knit the first and last stitch of every row for selvedges and work the center 92 stitches even in stockinette stitch for 4 rows, ending with a right-side row. On the next (wrong side) row, knit every stitch through the back loop to create a turning ridge.

Step 2: Lower Skirt

The lower part of this type of skirt is worked straight (the same number of stitches) from the hem to the top of the hips.

For our sample skirt, change to larger needles and work the selvedge stitches in garter stitch and the center 92 stitches in stockinette stitch until the piece measures 14" (35.5 cm) from the turning ridge, or 92 rows, ending with a wrong-side row.

Step 3: Upper Skirt

The upper part of this type of skirt involves decreasing from the hip width to the waist width. For our example, work the decreases over 7" (46 rows). To figure out how many stitches to decrease, subtract the number of stitches in the waist from the number of stitches at the hips.

94 stitches at hip − 72 stitches at waist = 22 stitches to decrease; 11 at each side

We want to work the first decrease on the first row of this section, which leaves 10 stitches to decrease at each side over the remaining 45 rows. The shaping formula tells us to decrease every 4th row 5 times and every 5th row 5 times. For a truly even distribution, alternate between decreasing every 4th and 5th rows as outlined on page 71.

For our sample skirt, decrease 1 stitch at each end of the next right-side row, then alternate decreasing every following 4th row and every 5th row 5 times—72 stitches remain.

Step 4: Waistband

In this step, change to smaller needles and work for the desired height of the waistband, ending with a right-side row. Knit 1 wrong-side row to create a turning ridge, then work for the same length again for the facing.

PROVISIONAL CAST-ON

With a crochet hook and contrasting waste yarn, make a crochet chain 2 or 3 stitches longer than needed to cast on. Cut the yarn and tie a loose knot at that end to identify the end to ravel from when it's time to expose the stitches to work in the other direction, or to seam a hem.

With the main yarn, knitting needle, and beginning 1 or 2 stitches in from the knotted end, pick up and knit 1 stitch through the back loop of each chain for the desired number of stitches. This is the first right-side knit row of the piece. The next row will be a wrong-side row.

To remove the temporary chain, slowly ravel the chain from the knotted end, placing the exposed stitches one by one onto a needle a few sizes smaller than the main needles.

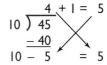

Use the shaping formula to determine an even spacing of the decreases. In this case, decrease every 4th row 5 times and every 5th row 5 times.

HIP-TO-WAIST TAPER SCHEDULE

Odd-numbered rows are right-side (RS) rows; even-numbered rows are wrong-side (WS) rows.

Garment Row	Shaping Row	Stitches Remaining
93	1	92
97	2	90
102	3	88
106	4	86
111	5	84
115	6	82
120	7	80
124	8	78
129	9	76
133	10	74
138	11	72

Total: 11 stitches decreased each side over 46 rows.

For our sample skirt, change to smaller needles and, maintaining selvedge stitches, work even in stockinette stitch for 1½" (3.8 cm), ending with a right-side row. Knit the next wrong-side row to create a turning ridge, then work even in stockinette stitch for 1½" (3.8 cm) more for the facing. Place the stitches on a waste-yarn holder in preparation for sewing the side seams.

Step 5: Finishing

All that's left is to sew the side seams, block the skirt, and sew the facings in place. Sew the side seams using a mattress stitch (see page 269), working just inside the selvedge stitches. After seaming, block the skirt, lightly pressing the hems in place along the turning ridges. With contrasting sewing thread and using large basting stitches, baste the hem in place, then with thin yarn (use just half the plies) threaded on a tapestry needle, use a whipstitch (see page 266) to sew the live stitches in place as described in the box below left. Repeat for the waistband, leaving 2" (5 cm) open on one side of the waistband for inserting elastic. Finish by inserting elastic in the waistband as described in the box below.

For our sample skirt, thread yarn on a tapestry needle and use the mattress stitch to sew the side seams, working from the hem to the waist on each side. Then block the skirt, sew the lower hem and waistband facings in place, and finish by inserting elastic into the waistband.

FOLDED HEM

A folded hem helps prevent the fabric from curling or stretching at the lower edge of a skirt or dress. Begin with a provisional cast-on, then work the facing for ¾" to 1" (2 to 2.5 cm) in a smooth stitch such as stockinette stitch, regardless of the stitch pattern used for the body. Work a turning ridge, then work the skirt or dress in the pattern stitch as desired. After the garment is finished, fold the facing along the turning ridge and baste in place.

To secure the hem, thread thin waste yarn on a tapestry needle and thread it through the exposed stitches as you carefully remove the waste yarn from the provisional cast-on. Then thread a length of working yarn on a tapestry needle and use a whipstitch (see page 266) to secure each live stitch to a corresponding purl loop on the wrong side of the skirt, removing the waste yarn after every five or six stitches.

WAISTBANDS

Waistbands are typically folded over to create a casing for elastic. The way this is done depends on whether you're working in rows or in rounds.

Worked in Rows

Begin by working the waistband for the desired length, work a turning ridge, then work the desired length of the facing. Sew the side seams and block the skirt to the finished measurements. To secure the facing, place the stitches on a length of waste yarn, then fold the facing to the wrong side along the turning ridge and whipstitch (see page 266) the live stitches to the purl loops on the wrong side, leaving a 2" (5 cm) gap so that elastic can be inserted in the casing. Cut a piece of 1" (2.5 cm) elastic long enough to fit comfortably around your waist, plus 1" (2.5 cm) for a securing overlap. Place a large safety pin through one end of the elastic and use it to guide the elastic through the casing. Overlap the ends of the elastic and sew them together securely. Using a whipstitch, secure the remaining live stitches of the 2" (5 cm) opening at the base of the waistband.

Worked in Rounds

Sometimes, the waistband looks best if it is knitted in a single piece in the round, even if the front and back were worked separately. After seaming the sides, transfer the front and back stitches onto a circular needle one or two sizes smaller than those used for the body of the skirt. Work the stitches in the round for the desired height of the waistband. Work a turning ridge, then work the facing for the same length as the waistband. Place the stitches on a waste-yarn holder. Finish as for a waistband worked flat.

STACKED CIRCULAR DECREASES

In this type of shaping, stitches are decreased evenly across the entire circumference at specific intervals as the garment is constructed. For the best results, the decreases neatly stack above one another as the width narrows so that the fabric pulls in evenly all around.

Our example straight skirt is worked circularly in a single piece from the hem to the waistband. It measures 44" (112 cm) around the lower edge (and hips) and 30" (76 cm) around the waist and is knitted in stockinette stitch. It has a 1" (2.5 cm) folded hem (worked on smaller needles), a 1½" (3.8 cm) waistband (also worked on smaller needles), and a 7" (18 cm) taper from the hips to the waist.

NEEDLES
Size U.S. 7 (4.5 mm)

GAUGE
Body (stockinette stitch): 5 stitches and 7 rounds = 1" (2.5 cm)

KEY MEASUREMENTS
Waist circumference: 28" (71 cm) + 2" (5 cm) ease = 30" (76 cm)

Hip circumference: 40" (101.5 cm) + 4" (10 cm) ease = 44" (112 cm)

Hem circumference: 40" (101.5 cm) + 4" (10 cm) ease = 44" (112 cm)

Length of hem facing: 1" (2.5 cm)

Length from hem to hipline: 15" (38 cm)

Length from hips to waist: 7" (18 cm)

Waistband height: 1½" (3.8 cm)

Notes

- Because this skirt is worked in one piece in the round, there are no selvedge stitches.
- For a longer or shorter skirt, add or subtract the desired number of rows in the lower skirt (i.e., before working the first decrease round in the upper skirt).
- When measuring, include the last decrease round in the part "worked even" between decrease rounds.
- About 1½" to 2" (3.8 to 5 cm) of stitches should be decreased in each decrease round. If the decrease rounds cannot be evenly spaced, the length between decrease rounds should be greater at the base and less near the waist.
- When the decreases are stacked, there should be one (1) less stitch between decreases in successive decrease rounds.

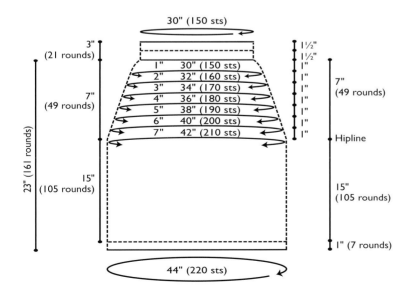

Schematic of the sample straight skirt worked circularly, annotated with numbers of stitches and rounds.

Conversion of Measurements to Numbers of Stitches and Rounds

Number of stitches at hem (hip circumference × stitch gauge)
    44" (112 cm) × 5 stitches/inch = 220 stitches

Number of stitches at hips (hip circumference × stitch gauge)
    44" (112 cm) × 5 stitches/inch = 220 stitches

Number of stitches in hipline 7" (18 cm) below waist (circumference × stitch gauge)
    42" (106.5 cm) × 5 stitches/inch = 210 stitches

Number of stitches at waist (waist circumference × stitch gauge)
    30" (76 cm) × 5 stitches/inch = 150 stitches

LENGTHS

Number of rounds in hem facing (length × round gauge)
    1" (2.5 cm) × 7 rounds/inch = 7 rounds

Number of rounds from hem to hipline (length × round gauge)
    15" (38 cm) × 7 rounds/inch = 105 rounds

Number of rounds from hipline to beginning of waist (length × round gauge)
    7" (18 cm) × 7 rounds/inch = 49 rounds

Number of rounds in waistband (length × round gauge)
    1½" (3.8 cm) × 7 rounds/inch = 10.5 rounds; round down to even number = 10 rounds

Number of rounds in waistband facing (length × round gauge)
    1½" (3.8 cm) × 7 rounds/inch = 10.5 rounds; round down to even number = 10 rounds

BODY

The body is worked in a single piece from the hem to the waistband.

Step 1: Cast-On and Hem Facing

For our sample skirt, use smaller needles and a provisional method (see page 157) to cast on 220 stitches. Place a marker, join for working in rounds, then knit every round for 7 rounds. Purl the next round to create a turning ridge.

Step 2: Lower Skirt

The lower part of the skirt is worked straight (the same number of stitches) from the hem to the top of the hips.

For our sample skirt, change to larger needles and knit every round until the piece measures 15" (38 cm), or 105 rounds.

Step 3: Upper Skirt

The upper part of this type of skirt involves decreasing from the hip circumference to the waist circumference, with the decreases distributed around the entire circumference in regularly spaced intervals. In our example, decrease 70 stitches over 49 rounds.

> 220 stitches at hips − 150 stitches at waist = 70 stitches to decrease
>
> 7" (18 cm) upper skirt length × 7 rounds/inch = 49 rounds over which to decrease

Next, decide how many decrease rounds to work in these 49 rounds and how many stitches to decrease on each decrease round. If we use 7 decrease rounds and divide that number into the rounds per inch, we'll work a decrease round every 1" (2.5 cm) as the hipline is shaped.

> 49 rounds ÷ 7 = 7 decrease rounds

At our round gauge of 7 rounds per inch, we'll work the decreases in 1" (2.5 cm) increments along the 7" (18 cm) length of the upper skirt. Divide the number of decrease stitches between the hip and waist by the number of decrease rounds to determine the number of stitches to decrease on each round. In our example, a total of 70 stitches are decreased in these 7 decrease rounds, or 10 stitches decreased per decrease round.

> 70 stitches to decrease ÷ 7 decrease rounds = 10 stitches decreased
> per decrease round

Divide the number of stitches in each decrease by the stitch gauge to determine the number of inches to be decreased on each decrease round. At our stitch gauge of 5 stitches per inch, decrease a total of 2" (5 cm) of width in each decrease round.

> 10 stitches ÷ 5 stitches/inch = 2" (5 cm)

For our example, decrease 2" (5 cm) of stitches at the beginning of the hip shaping. Then decrease 2" of stitches (10 stitches) after working 1" (2.5 cm), or 7 rounds, 6 additional times.

Finally, determine how to space the decreases so that they stack evenly atop one another. When working stacked decreases on a circular project, begin by planning a circular calculation summary. The key is to determine the number of decreases per round. This is easily done in three steps: First, subtract the number of stitches decreased per round from the starting number of stitches to establish a "baseline" number.

> 220 stitches − 10 stitches decreased = 210 stitches in baseline

Next, subtract the decrease amount from the baseline.

> 210 stitches in baseline − 10 stitches decreased = 200 stitches

Finally, divide the answer above by the number of stitches decreased per round to determine the number of stitches between decreases in the first decrease round.

> 200 stitches ÷ 10 stitches decreased = 20 stitches between decreases

The first decrease round will be worked as follows.

> *K20, k2tog; rep from *—210 stitches remain

To stack the decreases vertically in the remaining 6 decrease rounds, work 1 less stitch between decreases in each succeeding decrease round, ending by working 14 stitches between decreases, as shown in the box below. Note that each 2-stitch decrease counts as 1 stitch at the end of each decrease round so that after the first decrease round, there are 21 stitches in each of the 10 intervals (210 stitches). After the seventh decrease round (k14, k2tog), there are 15 stitches in each of the 10 intervals (150 stitches).

For our sample skirt, work the first decrease round as *k20, k2tog; rep from *, then work 6 rounds even. Work the remaining 6 decrease rounds every 7 rounds, working 1 less stitch between decreases in each decrease round and ending with *k14, k2tog; rep from *—150 stitches remain.

 tip There can be any number of decrease rounds, but the number of decreases in each round must fit evenly into the number of stitches on the needle.

Step 4: Waistband

For our sample skirt, change to smaller needles, knit 10 rounds, purl 1 round to create a turning ridge, then knit 10 more rounds for the facing.

Step 5: Finishing

For our sample skirt, work this step as for the straight skirt on page 155, omitting the side seams.

STACKED CIRCULAR DECREASE SCHEDULE

Decrease Round	Decrease Interval	Remaining Stitches
1	*K20, k2tog; rep from *	210
2	*K19, k2tog; rep from *	200
3	*K18, k2tog; rep from *	190
4	*K17, k2tog; rep from *	180
5	*K16, k2tog; rep from *	170
6	*K15, k2tog; rep from *	160
7	*K14, k2tog; rep from *	150

Total: 70 stitches decreased over 7 decrease rounds.

A-LINE SKIRT

An A-line skirt is similar to a straight skirt, but the width tapers continuously from the lower hem to the waist. The lower part of the skirt tapers from the hem width to the hip width, then the upper part tapers from the hip width to the waist width, just as for a straight skirt.

Our example A-line skirt measures 25" (63.5 cm) wide at the hem and 16" (40.5 cm) wide at the waist. It is knitted in stockinette stitch with a ¾" (2 cm) folded hem, a 1½" (3.8 cm) waistband and a 7" (18 cm) taper from the hips to the waist.

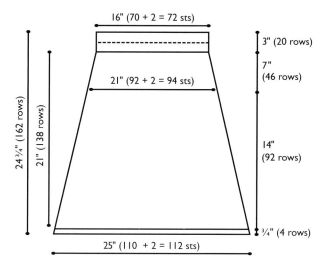

Schematic of the sample A-line skirt annotated with numbers of stitches and rows.

Conversion of Measurements to Numbers of Stitches and Rows

WIDTHS

Number of stitches at hem (hem width × stitch gauge + 2 selvedge stitches)
    25" (63.5 cm) × 4.40 stitches/inch + 2 selvedge stitches = 112 stitches

Number of stitches at hips (hip width × stitch gauge + 2 selvedge stitches)
    21" (53.5 cm) × 4.40 stitches/inch + 2 selvedge stitches
    = 94.4 stitches; round down to even number = 94 stitches

Number of stitches at waist (waist width × stitch gauge + 2 selvedge stitches)
    16" (40.5 cm) × 4.40 stitches/inch + 2 selvedge stitches
    = 72.4 stitches; round down to even number = 72 stitches

NEEDLES

Facing: Size U.S. 6 (4 mm)
Body: Size U.S. 7 (4.5 mm)

GAUGE

Facing (stockinette stitch): 4.57 stitches and 6.65 rows = 1" (2.5 cm)
Body (stockinette stitch): 4.4 stitches and 6.58 rows = 1" (2.5 cm)

KEY MEASUREMENTS

Waist circumference: 30" (76 cm) + 2" (5 cm) ease = 32" (81.5 cm)

Hip circumference: 38" (96.5 cm) + 4" (10 cm) ease = 42" (106.5 cm)

Hem circumference: 50" (127 cm)

Length of hem facing: ¾" (2 cm)

Length from top of hem facing to hipline: 14" (35.5 cm)

Length from hips to waist: 7" (18 cm)

Waistband height: 1½" (3.8 cm)

Notes

- The front and back are identical; make two pieces the same.
- A garter-stitch selvedge (knit every row) is added to each end of all rows to facilitate seaming.
- Rows are worked in pairs (a right-side row followed by a wrong-side row) so all row numbers are rounded to even numbers.
- Measurements include ease allowance.
- All shaping decreases are worked one stitch in from the edge (i.e., inside the selvedge stitches).

Decrease Row	Garment Row	Stitches Remaining
1	10	110
2	21	108
3	31	106
4	42	104
5	52	102
6	62	100
7	72	98
8	82	96
9	92	94

Total: 18 stitches decreased over 92 rows.

LENGTHS

Number of rows in hem facing (length × facing row gauge)

¾" (2 cm) × 6.65 rows/inch = 4.98 rows; round down to nearest even number = 4 rows

Number of rows from hem to hipline (length × body row gauge)

14" (35.5 cm) × 6.58 rows/inch = 92.12 rows; round to nearest even number = 92 rows

Number of rows from hipline to beginning of waist (length × body row gauge)

7" (18 cm) × 6.58 rows/inch = 46.06 rows; round down to nearest even number = 46 rows

Number of rows in waistband (length × body row gauge)

1½" (3.8 cm) × 6.58 rows/inch = 9.87 rows; round up to nearest even number = 10 rows

Number of rows in waistband facing (length × facing row gauge)

1½" (3.8 cm) × 6.65 rows/inch = 9.97 rows; round up to nearest even number = 10 rows

FRONT OR BACK

The front and back are worked the same.

Step 1: Cast-On and Hem Facing

Begin by casting on stitches for the hem with smaller needles. Work the facing in stockinette stitch for about ¾" (2 cm), then work a turning ridge.

For our sample skirt, use smaller needles and a provisional method (see page 157) to cast on 112 stitches. Knit the first and last stitch of every row for selvedge stitches and work the center 110 stitches even in stockinette stitch for 4 rows, ending with a right-side row. On the next (wrong side) row, knit every stitch through the back loop to create a turning ridge.

$$9 \overline{)\, 92} \quad \frac{10 + 1 = 11}{}$$
$$\underline{-90}$$
$$9 - 2 = 7$$

Use the shaping formula to determine even spacing of decreases. In this case, decrease every 10th row 7 times and every 11th row 2 times.

Step 2: Lower Skirt

The lower part of the skirt tapers from 112 stitches at the hem to 94 stitches at the hips. Therefore, 18 stitches are decreased in this section.

112 stitches at hem – 94 stitches at hip = 18 stitches to decrease; 9 stitches at each side

Use the shaping formula to space these decreases evenly along the 14" (35.5 cm), or 92 rows, in this section. The formula tells us to decrease every 10th row 7 times and every 11th row 2 times. For a truly even distribution, alternate between decreasing every 10th and 11th rows 2 times, then decrease every 10th row 5 times as outlined on page 70.

For our sample skirt, change to larger needles and work 9 rows even. Then decrease 1 stitch at each end (inside selvedge stitches) of the 10th row, then alternate decreasing every following 11th row and every 10th row 2 times, then every following 10th row 4 more times for a total of 18 stitches decreased over 92 rows.

Step 3 and Step 4: Upper Skirt and Finishing

These steps are worked the same as the straight skirt on page 155.

DRESSES

A knitted dress combines techniques for a skirt and a sweater. The construction is the same as a skirt from the hem to the waist and the same as a pullover or cardigan from the waist to the shoulders. A loose chemise is shaped as a long classic silhouette; a fitted dress is shaped as a long double-taper sweater.

Typically, dresses are knitted from the lower edge to the shoulders, but they can be worked from the top down as well. The hip, waist, and bust shaping can be worked along the sides or in intervals across the entire width.

To begin, take your body measurements as described on page 15, then measure a dress (or a sweater and a skirt) that fits comfortably to determine the ease amounts at the hips, waist, and bust. Be sure to plan for sufficient ease at the hemline for an unrestrained walking step. See the skirt measurement guidelines on page 154.

A chemise is worked like a long classic sweater. The key measurements are the hips and bust—the widest areas in upper and lower portions of the garment. Depending on the differences between these measurements, the dress can be worked as a classic, single taper, or reverse-taper silhouette, as described in Chapters 3 and 4.

**Ooh La Lace Dress and Stole,
first published in** *Lace Style*
(Interweave, 2007).
Photo: Chris Hartlove

CHEMISE SILHOUETTE OPTIONS

- If the bust width is equal to or 1" to 2" (2.5 to 5 cm) less than the hip width, work the body the same width from the cast-on to the beginning of the armhole shaping, as for a classic pullover (see page 69).

- If the bust width is equal to or more than 2" (5 cm) larger than the hip width, work the body the same width from the cast-on to the hip, then increase gradually to the full bust width, ending the increases 3" (7.5 cm) below the base of the armhole, as for a single taper pullover (see page 114).

- If the bust width is equal to or more than 3" (7.5 cm) smaller than the hip width, work the body the same width from the cast-on to the hip, then decrease gradually to the full bust width, ending the deceases 3" (7.5 cm) below the base of the armhole, as for a reverse-taper pullover (see page 116).

NEEDLES

Border: Size U.S. 3 (3.25 mm)
Body: Size U.S. 5 (3.75 mm)

GAUGE

Border (k1, p1 ribbing): 6.48 stitches and 10 rows = 1" (2.5 cm)

Body (stockinette stitch): 5.62 stitches and 7.9 rows = 1" (2.5 cm)

KEY MEASUREMENTS

Hip circumference: 39" (99 cm) + 2" (5 cm) ease = 41" (104 cm)

Bust circumference: 34½" (87.5 cm) + 2" (5 cm) ease = 36½" (92.5 cm)

Waist circumference: 31½" (80 cm) + 2" (5 cm) ease = 33½" (85 cm)

Cross-back width: 15½" (39.5 cm)

Neck width: 8½" (21.5 cm)

Shoulder width: 3½" (9 cm)

Length of border/ribbing: 1" (2.5 cm)

Length from top of border to hipline: 14⅞" (37.8 cm)

Length from hipline to base of waist: 5⅝" (14 cm)

Length of waist: 1⅝" (4 cm)

Length from top of waist to armholes: 5⅛" (13 cm)

Armhole depth: 8" (20.5 cm)

Front neck depth: 3" (7.5 cm)

Back neck depth: ¾" (2 cm)

Length from top of border to armholes: 27¼" (69 cm)

Notes

- A garter-stitch selvedge (knit every row) is added to each end of all rows in the stockinette-stitch portions to facilitate seaming.
- Rows are worked in pairs (a right-side row followed by a wrong-side row) so all row numbers are rounded to even numbers.
- Measurements include ease allowance.
- The front and back are worked identically to the beginning of the neck shaping; the front neck is shaped differently than the back neck.
- All shaping increases and decreases are worked one stitch in from the edge (i.e., inside the selvedge stitches).

TAPERED DRESS

A tapered dress follows the natural curves of the body—wider at the hips and bust and narrower at the waist. The key measurements are the hips, waist, bust, and shoulders. The part below the hips is worked like the lower part of a straight skirt (see page 155) and can have a straight, A-line, or flared shape. The part from the hips to the bust follows the shaping of a double-tapered sweater (see page 107).

Our example sleeveless dress has a straight skirt below the hipline, a double taper from hips to bust (a chemise would be worked straight in this area), a high round neckline, and unshaped shoulders. It is edged with ribbing (worked on smaller needles), and the body is worked in stockinette stitch. The front and back are worked separately from the hem to the shoulders.

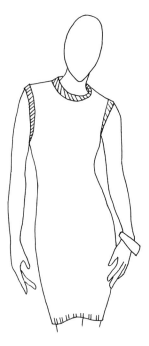

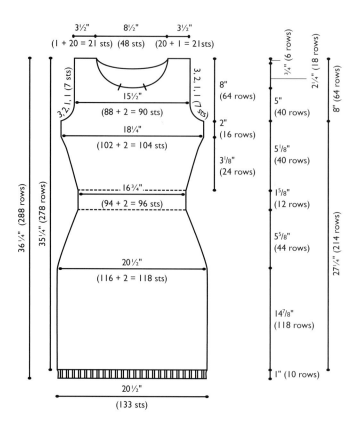

Schematic of the sample tapered dress, annotated with numbers of stitches and rows.

Conversion of Measurements to Numbers of Stitches and Rows

Number of stitches in border (hip width × border stitch gauge)

20½" (52 cm) × 6.48 = 132.84 stitches; round up to odd number = 133 stitches

Number of stitches at base of body (hip width × body stitch gauge + 2 selvedge stitches)

20½" (52 cm) × 5.62 stitches/inch + 2 selvedge stitches = 117.21 stitches; round up to nearest even number = 118 stitches

Number of stitches in waist width (waist width × body stitch gauge + 2 selvedge stitches)

16¾" (42.5 cm) × 5.62 stitches/inch + 2 selvedge stitches = 96.14 stitches; round down to nearest even number = 96 stitches

Number of stitches in bust width (bust width × body stitch gauge + 2 selvedge stitches)

18¼" (46.5 cm) × 5.62 stitches/inch + 2 selvedge stitches = 104.56 stitches; round down to nearest even number = 104 stitches

Number of stitches in cross-back width (width × body stitch gauge + 2 selvedge stitches)

15½" (39.5 cm) × 5.62 stitches/inch + 2 selvedge stitches = 89.11 stitches; round up to nearest even number = 90 stitches

Number of stitches in neck width (width × body stitch gauge)

8½" (21.5 cm) × 5.62 stitches/inch = 47.77 stitches; round up to nearest even number = 48 stitches

Number of stitches in each shoulder (width × body stitch gauge + 1 selvedge stitch)

3½" (9 cm) × 5.62 stitches/inch + 1 selvedge stitch = 20.67; round up to whole number = 21 stitches

Number of rows in border (length × border row gauge)

1" (2.5 cm) × 10 rows/inch = 10 rows

Number of rows from base of body to hipline (length × body row gauge)

14⁷⁄₈" (37.5 cm) × 7.9 rows/inch = 117.5 rows; round up to even number = 118 rows

Number of rows from hipline to base of waist (length × body row gauge)

5⁵⁄₈" (14.3 cm) × 7.9 rows/inch = 44.43 rows; round down to even number = 44 rows

Number of rows in waist (length × body row gauge)

1⁵⁄₈" (4 cm) × 7.9 rows/inch = 12.83 rows; round down to even number = 12 rows

Number of rows from top of waist to armhole (length × body row gauge)

5¹⁄₈" (13 cm) × 7.9 rows/inch = 40.48 rows; round down to nearest even number = 40 rows

Number of rows in armhole (length × body row gauge)

8" (20.5 cm) × 7.9 rows/inch = 63.2 rows; round up to nearest even number = 64 rows

Number of rows from armhole to beginning of front neck (length × body row gauge)

5" (12.5 cm) × 7.9 rows/inch = 39.5 rows; round up to nearest even number = 40 rows

Number of rows in front neck depth (length × body row gauge)

3" (7.5 cm) × 7.9 rows/inch = 23.7 rows; round up to nearest even number = 24 rows

Number of rows in back neck depth (length × body row gauge)

¾" (2 cm) × 7.9 rows/inch = 5.92 rows; round up to nearest even number = 6 rows

Total number of rows above border (body length × body row gauge)

35¼" (89.5 cm) × 7.9 rows/inch = 278.47 rows; round down to nearest even number = 278 rows

MATH CHECK!

The sum of the armhole shaping rows plus the number of rows worked even plus the number of rows in the neck shaping should match the total number of rows in the armhole.

8 armhole shaping rows
+ 32 rows worked even
+ 24 neck rows
= 64 rows

Step 1: Cast-On and Ribbing/Border

For our sample dress, use the smaller needles to cast on 133 stitches. Work k1, p1 ribbing for 10 rows, ending with a wrong-side row.

Step 2: Transition from Ribbing/Border to Body

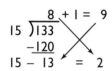

Use the shaping formula to determine an even spacing of decreases. In this example, decrease every 8th stitch 2 times and every 9th stitch 13 times.

To maintain the desired 20½" (52 cm) width in the stockinette-stitch gauge, 15 stitches must be decreased to achieve the necessary 118 stitches on the next row at the same time as a selvedge stitch is established at each edge. Use the shaping formula to determine an even distribution of decreases. The formula tells us to decrease every 8th stitch (i.e., k6, k2tog) 2 times and every 9th stitch (i.e., k7, k2tog) 13 times. To prevent the last decrease from occurring at the end of the row, split one of the 8-stitch intervals between the beginning and end of the row and designate the first and last stitch of the row as selvedge stitches.

For our sample dress, work this right-side row as k1 (selvedge), k1, k2tog, k6, k2tog, [k7, k2tog] 13 times, k3, k1 (selvedge)—118 stitches remain.

Step 3: Lower Body

Just like the lower body of a double-taper pullover (see page 107), the lower body of this dress is divided into five sections—the first section is worked even from the hem to the hipline, the second section tapers from the hipline to the waist, the third section is worked straight for the waist, the fourth section tapers from the waist to the bust, and the fifth section is worked straight to the armholes.

Section 1: Hem to Hipline
This section includes the shaping of the lower skirt, which is straight for this dress, but would taper for an A-line silhouette (see page 163).

For our sample dress, change to larger needles and work the selvedge stitches in garter stitch and the center 116 stitches even in stockinette stitch for 118 rows, or until the piece measures 14⅞" (37.8 cm) from the top of the ribbing, ending with a wrong-side row.

Section 2: Hip-to-Waist Taper
In this section, decrease from 118 stitches at the hips to 96 stitches at the waist over the course of 5⅝" (14.3 cm), or 44 rows.

118 stitches at hips − 96 stitches at waist = 22 stitches to decrease

Use the shaping formula to determine an even spacing of decreases. In this example, decrease every 4th row 7 times and every 5th row 3 times.

Work the decreases in pairs—one stitch at each edge of the piece—to decrease 11 stitches at each side. Decrease on the first row of this section, then space the remaining 10 decreases evenly over the remaining 43 rows. The shaping formula tells us to decrease every 4th row 7 times and every 5th row 3 times.

For our sample dress, decrease at each end of the next row, then every following 4th row 7 times, then every following 5th row 3 times—96 stitches remain.

Section 3: Waist
For our sample dress, work even on 96 stitches for 1⅝" (4 cm), or 12 rows.

Section 4: Waist-to-Bust Taper
In this section, increase from 96 stitches at the waist to 104 stitches at the bust over the course of 3⅛" (8 cm), or 24 rows.

104 stitches at bust – 96 stitches at waist = 8 stitches to increase

Again, work the increases in pairs over 4 increase rows. To maximize ease of movement, position the last increase 2" (5 cm) before the beginning of the armholes. Therefore, shape this section on just the first 3⅛" (7.95 cm), or 24 rows, of the 5⅛" (13 cm) length between the waist and the armholes. Increase on the first row of this section, then space the remaining 3 increases evenly over the remaining 23 rows. The shaping formula tells us to increase every 7th row 1 time and every 8th row 2 times.

For our sample dress, increase at each end of the next row, then on the following 7th row 1 time, then every following 8th row 2 times—104 stitches.

Section 5: Bust to Armholes
In this section, work even to the beginning of the armhole.

For our sample dress, work even on 104 stitches for 2" (5 cm), or 16 rows, ending with a wrong-side row.

$$\begin{array}{r} 7 \\ 3\overline{)23} \\ -21 \\ \hline 3 \end{array} \quad +1 = 8$$
$$3 - 2 = 1$$

Use the shaping formula to determine an even spacing of increases. In this example, increase every 7th row 1 time and every 8th row 2 times.

Step 4: Armhole Shaping

In this step, decrease 14 stitches (from 104 stitches at the bust to 90 stitches at the cross-back). Half of these stitches—7 stitches—are decreased at each armhole edge. Beginning with about ½" (1.3 cm) of stitches and tapering to 1 stitch as described on page 75, plot the decreases on graph paper to ensure a smooth, even curve over about 1" (2.5 cm) of rows.

For our sample dress, follow the shaping schedule in the box at right to decrease to 90 stitches. Then reestablish the selvedge stitches and work even on these stitches until the armholes measure 5" (12.5 cm) and a total of 254 rows of stockinette stitch have been worked, ending with a wrong-side row.

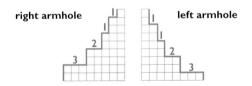

Plot of the armhole decreases for the left and right armhole.

ARMHOLE BIND-OFF SCHEDULE
Odd-numbered rows are right-side (RS) rows; even numbered rows are wrong-side (WS) rows.

Shaping Row	Garment Row	Stitches Decreased
1 (RS)	215	3
2 (WS)	216	3
3	217	2
4	218	2
5	219	1
6	220	1
7	221	1
8	222	1

Total: 14 stitches (7 stitches each side) bound off over 8 rows.

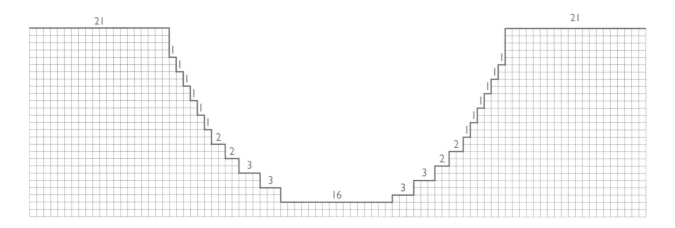

Plot of the neck shaping. In this example, one-third of the stitches are removed in the initial bind-off.

FRONT NECK SHAPING SCHEDULE

Odd-numbered rows are right-side (RS) rows; even numbered rows are wrong-side (WS) rows.

Shaping Row	Garment Row	Stitches Decreased
1 (RS)	255	16
2 (WS)	256	3
3	257	3
4	258	3
5	259	3
6	260	2
7	261	2
8	262	2
9	263	2
10	264	1
11	265	1
12	266	1
13	267	1
14	268	1
15	269	1
16	270	1
17	271	1
18	272	1
19	273	1
20	274	1
21	275	1

Total: 48 stitches decreased over 21 rows.

Step 5: Front Neck Shaping

The front neck in our example is 8½" (20.5 cm), or 48 stitches, wide. Using the one-third initial bind-off method (see page 77), bind off the center 16 stitches on the first row of shaping, then bind off 16 stitches at each side in a series of steps to produce a rounded shape over the course of the next 20 rows. Work the final ½" (1.3 cm), or 3 rows, of length even, so the entire front neck section will take place over 24 rows. The shaping sequence is shown in the box at left.

For our sample dress, bind off the center 16 stitches on the first row. Work the right and left sides separately, using the sloped bind-off described on page 77 to decrease 16 stitches at each side as described in the box at left—21 stitches remain at each side. Work even on these 21 stitches until the armholes measure 8" (20.5 cm) and a total of 278 rows of stockinette stitch have been worked.

Step 6: Shoulder Shaping

For our sample dress, bind off all 21 stitches at once.

Step 7: Back

The back is worked exactly as the front through the 8 armhole shaping rows. In our example, the back neck begins when the armholes measure 7¼" (18.5 cm), or 58 rows.

For our sample dress, repeat Step 1 through Step 4, but continue working the upper body even until 58 rows have been worked from the beginning of the armhole (272 rows total of stockinette stitch), ending with a wrong-side row.

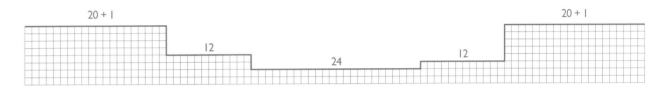

20 + 1   12   24   12   20 + 1

Shape the back neck in two steps—the initial bind-off followed by one set of bind-offs on each side.

Step 8: Back Neck and Shoulder Shaping

The back neck width is the same width as the front neck—48 stitches—but it is worked over just ¾" (2 cm), or 6 rows. Using the one-half initial bind-off method (see page 78), bind off the center 24 stitches on the first row of shaping, then bind off 12 stitches at each side.

For our sample dress, work across 33 stitches (21 shoulder stitches plus 12 side neck stitches) to the center neck, then bind off the center 24 stitches, then work to end of the row—33 stitches remain at each side. Working each side separately, bind off 12 stitches at each neck edge once—21 sts rem at each side. Work even on these stitches until 6 rows have been worked from the start of the neck shaping, then bind off the remaining stitches.

chapter seven
Alternate Armhole Shaping

In addition to the set-in, drop-shoulder, and modified drop-shoulder armholes presented in Chapter 4, the armholes and upper bodies of sweaters can also be shaped to produce raglan, saddle-shoulder, and circular-yoke silhouettes. Because the techniques for all of these alternatives begin at the armholes, you can use the lower body silhouettes previously described, depending on whether you want to knit a pullover or cardigan.

CLASSIC RAGLAN

The raglan shaping is named after the 1st Baron Raglan (1788–1855), a distinguished British military officer who, before he was ennobled, lost his right arm while serving as a Field Marshall in the Crimean War. To give him more mobility, his tailor designed a sleeve cap that extended from the underarm to the collarbone along a diagonal seam.

In raglan construction, the armhole shaping decreases the width of the garment from the bust to the neck width instead of from the bust to the cross-back width, as in a classic silhouette. The long diagonal lines extending from the armhole to the neckline become a focal point of this type of silhouette and provide key areas for adding decorative elements such as paired decreases or eyelets.

The Sleek Cabled Raglan, from the Fall 2002 issue of *Interweave Knits,* **is an example of a pullover with classic raglan shaping.**
Photo: Chris Hartlove

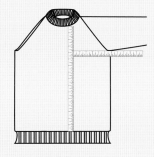

The raglan depth is the vertical length from the underarm to just below the neck bone.

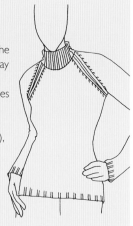

FULL-FASHIONED DECREASES

The creative design details that the eye follows along the length of the diagonal seams are a key focal point of raglan designs. A common way to enhance the diagonal lines is to work directional decreases (left-leaning at one edge and right-leaning at the other edge) a few stitches in from the selvedge stitches on right-side rows.

Right-Slant Single Decrease: (beginning of row) K1 (selvedge stitch), k2, k1, slip the first stitch on the right-hand needle to the left-hand needle, then use the right-hand needle to reach across the slipped stitch, lift the next stitch on the left-hand needle over the slipped stitch and off the needle, then return the slipped stitch to the right-hand needle—1 stitch decreased.

Left-Slant Single Decrease: (end of row) Work to the last 5 stitches, slip 1 stitch, k1, pass the slipped stitch over the knitted stitch (abbreviated psso), k2, k1 (selvedge stitch).

Right-Slant Double Decrease: (beginning of row) K1 (selvedge stitch), k2, ssk, slip the resulting decreased stitch back onto the left-hand needle, use the right-hand needle to reach across the slipped stitch, lift the next stitch on the left-hand needle over the slipped stitch and off the needle, then return the slipped stitch to the right-hand needle—2 stitches decreased.

Left-Slant Double Decrease: (end of row) Work to the last 6 stitches, slip 1 stitch, k2tog, use the left-hand needle to lift the slipped stitch over the decreased stitch and off the needle, k2, k1 (selvedge stitch)—2 stitches decreased.

Pattern Play, from the Winter 2001/2002 issue of *Vogue Knitting,* is an example of a classic raglan silhouette.

Photo: Paul Amato

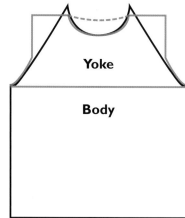

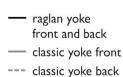
— raglan yoke front and back
— classic yoke front
--- classic yoke back

The armhole in a raglan silhouette extends from the underarm to the collarbone along a diagonal line, whereas the armhole in a classic silhouette extends straight from the underarm shaping to the shoulder bone.

tip The neck circumference includes the width at the top of the front, back, and each sleeve.
The neck circumference includes the front and back neck widths along with the top width of each sleeve (shown by dotted lines). Because the tops of the sleeves contribute to the neck depth, the wider the tops of the sleeves are, the shallower the neck depth needs to be. Plan the neckline—round, V, or square—at the center of the garment top after planning the raglan decreases.

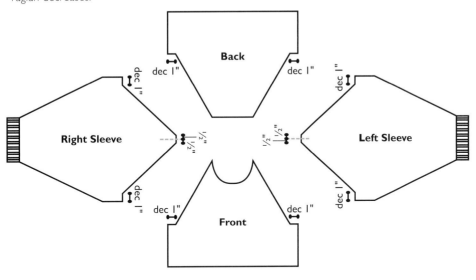

Our example raglan shaping is for a pullover with a 37" (94 cm) body circumference, 15¼" (38.5 cm) upper arm width, 8¼" (21 cm) yoke depth, 1" (2.5 cm) upper sleeve width, and 7" (18 cm) high round neck width.

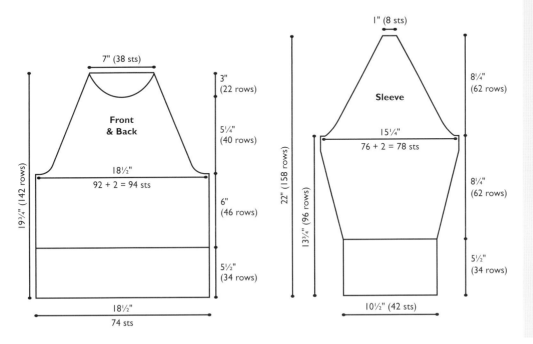

Schematic of the sample raglan pullover, annotated with numbers of stitches and rows.

GAUGE

Border (garter stitch): 4 stitches and 6.18 rows = 1" (2.5 cm)
Body (stockinette stitch): 5 stitches and 7.5 rows = 1" (2.5 cm)

KEY MEASUREMENTS

Bust circumference: 35" (89 cm) + 2" (5 cm) ease = 37" (94 cm)
Bust width: 18½" (47 cm)
Neck width: 7" (18 cm)
Armhole depth: 7¾" (19.5 cm)
Yoke depth: (armhole depth + 1" [2.5 cm]) 8¾" (22 cm)
Neck depth: 3" (7.5 cm)
Adjusted yoke depth (yoke depth − ½ top sleeve width)
    8¾" (22 cm) − ½" (1.3 cm) = 8¼" (21 cm)
Upper arm width: 15¼" (38.5 cm)
Top sleeve width: 1" (2.5 cm)

Conversion of Measurements to Numbers of Stitches and Rows

WIDTHS

Number of stitches in bust (bust width × body stitch gauge + 2 selvedge stitches)

18½" (47 cm) × 5 stitches/inch + 2 selvedge stitches = 94.5 stitches;

round down to nearest even number = 94 stitches

Number of stitches in neck (neck width × body stitch gauge + 4 selvedge stitches)

7" (19 cm) × 5 stitches/inch + 4 selvedge stitches = 39 stitches;

round down to even number = 38 stitches

Number of stitches in upper arm (upper arm width × body stitch gauge + 2 selvedge stitches)

15¼" (38.5 cm) × 5 stitches/inch + 2 selvedge stitches = 78.25 stitches;

round down to even number = 78 stitches

Number of stitches in sleeve top (width × body stitch gauge + 2 selvedge stitches)

1" (2.5 cm) × 5 stitches/inch + 2 selvedge stitches = 7 stitches;

round up to even number = 8 stitches

LENGTHS

Number of rows in adjusted yoke (length × body row gauge)

8¼" (21 cm) × 7.5 rows/inch = 61.8 rows;

round up to nearest even number = 62 rows

Number of rows from armhole to base of front neck (length × body row gauge)

5¼" (13.5 cm) × 7.5 rows/inch = 39.37 rows;

round up to nearest even number = 40 rows

Number of rows in front neck (depth × body row gauge)

3" (7.5 cm) × 7.5 rows/inch = 22.5 rows;

round down to nearest even number = 22 rows

Number of rows in sleeve cap (match adjusted yoke length)

62 rows

BACK
. . . .

Step 1: Determine Number of Raglan Stitches to Decrease

Above the armhole, the body changes from the bust width of 94 stitches to the neck width of 38 stitches (which includes 4 selvedge stitches; 2 on each side). In our example, decrease a total of 56 stitches along the raglan armholes.

94 bust stitches − 38 neck stitches = 56 stitches to decrease

This shaping begins with about 1" (2.5 cm), or 5 stitches, bound off at each edge at the base of the armholes, then the remaining decreases are evenly spaced over the entire length to the neck. In our example, bind off 5 stitches at each edge, which will leave 46 stitches to decrease along the raglan edges.

56 stitches to decrease − 10 bind-off stitches = 46 stitches to decrease;
23 stitches at each side

For our sample back, decrease 23 stitches at each side along the raglan edges.

Step 2: Determine Number of Rows for Raglan Decreases

The raglan depth for the body is 8¼" (21 cm), or 62 rows. The initial bind-offs are worked on the first 2 of these rows, leaving 60 rows for the remaining raglan decreases.

For our sample back, work the raglan decreases over 60 rows.

Step 3: Determine Raglan Decrease Schedule

Because all of the raglan decreases are worked on right-side rows, only 30 of the 60 rows are available for decreases. Using the shaping formula, divide these 30 right-side rows by 23 decreases to determine how to space the decreases evenly. The formula tells us to decrease every right-side (i.e., every 2nd) row 16 times and every 2nd right-side (i.e., every 4th) row 7 times. To give the illusion of perfectly spaced decreases, work the interval with the fewest number of repeats first by decreasing every 4th row 7 times, then decrease every 2nd row 16 times.

 tip To give the illusion of perfectly spaced raglan decreases, work the interval with the fewest number of repeats first.

For our sample back, bind off 5 stitches at the beginning of the first 2 rows, then decrease 1 stitch at each side (inside the selvedge stitches) every 4th row 7 times, then every 2nd row 16 times, working all decreases on right-side rows—38 stitches remain. Of these 38 stitches, the outermost stitch at each side is used to seam the back to the sleeves. The adjacent stitch at each side is used for picking up stitches around the neck.

FRONT

The front is worked exactly as the back, but includes front neck shaping. For our example, the front neck is 3" (7.5 cm) deep, which translates to the last 22 rows of the raglan shaping.

Step 1: Determine Number of Stitches to Decrease

For our sample front, bind off 5 stitches at each armhole, then decrease 23 stitches at each side along the raglan edges.

Step 2: Determine Number of Rows for Decreases

For our sample front, work the raglan decreases over 60 rows.

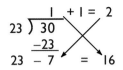

Use the shaping formula to determine an even distribution of raglan decreases. In this example, decrease every right-side (every 2nd) row 16 times and every other right-side (every 4th) row 7 times.

Step 3: Determine Raglan Decrease Schedule

For our sample front, bind off 5 stitches at the beginning of the first 2 rows, then decrease 1 stitch at each side (inside the selvedge stitches) every 4th row 7 times, then every 2nd row 16 times, working all decreases on right-side rows. At the same time, shape the front neck on the last 22 rows as described below.

Step 4: Determine Front Neck Shaping

After 5¼" (13.5 cm), or 40 rows of the raglan decreases have been worked, shape the front neck using the one-third initial bind-off technique (see page 77). Because there are 34 stitches in the neck, decrease 12 stitches in the initial bind-off and decrease 11 stitches along each side.

34 stitches ÷ 3 = 11.33 stitches; round up to even number = 12 stitches in initial bind-off

34 stitches − 12 initial bind-off stitches = 22 stitches to decrease; 11 stitches at each side

Plot the decreases on graph paper to ensure a smooth, even slope along the neckline.

For our sample front, the front neck begins after 40 rows of the raglan shaping have been worked, and the neck shaping is worked at the same time as the raglan shaping continues at the armholes. On the first row of neck shaping, bind off the center 12 stitches, then, at each neck edge, bind off 2 stitches 2 times, then bind off 1 stitch 7 times—2 stitches remain at each side after all raglan and neck shaping has been completed.

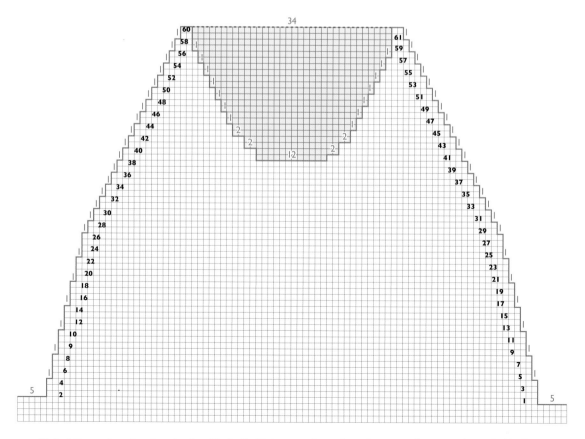

Plot of the neck and raglan shaping. Bind-off stitches are shown in red; row numbers are shown in black.

Step 1: Determine Number of Raglan Stitches to Decrease

At the armhole, the sleeve changes from 78 stitches at the upper arm to 8 stitches at the neck edge (top of sleeve). Therefore, decrease 70 stitches in the sleeve cap.

78 upper arm stitches – 8 neck stitches = 70 stitches to be decreased

To match the initial shaping of the body, begin by binding off 5 stitches at each edge, leaving 60 stitches for the raglan decreases.

70 stitches to decrease – 10 bind-off stitches = 60 stitches to decrease;
30 stitches at each side

For our sample sleeve, decrease 30 stitches at each side along the raglan shaping.

Step 2: Determine Number of Rows for Raglan Decreases

In raglan shaping, there must be the same number of rows in the sleeve cap as in the body armhole.

For our sample sleeve, work the raglan decreases over 60 rows.

 tip   The number of rows in a raglan sleeve cap shaping must match the number of rows in the raglan armhole shaping on the body.

Step 3: Determine Raglan Decrease Schedule

Again, work the decreases on right-side rows only, so only 30 of these 60 rows are available for decreases. Using the shaping formula, divide the 30 right-side rows by 30 decreases to determine an even spacing of the decrease rows. In this case, decrease 1 stitch at each edge of every right-side (i.e., every 2nd) row 30 times.

$$30 \overline{)\,30}^{\,1}$$

The shaping formula tells us to decrease 1 stitch at each edge every right-side row.

For our sample sleeve, bind off 5 stitches at the beginning of the next 2 rows, then decrease 1 stitch at each side (inside the selvedge stitches) every right-side row 30 times—8 stitches remain.

Note that 30 stitches are decreased on each side of the sleeve cap, but only 23 stitches are decreased on each side of the body over the same 60 rows. Therefore, 7 decrease rows on the sleeve cap are worked without a matching yoke decrease. In other cases, it may be necessary to work more than one decrease every right-side row on one of the pieces, in which case double decreases (see page 174) are used. In either scenario, work the mismatched rows at the beginning of the raglan slope, closest to the underarm, where they will be less noticeable.

The Eyelet Lace Tunic, from the Spring/Summer 1999 issue of *Vogue Knitting,* **is an example of a circular-yoke silhouette.**
Photo: Paul Amato

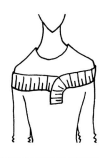

CIRCULAR YOKE

Sweaters with circular-yoke constructions are flattering on most body types and allow for colorful patterns to encircle the upper bodies, such as traditional Icelandic patterns.

Circular-yoke sweaters combine construction techniques used for raglan sweaters and circular skirts. The lower part of the yoke has raglan shaping while the upper part, which is worked in rounds, is shaped with a series of concentric decreases, similar to how the skirt was shaped on page 159. The key measurements for planning a circular-yoke sweater are the shoulder circumference (including ease) and the desired finished neck circumference. The shoulder circumference is taken around the upper part of the body, just below the shoulder bone.

Our example circular-yoke shaping is for a pullover with a 36" (91.5 cm) bust circumference, 9¼" (23.5 cm) raglan depth, and 15½" (39.5 cm) upper arm width. The raglan shaping occurs over the first 4" (10 cm) of the yoke. The front neck shaping begins 2" (5 cm) above the base of the armhole with a one-third initial bind-off (see page 77) and the neck circumference is 48% of the circumference at the top of the shoulder shaping. The back neck is also shaped, but differently than the front.

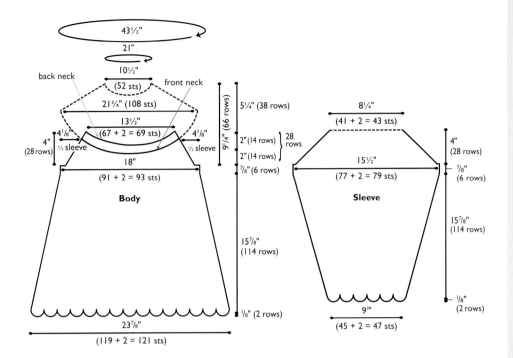

Schematic of the sample circular-yoke pullover, annotated with numbers of stitches and rows.

KEY MEASUREMENTS

Bust circumference: 34" (86.5 cm) + 2"
(5 cm) ease = 36" (91.5 cm)

Neck width at top of raglan shaping: 13½"
(34.5 cm)

Neck circumference: (48% of shoulder
circumference)
 43½" (110.5 cm) × 48% = 20.88"; round
 up to nearest quarter inch = 21" (53.5 cm)

Neck width at top of circular-yoke shaping:
10½" (26.5 cm)

Front neck depth: 2" (5 cm)

Back neck depth: ¾" (2 cm)

Base of front neck shaping: 2" (5 cm) above
base of armhole

Raglan armhole depth: 9¼" (23.5 cm)

Raglan armhole shaping depth: 4" (10 cm

Circular-yoke depth: (raglan armhole depth –
raglan shaping depth)
 5¼" (13.5 cm)

Upper arm width: 15½" (39.5 cm)

Top of cap width: 8¼" (21 cm)

Shoulder circumference: (left cap width +
front width + right cap width + back width)
 8¼" (21 cm) + 13½" (34.5 cm)
 + 8¼" (21 cm) + 13½" (34.5 cm)
 = 43½" (110.5 cm)

Notes

• The raglan shaping portion of the
yoke is worked back and forth in
rows; the circular yoke portion is
worked in rounds.

• The front and back are worked
identically to the beginning of the
front neck shaping; the back neck is
shaped differently.

• Both sleeves are worked identically.

Conversion of Measurements to Numbers of Stitches and Rows

WIDTHS

Number of stitches in bust (bust width × stitch gauge + 2 selvedge stitches)
 18" (45.5 cm) × 5 stitches/inch + 2 selvedge stitches = 92 stitches;
 round up to odd number = 93 stitches

Number of stitches in neck (neck width × stitch gauge)
 10½" (26.5 cm) × 5 stitches/inch = 52.5 stitches; round down to nearest
 even number = 52 stitches

Number of stitches in neck width at top of raglan shaping (top raglan width × stitch gauge
+ 2 selvedge stitches)
 13½" (34.5 cm) × 5 stitches/inch + 2 selvedge stitches = 69.5 stitches;
 round down to nearest odd number = 69 stitches

Number of stitches in raglan shaping (bust stitches – neck stitches at top of armhole)
 93 bust stitches – 69 neck stitches = 24 stitches in raglan shaping; 12 stitches each side

Number of stitches at beginning of circular yoke (bust stitches – stitches in raglan shaping)
 93 bust stitches – 24 stitches decreased in raglan shaping
 = 69 stitches at beginning of circular yoke

Number of stitches in upper arm (upper arm width × stitch gauge + 2 selvedge stitches)
 15½" (39.5 cm) × 5 stitches/inch + 2 selvedge stitches = 79.5 stitches;
 round down to nearest odd number = 79 stitches

- Circular-yoke construction begins with raglan decreases for the first 2" to 4" (5 to 10 cm) of the yoke (worked in rows) and ends with stacked circular decreases (worked in rounds) to the neck edge.
- The same number of rows is worked in the raglan shaping portions of the front, back, and sleeves.
- The yoke depth is based on the raglan depth, which is typically 1" (2.5 cm) longer than the armhole depth for a classic silhouette.
- The neck circumference is typically 40% to 50% of the shoulder circumference.

Number of stitches at top of sleeve cap (top of cap width × stitch gauge + 2 selvedge stitches)

8¼" (21 cm) × 5 stitches/inch + 2 selvedge stitches = 43.25 stitches; round down to nearest odd number = 43 stitches

Number of raglan decrease stitches on sleeve (upper arm stitches − cap top stitches)

79 stitches in upper arm − 43 stitches at top of cap = 36 stitches for raglan shaping; 18 stitches on each side

Number of stitches at base of sleeve yoke (upper arm stitches − raglan decrease stitches)

79 stitches in upper arm − 36 stitches decreased in raglan shaping = 43 sleeve stitches at beginning of circular yoke

Total number of stitches at beginning of yoke (front stitches + back stitches + 2 × sleeve stitches)

69 front stitches + 69 back stitches + 43 sleeve stitches + 43 sleeve stitches = 224 stitches

Total number of stitches at top of neck (front stitches + back stitches)

52 front stitches + 52 back stitches = 104 stitches

LENGTHS

Number of rows in armhole (raglan armhole length × row gauge)

9¼" (23.5 cm) × 7.25 rows/inch = 67 rows; round down to nearest even number = 66 rows

Number of rows in raglan shaping (raglan shaping length × row gauge)

4" (10 cm) × 7.25 rows/inch = 29 rows; round down to nearest even number = 28 rows

Number of rows from base of armhole to base of front neck (length × row gauge)

2" (5 cm) × 7.25 rows/inch = 14.5 rows; round down to nearest even number = 14 rows

Number of rows in circular-yoke shaping (rows in armhole − rows in raglan shaping)

66 rows in armhole − 28 rows in armhole shaping = 38 rows in circular-yoke shaping

Number of inches in circular-yoke shaping (rows in circular-yoke shaping ÷ row gauge)

38 rows ÷ 7.25 rows/inch = 5.24 inches; round to nearest quarter inch = 5¼" (13.5 cm)

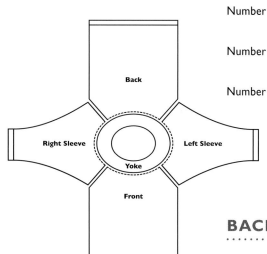

Illustration of how the pieces of a circular-yoke pullover fit together.

BACK RAGLAN

Step 1: Determine Number of Stitches to Decrease in Raglan Shaping

In this type of silhouette, ½" to 1" (1.3 to 2.5 cm) of width is bound off at the base of the armholes. At a gauge of 5 stitches/inch (2.5 cm), this translates to 3 stitches at each edge. Therefore, a total of 6 stitches are bound off on the first 2 rows of the armhole. In our example, bind off a total of 24 stitches during the raglan portion of the shaping, leaving 18 stitches for the raglan decreases.

24 stitches to decrease − 6 bind-off stitches = 18 stitches to decrease along raglan; 9 stitches each side

For our sample back, decrease 9 stitches at each side along the raglan shaping.

Step 2: Determine Number of Rows for Raglan Decreases

Work the raglan shaping over the first 4" (10 cm), or 28 rows, of the armhole. The first 2 rows will be used for the initial bind-offs, leaving 26 rows for the base raglan decreases.

28 rows in raglan section – 2 bind-off rows = 26 rows for raglan decreases

For our sample back, work the raglan decreases over 26 rows.

Step 3: Determine Raglan Decrease Schedule

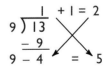

Because the raglan decreases are worked on right-side rows, only 13 of the remaining 26 rows are available for decreases. Using the shaping formula, divide these 13 right-side rows by 9 decreases to determine how to space the decreases evenly. The formula tells us to decrease every right-side (i.e., every 2nd) row 5 times and every 2nd right-side (i.e., every 4th) row 4 times. To give the illusion of perfectly spaced decreases, work the interval with the fewest number of repeats first by decreasing every 4th row 4 times, then every 2nd row 5 times.

Use the shaping formula to determine an even distribution of the raglan decreases. In this example, decrease every right-side (every 2nd) row 5 times and every 2nd right-side (every 4th) row 4 times.

Step 4: Determine Back Neck Shaping

The back neck is shaped over the final 1" (2.5 cm), or 8 rows, of the raglan shaping, using the one-half initial bind-off technique (see page 78). In our example, there are 69 stitches at the beginning of the neck shaping. Therefore, decrease 35 stitches in the initial bind-off row, leaving 17 stitches at each side.

69 stitches ÷ 2 = 34.5 stitches; round up to nearest odd number
= 35 stitches in initial bind-off

69 stitches – 35 initial bind-off stitches = 34 stitches; 17 stitches at each side.

To end up with 2 stitches at each side, decrease 15 stitches at each side. Plot the decreases on graph paper to ensure a smooth even curve.

For our sample back, bind off 3 stitches at the beginning of the first 2 rows, then decrease 1 stitch at each side (inside the selvedge stitches) every 4th row 4 times, then every 2nd row 5 times, working all decreases on right-side rows. At the same time, after a total of 20 rows have been worked, begin the neck shaping by binding off the center 35 stitches. Working each side separately, at each neck edge, bind off 7 stitches once, then bind off 8 stitches once, then work even until 28 rows have been completed—2 stitches remain at each side. Place these remaining stitches on holders in preparation for picking up stitches for the circular-yoke section.

Plot of the back neck shaping. Bind-off stitches are shown in red; row numbers are shown in black.

FRONT RAGLAN AND NECK DECREASE SCHEDULE

After working the initial armhole bind-offs, the raglan decreases are evenly spaced over the remaining rows of the raglan section of the armhole. **Note:** Odd-numbered rows are right-side (RS) rows and even-numbered rows are wrong-side (WS) rows. All raglan decreases are worked on right-side rows.

Row Number	Raglan Decreases (1 stitch at each edge)	Neck Decreases
1 (RS)		
2 (WS)		
3		
4		
5	2	
6		
7		
8		
9	2	
10		
11		
12		
13	2	
14		
15		21
16		5
17	2	5
18		4
19	2	4
20		4
21	2	4
22		3
23	2	3
24		3
25	2	3
26		3
27	2	3

Total: 18 stitches decreased along raglan lines and 65 stitches decreased at neck; 2 stitches remain at each side.

FRONT RAGLAN

Step 1: Match Back Raglan

The raglan decreases on the front must match those of the back.

For our sample front, work the raglan shaping exactly the same as the back.

Step 2: Determine Front Neck Shaping

The neck in our example begins with one-third of the stitches bound off at the center on the next row, and one-third of the stitches are bound off at each side to create a smooth curve (see page 77). There are 69 stitches at the beginning of the neck shaping. To end with 2 stitches at each side, 65 stitches are decreased during the neck shaping. Of these 65 stitches, bind off 21 on the first row of neck shaping.

> 65 stitches to decrease ÷ 3 sections = 21.6 stitches; round down to nearest odd number = 21 stitches

> 65 stitches to decrease − 21 initial bind-off stitches = 44 stitches to decrease; 22 stitches each side

Plot the neck shaping on graph paper to ensure a smooth, even curve.

For our sample front, bind off 3 stitches at the beginning of the first 2 rows, then decrease 1 stitch at each side (inside the selvedge stitches) every 4th row 4 times, then every 2nd row 5 times, working all decreases on right-side rows. At the same time, after a total of 14 rows have been worked, begin the neck shaping by binding off the center 21 sts. Working each side separately, bind off 22 stitches at each side over the next 2" (5 cm), or 14 rows. At each neck edge, bind off 5 stitches once, then bind off 4 stitches 2 times, then bind off 3 stitches 3 times—2 stitches remain at each side. On the right-hand side, work one wrong-side row even to complete the 14 rows of shaping. Place the remaining 2 stitches at each side on holders in preparation for picking up stitches for the circular-yoke section.

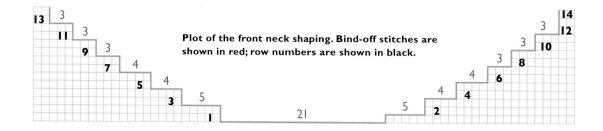

Plot of the front neck shaping. Bind-off stitches are shown in red; row numbers are shown in black.

SLEEVE RAGLAN SECTION

Step 1: Determine Number of Stitches to Decrease

For the raglan section of each sleeve, decrease 36 stitches, from 79 stitches at the upper arm to 43 stitches at the top of the sleeve cap.

> 79 upper arm stitches – 43 stitches at top of raglan = 36 stitches to be decreased

To match the initial shaping of the body, begin by binding off 3 stitches at each edge, leaving 30 stitches for the raglan decreases, or 15 stitches at each side.

> 36 stitches for raglan decreases – 6 bind-off stitches = 30 stitches for raglan decreases; 15 stitches at each side

For our sample sleeve, decrease 15 stitches at each side along the raglan line.

Step 2: Determine Number of Rows for Raglan Decreases

The raglan section is worked over 4" (10 cm), or 28 rows. The initial bind-offs are worked on the first 2 of these rows, leaving 26 rows for the raglan decreases.

> 28 rows in raglan section – 2 bind-off rows = 26 rows for raglan decreases

For our sample sleeve, work the raglan decreases over 26 rows.

Step 3: Determine Raglan Decrease Schedule

The raglan decreases are worked on right-side rows, so only 13 of the remaining 26 rows are available for decreases. In this case, the number of stitches to decrease at each edge (15) is larger than the number of rows available for decreases (13). Therefore, we have to use double decreases. To determine the number of double decreases, subtract the number of rows available for decreases from the number of stitches to decrease. In this case, work 2 double decreases.

> 15 stitches to decrease – 13 decrease rows = 2 extra decreases

For our sample sleeve, use double decreases (see page 174) to decrease 2 stitches at each end of each right-side row 2 times, then decrease 1 stitch at each end of every following right-side row 11 times—43 stitches remain. Place these stitches on holders in preparation for working the circular-yoke section.

CIRCULAR-YOKE SECTION

In preparation for working the circular-yoke section, begin by blocking (see page 261) all of the pieces. With yarn threaded on a tapestry needle, sew the side and sleeve seams (see page 269). Next, sew the sleeves to the front and back along the raglan lines from the base of the armhole to the held stitches to give the garment structure as the yoke is worked.

Step 1: Pick Up Stitches

With the appropriate size circular needle and beginning at the left sleeve, slip the held stitches and pick up and knit the bind-off stitches.

 tip To ensure a smooth pick-up, slip the held stitches onto the circular needle without working them and pick up and knit the bound-off stitches. To do this, the working yarn will be cut at the beginning of each section of held stitches and rejoined at the beginning of each pick-up section. Pick up stitches for the yoke beginning with the left sleeve, followed by the front, followed by the right sleeve, and ending with the back.

For our sample yoke, slip the 43 held left sleeve stitches, then the 2 held left front shoulder stitches onto a circular needle. Then join the working yarn and pick up and knit 22 stitches along the left neck edge, 21 stitches across the center front neck, and 22 stitches along the right neck edge, then slip the 2 held right front shoulder stitches onto the same needle (112 left sleeve and front stitches on the needle). Next, slip the 43 held right sleeve stitches, then the 2 held right back shoulder stitches onto the same needle. Then join the working yarn again and pick up and knit 15 stitches along the right neck edge, 35 stitches across the center back, and 15 stitches along the left neck edge. Finally, slip the 2 held left back shoulder stitches onto the needle (112 right sleeve and back stitches)—224 stitches total. Place a marker on the needle to designate the beginning of the round.

Step 2: Determine Number of Stitches to Decrease in Circular Yoke

To determine the number of stitches to decrease in the circular-yoke section, subtract the number of stitches in the neckline from the number of stitches at the beginning of this section.

224 circular-yoke stitches − 104 neckline stitches = 120 stitches to decrease

For our sample yoke, decrease 120 stitches in the circular-yoke section.

Step 3: Determine Number of Rounds for Circular-Yoke Decreases

The schematic tells us there are 38 rounds in this section.

Step 4: Determine Yoke Decrease Schedule

If the standard decrease of 2" (5 cm), or, in our case 10 stitches, is used for each decrease round, 12 decrease rounds are necessary to decrease to the desired number of neck stitches. However, our 10-stitch decrease does not evenly divide into the total number of beginning stitches on the needle.

224 stitches ÷ 10 decreases = 22.4 stitches between decreases

Stacked decreases must begin with a number of stitches divisible by the number of stitches in each decrease round (10 stitches). In our example, we need to decrease 4 stitches to achieve a number that's divisible by 10. Therefore, decrease 4 stitches on the first round to set up for stacked decreases of 10 decreases per decrease round.

224 stitches – 4 stitches = 220 stitches

$$\begin{array}{r} 56 \\ 4\overline{)224} \end{array}$$

Use the shaping formula to determine an even distribution of decreases. In this example, decrease every 56th stitch (k54, k2tog).

Use the shaping formula to determine how to space the initial 4 stitches evenly over the 224 stitches at the beginning of the yoke. Because there is no remainder in this case, simply decrease every 56th stitch by working [k54, k2tog] 4 times—220 stitches remain.

Based on the schematic, there must be 104 stitches after all of the yoke decreases have been completed. The number of stitches that are needed at the end (104) is not evenly divisible by the multiple of 10. The solution is to calculate the decrease rounds based on 10 decreases to the last round, then work 4 fewer decreases (i.e., decrease only 6 stitches) on the last decrease round.

120 stitches to decrease ÷ 10 stitches per decrease round = 12 decrease rounds

In this case, work 12 stacked decrease rounds during the 38 rounds in the yoke. Set up for the stacked decreases by decreasing 4 stitches on the first round of the yoke. Because only 6 stitches will be decreased on the last stacked decrease round, 110 stitches are involved in the remaining 11 stacked decrease rounds.

120 stitches to decrease – 4 initial decreases – 6 decreases in last decrease round
= 110 stitches to decrease in stacked decreases

12 stacked decrease rounds – 1 round of only 6 decreases
= 11 stacked decrease rounds

We'll plan to work the initial 4-stitch decrease on the first round of the yoke, then work 1 round even before starting the stacked decreases. We'll also plan to work the 6-stitch decrease round 3 rounds before the end of the yoke (i.e., work the last 2 rounds even). Therefore, work the 11 stacked decrease rounds over 33 rounds.

38 rounds in yoke – 5 rounds = 33 rounds for stacked decreases

To determine how to space the decrease rounds, divide the number of rounds available for stacked decreases by the number of decrease rounds. In our case, work the stacked decreases every 3rd round.

33 rounds for stacked decreases ÷ 11 stacked decrease rounds = 3 rounds per decreases; or 2 rounds between decrease rounds

Next, determine how to space the decreases to stack the stitches in the decrease rounds. In the first decrease round, decrease 10 stitches, from 220 stitches to 210 stitches. Set up the baseline for stacking as for the circular skirt on page 159. Begin by subtracting two times the decrease amount from the beginning stitch count. Then divide the answer by the decrease amount.

220 stitches – 20 stitches = 200 stitches

200 stitches ÷ 10 decreased stitches = 20 stitches between decreases

This tells us there are 20 stitches to work even between decreases. Work the first decrease round as *k20, k2tog; repeat from * to decrease 10 stitches. Note that 1 stitch remains after every k2tog, which leaves ten sections of 21 stitches each, or a total of 210 stitches. To stack the decreases on subsequent decrease rounds, work 1 less stitch between decreases on each decrease round through *k10, k2tog; repeat from *. After working the 11 stacked decrease rounds, there will be 110 stitches on the needles, as shown in the decrease schedule in the box on page 189.

To space the 6 stitches in the last decrease round evenly, use the shaping formula to divide the remaining 110 stitches by the 6 stitches left to decrease. The formula tells us to decrease every 18th stitch (k16, k2tog) 4 times and every 19th stitch (k17, k2tog) 2 times.

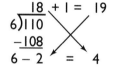

Use the shaping formula to determine an even distribution of decreases. In this example, decrease every 18th stitch (k16, k2tog) 4 times and every 19th stitch (k17, k2tog) 2 times.

For our sample yoke, decrease 4 stitches on the first row by working [k54, k2tog] 4 times—220 stitches remain. Then work stacked decreases every 3 rounds, beginning by working [k20, k2tog] 10 times for the first decrease round, working 1 less stitch between decreases on the next 9 decrease rounds, and ending by working [k10, k2tog] 10 times on the last decrease round—110 stitches remain. Then work 2 rounds even, then decrease 6 stitches on the next round by working [k16, k2tog] 4 times, [k17, k2tog] 2 times—104 stitches remain. Work the final 2 rounds even, then bind off all of the stitches.

 tip When working the circular portion of the yoke, change to progressively shorter circular needles as the number of stitches decreases so that the stitches are not stretched on the needles.

 tip If there are different patterns in the yoke, plan to work the decrease rows in a "separation" stitch pattern so that the decreases don't interrupt the individual patterns. For example, if color patterns are used, work the decreases in solid-color rows.

CIRCULAR-YOKE DECREASE SCHEDULE

Note: There is 1 stitch less between decreases in the second through the twelfth decrease rounds.

Round Number	Decrease Round	Decrease Interval	Stitches Remaining
1	1	*k54, k2tog; rep from * 3 more times	220
4	2	*k20, k2tog; rep from * 9 more times	210
7	3	*k19, k2tog; rep from * 9 more times	200
10	4	*k18, k2tog; rep from * 9 more times	190
13	5	*k17, k2tog; rep from * 9 more times	180
16	6	*k16, k2tog; rep from * 9 more times	170
19	7	*k15, k2tog; rep from * 9 more times	160
22	8	*k14, k2tog; rep from * 9 more times	150
25	9	*k13, k2tog; rep from * 9 more times	140
28	10	*k12, k2tog; rep from * 9 more times	130
31	11	*k11, k2tog; rep from * 9 more times	120
34	12	*k10, k2tog; rep from * 9 more times	110
37	13	[k16, k2tog] 4 times, [k17, k2tog] 2 times	104

SLEEVELESS-YOKE VARIATION

To work a sleeveless pullover with circular-yoke shaping, omit the raglan shaping at the base of the yoke. When picking up stitches for the yoke, pick up the appropriate number of stitches across the back, cast on the appropriate number of stitches for the left sleeve, pick up the appropriate number of stitches across the front, and cast on the appropriate number of stitches for the right sleeve.

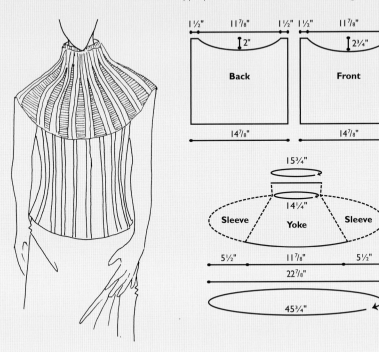

tip
> If you do not want to vertically stack the decreases in the circular portion of the yoke shaping, calculate each decrease round separately using the shaping formula by dividing the number of stitches to be decreased into the number of stitches on the needles.

OFF-THE-SHOULDER VARIATION WITH TURN-BACK COLLAR

For off-the-shoulder styles in which a pattern stitch is worked in a fold-over collar, make certain that the pattern stitch flows continuously above the joining row. To begin, work 1½" to 2" (3.8 to 5 cm) of ribbing to provide necessary elasticity at the shoulders and delineation between the two parts of the garment. Next, work a round of stockinette stitch, increasing or decreasing stitches (typically these adjustments will be made at the boundaries between the body and sleeves) as necessary to achieve full multiples of the collar stitch pattern. In the example shown here, the collar includes 12 repeats of a pattern that repeats over 20 stitches. Instead of working increases to widen the circumference of the collar, increase the needle size every 1" to 3" (2.5 to 7.5 cm).

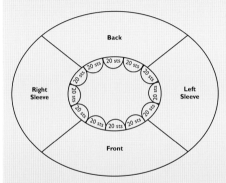

Interlocking Cables, from the Interweave website in conjunction with the **Winter 2004** issue of *Interweave Knits,* is an example of a pullover with off-the-shoulder circular-yoke shaping and a fold-over collar. *Photo: Chris Hartlove*

Plan the stitch pattern to be continuous around the full shoulder circumference.

CLASSIC SADDLE SHOULDER

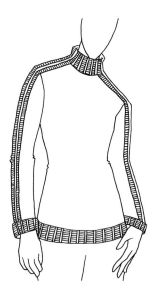

A classic saddle-shoulder silhouette is constructed much the same as a classic raglan. For both styles, the top of the sleeve contributes part of the neck and shoulder measurement. The saddle is an extension of the top of a set-in sleeve that resembles a strap. It extends across the shoulder (or "straddles" the shoulder) to the neck edge.

There are several reasons to design garments with saddle shoulders. Creatively, saddle-shoulder construction allows for design elements in the sleeves (cables, for example) to be extended to the neck edge. Practically, this type of construction divides the weight of the shoulder area between two shoulder seams (one on each side of the saddle), which is particularly advantageous for heavy garments. In their simplest form, the saddles contribute the entire neck depth on the front and back.

CLASSIC SADDLE-SHOULDER CHARACTERISTICS

- The front and back are worked exactly the same as for a classic silhouette (see page 66), but the upper body lengths are shortened by one-half of the saddle-width measurement.

- The sleeves are worked exactly the same as for set-in sleeves for a classic silhouette (see page 81), but the top of the cap is extended for the saddle that continues across the shoulder to the neck edge.

- A typical saddle is between 2" and 5" (5 and 12.5 cm) wide.

- The planned armhole-to-shoulder depth for both the front and back yokes is shorter than that for a classic body. This is because half of the saddle width contributes to the overall length and neck depth of the body front and half contributes to the overall length and neck depth of the body back.

- The length (rows) of the saddle must measure the same as the width (stitches) in the shoulder.

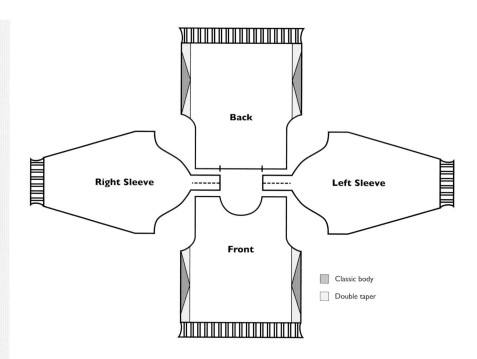

The tops of the sleeves contribute to both the front and back body length.

Our example saddle-shoulder shaping for a pullover with a high round neck, set-in sleeves, 3" (7.5 cm) saddle length, 3" (7.5 cm) shoulder width, 7" (18 cm) neck width, and 3½" (9 cm) front neck depth.

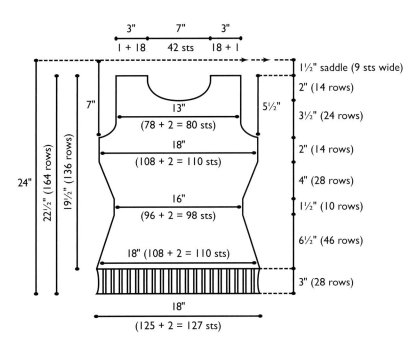

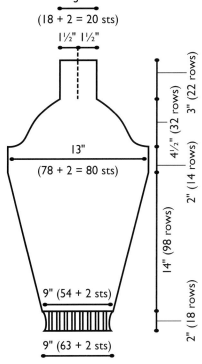

Schematic of the sample classic saddle-shoulder pullover, annotated with numbers of stitches and rows. Note: Dotted lines represent additional body length contributed by the saddles.

 tip The length of the side of the saddle strap (measured in rows) must match the shoulder width (measured in stitches).

Conversion of Measurements to Numbers of Stitches and Rows

WIDTHS

Number of stitches in saddle (saddle width × stitch gauge + 2 selvedge stitches)

3" (7.5 cm) × 6 stitches/inch + 2 selvedge stitches = 20 stitches

Number of stitches in shoulder width (shoulder width × stitch gauge + 1 selvedge stitch)

3" (7.5 cm) × 6 stitches/inch + 1 selvedge stitch = 19 stitches

LENGTH

Number of rows in saddle (length × row gauge)

3" (7.5 cm) × 7 rows/inch = 21 rows; round up to nearest even number = 22 rows

GAUGE

Border (k1, p1 ribbing): 6.94 stitches and 9 rows = 1" (2.5 cm)

Body (stockinette stitch): 6 stitches and 7 rows = 1" (2.5 cm)

KEY MEASUREMENTS

Neck width: 7" (18 cm)

Shoulder width: 3" (7.5 cm)

Total armhole depth: 7" (18 cm): 5½" (14 cm) in body + 1½" (3.8 cm) in saddle

Front neck depth: 3½" (9 cm): 2" (5 cm) in body + 1½" (3.8 cm) in saddle

Upper arm width: 13" (33 cm)

Saddle width: 3" (7.5 cm)

Saddle length: 3" (7.5 cm)

BACK

Step 1: Determine Length of Back Armhole

The upper back of a double-tapered saddle-shoulder silhouette is worked exactly like the upper back of a classic double-tapered silhouette with similar armhole shaping (in this case, set-in sleeves), except that the armhole is worked shorter to account for the length that will be contributed by the saddle. The saddle in our example is 3" (7.5 cm) wide. Half of the saddle width, or 1½" (3.8 cm), will contribute to the front length and half will contribute to the back length. Therefore, work the back until the armholes measure 5½" (14 cm).

> 7" (18 cm) total armhole depth − 1½" (3.8 cm) saddle depth
> = 5½" (14 cm) body armhole depth

For our sample back, shape the armhole as for a set-in sleeve (see page 75), work the upper back even until the armhole measures 5½" (14 cm), then bind off all the stitches.

FRONT

Step 1: Determine the Length of the Front Armhole

The front is worked exactly the same as the back, but the neck is shaped over the last 2" (5 cm), or 14 rows.

For our sample front, work the front exactly the same as the back until the armhole measures 3½" (9 cm), or 24 rows. Then shape the front neck using the one-third initial bind-off technique (see page 77) over the last 2" (5 cm), or 14 rows.

Step 2: Determine Front Neck Shaping

Using the one-third initial bind-off technique, shape the front neck over the last 14 rows as for a high round neck for a classic silhouette (see page 76).

SLEEVES

The sleeve for a saddle-shoulder silhouette is worked in four parts, the same as a set-in sleeve for a classic silhouette (see page 81). For our example, there are 80 stitches in the upper arm and the cap is shaped over 4½" (11.5 cm), or 32 rows, ending with 20 stitches for the saddle. Although the sections are knitted in order, work the calculations for Section 1 first, followed by Section 4, Section 3, then Section 2. Then work the remaining 20 stitches (18 saddle stitches + 2 selvedge stitches) even until the length of the saddle matches the width of the shoulders, which is 3" (7.5 cm), or 22 rows. Bind off all stitches in preparation for evenly picking up the end of the saddle strap as part of the neck finishing.

Section 1: Armhole Bind-Off Match
In this section, match the armhole bind-off on the body. Let's say that the armhole on the body involved decreasing 30 stitches (15 stitches at each side) over 12 rows and that the decreases were worked by binding off 6 stitches at the beginning of the first 2 rows, then binding off 3 stitches at the beginning of the next 2 rows, then binding off 2 stitches at the beginning of the next 4 rows, then binding off 1 stitch at the beginning of the next 4 rows.

Section 4: Saddle-Shoulder Stitches
This section corresponds to the final bind-off of a set-in sleeve (see page 85), but instead of binding off the stitches at the top of the sleeve cap, work them for the desired saddle length. In this case, the saddle is 3" (7.5 cm), or 20 stitches, wide and 3" (7.5 cm), or 22 rows, long.

Section 3: Top Slope
In this section, decrease 2" (5 cm) of stitches, or 12 stitches, over the last ½" (1.3 cm), or 4 rows of the cap. Therefore, bind off 3 stitches at the beginning of the last 4 rows of cap shaping.

Section 2: Center Cap
In this section, decrease from 50 stitches at the top of the armhole shaping to 32 stitches at the top slope (20 saddle stitches + 12 top-slope bind-off stitches), for a total of 18 stitches decreased. Work these decreases over 16 rows (32 cap rows – 12 armhole rows – 4 top-slope rows = 16 rows). In this case, decrease 18 stitches (9 stitches each side) over 16 rows by binding off 2 stitches at the beginning of 2 rows, then binding off 1 stitch at the beginning of the next 14 rows.

For our sample sleeve, use the sloped method (see page 77) to bind off 6 stitches at the beginning of the first 2 rows, then bind off 3 stitches at the beginning of the next 2 rows, then bind off 2 stitches at the beginning of the next 4 rows, then bind off 1 stitch at the beginning of the next 4 rows—50 stitches remain. Bind off 2 stitches at the beginning of the next 2 rows, then bind off 1 stitch at the beginning of the following 14 rows—32 stitches remain. Bind off 3 stitches at the beginning of the next 4 rows—20 stitches remain. Work the 20 saddle stitches for 22 rows, then bind off all the stitches.

chapter eight
Sleeves and Cuffs

In addition to the classic tapered sleeve presented on page 81, there are a number of variations that offer more design possibilities—straight, lantern, gathered top, pleated top, and cap (short sleeve). There are also a number of cuff variations that add even more possibilities.

All of the sleeves described in this book are worked upward from the lower (cuff) edge. The construction is based on the structure of the arm—narrower at the wrist and wider at the upper arm—with symmetrical increases worked along the way at each edge of the piece. In general, the increases end between 1" and 3" (2.5 and 7.5 cm) before the beginning of the cap section and allow for 2" (5 cm) of ease to allow for comfort in movement when raising and lowering arms and shoulders.

We'll begin with a straight sleeve with a set-in cap. Other types of sleeves will then be easy to plan because they follow the same construction principles.

SLEEVE CHARACTERISTICS

- Because the wrist is narrower than the upper arm, long sleeves are planned to taper from a comfortable cuff measurement to a comfortable upper arm measurement.

- There is typically 1" (2.5 cm) of ease at the cuff and 2" (5 cm) of ease at the upper arm (this extra ease allows for comfort in movement when raising the arms and shoulders).

- Measure around the knuckles when planning the cuff width to ensure that the sleeve will fit over the hand without difficulty.

- The increases are typically divided between the two edges so that an equal number of increases are made at each side, ending 1" to 3" (2.5 cm to 7.5 cm) before the desired length to the armhole (this work-even section provides sufficient width for ease of movement in the upper arm area).

The Copper Tone Pullover, first published in the Fall 2002 20th Anniversary Issue of *Vogue Knitting* **is an example of a pullover with fold-back cuffs.**
Photo: Paul Amato

STRAIGHT SLEEVE

GAUGE
Border (p4, k2 ribbing): 4.5 stitches and
    5.6 rows = 1" (2.5 cm)
Body (stockinette stitch): 5 stitches
    and 7 rows = 1" (2.5 cm)

KEY MEASUREMENTS
Cuff width: 12" (30.5 cm)
Upper arm width: 12" (30.5 cm)
Cuff length: 4¾" (12 cm)
Length from cuff to armhole: 12¼" (31 cm)

Straight sleeves are worked without any increases between the cast-on edge and the armhole. In this type of sleeve, the cuff width is the same as the upper arm width. The calculations are therefore based on the upper arm width including ease. This shape is ideal for uninterrupted stitch or color patterns. It is also a practical choice for sporty garments where more ease is desired at the cuff and lower arm.

Our example straight sleeve measures 12" (30.5 cm) wide from the cast-on edge to the armhole with a border that is worked in p4, k2 ribbing for 4¾" (12 cm). The sleeve in this example is shown with a set-in cap, but any other cap style could be substituted.

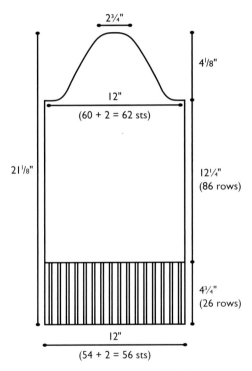

Schematic of the sample straight sleeve.

Conversion of Measurements to Numbers of Stitches and Rows

WIDTHS

Number of stitches in cuff (cuff width × border stitch gauge + 2 selvedge stitches)
    12" (30.5 cm) × 4.5 stitches/inch + 2 selvedge stitches = 56 stitches

Number of stitches at base of sleeve (cuff width × body stitch gauge + 2 selvedge stitches)
    12" (30.5 cm) × 5 stitches/inch + 2 selvedge stitches = 62 stitches

Number of stitches at upper arm (upper arm width × body stitch gauge + 2 selvedge stitches)
    12" (30.5 cm) × 5 stitches/inch + 2 selvedge stitches = 62 stitches

Number of rows in cuff (cuff length × border row gauge)
4¾" (12 cm) × 5.6 rows/inch = 26.6 rows;
round down to nearest even number = 26 rows

Number of rows from cuff to armhole (length × body row gauge)
12¼" (31 cm) × 7 rows/inch = 85.75 rows;
round up to nearest even number = 86 rows

Step 1: Cast-On and Ribbing/Border

For our sample sleeve, use the smaller needles to cast on 56 stitches. Center the p4, k2 rib on a right-side row as: k1 (selvedge), p2, *k2, p4; rep from * to last 5 stitches, k2, p2, k1 (selvedge). Then work the ribbing as established until the piece measures 4¾" (12 cm), or 26 rows, ending with a wrong-side row.

Step 2: Transition from Ribbing/Border to Sleeve

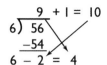

Use the shaping formula to determine an even distribution of increases. In this example, increase every 9th stitch 4 times and every 10th stitch 2 times.

To maintain the desired 12" (30.5 cm) width in the body stitch gauge, increase 6 stitches on the first row of stockinette stitch.

62 body stitches – 56 cuff stitches = 6 stitches to increase

Using the shaping formula, divide the 56 cuff stitches by 6 increases to determine how to space these increases evenly. The formula tells us to increase every 9th stitch 4 times and every 10th stitch 2 times. To prevent the last increase from falling at the end of the row, divide one of the 10-stitch intervals between the beginning and end of the row.

For our sample sleeve, use the M1 method of increasing (see box below) and work this right-side row as: k1 (selvedge stitch), k4, M1, [k9, M1] 4 times, k10, M1, k4, k1 (selvedge stitch)—62 stitches.

M1 INCREASE

This technique uses the strand of yarn between two stitches to make an extra stitch. It can be worked to slant to the right or left.

Right Slant: Insert the left needle tip from back to front under the horizontal strand between the two needles (Figure 1). Use the right needle to knit through the front of this lifted strand (Figure 2).

Left Slant: Insert the left needle tip from front to back under the horizontal strand between the two needles (Figure 3). Use the right needle to knit through the back of this lifted strand (Figure 4).

Figure 1

Figure 2

Figure 3

Figure 4

Step 3: Sleeve Taper to Upper Arm

There is no shaping between the cuff and armhole of a straight sleeve.

For our sample sleeve, change to larger needles and work even in stockinette stitch until the piece measures 12¼ " (31 cm), or 86 rows, from the transition row.

Step 4: Cap Shaping

Shape the cap for a set-in, raglan, or saddle shoulder as desired.

LANTERN SLEEVE

Lantern sleeves are similar to straight sleeves, but they have a snug fit at the cuff. Stitches are increased to the full upper arm width on the transition row between the cuff and the sleeve to produce blouson-type fullness above the fitted cuff. The sleeve is then worked straight to the armhole, just like a straight sleeve. Typically, the cuff of a lantern sleeve is worked in ribbing, but any pattern can be used.

Our example lantern sleeve measures 8" (20.5 cm) wide at the cuff and 14" (35.5 cm) wide at the upper arm, and has a cuff border that is worked in k1, p1 ribbing for 3" (7.5 cm) on smaller needles. The sleeve is shown with a set-in cap, but any other cap style could be substituted.

GAUGE

Border (k1, p1 ribbing): 7 stitches and 9 rows = 1" (2.5 cm)
Body (cable pattern): 5 stitches and 7 rows = 1" (2.5 cm)

KEY MEASUREMENTS

Cuff width: 8" (20.5 cm)
Upper arm width: 14" (35.5 cm)
Cuff length: 3" (7.5 cm)
Length from cuff to armhole: 15" (38 cm)

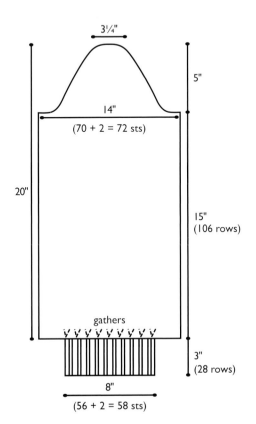

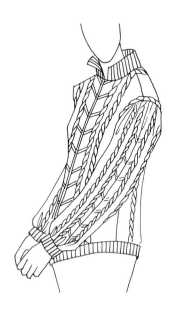

Schematic of the sample typical lantern sleeve.

Conversion of Measurements to Numbers of Stitches and Rows

Number of stitches in cuff (cuff width × border stitch gauge + 2 selvedge stitches)

8" (20.5 cm) × 7 stitches/inch + 2 selvedge stitches = 58 stitches

Number of stitches at base of sleeve (upper arm width × body stitch gauge + 2 selvedge stitches)

14" (35.5 cm) × 5 stitches/inch + 2 selvedge stitches = 72 stitches

Number of stitches at upper arm (upper arm width × body stitch gauge + 2 selvedge stitches)

14" (35.5 cm) × 5 stitches/inch + 2 selvedge stitches = 72 stitches

LENGTHS

Number of rows in cuff (cuff length × border row gauge)

3" (7.5 cm) × 9 rows/inch = 27 rows; round up to even number = 28 rows

Number of rows from cuff to armhole (length × body row gauge)

15" (38 cm) × 7 rows/inch = 105 rows; round up to even number = 106 rows

Step 1: Cast-On and Ribbing/Border

For our sample sleeve, use the smaller needle to cast on 58 stitches. Work k1, p1 ribbing until the piece measures 3" (7.5 cm), or 28 rows, ending with a wrong-side row.

Step 2: Transition from Ribbing/Border to Sleeve

In this step, increase 14 stitches from 58 stitches at the cuff to 72 stitches for the upper arm.

72 stitches at upper arm – 58 stitches at cuff = 14 stitches to increase

$$14 \overline{)58} \quad \begin{array}{r} 4 \\ -56 \\ \hline 2 \end{array}$$

Use the shaping formula to determine an even distribution of increases. In this example, increase every 4th stitch 14 times, then work the remaining 2 stitches.

Using the shaping formula, divide the 58 cuff stitches by 14 increases to determine how to space these increases evenly. The formula tells us to increase every 4th stitch 14 times, then work the remaining 2 stitches.

For our sample sleeve, use the M1 method of increasing (see page 196) and work this right-side row as: k1 (selvedge stitch), k3, M1, [k4, M1] 13 times, k1, k1 (selvedge stitch)—72 stitches.

Step 3: Sleeve Taper to Upper Arm

There is no shaping between the top of the cuff and the armhole of a lantern sleeve.

For our sample sleeve, change to larger needles and work even in the cable pattern until the piece measures 15" (38 cm), or 106 rows, from the transition row.

Step 4: Cap Shaping

Shape the cap for a set-in, raglan, or saddle shoulder as desired.

GATHERED-TOP SLEEVE

A sleeve with a gathered top has extra fullness at the top of the cap where the sleeve meets the shoulder. The billow created by the gathers adds softness to the overall look of a garment and is commonly used for dressy styles.

This type of sleeve is similar to a classic set-in sleeve (see page 81) through the armhole shaping, but the upper arm typically has 2" to 3" (5 to 7.5 cm) more ease, and after the initial armhole shaping, the cap is worked straight to the last 1" (2.5 cm) where it is slightly tapered to round out the top edges. To provide the extra length needed for the top gathers, the cap of a gathered sleeve is typically 1" (2.5 cm) longer than that for a classic sleeve cap. There are two important measurements for planning the top shaping: the finished knitted measurement before the cap is gathered and the gathered width, which is typically 15% of the upper arm width.

Our example sleeve with a gathered top measures 18" wide (45.5 cm) at the upper arm, 14" (35.5 cm) wide at the center cap, 12" (30.5 cm) wide before gathering, 3" (7.5 cm) wide after gathering, and has a cap that is 5" (12.5 cm) long.

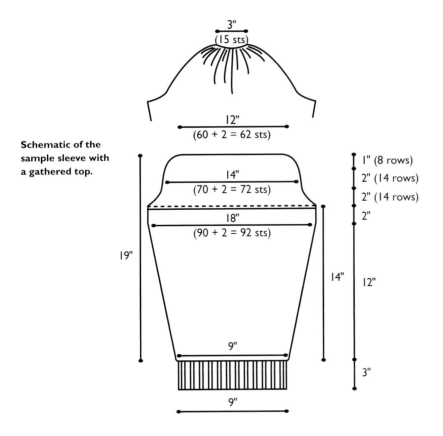

Schematic of the sample sleeve with a gathered top.

GAUGE
5 stitches and 7 rows = 1" (2.5 cm)

KEY MEASUREMENTS
Upper arm width: 18" (45.5 cm)
Center cap width: 14" (35.5 cm)
Finished gathered width: (upper arm width × 15%; rounded to nearest whole number)
18" (45.5 cm) × 15% = 2.7";
round up to nearest whole number
= 3" (7.5 cm)
Knitted width at top of cap: (finished gathered width × 4)
3" (7.5 cm) × 4 = 12" (30.5 cm)
Total cap length: 5" (12.5 cm)
Length to match armhole shaping: 2" (5 cm)
Length of top-of-cap shaping: 1" (2.5 cm)
Length of center cap: (total cap length − length to match armhole shaping − top of cap shaping length)
5" (12.5 cm) − 2" (5 cm) − 1" (2.5 cm)
= 2" (5 cm)

Conversion of Measurements to Numbers of Stitches and Rows

WIDTHS

Number of stitches at upper arm (upper arm width × body stitch gauge + 2 selvedge stitches)
18" (45.5 cm) × 5 stitches/inch + 2 selvedge stitches = 92 stitches

Number of stitches in center cap (center cap width × body stitch gauge + 2 selvedge stitches)
14" (35.5 cm) × 5 stitches/inch + 2 selvedge stitches = 72 stitches

Number of stitches to decrease in length to match armhole shaping (upper arm stitches – center cap stitches)

> 92 upper arm stitches – 72 center cap stitches = 20 stitches to decrease at armhole; 10 stitches at each side

Number of stitches at top of cap (top of cap width × body stitch gauge + 2 selvedge stitches)

> 12" (30.5 cm) × 5 stitches/inch + 2 selvedge stitches = 62 stitches

Number of stitches to bind-off in last 2 rows of cap shaping (number of stitches in center cap – number of stitches at top of cap)

> 72 center cap stitches – 62 top of cap stitches = 10 stitches to bind off; 5 stitches at each side

Number of stitches in gathered final row (finished gathered width × body stitch gauge)

> 3" (7.5 cm) finished gathered width × 5 stitches/inch = 15 stitches

Number of stitches to decrease for the gathered final top width

> 62 top of cap stitches – 15 stitches in gathered final row = 47 stitches to decrease

LENGTHS

Number of rows in length to match armhole shaping (length × body row gauge)

> 2" (5 cm) in armhole shaping × 7 rows/inch = 14 rows

Number of rows in work-even section of center cap (length × body row gauge)

> 2" (5 cm) in work-even length × 7 rows/inch = 14 rows

Number of rows in top cap shaping (length × body row gauge)

> 1" (2.5 cm) × 7 rows/inch = 7 rows; round up to even number = 8 rows

For sufficient gathering width, the top of the cap should measure four times the desired gathered width. In our example of a finished gathered width of 3" (7.5 cm), the top of the cap must therefore measure 12" (30.5 cm).

> 3" (7.5 cm) gathered width × 4 = 12" (30.5 cm) before gathering

 tip The cap can be bound off straight, then gathered by hand, or the gathers can be produced by decreases worked on the last 2 rows of the cap.

Step 1: Cast On for Ribbing/Border through Step 3: Sleeve Taper to Upper Arm

For our sample sleeve, work the sleeve to the armhole as for a classic tapered sleeve (see page 81), following the gauge and schematic shown on page 199.

Step 4: Cap Shaping

Like a classic set-in cap (see page 84), the cap of gathered sleeve is worked in four sections.

Section 1: Armhole Bind-Off Match

The cap shaping begins with at least the same first two rows of bind-offs that were worked at the armhole of the sweater body so that the base of the sleeve matches the base of the armhole. For our example, we'll say this section was worked as: bind off 3 stitches at the beginning of the first 2 rows, then bind off 2 stitches at the beginning of the next 2 rows, then bind off 1 stitch at the beginning of every row 10 times.

For our sample sleeve, begin with 92 stitches, then bind off 20 stitches over the first 2" (5 cm), or 14 rows as follows: bind off 3 stitches at the beginning of the first 2 rows, then bind off 2 stitches at the beginning of the next 2 rows, then bind off 1 stitch at the beginning of every row 10 times—72 stitches remain.

Section 2: Center Cap
For a gathered sleeve, this section is worked without shaping for 2" (5 cm).

For our sample sleeve, work even on 72 stitches for 2" (5 cm), or 14 rows, ending with a wrong-side row.

Section 3: Top Slope
In this section, decrease 10 stitches over the next 1" (2.5 cm), or 8 rows.

For our sample sleeve, bind off 2 stitches at the beginning of the next 2 rows, then bind off 1 stitch at the beginning of the following 6 rows, ending with a wrong-side row—62 stitches remain.

Section 4: Gathered Top
In this section, decrease 47 stitches from 62 stitches to the desired top width of 15 stitches. Because 62 is less than 2 times 47 and because decreases involve at least 2 stitches (k2tog, for example), work these decreases in a series of 2 decrease rows.

To determine the number of decreases to work on the first decrease row, divide the number of stitches in the gathered top by 2 (the number of stitches involved in a single decrease).

62 stitches ÷ 2 stitches per decrease = 31 decreases

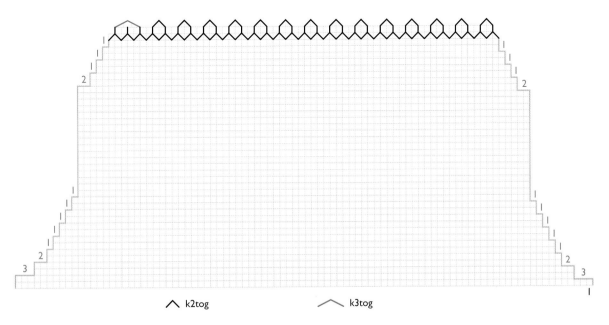

⋀ k2tog   ⌢ k3tog

Plot of the cap on graph paper. Bind-off stitches are shown in red.

PLEATED-TOP SLEEVE

A pleated cap is worked much the same as a gathered top. Like a gathered top, the top of a pleated cap is considerably wider than that of a classic set-in sleeve to allow for the pleats. Pleated sleeve tops add softness to a silhouette and are commonly used for dressy styles.

- Before pleating, the cap is 3 times as wide as the pleated width, which is 20% of the upper arm width.

- The cap is typically 1½" (3.8 cm) shorter than the length of the armhole.

- An additional 2" to 4" (5 to 10 cm) of ease is added to the standard 2" (5 cm) of ease in the upper arm circumference.

- The cap can be bound off straight, then pleated by hand, or the pleats can be formed while working a three-needle bind-off on the final row of the cap.

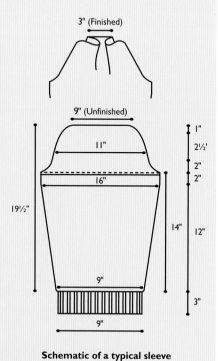

Schematic of a typical sleeve with a pleated top.

This will leaves 31 stitches for the second decrease row.

> 62 stitches – 31 stitches decreased = 31 stitches remain

To determine the number of decreases to work on the second decrease row, subtract the desired final number of stitches from the number of stitches remaining.

> 31 stitches after first decrease row – 15 stitches in final bind-off row
> = 16 stitches to decrease

Because we want to end up with fewer stitches (15) than the number of decreases that must be worked (16), some double decreases (k3tog) must be worked in the final decrease row. To determine the number of double decreases necessary, subtract the number of final stitches from the number of decreases.

> 16 decreases – 15 final stitches = 1 extra stitch

Therefore, on the final decrease row there will be 14 single (k2tog) decreases and 1 double (k3tog) decrease.

 MATH CHECK!

> The sum of the numbers of single and double decreases must match the desired final stitch count. In our example, work 14 single decreases (28 stitches reduced to 14) and 1 double decrease (3 stitches reduced to 1) for a total of 16 decreases and 15 stitches remaining.

For our sample sleeve, work this right-side row as *k2tog; repeat from * 30 more times—31 stitches remain. Purl the next wrong-side row, then work the next right-side row as *k2tog; rep from * 13 more times, k3tog—15 stitches remain. Purl the next wrong-side row, then bind off all of the stitches.

 tip

> Each decrease will result in 1 stitch on the needle, whether a single (k2tog) or double (k3tog) decrease is made. In our example, we decreased from 31 stitches to 15 stitches by working k2tog 14 times and working k3tog 1 time.

 tip

> Instead of using decreases to gather the top of the cap, you can simply bind off all the stitches (62 stitches in our example) on the last row. Then work two rows of basting stitches across the top of the cap and gently pull on both ends of the basting thread to gather the top edge to the desired width (3" [7.5 cm] in our example) before sewing the sleeve into the armhole.

SHORT SLEEVE

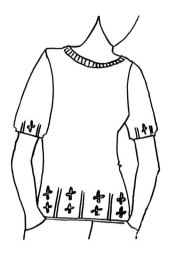

A short sleeve is worked just like any other sleeve, but with a shorter length between the cuff and armhole. For a true cap sleeve, the upper arm is worked for just 1" (2.5 cm) before beginning the cap. The key measurements are the upper arm width and the desired length of the sleeve to the armhole.

Our example short sleeve has a classic taper shape (see page 81) that measures 12" (30.5 cm) wide at the cuff (worked in k1, p1 ribbing on smaller needles), 14½" (37 cm) wide at the upper arm, and 5" (12.5 cm) long from the base of the cuff to the armhole.

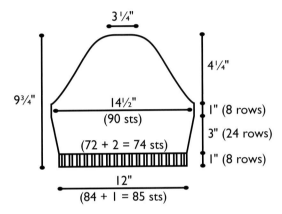

Schematic of the sample short sleeve.

Conversion of Measurements to Numbers of Stitches and Rows

WIDTHS

Number of stitches at border/cuff (arm circumference × ribbing stitch gauge + 1 symmetry stitch)

> 12" (30.5 cm) × 7 stitches/inch + 1 symmetry stitch = 85 stitches

Number of stitches at base of sleeve (arm circumference × body stitch gauge + 2 selvedge stitches)

> 12" (30.5 cm) × 6 stitches/inch + 2 selvedge stitches = 74 stitches

Number of stitches at upper arm (upper arm circumference × body stitch gauge + 2 selvedge stitches)

> 14½" (37 cm) × 6 stitches/inch + 2 selvedge stitches = 89 stitches; round up to even number = 90 stitches

LENGTHS

Number of rows in border/cuff (length × border row gauge)

> 1" (2.5 cm) × 9 rows/inch = 9 rows; round down to even number = 8 rows

Number of rows from top of border to armhole (length × body row gauge)

> 4" (12.5 cm) × 8 rows/inch = 32 rows

Step 1: Cast-On and Ribbing/Border

For our sample sleeve, use the smaller needles to cast on 85 stitches. Work k1, p1 ribbing on 85 stitches for 1" (2.5 cm), or 8 rows.

Step 2: Transition from Border to Body

In this step, decrease 11 stitches from 85 stitches at the border to 74 stitches at the top of the border.

74 stitches at top of border – 85 stitches at border = 11 stitches to decrease

Divide the 85 stitches in the border by 11 decreases to determine how to space these decreases evenly. The shaping formula tells us to decrease (k2tog) every 6th and 7th stitches 3 times and every 7th and 8th stitches 8 times. To prevent the last decrease from occurring at the end of the row, divide one of the 8-stitch intervals between the beginning and the end of the row.

For our sample sleeve, work this right-side row as: k1 (selvedge stitch), k1, k2tog, [k5, k2tog] 3 times, [k6, k2tog] 7 times, k3, k1 (selvedge stitch)—74 stitches.

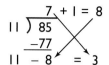

Use the shaping formula to determine an even distribution of decreases. In this example, decrease (k2tog) every 6th and 7th stitches 3 times and every 7th and 8th stitches 8 times.

Step 3: Sleeve Taper to Upper Arm

In this step, increase 16 stitches from 74 stitches at the base of the sleeve to 90 stitches at the upper arm.

90 stitches at upper arm – 74 stitches at the base of the sleeve
= 16 stitches to increase; 8 stitches at each side

The length from the base of the sleeve body to armhole is 4" (10 cm), or 32 rows. To provide sufficient ease of movement in the upper arm area, work the last 1" (2.5 cm), or 8 rows, even. Therefore, work the increases over 24 rows.

32 rows total – 8 rows worked even at top = 24 rows for shaping

Divide 24 rows by 8 increase rows to determine how to space these increases evenly. In this case, increase every 3rd row 8 times.

For our sample sleeve, change to larger needles and stockinette stitch and increase 1 stitch at each edge (inside the selvedge stitches) every 3rd row 8 times—90 stitches. Work even for 8 rows until a total of 32 rows have been worked and the piece measures 5" (12.5 cm) from the cast-on edge.

Use the shaping formula to determine an even distribution of increases. In this example, increase every 3rd row 8 times.

Step 4: Cap Shaping

Shape the cap for a set-in (as shown here), raglan, or saddle shoulder as desired.

CUFFS

Cuffs, like collars, are small designer details that can significantly enhance the look of a garment. A fold-back cuff can give an aura of sophistication to an otherwise plain jacket. A lacy bell cuff can add a feeling of femininity to an otherwise plain sleeve. A buttoned placket can add a professional look to a jacket made for the office. The list goes on. The three most common cuff designs are fold-back, bell, and buttoned.

CLASSIC FOLD-BACK CUFF

A straight fold-back cuff is the easiest to make. It can be worked at the beginning of the sleeve or, if a provisional cast-on is used, it can be added after the sleeve is completed. The fold-back portion of the cuff can be worked in any stitch pattern. Typically, this portion of the cuff measures the same width as the cuff, which is designed for a snug fit. Because this type of cuff is usually longer than the typical ribbed cuff described for a classic silhouette (see page 81), the tapered part of the sleeve is worked over fewer rows.

Our example sleeve with a fold-back cuff measures 10½" (26.5 cm) wide at the cuff, with a 4½" (11.5 cm) long cuff that folds back 4" (10 cm). Begin by casting on stitches for the fold-back portion of the cuff.

GAUGE
7 stitches and 9 rows = 1" (2.5 cm)

KEY MEASUREMENTS
Cuff width: 10½" (26.5 cm)
Fold-back cuff width: 10½" (26.5 cm)
Cuff length: 4½" (11.5 cm)
Fold-back cuff length: 4" (10 cm)

> *tip* The right side of the fold-back section corresponds to the wrong side of the cuff and sleeve.

> *tip* To clearly mark the boundary between the cuff and the turn-back section, purl one right-side row or knit one wrong-side row to form a turning ridge.

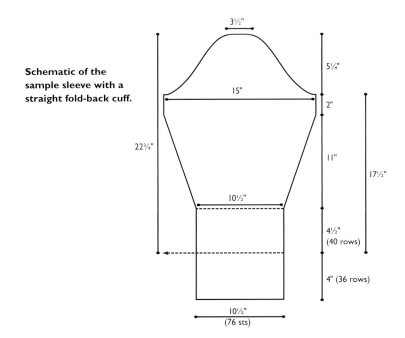

Schematic of the sample sleeve with a straight fold-back cuff.

3½"
5¼"
15"
2"
22¾"
11"
17½"
10½"
10½"
4½" (40 rows)
4" (36 rows)
10½" (76 sts)

Conversion of Measurements to Numbers of Stitches and Rows

WIDTHS

Number of stitches in cuff (cuff width × border stitch gauge + 2 selvedge stitches)

10½" (26.5 cm) × 7 stitches/inch + 2 selvedge stitches = 75.5 stitches; round up to nearest even number = 76 stitches

LENGTHS

Number of rows in cuff (cuff length × border row gauge)

4½" (11.5 cm) × 9 rows/inch = 40.5 rows; round down to nearest even number = 40 rows

Number of rows in fold-back cuff (fold-back cuff length × border row gauge)

4" (10 cm) × 9 rows/inch = 36 rows

Step 1: Cast-On and Ribbing/Border

In this step, cast on for the turn-back portion of the cuff.

For our sample sleeve, cast on 76 stitches.

Step 2: Cuff

In this step, work the desired number of rows for the turn-back section, purl one right-side row to create a turning ridge, then work the desired number of rows for the actual cuff.

For our sample sleeve, work the border pattern for 4" (10 cm), or 36 rows, for the turn-back portion of the cuff, ending with a wrong-side row. Purl the next right-side row to form a turning ridge, then continue in pattern as established for 4½" (11.5 cm), or 40 rows, more for the cuff. Because the cuff is turned back, the right side of the sleeve will correspond to the wrong side of the cuff, beginning with the first right-side row following the turning ridge.

GAUGE
5 stitches and 6 rows = 1" (2.5 cm)

KEY MEASUREMENTS
Cuff width at top of bell: 9" (23 cm)
Bell width at widest point: 15" (38 cm)
Length of bell: 6" (15 cm)
Decrease interval: 1" (2.5 cm)
Number of decrease rows: (bell length ÷ length between decreases)
6" (15 cm) bell length ÷ 1" (2.5 cm) per interval between each decrease row = 6 decrease rows

BELL CUFF

A bell cuff is worked at the beginning of a classic sleeve and is appropriate for all types of silhouettes. It typically measures between 4" to 6" (10 to 15 cm) long and between 13" to 16" (33 to 40.5 cm) wide. The narrowest part of the bell corresponds to the circumference of the arm (including ease) at the desired position for the top of the bell. The bell can be shaped by decreasing along the side edges or in bands across the entire width. At the top of the bell, the sleeve begins to taper out to the upper arm measurement.

Our example bell cuff measures 6" (15 cm) long and tapers from 15" (38 cm) at the base to 9" (23 cm) at the top, following the method used to shape a circular skirt (see page 159). Begin by planning the amount of width to be decreased on each decrease row and spacing these decrease rows 1" (2.5 cm) apart.

tip

To avoid a slight undulation (peak) at the base of the bell, do not stack the decreases along the side edges. Instead, either plan a different decrease schedule for each decrease row or plan the decreases a few inches away from the side seams.

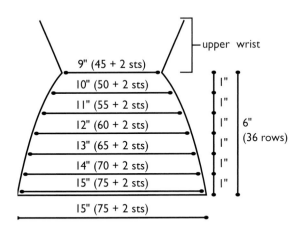

9" (45 + 2 sts)
10" (50 + 2 sts)
11" (55 + 2 sts)
12" (60 + 2 sts)
13" (65 + 2 sts)
14" (70 + 2 sts)
15" (75 + 2 sts)
15" (75 + 2 sts)

upper wrist

1"
1"
1"
1"
1"
1"

6"
(36 rows)

Schematic of the sample bell cuff.

 tip

If you prefer to work the decreases along the side edges, subtract the number of stitches in the wrist from the number of stitches at the base of the bell, divide this number in half, then use the shaping formula to divide that answer into the number of rows planned for the cuff. This will give you a single side-edge decrease schedule where 1 stitch will be decreased at each edge on specific rows over the length of the cuff.

Conversion of Measurements to Numbers of Stitches and Rows

WIDTHS

Number of stitches at base of bell (width × stitch gauge + 2 selvedge stitches)
15" (38 cm) × 5 stitches/inch + 2 selvedge stitches = 77 stitches

Number of stitches at top of bell (width × stitch gauge + 2 selvedge stitches)
9" (23 cm) × 5 stitches/inch + 2 selvedge stitches = 47 stitches

LENGTHS

Number of rows in bell: (length × row gauge)
6" (15 cm) × 6 rows/inch = 36 rows

Number of rows in each decrease interval: (length × row gauge)
1" (2.5 cm) × 6 rows/inch = 6 rows

Step 1: Cast On

For our sample cuff, cast on 77 stitches.

Step 2: Cuff

The decreases are based on the stitch counts excluding selvedge stitches. In our example, decrease 30 stitches from 75 stitches (excluding selvedge stitches) at the base of the bell to 45 stitches (excluding selvedge stitches) at the top of the bell.

75 stitches at base of bell – 45 stitches to top of bell = 30 stitches to decrease

We know that we want to work the decreases in 6 sections of 6 rows each. To determine how many stitches to decrease in each interval, divide the total number of stitches to decrease by the number of decrease rows.

30 stitches to decrease ÷ 6 decrease rows = 5 stitches to decrease per decrease row

Using the shaping formula, divide the 75 cast-on stitches by 5 decreases to determine how to space these decreases evenly on the first decrease row. The formula tells us to decrease every 15th stitch. Because 2 stitches are involved in each decrease (k2tog), work the first decrease row as [k13, k2tog] 5 times to end with 70 stitches. To prevent the last decrease from occurring at the end of the row, divide one interval evenly between the beginning and end of the row. In this case, work the center 75 stitches of this row as: k6, k2tog, [k13, k2tog] 4 times, k7 to end with 70 stitches (excluding selvedge stitches). Work 1 less stitch between decreases in each of the 5 remaining decrease intervals.

For our sample cuff, decrease 5 stitches every 6 rows following the decrease schedule described in the box at the top of page 209.

$$5\overline{)75} = 15$$

Omit the selvedge stitches and use the shaping formula to determine an even distribution of decreases. In this example, decrease every 15th stitch (k2tog) 5 times.

DECREASE SCHEDULE FOR WORKING IN ROUNDS

Decrease Round	Decrease Interval	Stitches Remaining (excluding selvedge stitches)
1	[k13, k2tog] 5 times	70
2	[k12, k2tog] 5 times	65
3	[k11, k2tog] 5 times	60
4	[k10, k2tog] 5 times	55
5	[k9, k2tog] 5 times	50
6	[k8, k2tog] 5 times	45

DECREASE SCHEDULE FOR WORKING IN ROWS

Decrease Row	Decrease Interval	Stitches Remaining (excluding selvedge stitches)
1	k6, k2tog, [k13, k2tog] 4 times, k7	70
2	k6, k2tog, [k12, k2tog] 4 times, k6	65
3	k5, k2tog, [k11, k2tog] 4 times, k6	60
4	k5, k2tog, [k10, k2tog] 4 times, k5	55
5	k4, k2tog, [k9, k2tog] 4 times, k5	50
6	k4, k2tog, [k8, k2tog] 4 times, k4	45

PLACKET CUFF

A placket adds a tailored and polished look to the base of a jacket or cardigan sleeve. Depending on the size and type of buttons chosen, the overall look can be anything from sporty and casual to dressy. When buttoned, just one side of the placket (the side that overlaps) contributes to the overall cuff width. Plackets are worked as mirror images on the two sleeves—the wider section is worked on the right-hand side of the right sleeve and on the left-hand side of the left sleeve. The narrower section tucks under the wide section. A placket is planned the same way as overlapping button bands described on page 127. Typically, the wide section is 65% of the total cuff width minus half of the placket overlap width. Because the placket overlaps, it does not contribute any additional width to the cuff and, when the placket is buttoned, the width will be the same as the cuff.

To begin, decide on the cuff width and calculate the sleeve-shaping schedule. Then plan the placket calculations. Initially, the sleeves are worked in two pieces for the desired length of the placket. At the top of the placket, the stitches are joined and the sleeve is worked in a single piece to the armhole as usual.

The length of the placket depends on the number of buttons and the width depends on the size of the buttons. In general, a placket should be twice the width of the buttons. To determine a suitable length, arrange the buttons on your gauge swatch until you find a spacing you like. You can choose whether or not to add buttonholes to the placket. If you decide to omit buttonholes, simply sew the buttons through all layers of the overlapped placket.

Our example placket cuff has three ½" (1.3 cm) buttons with an overlap that measures 1" (2.5 cm) wide and 4" (10 cm) long. The cuff measures 9½" (24 cm) wide (including the placket), of which 1" is contributed by the overlap, 2¾" (7 cm) is contributed by the narrow side, and 5¾" (14.5 cm) is contributed by the wide side. Instead of working buttonholes, the buttons are sewn through all layers of the overlapped placket.

GAUGE
5 stitches and 9 rows = 1" (2.5 cm).

KEY MEASUREMENTS
Cuff width: 9½" (24 cm)

Upper arm width: 15¾" (40 cm)

Placket overlap width: 1" (2.5 cm)

Width of wide section of cuff, including placket: (cuff width × 65%) 9½" (24 cm) × 65% = 6.175"; round up to nearest quarter inch = 6¼" (16 cm)

Width of wide section of cuff, excluding placket: (width including placket – ½ placket overlap width) 6¼" (16 cm) – ½" (1.3 cm) overlap = 5¾" (14.5 cm)

Width of narrow section of cuff, excluding placket: (cuff width – wide section width– ½ placket overlap width) 9½" (24 cm) – 6¼" (16 cm) – ½" (1.3 cm) overlap = 2¾" (7 cm)

Placket length: 4" (10 cm)

Total sleeve length: 17" (43 cm)

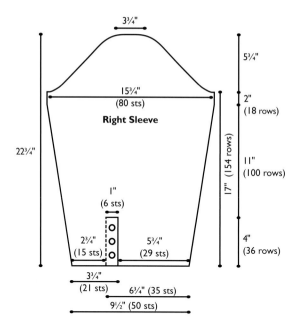

Schematic of the sample sleeve with a placket cuff.

✳ *tip* The placket is worked at the same time as increases are worked along the sides to taper the sleeve.

✳ *tip* The placket width is added to both the wide section and the narrow section of the cuff as they are worked. Because the placket overlaps, only one placket width contributes to the overall cuff width when the placket is fastened.

Conversion of Measurements to Numbers of Stitches and Rows

WIDTHS

Number of stitches at base of sleeve (cuff width × stitch gauge + 2 selvedge stitches)

9½" (24 cm) × 5 stitches/inch + 2 selvedge stitches = 49.5 stitches;
round up to nearest even number = 50 stitches

Number of stitches in placket overlap (placket width × stitch gauge)

1" (2.5 cm) × 5 stitches/inch = 5 stitches; round up to even number = 6 stitches

Number of stitches in wide section, without placket overlap (width × stitch gauge + 1 selvedge stitch)

5¾" (14.5) × 5 stitches/inch + 1 selvedge stitch = 29.75 stitches;
round down to whole number = 29 stitches

Number of stitches in wide section, including placket overlap (width × stitch gauge + 1 selvedge stitch + 6 placket stitches)

> 5¾" (14.5 cm) × 5 stitches/inch + 1 selvedge stitch + 6 placket stitches = 35.75 stitches; round down to nearest whole number = 35 stitches

Number of stitches in narrow section, without placket overlap (width × stitch gauge + 1 selvedge stitch)

> 2¾" (7 cm) × 5 stitches/inch + 1 selvedge stitch = 14.75; round up to nearest whole number = 15 stitches

Number of stitches in narrow section, including placket overlap (width × stitch gauge + 1 selvedge stitch + 6 placket stitches)

> 2¾" (7 cm) × 5 stitches/inch + 1 selvedge stitch + 6 placket stitches
> = 20.75 stitches; round up to nearest whole number = 21 stitches
> (6 of these stitches will be tucked behind the overlap)

Number of stitches at upper arm (upper arm width × stitch gauge + 2 selvedge stitches)
> 15¾" (40 cm) × 5 stitches/inch + 2 selvedge stitches = 80.75 stitches;
> round down to nearest even number = 80 stitches

LENGTHS

Number of rows in total sleeve length (total length × row gauge)
> 17" (43 cm) × 9 rows/inch = 153 rows; round up to even number = 154 rows

Number of rows in placket (placket length × row gauge)
> 4" (10 cm) × 9 rows/inch = 36 rows

Step 1: Cast On

For our sample cuff, begin with the right sleeve and cast on 35 stitches (29 cuff stitches plus 6 placket overlap stitches) for the wide side, and with separate needles, cast on 21 stitches (15 cuff stitches plus 6 placket overlap stitches) for the narrow side. Remember, only the placket stitches on the wide side contribute to the cuff width.

 MATH CHECK!

When buttoned, the placket width should be the same as a sleeve cuff that had no placket. The total cuff width should equal the sum of the widths of the wide section including the overlap stitches plus the narrow section without the overlap stitches.

> 5¾" (14.5 cm) width + 2¾" (7 cm) narrow width + 1" (2.5 cm)
> overlap = 9½" (24 cm)

The total number of stitches cast on (excluding the underlap stitches of the narrow section, which will be hidden) should equal the number of stitches for the cuff measurement without a placket.

> 35 stitches in wide side + 15 stitches in narrow side = 50 stitches total

Step 2: Cuff

In this step, work the two sides of the placket separately for 4" (10 cm), or 36 rows, to the top of the placket and at the same time begin increasing 30 stitches (15 stitches each side) from 50 stitches in the cuff to 80 stitches in the upper arm.

80 upper arm stitches − 50 cuff stitches = 30 stitches to increase;
15 stitches at each side

Work these increases over 15" (38 cm) of the 17" (43 cm) of the total sleeve length to the armhole, leaving the last 2" (5 cm) to work even to allow for sufficient ease of movement in the upper arm area. In this example, the increases are worked over 136 rows.

15" (38 cm) × 9 rows/inch = 135 rows; round up to even number = 136 rows

Using the shaping formula, divide 136 rows by 15 increases to determine how to space these increases evenly. The formula tells us to increase every 9th row 14 times and every 10th row 1 time.

We now know to work the first 4 increase rows during the 36 placket rows and the remaining 11 increase rows during the remaining 100 rows, after the two sides of the placket have been joined.

For our sample right sleeve, work the two sides of the placket separately and increase 1 stitch at each side edge (inside the selvedge stitches) every 9th row 4 times, then every 10th row 1 time, and at the same time, when each placket measures about 4" (10 cm), or a total of 36 rows have been worked, join the two sides of the placket as follows.

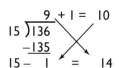

Use the shaping formula to determine an even distribution of the increases. In this example, increase every 9th row 14 times, then every 10th row 1 time.

Step 3: Sleeve Taper to Upper Arm

In this section, join the two sides of the placket and continue working the sleeve in a single piece to the armhole.

For our sample right sleeve, join the two sides of the placket on the next right-side row by working across the wide section (work across the short section first for the left sleeve) to the last 6 stitches (the placket overlap stitches), placing the short section behind the wide section, then working the 6 placket stitches of the short section together with the 6 placket stitches of the wide section by knitting through both sets of stitches as if to k2tog. Then work to the end of the short section. Continue to work the sleeve in a single piece to the armhole. There will be 80 stitches after all of the side increases have been worked and a total of 136 rows have been worked. Work even on 80 stitches for 2" (5 cm), or 18 rows, ending with a wrong-side row.

Step 4: Cap Shaping

Shape the cap for a set-in as in this example, raglan, or saddle shoulder as desired.

 tip To maintain a continuous flow of a pattern stitch across the two sides of the overlap, the same part of the pattern repeat should be worked on each part of the overlap. In our example that has a 6-stitch overlap, the first 6 pattern stitches of the smaller side must be the same as the last 6 pattern stitches of the wider side of the placket.

chapter nine
Necklines

The neckline is a key element in garment design. The width and depth of the neckline are important structural components in the overall fit around the top half of a garment. In addition, the neckline falls at the center of the garment and a poor fit in this area will detract from the appearance of even the most finely crafted sweater.

Necklines can take on a variety of shapes from straight (boat) to square, round, or V. Vary the width or depth of any of these, or combine techniques, and the possibilities become endless. For example, a neckline can transition from a V at the base to a classic round shape at the top or from a wide V at the base to a square at the top. In addition, the shape can be different on the front and back, such as a high round neck on the front paired with a deep narrow V on the back.

The following examples illustrate how to plan the most popular necklines. These examples are for shaping the front neck only; the back neck can be shaped as desired.

NECKLINE NOTES

- A neck opening must be large enough to accommodate the head. In general, the narrower the width, the deeper the length should be, unless the neckline includes a button placket.

- Neck widths are calculated as percentages of cross-back widths. They vary from 65% to 70% of this width for a wide boatneck to just 35% to 45% for a high round or V-neckline.

- Most neck shaping begins after the armholes have been shaped.

- Shoulder shaping will contribute to the neck depth. For example, shoulders that are shaped over 1" (2.5 cm) will add 1" (2.5 cm) to the neck depth.

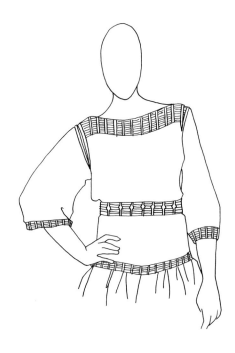

CLASSIC BOATNECK

The classic boatneck, which involves no neckline shaping, is the easiest to plan. (In non-classic versions, the back and front neck can be shaped over 1" [2.5 cm]). This type of neck (including border) is planned to fall at the raglan depth of just below the back neck bone. A typical boatneck is 65% to 70% of the cross-back width. The shoulders are bound off straight, with the last 1" to 3" (2.5 to 7.5 cm) worked in a stabilizing ribbed pattern, or the neck edge can be trimmed with a row of crochet to prevent curling. The top edges can abut or overlap at the shoulders (in which case, plan for the extra length of the overlap). To finish a boatneck, simply sew together the front and back along the shoulders, leaving the planned neck width open at the center.

Our example boatneck shaping is for a pullover that measures 16½" (42 cm) wide below the armholes and 12½" (31.5 cm) wide at the cross-back. The armholes are 7" (18 cm) long to the shoulders with 1" (2.5 cm) added for the raglan depth. The body is worked in stockinette stitch to 2" (5 cm) below the raglan depth, then k1, p2 ribbing is worked for the last 2" (5 cm).

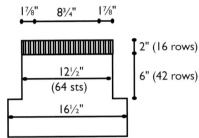

Schematic of the sample upper body with classic boatneck shaping.

Conversion of Measurements to Numbers of Stitches and Rows

WIDTHS

Number of body stitches in cross-back width (width × stitch gauge + 2 selvedge stitches)
    12½" (31.5 cm) in cross-back width × 5 stitches/inch + 2 selvedge stitches = 64.5 stitches; round down to nearest even number = 64 stitches

Number of border stitches in cross-back width (width × stitch gauge)
    12½" (31.5 cm) in cross-back width × 6 stitches/inch = 75 stitches; round down to even number = 74 stitches

Number of border stitches in neck width (width × stitch gauge + 2 selvedge stitches)
    8¾" (22 cm) in neck width × 6 stitches/inch + 2 selvedge stitches = 54.5 stitches; round down to nearest even number = 54 stitches

Number of stitches in shoulders (border stitches in cross-back – border stitches in neck)
    74 cross-back stitches – 54 neck stitches = 20 stitches; 10 stitches each side

LENGTHS

Number of rows in raglan (length × body row gauge)
    8" (20.5 cm) × 7 rows/inch = 56 rows

Number of rows in armhole to base of border (length × body row gauge)
    6" (2.5 cm) × 7 rows/inch = 42 rows

Number of rows in border (length × border row gauge)
    2" (5 cm) × 8 rows/inch = 16 rows

Step 1: Work to Base of Border

In this step, work even to the base of the neck border

For our sample neck, work even on the 64 cross-back stitches until a total of 42 armhole rows have been worked—piece measures 6" (15 cm) from base of armholes.

GAUGE

Border (k1, p2 ribbing): 6 stitches and 8 rows = 1" (2.5 cm)

Body (stockinette stitch): 5 stitches and 7 rows = 1" (2.5 cm)

KEY MEASUREMENTS

Bust width: 16½" (42 cm)

Cross-back width: 12½" (31.5 cm)

Neck width: (cross-back width × 70%) 12½" (31.5 cm) × 70% = 8¾" (22 cm)

Armhole length: 7" (18 cm)

Raglan length: 8" (20.5 cm)

Border depth: 2" (5 cm)

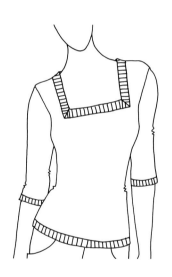

$$10 \overline{)\,\begin{matrix} 6 \\ 64 \\ -60 \\ \hline 4 \end{matrix}}$$

Use the shaping formula to determine an even distribution of increases. In this example, increase every 6th stitch 10 times, then work the remaining 4 stitches.

Step 2: Border

The border is worked as a continuation of the body. In this step, increase 10 stitches from 64 body stitches to 74 border stitches so that the width remains the same in the border stitch pattern.

Using the shaping formula, divide the 64 body stitches by 10 increases to determine how to space these increases evenly. The formula tells us to increase every 6th stitch 10 times, then work the remaining 4 stitches.

For our sample neck, increase 10 stitches by working [k6, M1 (see page 196)] 10 times, k4—74 stitches. Center the k1, p2 pattern of the border on the next right-side row by working k1, p1, [k1, p2] 23 times, k1, p1, k1. Work in ribbing as established for 2" (5 cm)—piece measures 8" (20.5 cm) from base of armholes.

Step 3: Initial Bind-Off

For a boatneck, all of the stitches are bound off at once.

For our sample neck, bind off all stitches.

SQUARE NECKLINE

In a square neckline, the entire neck width is bound off in a single step, then each side is worked separately to the shoulder. A square neckline can be wide or narrow, shallow, or deep. This type of neckline is ideal for sleeveless tops that have narrow straps. In addition to simple neckbands, square necks can be finished with cross-over shawl collars (see page 235).

Our example square neck shaping is for a sleeveless pullover top that measures 16½" (42 cm) wide at the bust, 13" (33 cm) wide at the cross-back, 9" (23 cm) wide at the neck, and 2" (5 cm) wide at the shoulders. The armholes measure 7" (18 cm) long and the front neck is 3" (7.5 cm) deep.

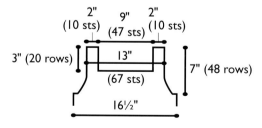

Schematic of the sample square neck shaping.

GAUGE
5 stitches and 7 rows = 1" (2.5 cm)

KEY MEASUREMENTS
Bust width: 16½" (42 cm)
Cross-back width: 13" (33 cm)
Neck width: 9" (23 cm)
Shoulder width: 2" (5 cm)
Armhole length: 7" (18 cm)
Front neck depth: 3" (7.5 cm)

Conversion of Measurements to Numbers of Stitches and Rows

WIDTHS

Number of stitches in cross-back (width × stitch gauge + 2 selvedge stitches)
 13" (33 cm) cross-back width × 5 stitches/inch + 2 selvedge stitches = 67 stitches

Number of stitches in neck width (width × stitch gauge + 2 selvedge stitches)
 9" (23 cm) neck width × 5 stitches/inch + 2 selvedge stitches = 47 stitches

Number of stitches in shoulders (stitches in cross-back – stitches in neck)

> 67 cross-back stitches – 47 neck stitches = 20 stitches; 10 stitches each side

LENGTHS

Number of rows in armhole (length × row gauge)

> 7" (18 cm) × 7 rows/inch = 49 rows; round down to even number = 48 rows

Number of rows in front neck depth (length × row gauge)

> 3" (7.5 cm) × 7 rows/inch = 21 rows; round down to even number = 20 rows

Number of rows in armhole to front neck (total armhole rows – number of rows in front neck)

> 48 total rows – 20 rows in front neck = 28 rows to base of front neck

Step 1: Work to Base of Neck

For our sample neck, work even on 67 cross-back stitches until a total of 28 rows have been worked in the armhole.

Step 2: Initial Bind-Off

For a square neckline, all of the neck stitches are bound off on a single row. In our example, begin with 67 stitches and bind off the center 47 stitches, leaving 10 stitches at each side.

For our sample neck, work 10 stitches, bind off the center 47 stitches, then work the remaining 10 stitches.

Step 3: Side Neck Shaping

There is no side shaping on a classic square neckline.

For our sample neck, work each side separately for 3" (7.5 cm), or 20 rows; then bind off all stitches.

ROUND NECKLINE

Round necklines are probably the most common type of neck shaping. This type of neckline was detailed on page 76 for the classic pullover silhouette. In general, the center portion of the front neck is bound off in a single step, then the sides are shaped to the shoulders. For a more tailored fit along the upper body, work round necks in conjunction with back neck and shoulder shaping. Round-neckline shaping can be paired with straight, split, turtleneck, mock turtleneck, cowl, Peter Pan, and large round collars (see pages 227 to 234).

Our example low round, or scooped, neck shaping is for a pullover that measures 16½" (42 cm) wide at the bust, 13" (33 cm) wide at the cross-back, 9" (23 cm) wide at the neck, and 2" (5 cm) wide at the shoulders. The armholes measure 7" (18 cm) long and the shoulders are shaped over 1" (2.5 cm). The neck has a one-half initial bind-off (see page 78) that begins 3" (7.5 cm) below the top of the armhole and the sides of the neck are shaped over 1½" (3.8 cm) of rows.

GAUGE
5 stitches and 7 rows = 1" (2.5 cm)

KEY MEASUREMENTS
Bust width: 16½" (42 cm)
Cross-back width: 13" (33 cm)
Neck width: 9" (23 cm)
Shoulder width: 2" (5 cm)
Armhole length: 7" (18 cm)
Shoulder shaping depth: 1" (2.5 cm)
Neck depth: 3" (7.5 cm) below beginning
   of shoulder shaping

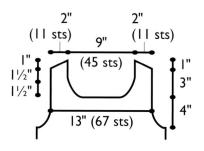

Schematic of the sample scooped-neck shaping.

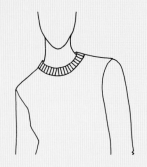

High Round Neck (crewneck):
Begins 2" to 2½" (5 to 6.5 cm) before the beginning of the shoulder shaping; shoulder shaping adds to the neck depth.

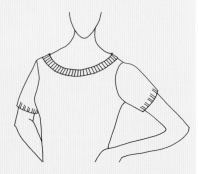

Medium Round Neck:
Begins 2½" to 3" (6.5 to 7.5 cm) before the beginning of the shoulder shaping; shoulder shaping adds to the neck depth.

Low Round Neck (scooped neck):
Begins 3" to 3½" (7.5 to 9 cm) or more below the beginning of the shoulder shaping; shoulder shaping adds to the neck depth.

Conversion of Measurements to Numbers of Stitches and Rows

WIDTHS

Number of stitches in cross-back (width × stitch gauge + 2 selvedge stitches)

13" (33 cm) cross-back width × 5 stitches/inch + 2 selvedge stitches = 67 stitches

Number of stitches in neck width (width × stitch gauge)

9" (23 cm) neck width × 5 stitches/inch = 45 stitches

Number of stitches in initial neck bind-off (stitches in neck × 50%)

45 stitches × 50% = 22.5 stitches; round up to whole number = 23 stitches

Number of stitches in shoulders (width × stitch gauge + 1 selvedge stitch)

2" (5 cm) × 5 stitches/inch + 1 selvedge stitch = 11 stitches

LENGTHS

Number of rows in armhole (length × row gauge)

7" (18 cm) × 7 rows/inch = 49 rows; round up to even number = 50 rows

Number of rows in armhole shaping (length × row gauge)

1½" (3.8 cm) × 7 rows/inch = 10.5 rows; round down to even number = 10 rows

Number of rows in neck depth (length × row gauge)

3" (7.5 cm) × 7 rows/inch = 21 rows; round up to even number = 22 rows

Number of rows in armhole to base of neck (total armhole rows − number of rows in front neck)

50 total rows − 22 rows in front neck = 28 rows to base of front neck

✳ *tip* The shoulder shaping will contribute to the overall neck length. In our example, the shoulder shaping will add 1" (2.5 cm) to the 3" (7.5 cm) neck length for a total length of 4" (10 cm).

Step 1: Work to Base of Neck

For our sample neck, work even on 67 cross-back stitches until a total of 28 rows have been worked in the armhole.

Step 2: Initial Bind-Off

In our example, bind off one-half of the neck width, or 23 stitches, on the first neck row, leaving 22 stitches, or 11 stitches to decrease at each side.

> 45 neck stitches ÷ 2 = 22.5 stitches;
> round up to whole number = 23 stitches in initial bind-off
>
> 45 neck stitches – 23 stitches in initial bind-off = 22 stitches;
> 11 stitches each side

For our sample neck, work across 22 stitches (11 shoulder stitches plus 11 neck stitches), bind off the center 23 stitches, then work 22 stitches (11 shoulder stitches plus 11 neck stitches) to the end of the row—22 stitches remain each side.

Step 3: Side Neck Shaping

In our example, bind off 11 stitches at each side of the neck over the first 1½" (3.8 cm), or 10 rows of the neck.

> 1½" (3.8 cm) × 7 rows/inch = 10.5; round down to even number = 10 rows

Plot the 11 decreases over the next 10 rows on graph paper to ensure a smooth, even curve. Then work even until the armhole measures 7" (18 cm), or a total of 50 rows have been worked.

For our sample neck, work the two sides separately and, at each neck edge, bind off 4 stitches once, then bind off 3 stitches once, then bind off 2 stitches once, then bind off 1 stitch 2 times—11 shoulder stitches remain. Work even on these 11 stitches until a total of 50 armhole rows have been worked. Shape the shoulders over the next 1" (2.5 cm), or 6 rows.

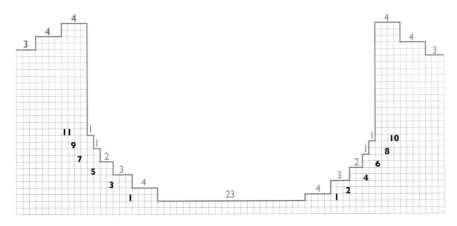

Plot of the neck decreases. Bind-off stitches are shown in red; row numbers are shown in black.

PLACKETS

Add a placket to add a different look to a round neckline. Most plackets are between 1" and 3" (2.5 and 7.5 cm) wide and may extend only a few inches below the neckline or all the way to the base of the armhole. To set up for a placket, work the front to the desired placket depth. Work across the next row to the desired placket placement, then either bind off the desired number of placket stitches (for a horizontal finish) or place these stitches on a holder (for a vertical finish), join a second ball of yarn, and work to the end of the row. Work the two sides separately to the shoulders. If you want to add buttons, plan and work their placement as with any buttonhole band.

For a horizontal finish (shown here), pick up and knit stitches along one side of the opening, work these stitches in the desired stitch pattern until the band is the same width as the bind-off at the base of the placket, then repeat for the other side. Overlap the two bands (with the buttonhole band on top) and sew them to the base of the opening. Add a neckband or collar as desired.

For a vertical finish, slip the held stitches onto a needle, increase 1 selvedge stitch at the seaming edge, and work in the desired stitch pattern for the length of the opening. Plan and work buttonholes as desired on this band. For the other band, pick up and knit the same number of stitches from behind the base of the first band and work it for the same length. When finished, sew the side of each band to the front. Add a neckband or collar as desired.

You can also knit the bands separately and sew them into the opening. If you do so, be sure to include a selvedge stitch for seaming.

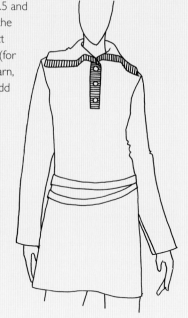

V-NECKLINE

A V-neckline looks good both on the front and back of a garment. This type of neckline can be most any length. Typically, longer Vs are paired with narrower neck widths and vice versa. The shaping at the top generally ends ½" to 1" (1.3 to 2.5 cm) before the top of the neckline. In addition to mitered and overlapped neckbands, V-necklines can be paired with a variety of shawl collars (see page 237 to 249).

 tip If there is an odd number of stitches in the body, bind off 1 stitch at the base of the V; if there is an even number of stitches in the body, bind off 2 stitches at the base of the V. This will ensure the same number of stitches on each side of the centered V.

 tip For a good fit at the neckline, plan the width at the top of the V, including the width of the border, to be the same as the neck width. This is especially important for a V that is more than 6" (15 cm) long.

Our example V-neck shaping is for a pullover that measures 20" (51 cm) wide at the bust, 17" (43 cm) wide at the cross-back, 7" (18 cm) wide at the neck, and 5" (12.5 cm) wide at the shoulders. The armholes measure 8" (20.5 cm) long and the neck measures 6¾" (17 cm) deep.

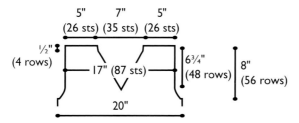

Schematic of the sample V-neck shaping.

Conversion of Measurements to Numbers of Stitches and Rows

WIDTHS

Number of stitches in cross-back (width × stitch gauge + 2 selvedge stitches)

17" (43 cm) × 5 stitches/inch + 2 selvedge stitches = 87 stitches

Number of stitches in neck width (width × stitch gauge)

7" (18 cm) × 5 stitches/inch = 35 stitches

Number of stitches in shoulder width (width × stitch gauge + 1 selvedge stitch)

5" (12.5 cm) × 5 stitches/inch + 1 selvedge stitch = 26 stitches

Number of stitches to decrease in neck (total neck stitches − initial bind-off)

35 neck stitches − 1 initial bind-off stitch = 34 stitches to decrease; 17 stitches each side

LENGTHS

Number of rows in V-neck (length × row gauge)

6¾" (17 cm) × 7 rows/inch = 47.25 rows; round up to nearest even number = 48 rows

Number of rows to work-even section at top of V (length × row gauge)

½" (1.3 cm) × 7 rows/inch = 3.5 rows; round up to even number = 4 rows

Number of rows in armhole (length × row gauge)

8" (20.5 cm) × 7 rows/inch = 56 rows

Number of rows in armhole to base of neck (total armhole rows − number of rows in V-neck)

56 total rows − 48 rows in V-neck = 8 rows to base of front neck

Step 1: Work to Base of Neck

For our sample neck, work even on 87 cross-back stitches until a total of 8 rows have been worked in the armhole.

Step 2: Initial Bind-Off

Because there is an odd number of stitches, bind off 1 stitch at the base of the V, leaving the same number of stitches on each side.

For our sample neck, work across 43 stitches (26 shoulder stitches and 17 side neck stitches), bind off the center stitch, then work remaining 43 stitches (17 side neck stitches and 26 shoulder stitches)—43 stitches remain each side.

Step 3: Side Neck Shaping

In this example, bind off 17 stitches evenly spaced at each side of the neck. The decreases will be completed ½" (1.3 cm), or 4 rows before the top of the armhole, and 2 rows are used to work the initial bind-off (and the return wrong-side row). Therefore, the neck is shaped over the next 42 rows.

48 neck rows − 2 initial bind-off rows − 4 work-even rows = 42 rows

Because bind-offs worked in a series need to be worked on alternate rows, only 21 of these 42 rows will be available for shaping. Using the shaping formula, divide the 21 available rows by 17 decreases to determine how to space these decreases evenly. The formula tells us to decrease every right-side (i.e., every 2nd) row 13 times and every 2nd right-side (i.e., every 4th) row 4 times—26 shoulder stitches remain. Working all of the shorter intervals first followed by all of the longer intervals will impart a concave taper to our neckline, as described in the box on page 223. Then work even on the shoulder stitches for 4 rows until a total of 48 neck rows have been worked.

For our sample neck, work the two sides separately and, at each neck edge, bind off 1 stitch every 2nd row 13 times, then every 4th row 4 times. Work even for 4 rows on the right-hand side (left neck) and 5 rows on the left-hand side (right neck) until a total of 48 neck rows and 56 armhole rows have been worked.

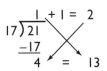

Use the shaping formula to determine an even distribution of bind-offs. In this example, bind off 1 stitch every right-side (every 2nd) row 13 times and every 2nd right-side (every 4th) row 4 times.

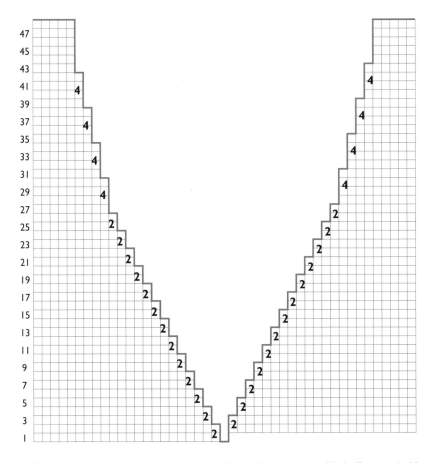

Plot of the V-neck shaping labeled with numbers of rows between bind-offs on each side.

THE SHAPE OF A V-NECK

Depending on the sequence and spacing of the decreases, the edges of a V-neck can take on a concave, convex, or straight shape. A concave neckline, which opens more quickly at the base than at the top, is shaped by working the shorter decrease intervals first, followed by the longer intervals. A convex neckline, which opens more slowly at the base than at the top, is shaped by working the longer decrease intervals first, followed by the shorter intervals. A straight neckline, which opens at a constant rate from the base to the top, is shaped by alternating the decrease intervals.

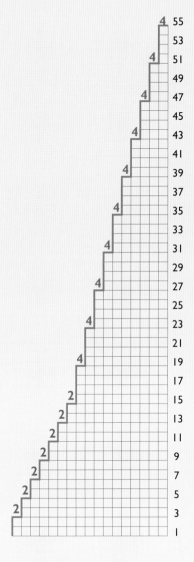

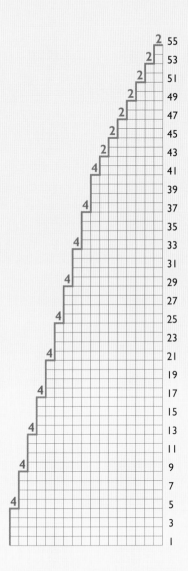

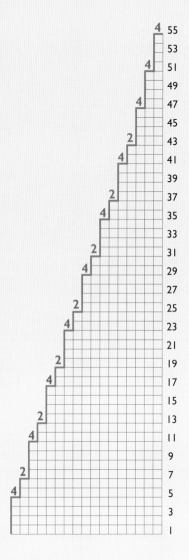

A concave taper is created if all of the decreases (red) worked at shorter intervals (2 rows) are worked first, followed by all of the decreases worked at longer intervals (4 rows).

A convex taper is created if all of the decreases (red) worked at longer intervals (4 rows) are worked first, followed by all of the decreases worked at shorter intervals (2 rows).

A straight taper is created when the two decrease intervals are as evenly spaced as possible from the bottom to the top.

chapter ten

Neckbands, Collars, and Lapels

This chapter provides design techniques that can bring variety to the classics and create looks that range from elegant to casual.

Round collar.

V-neck collar.

Square collar.

NECKBANDS AND COLLARS

A neckband or collar provides the finishing touch to a neckline. From decorative to utilitarian, this part of the sweater becomes the focal point closest to the face. Almost any neckband or collar can be worked from stitches picked up around the neckline or worked as a separate piece and sewn in place. The instructions below are for picking up stitches around the neckline. If you prefer to knit the neckband or collar separately, simply cast on the same number of stitches as would be picked up.

NECKBANDS

Neckbands are the simplest way to finish a neckline. Most neckbands are about 1" (2.5 cm) wide and are worked in a ribbed pattern. Be sure to work the neckband on a number of stitches that fits evenly into the pattern multiple.

Sew live stitches to the wrong side of the first row of the neckband.

Medium round neckband.

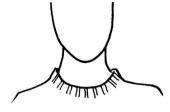

High round neckband.

Round Neckband

Pick up the appropriate number of stitches around the neck opening (see Notes at right) and work the band in the desired edging pattern. For a single-layer neckband, bind off the stitches in pattern, making sure to bind off loosely enough so that the bind-off edge does not pull in and prevent the head from passing through. For a double-layer neckband, work the band to twice the planned depth, then slip the stitches onto a length of yarn. Fold the neckband in half to the inside, baste it in place, then loosely stitch the live stitches to pick-up row, matching stitch for stitch, as shown in the box on page 224. Alternately, fold the neckband to the outside and use backstitches (see page 267) to sew the live stitches to the base of the band.

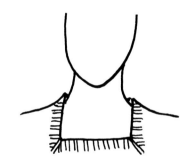

Square neckband with mitered corners.

Square Neckband

Pick up the appropriate number of stitches around the neck opening (see Notes), picking up an odd number of stitches in each vertical and horizontal section, including one "axis" stitch in each of the four corners. Working in the round and keeping in the rib pattern as established, miter the corners by working to two stitches before each axis stitch, working a k2tog decrease, knitting the axis stitch, then working a k2tog decrease after each axis stitch every other round. For tidy corners, bind off on a decrease row.

- To determine the number of stitches to pick up (or cast on, if you plan to knit the neckband separately and sew it in place), sew the shoulder seams, then lay the garment right side up on a flat surface. Turn a tape measure on its side and measure the inner circumference of the neck opening. Multiply this measurement by the appropriate stitch gauge to determine how many stitches to pick up. For an even distribution of picked-up stitches, place a marker at the center back neck and another at the center front, then pick up half of the total number of stitches in each half.

- To eliminate neckband seams, work neckbands in the round on short circular needles. If there are too many stitches to work comfortably on a 16" (40 cm) needle, use a 24" (60 cm) needle, keeping in mind that if the needle is too long, you'll risk distorting the neckline as the stitches are stretched to fit on the needle.

- Neckbands and collars are typically knitted in firm, reversible stitch patterns such as garter stitch, moss stitch, and ribbing.

- To avoid gapping or drooping necklines, very wide collars should be paired with narrower neck widths. To avoid choking, very tight collars should be paired with wider neck widths.

- Most collars can be widened by working increases or changing to larger needles; most can be narrowed by working decreases or changing to smaller needles.

- Large collars or those that involve a number of construction techniques are best knitted separately to eliminate having to handle the entire garment, plus the large collar, which is bulky and awkward.

- Collars that are sewn in place can add valuable structure and help prevent sagging necklines. Use small whipstitches (see page 266) for strong seams without unsightly seam allowances.

- Unless otherwise specified, neckbands and collars are worked after the shoulders have been seamed.

V-neckband with a mitered base.

Detail of mitered V.

MITERS

Miters are worked at "corners" where stitches that run vertically meet stitches that run horizontally and create a smooth diagonal line of stitches (typically worked in stockinette stitch) that transitions between the vertical and horizontal stitches. Areas that become smaller as they are filled in with fabric (such as square and V-neckbands) are called "decreasing" or "inner" miters; areas that become wider as more width is added (such as the outer edges of cardigan bands) are called "increasing" or "outer" miters.

To create a miter, decreases or increases are worked on each side of one (or more) corner or axis stitch. Different types of decreases and increases will give different looks. For example, a k2tog decrease can be worked on each side of the axis stitch, a ssk decrease (see page 326) can be worked on each side, or a k2tog decrease worked on one side and the ssk decrease worked on the other—experiment to see what you like best for each project.

V-neckband with an overlapping base.

Detail of overlapping V.

V-Neckband

For a mitered base, pick up the appropriate number of stitches around the neck opening (see Notes on page 225), picking up an even number of stitches on each side of one axis stitch at the base of the V. Working in the round and maintaining the rib pattern as established, miter the base by working a ssk decrease before the axis stitch, knitting the axis stitch, then working a k2tog decrease after the axis stitch every round. For a sharp point, bind off on a decrease row.

For an overlapping base, there is no shaping at the base of the V. Simply pick up the appropriate number of stitches around the neck opening (see Notes), beginning and ending at the base of the V. Work the neckband back and forth in rows as desired, then bind off in pattern. Overlap the edges at the base of the V and sew them in place with whipstitches (see page 266).

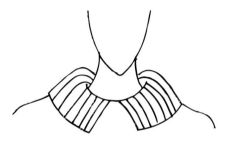

A straight collar folds over at the neckline.

STRAIGHT COLLAR

As the name implies, a straight collar is worked without increases or decreases. It is typically combined with round-neck shaping. The picked-up or cast-on edge of a straight collar should match the circumference of the neck opening. Collars that are very short, such as 1" to 2" (2.5 to 5 cm), for example, will stand up straight; longer collars will fold over and lay against the upper body. To add fullness and shaping to a fold-over length, change to a larger needle size every 1" to 2" (2.5 to 5 cm) along the way. The more width that's added, the more pointed the corners will become.

STRAIGHT-COLLAR VARIATIONS

A standard polo collar is about an inch longer than a straight collar so that it will lie flat on each side. An Eaton or pointed polo collar has more exaggerated points. To exaggerate the points, cast on 1½ to 2 times the number of stitches for the neck circumference and decrease at each edge (inside a selvedge stitch) every other row until the desired neck width is achieved, then bind off the stitches and attach the bind-off edge to the neck opening. Alternately, pick up the appropriate number of stitches around the neck opening (see Notes on page 225) and use the M1 method (see page 196) to increase 1 stitch inside each edge stitch every right-side row, working the increased stitches in the established pattern. If the collar is worked in ribbing, either add a garter-stitch selvedge (knit every row) at each edge or make certain that the edge stitches are knit stitches on right-side rows. The more increases you work, the more exaggerated the points will be.

A standard polo collar is about an inch longer than a straight collar.

An Eaton collar has exaggerated points.

 tip Straight and split collars can be worked horizontally (from neck edge to outer edge) or vertically (from one short edge to the other) and sewn in place.

Step 1: Pick Up Stitches

With the right side facing and beginning at the center front, pick up and knit the appropriate number of stitches around the neck opening (see Notes), ending where you began.

Step 2: Shape the Collar

Working back and forth in rows, work the desired stitch pattern to the desired length, changing to progressively larger needles every 1" to 2" (2.5 to 5 cm) to add fullness, if desired.

Step 3: Bind Off Stitches

Bind off the stitches in pattern.

SPLIT COLLAR

A split collar is similar to a straight collar but begins with a few rounds worked around the entire neck opening before the split is made, at which point the collar is worked back and forth in rows. Alternately, it can be worked separately and sewn to the neck opening with the split at the desired position. A split collar is typically combined with round neck shaping. As with a straight collar, it can be shaped by gradually increasing the needle size from the neck edge to the outer edge. For an asymmetrical look, the split can be offset on one side of the neck. To make the back of the collar stand higher, work extra short-rows at the back neck when working the initial rounds.

Step 1: Pick Up Stitches

With the right side facing and beginning where you want the split, pick up and knit the appropriate number of stitches around the neck opening (see Notes), ending where you began. Join for working in rounds.

Step 2: Shape the Collar

Work the desired stitch pattern for the desired number of rounds. Beginning at the desired position of the split, work back and forth in rows to the desired length, changing to progressively larger needles every 2" to 3" (5 to 7.5 cm) to add fullness, if desired. Work the edge stitches so that they appear as knit stitches on right-side rows.

Step 3: Bind Off Stitches

Bind off the stitches in pattern.

A split collar is a straight collar worked as a continuation of a neckband.

Place the split at the side for an asymmetrical look.

TURTLENECK COLLAR

A turtleneck is a long tube picked up and worked in rounds from a high round neckline. To ensure that the tube will fit over the head, the neck width should be 50% of the cross-back width. Turtlenecks are typically between 6" and 9" (15 and 23 cm) long, depending on the length of the wearer's neck. To provide extra width for the upper half to fold over the lower half, change to progressively larger needles every 3" (7.5 cm). Turtlenecks are typically worked in a ribbing or cable pattern. If using a pattern that has a right and wrong side, be sure to reverse the right and wrong sides (see the tip below) when the tube reaches the fold length so that the right side of the stitch pattern will be visible when the tube is folded down.

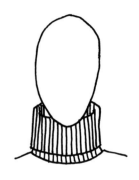

A turtleneck is a long tube worked on a high round neckline.

Step 1: Pick Up Stitches

With the right side facing and beginning at one shoulder seam, pick up and knit the appropriate number of stitches around the neck opening (see Notes on page 225), ending where you began. Join for working in rounds.

Step 2: Shape the Collar

Work the desired stitch pattern for the desired number of rounds, changing to progressively larger needles every 3" (7.5 cm) if desired to add fullness to the fold-over section, and reversing the right and wrong sides at the fold line so that the right side of the collar will show when it is folded over.

Step 3: Bind Off Stitches

Bind off the stitches in pattern.

 tip To change the stitch pattern from one face of the collar to the other (so the right side will show both above and below the fold), begin knitting in the opposite direction (work counterclockwise instead of clockwise). To do this, work the rounds at the "far" side of the circle so that the right side of the knitting is on the inside of the round.

 tip A turtleneck can be worked back and forth in rows and seamed at one shoulder. When sewing the seam, be sure to reverse the seam allowance at the fold so that the right side of the seam faces out when the turtleneck is folded down.

A mock turtleneck is a short turtleneck.

MOCK-TURTLENECK COLLAR

A mock turtleneck is simply a short turtleneck. Stitches are picked up from a high round neckline, then worked in rounds for 3" to 4" (7.5 to 10 cm). For a firmer band, a mock turtleneck can be worked to twice the desired length, then folded in half to the inside and sewn in place.

> *tip* For a more comfortable fit below the chin, shape the front of the neck over the last 1" (2.5 cm). Begin by binding off half of the center front stitches, then work back and forth in rows and bind off the remaining side front stitches in two steps (each including one-eighth of the front stitches), then bind off the remaining stitches for the back neck.

Step 1: Pick Up Stitches

With the right side facing and beginning at one shoulder seam, pick up and knit the appropriate number of stitches around the neck opening (see Notes on page 225), ending where you began. Join for working in rounds.

Step 2: Shape the Collar

Work the desired stitch pattern until the collar measures the desired length (or twice the desired length for a double thickness). Shape the front neck over the last 1" (2.5 cm) for a more tailored fit if working single thickness.

Step 3: Bind Off Stitches

For a single thickness, bind off the stitches in pattern. For a double thickness, fold the collar to the inside and use a whipstitch (see page 266) to sew the live stitches to the pick-up round.

COWL COLLAR

A cowl collar is loose and drapey.

A cowl collar is essentially a very long and wide turtleneck that forms loose, drapey folds. Like a turtleneck, a cowl is best worked in rounds and the right and wrong sides are reversed when the tube reaches the fold length so that the right side of the collar will show when it is folded over. A cowl collar can be paired with high, medium, or scooped round necklines and can be worked in any stitch pattern. A typical deep cowl worked on a scooped neckline should be 9" to 11" (23 to 28 cm) long to produce enough fabric to fold and drape nicely. If worked on a high or medium round neckline, however, the number of stitches should double between the neck and bind-off edges. To produce the appropriate drape on a high round neckline, pick up the appropriate number of stitches around the neckline, work in the round for about ¾" (2 cm), then increase to at least twice the number of picked-up stitches on the next round and work even for the desired length. For a wide tube with a fitted neck, increase to the desired width on the first row, then work even for the remaining length. For more tapered shaping, work the increases over a number of rows, following the method for working decreases for the circular skirt on page 159. For a removable cowl, knit a rectangle that measures 9" to 11" (23 to 28 cm) wide and 19" to 24" (48.5 to 61 cm) long and sew the short ends together. Alternately, knit the cowl in the round as a separate tube.

Step 1: Pick Up Stitches

With the right side facing and beginning at the left shoulder seam, pick up and knit the appropriate number of stitches around the neck opening (see Notes on page 225), ending where you began. Join for working in rounds.

Step 2: Shape the Collar

Work the desired stitch pattern for the desired number of rounds, increasing to double the number of stitches after about ¾" (2 cm), and reversing the right and wrong sides so that the right side of the collar will show when it is folded over.

Step 3: Bind Off Stitches

Bind off the stitches in pattern.

A Peter Pan collar has rounded edges and is typically worked in stockinette stitch and edged with ribbing or other non-curling border stitch.

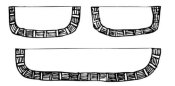

A Peter Pan collar can be worked in a single piece with the split at the center front, or in two pieces with splits at both the center front and center back.

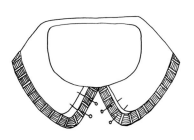

Sew the extra width of the border to the selvedge edges of the collar.

PETER PAN COLLAR

A Peter Pan collar is worked much the same as a straight collar (see page 227), but it is bordered with a noncurling stitch pattern, the edges are rounded, and the edges meet at the center front. This type of collar is typically paired with a high round neckline. Because of the close fit, there must be a placket opening at the front or back of the garment. This type of collar can be worked in a single piece that splits at the front or it can be worked in two pieces that split at both the front and back. There is no gap between the two sides at the split; instead, the edges butt together. A typical Peter Pan collar is worked in stockinette stitch with a short ribbed border to prevent curling. Most measure 1½" to 2½" (3.8 to 6.5 cm) long.

This type of collar can be either picked up from the edge of the neckline or knitted separately and sewn in place. If working from picked-up stitches, the first row is a wrong-side row of the garment and a right-side row of the collar so that the right side of the collar will be visible when it is folded back.

Step 1: Pick Up Stitches

With the right side facing and beginning at the width of the border to the left of the center front (as the piece faces you), pick up and knit the appropriate number of stitches around the neck opening (see Notes on page 225), ending at the width of the border to the right of the center front if working the collar in one piece, or ending at the center back if working the collar in two pieces. For example, for a 1" (2.5 cm) border, begin 1" (2.5 cm) to the left of the center front and end 1" (2.5 cm) to the right of the center front so that there is a 2" (5 cm) gap at the center front. This gap will be filled in by the borders.

Step 2: Shape the Collar

Work the desired stitch pattern back and forth in rows for the desired length, excluding the length of the edging. For example, for a collar that is 3" (7.5 cm) long with a 1" (2.5 cm) border, work for 2" (5 cm). Next, change to smaller needles and work a non-curling border pattern and cast on the appropriate number of stitches at each edge to equal the total desired collar length. For our example, cast on the number of stitches that will equal 3" (7.5 cm) at each edge. This additional length will be sewn to the center front edges on each side after the collar is bound off. The depth of the entire border will be equal to half the width of the gap at the center front, or 1" (2.5 cm) in our example.

Step 3: Bind Off Stitches

Bind off the stitches in pattern. Then sew the cast-on edge of the extra border stitches to the selvedge edges of the collar and sew the bind-off edges of the borders to the center front of the neck opening so that they touch.

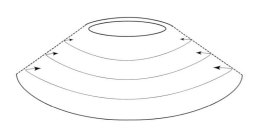

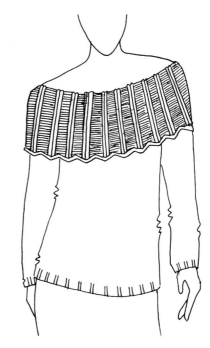

A large round-yoke collar is shaped with stacked interval increases or decreases.

A large round-yoke collar typically covers the shoulder circumference.

LARGE ROUND-YOKE COLLAR

A large round-yoke collar is typically paired with a high or medium round neckline and is most commonly worked in the round and shaped the same as the circular yoke of a pullover (see page 180). It can be picked up around the neckline or it can be worked separately and sewn in place. This type of collar can be from 4" to 8" (10 to 20.5 cm) long. The wide base circumference is based on the body width at the desired collar length. The collar can be shaped with increases from the narrow neck circumference to the wide base or it can be shaped with decreases from the wide base to the narrow neck. First, determine the number of rows in the length, then decide on the number of shaping rows and the number of stitches to increase or decrease, following the method outlined for the circular skirt on page 159. This type of collar can be worked in any stitch pattern.

Step 1: Cast On Stitches

Cast on (or pick up) the appropriate number of stitches (see Notes on page 225). Join for working in rounds.

Step 2: Shape the Collar

Work the desired stitch pattern for the desired number of rounds, using the stacked interval method (see page 159) to increase stitches if working from the narrower neck circumference to the wider outer edge, or to decrease stitches if working from the wider outer edge to the narrower neck circumference. Plan the shaping intervals to be spaced ½" to 1" (1.3 to 5 cm) apart and work longer intervals at the base and shorter intervals at the top if the intervals are not all the same length.

Step 3: Ending

Bind off the stitches in pattern.

LARGE ROUND COLLAR

A large round collar extends from the neck to the shoulders and is fastened at the front for a close fit at the neck, much the same as a Peter Pan collar (see page 232). This type of collar is paired with high round necklines and is typically worked separately on circular needles (to accommodate the large number of stitches at the outer edge), then sewn in place. Generally, a large round collar measures between about 45" and 55" (114.5 and 139.5 cm) around the outer edge (depending on the amount of drape), between about 18" and 20" (45.5 and 51 cm) around the neck edge, and between about 5" and 7" (12.5 and 18 cm) long. It is constructed by casting on stitches for the outer circumference, working the chosen border for the desired length, then working stacked decreases as described for a circular-yoke pullover (see page 180) to decrease to the neck circumference. The number and spacing of the stacked decreases will depend on the gauge, collar length, and number of stitches to decrease between the outer edge and neck circumference.

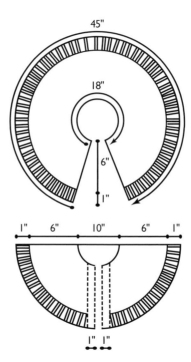

A large round collar covers most of the shoulder area.

Schematic of a typical large round collar that measures 18" (45.5 cm) at the neck edge, 45" (114.5 cm) at the outer edge, and 6" (15 cm) long with a 1" (2.5 cm) border.

Step 1: Cast On Stitches

Cast on the appropriate number of stitches for the wider outer edge, excluding the width that the border will add to each side, as for a Peter Pan collar (see page 232). The border will be worked along with the front bands.

Step 2: Shape the Collar

Work the desired stitch pattern for the desired number of rows, using the stacked interval method (see page 159) to decrease stitches to the desired neck circumference.

Step 3: Bind Off Stitches

Bind off the stitches in pattern.

HORIZONTAL SHAWL COLLAR

This type of shawl collar is paired with a square neckline. It is worked separately as a rectangle of fabric, typically in ribbing or garter stitch, then sewn in place. The short edges of the rectangle match the width of the base of the neck opening; the long edges match the neckline opening from the base of the center front, around the back neck, and back to the base of the center front. The two short ends overlap one another at the center front and the extra fabric along the back neck folds over to form a shawl. For optional shaping at the center back, work short-rows over the center 50% of the stitches.

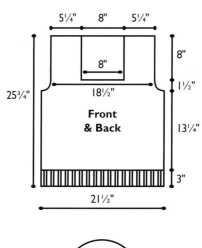

Schematic of a typical square-neck pullover and horizontal shawl collar.

A horizontal shawl collar is paired with a square neckline.

Step 1: Cast On Stitches

Cast on the appropriate number of stitches for the neck opening (see Notes on page 225), omitting the section at the base of the center front (the selvedge edges will overlap and fill in the center front).

Step 2: Shape the Collar

Work the desired stitch pattern until the length matches the width of the front neck, working short-rows across the back neck (see the Short-Rows box on page 236) to add extra fabric for a shawl, if desired.

Step 3: Bind Off Stitches and Finish

Bind off the stitches in pattern. Overlap the left front collar edge over the right front collar edge and sew both layers to the bind-off row at the base of the front neck.

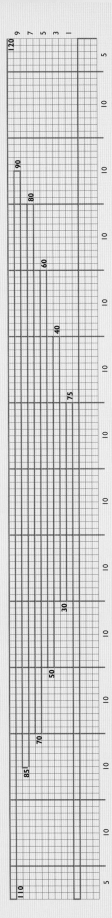

SHORT-ROWS

Short-rows are a technique used to add length (i.e., rows) to just part of a section of knitting. When working shawl collars, the center stitches (those that correspond to the back neck) are worked for more rows than the edge stitches (those that correspond to the front neck). For a smooth transition between the extra rows in the back, the short-rows include progressively more stitches each row until all of the stitches have been worked.

The back neck of a horizontal shawl collar is shaped by working short-rows across the back neck stitches, working progressively more stitches on each row (as shown in red) to add extra length to the back neck without adding length to the sides. This is done to provide more turn-back fabric in the center of the collar.

Timeless Burgundy, first published in the Fall 1997 issue of *Knitter's Magazine* and later in *Jackets: For Work and Play,* is an example of a jacket with a classic vertical shawl collar.
Photo: Alexis Xenakis

BANDS WORKED SEPARATELY

If the band and collar are worked at a different gauge than the garment body, they will have to be knitted separately and sewn in place. Subtract the width of the band from the number of stitches to cast on for each front and work the fronts to the shoulder, shaping the V as desired. Cast on and work the band stitches separately, adding a selvedge stitch for seaming the band to the body and calculating the V increases along the side of the band to match the body.

As the band is worked, baste or tack it to the front to ensure a snug fit without pulling or puckering. Work the buttonband side first, then mark the position of the buttons. Work the buttonhole side next, working buttonholes opposite the marked button locations. Work the neck shaping as necessary, then work even on the band stitches until the band's length from the shoulder measures one-half the center back neck width.

If the bottom border is worked in the same pattern stitch as the front bands, begin by casting on stitches for the border as well as the band. Work the border for the desired length, place the band stitches on a holder while the front is worked to the shoulder, then work the band stitches to the desired length and sew the edge of the band to the edge of the front.

CLASSIC VERTICAL SHAWL COLLAR

A classic vertical shawl collar is paired with cardigans with V-neck shaping. The fold-back shawl on this type of collar is created by working the center front without shaping from the bust to the top of the collar as the V shape is delineated by a change in the stitch pattern along the upper front. At the shoulders, the body stitches are bound off, then the collar stitches are worked even for the distance that corresponds to half of the back neck width. To finish, the left front and right front components are seamed together and the selvedge edge is sewn along the back neck.

This type of collar is typically knitted as a continuous part of each cardigan front. Therefore, the V shaping is calculated and charted on graph paper as usual, but instead of working decreases along the shaping lines, the stitches are switched to the collar stitch pattern along the shaping lines. The neckline V typically begins about ½" (1.3 cm) above the top buttonhole and ends about 1" (2.5 cm) below the shoulder.

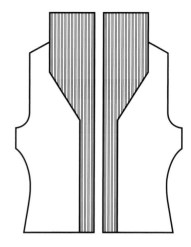

The center front edges of a classic vertical shawl collar are straight from the lower front edge to the top of the collar; the collar fills in the area of the fronts removed by V-neck shaping.

 tip   Instead of working decreases along the front neck edge, this edge is worked even while the portion of the front designated as collar is increased at the expense of the portion of the front designated as body.

Because this type of collar folds over to expose the wrong side of the fabric, it is best to use a reversible pattern such as ribbing or garter stitch or plan to convert (reverse) the pattern as the collar is knitted. The collar stitches are typically worked as the wrong side of the stitch pattern. For a shallow shawl collar that involves converting a stitch pattern, first plan the V-neck shaping. But instead of using the shaping schedule to decrease for the V, follow the schedule to convert the stitch pattern along the planned V lines. For example, if the V-neck shaping indicates that 3 stockinette stitches should be decreased, instead of decreasing those stitches, work them in reverse stockinette stitch. The number of reverse stockinette stitches (representing the collar) increases as the number of stockinette stitches (representing the front of the body) decreases along the line of the V.

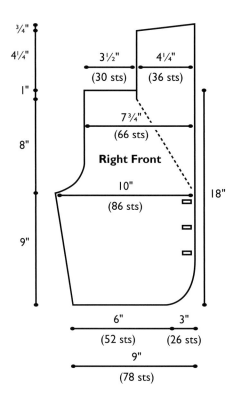

Schematic of a typical vertical shawl collar worked simultaneously with the cardigan front.

Step 1: Calculate Slope of V Shaping

Calculate the slope of the V shaping as described on page 222, reversing the shaping for the right and left front.

Step 2: Shape the Collar

Work the fronts, switching from the collar stitch pattern to the body stitch pattern along the shaping lines of the V. At the shoulders, bind off the shoulder stitches as usual, then continue working the collar stitches for the length that corresponds to half of the back neck width.

Step 3: Bind Off Stitches and Finish

Bind off the collar stitches and sew the left front collar to the right front collar (or use the Kitchener stitch to graft the two sets of stitches together). Sew the selvedge edge of the joined collar to the bind-off edge along the back neck.

WIDE VERTICAL SHAWL COLLAR

A wide vertical shawl collar is paired with cardigans or jackets with V-neck shaping. Increases are worked along the outside front edge to increase the width of the fold-back section by about 1¾" (4.5 cm) and increases are worked along the inside front edge to match the V-neckline shaping on the body. This type of collar is typically knitted separately and sewn in place. The dimensions are based on the length of the V-neckline of the garment body and the right and left halves are worked as mirror images of each other, just like the right and left fronts of the garment. The bind-off edge at the top of the collar is worked in several steps to provide more fabric at the center back of the collar for an unrestrained turn-back. Typically, the bind-offs are worked over between 1" and 2" (2.5 and 5 cm) of length, depending on the width of the collar, to prevent puckering or pulling when the collar is turned back.

Our example shawl collar is for a neck that is 8½" (21.5 cm) wide and 8¾" (22 cm) long. The V on the collar is shaped over 8" (20.5 cm) and has a maximum width of 6" (15 cm) with 1¾" (4.5 cm) of this width along the outside front edge and 4¼" (11 cm) along the inside front edge. The bind-off is worked over 1½" (3.8 cm) for a smooth turn-back edge.

A wide vertical shawl collar covers most of the shoulders.

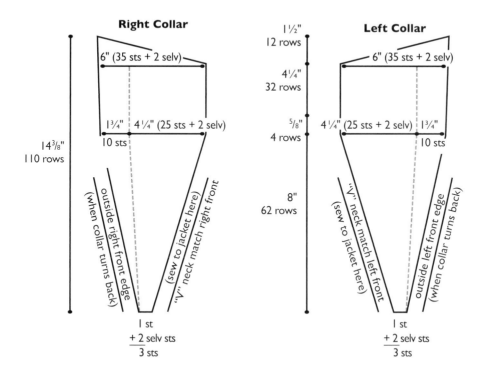

Schematic of the sample wide vertical shawl collar, annotated with numbers of stitches and rows.

KEY MEASUREMENTS

Neck width: 8½" (21.5 cm)
V-shaping depth: 8" (20.5 cm)
Work-even section at top of shaping:
⅝" (1.6 cm)
Half back neck width: (neck width ÷ 2)
4¼" (11 cm)
Neck depth: 8¾" (22 cm)
Maximum collar width: 6" (15 cm)
Increased width along outside front edge:
1¾" (4.5 cm)
Increased width along inside (V) front edge:
(same half back neck width)
4¼" (11 cm)

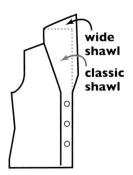

wide shawl

classic shawl

A wide vertical shawl collar is larger than a classic vertical shawl collar and includes shaping along the center front edge and at the back neck.

WIDTHS

Number of stitches at cast-on (1 collar stitch + 2 selvedge stitches)

1 collar stitch + 2 selvedge stitches = 3 stitches

Number of stitches at maximum width ([width × stitch gauge] + 2 selvedge stitches)

[6" (15 cm) × 5.71 stitches/inch] + 2 selvedge stitches = 36.26 stitches;
round up to odd number = 37 stitches

Number of stitches at maximum outside front edge (width × stitch gauge)

1¾" (4.5 cm) × 5.71 stitches/inch = 9.99 stitches;
round up to nearest number = 10 stitches

Number of stitches at maximum inside (V) front edge ([width × stitch gauge] + 2 selvedge stitches)

[4¼" (11 cm) × 5.71 stitches/inch] + 2 selvedge stitches = 26.26;
round up to nearest odd number = 27 stitches

LENGTHS

Number of rows in V shaping (length × row gauge)

8" (20.5 cm) × 7.63 rows/inch = 61.04 rows;
round up to nearest even number = 62 rows

Number of rows from top of V to shoulder (length × row gauge)

⅝" (1.6 cm) × 7.63 rows/inch = 4.76 rows;
round down to nearest even number = 4 rows

Number of rows in half back neck width (width × row gauge)

4¼" (11 cm) × 7.63 rows/inch = 32.4 rows;
round down to nearest even number = 32 rows

Number of rows in bind-off (length × row gauge)

1½" (3.8 cm) × 7.63 rows/inch = 11.44;
round up to nearest even number = 12 rows

Step 1: Cast On Stitches

Cast on 3 stitches (1 collar stitch and 2 selvedge stitches).

Step 2: Shape Collar

The inside front edge matches the slope of the V-neckline shaping on the garment front. The outside front edge increase 1¾" (4.5 cm) in width along the length of the V-neckline shaping. Therefore, the shaping is calculated separately for each side although they are worked simultaneously as the collar is knitted.

Section 1: Calculate Increases for Inside Front Edge
Along this edge, increase 24 stitches from 3 stitches at the base of the collar to 27 stitches at the widest point.

27 stitches at widest point – 3 initial stitches = 24 stitches to increase

Increase these 24 stitches evenly spaced over the 8" (20.5 cm) length of the V shaping, or 62 rows. The increases are all worked on right-side rows, so only 31 of these 62 rows are available for shaping. Using the shaping formula, divide the 31 available rows by 24 increases to determine how to space the increases evenly. The formula tells us to increase every right-side (i.e., every 2nd) row 17 times and every 2nd right-side (i.e., every 4th) row 7 times. For truly even increases, alternate the two intervals.

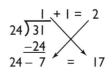

Use the shaping formula to determine an even distribution of increases on the inside front edge. In this example, increase every right-side (every 2nd) row 17 times and every 2nd right-side (every 4th) row 7 times.

Right Collar

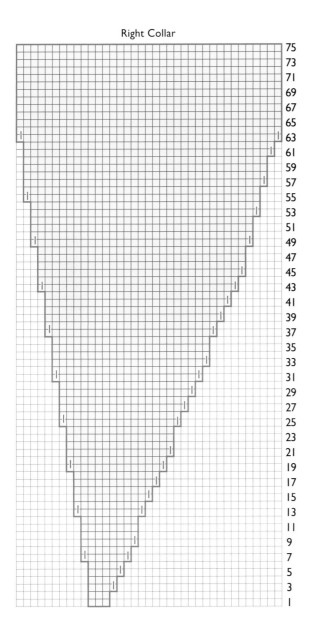

Plot of the right collar. Bind-off stitches are shown in red; row numbers are shown in black.

Left Collar

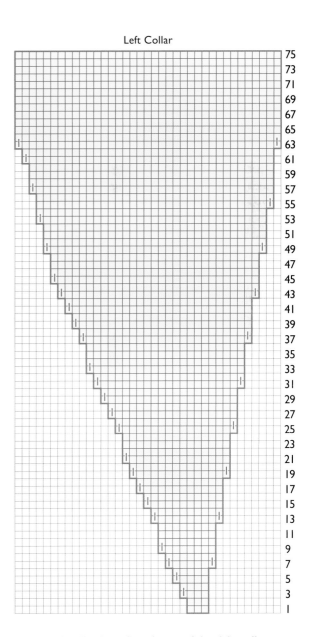

The left collar is a mirror image of the right collar.

For our sample collar, increase 1 stitch inside the selvedge stitch at the inside edge beginning on the 3rd row, then every following 2nd row 3 times, then on the 4th row 1 time, then [every 2nd row 4 times, then every 4th row 1 time] 3 times, then every 4th row 3 times, then every 2nd row 1 time—24 stitches increased over 62 rows. Then work 4 rows even to reach the shoulder.

Section 2: Calculate Increases for Outside Front Edge
Along this edge, increase 10 stitches evenly spaced over the 62 rows of the V shaping. Again, only right-side rows are available for shaping. Using the shaping formula, divide the 31 available rows by 10 increases to determine how to space the increases evenly. The formula tells us to increase every 3rd right-side (i.e., every 6th) row 9 times and every 4th right-side (i.e., every 8th) row 1 time. Begin shaping for this side on the 7th row so that the outside edge increases are worked on the same rows that increases are worked on the inside edge. Plot the shaping on graph paper (see page 241) to see the relationship between the two sides.

For our sample collar, increase 1 stitch at the outside edge every 6th row 9 times, then every 8th row 1 time—37 stitches after increases at both inner and outer edges are complete. Then work 4 rows even to reach the shoulder, then 32 more rows to reach the back neck.

Step 3: Back Neck and Bind-Off

In this step, work the remaining stitches even through row 97 on the left collar and row 98 on the right collar to reach the center back neck. Then, beginning with row 98 on the left collar and row 99 on the right collar, bind off the stitches in a series of steps to add fullness to the outer edge of the back neck. In our example, bind off the stitches over 1½" (3.8 cm), or 12 rows. Because bind-offs can only be worked at the beginning of rows, only 6 of these 12 rows will be available for shaping on each collar. Using the shaping formula, divide the 37 stitches by 6 available shaping rows to determine how to space the increases evenly. The formula tells us to bind off 6 stitches 5 times and 7 stitches 1 time.

For our sample collar, work even on 37 stitches for 36 rows until the top of the collar reaches the center of the back neck. Then use the sloped method (see page 77) to bind off 6 stitches at the inside edge 5 times, then bind off the remaining 7 stitches.

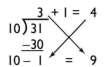

Use the shaping formula to determine an even distribution of increases on the outside front edge. In this example, increase 1 stitch every 3rd right-side (every 6th) row 9 times, then every 4th right-side (every 8th) row 1 time.

Use the shaping formula to determine an even distribution of bind-offs. In this example, bind off 6 stitches 5 times, then 7 stitches 1 time.

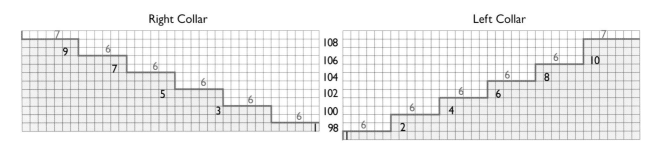

Plot of the sloped bind-offs at the top of the collar. Bind-off stitches are shown in red; row numbers are shown in black.

SHAWL COLLAR WORKED HORIZONTALLY

When worked horizontally, a shawl collar can be worked separately and sewn in place. The collar measurements are based on the neck shaping of the garment fronts and back. The collar begins with stitches cast on to represent the back neck width of the outside collar edge (the edge farthest from the neck). Additional stitches are cast on at each end of the needle in a series of steps until the total length represents the circumference of the neck opening, then the stitches are bound off in a series of steps to end with the back neck width of the inside neck edge (the edge closest to the neck).

Our example horizontal shawl collar is to fit a back neck that measures 7¼" (18.5 cm) wide and 9" (23 cm) deep. The collar measures 25¼" (64 cm) from the base of the right front neck shaping to the right shoulder, across the back neck to the left shoulder, and down to the base of the left front neck shaping. The outer edge (the part that folds over) is worked first, followed by the inner edge (the edge that will be sewn to the garment). The collar measures ½" (1.3 cm) at the ends that correspond to the base of the V at the center front and 7" (18 cm) at the center back, 3¼" (8.5 cm) of which will fold over.

The Diamonds are Forever Mosaic Coat, first published in the Holiday 2003 issue of *Vogue Knitting*, is an example of a shawl collar worked horizontally.

Photo: Paul Amato

Knitting View

Vertical View

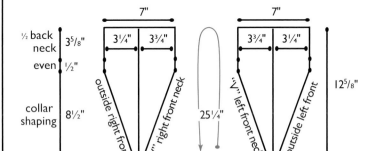

Schematic of the sample shawl collar worked horizontally.

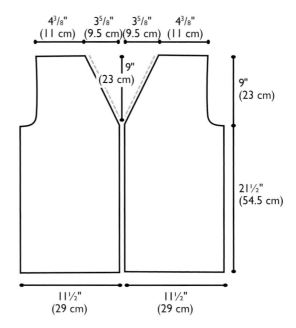

GAUGE

2.4 stitches and 3.6 rows = 1" (2.5 cm)

KEY MEASUREMENTS

Back neck width: 7¼" (18.5 cm)

Front V-neck depth: 9" (23 cm)

Collar width: 7" (18 cm)

Total collar length: (left neck depth + neck width + right neck depth)
9" (23 cm) + 7¼" (18.5 cm) + 9" (23 cm) = 25¼" (64 cm)

Collar length from initial cast-on to maximum width: 3¼" (8.5 cm)

Work-even section between collar shaping sections: ½" (1.3 cm)

Collar length from maximum width to final bind-off: 3¼" (8.5 cm)

Schematic of a typical cardigan body with V-neckline shaping.

Conversion of Measurements to Numbers of Stitches and Rows

WIDTHS

Number of stitches at cast-on ([work-even section of right front + back neck width + work-even section of left front] × stitch gauge)

> [½" (1.3 cm) + 7¼" (18.5 cm) + ½" (1.3 cm)] × 2.4 stitches/inch = 19.8 stitches; round up to nearest whole number = 20 stitches

Number of stitches along V-neck edge (neck depth × stitch gauge)
> 8½" (21.5 cm) × 2.4 stitches/inch = 20.4 stitches; round down to nearest whole number = 20 stitches

Number of stitches along maximum width (total collar length × stitch gauge)
> 25¼" (64 cm) × 2.4 stitches/inch = 60.6 stitches; round up to nearest odd number = 61 stitches

Number of stitches increased/decreased at each side ([maximum stitches – cast-on stitches] ÷ 2)

> [61 maximum stitches – 20 cast-on stitches] ÷ 2 = 20.5 stitches; we can't increase or decrease partial stitches, so we'll call this 20 stitches and add the extra stitch to the cast-on (i.e., cast on 21 stitches instead of 20)

LENGTHS

Number of rows from initial cast-on to maximum collar width (width × row gauge)
> 3¼" (8.5 cm) × 3.6 rows/inch = 11.7 rows; include initial cast-on row and return row before first side cast-on = 12 rows

Number of work-even rows in maximum collar width (width × row gauge)
> ½" (1.3 cm) × 3.6 rows/inch = 1.8 rows; round up to nearest even number = 2 rows

Number of rows from end of work-even section to final bind-off (width × row gauge)

3¼" (8.5 cm) × 3.6 rows/inch = 11.7 rows; round up to whole number = 12 rows

Number of total rows in collar (total width × row gauge)

7" (18 cm) × 3.6 rows/inch = 25.2 rows; round up to nearest even number = 26 rows

 tip | For simplicity, plot the right front neck shaping vertically on graph paper, then turn the graph on its side and add the left front neck shaping as a mirror image of the right front shaping.

Step 1: Cast On Stitches

To begin, cast on the number of stitches equal to the sum of the back neck width and the work-even sections above the V shaping of each front. For our example, the back neck measures 7¼" (18.5 cm) and each work-even section measures ½" (1.3 cm) for a total of 8¼" (21 cm).

For our sample collar, cast on 21 stitches.

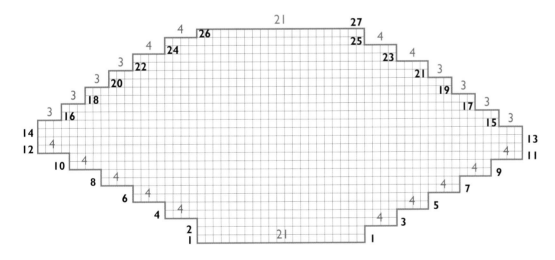

Plot of the horizontal shawl. Cast-on and bind-off stitches are shown in red; row numbers are shown in black.

Step 2: Shape Collar

This type of collar is shaped in two sections. In the first section, stitches are cast on at each side to the desired maximum width. In the second section, stitches are bound off at each side to end up with the same number of stitches that were cast on initially.

$$5 \overline{)20}^{\,4}$$

Use the shaping formula to determine an even distribution of cast-on stitches. In this example, cast on 4 stitches at each edge 5 times.

Section 1: Cast On in Increments to Maximum Width

Begin by working the return (wrong-side) row of the initial 21 cast-on stitches, then cast on a total of 20 additional stitches at each side over the next 10 rows. Because the cast-ons are worked at the beginning of rows, only 5 of these 10 rows are available for cast-ons. Using the shaping formula, divide the 20 stitches to be cast on at each side by 5 available rows to determine an even distribution of cast-ons. The formula tells us to cast on 4 stitches at each side 5 times.

For our sample collar, cast on 4 stitches at the beginning of the next 10 rows—20 stitches cast on at each edge over 10 rows; 61 stitches total. Then work 2 rows even to bring us to a total of 14 rows.

Section 2: Bind off in Increments to Initial Cast-On Width

In this section, bind off 20 stitches at each side over 12 rows. Like cast-ons, bind-offs are worked at the beginning of rows, so only 6 of these 12 rows are available for bind-offs. Using the shaping formula, divide the 20 stitches to be bound off on each side by 6 available rows to determine an even distribution of the bind-offs. The formula tells us to bind off 3 stitches 4 times and 4 stitches 2 times.

For our sample collar, bind off 3 stitches at the beginning of the next 8 rows, then bind off 4 stitches at the beginning of the next 4 rows—20 stitches bound off at each side over 12 rows; 21 stitches remain.

Step 3: Bind Off Stitches and Finishing

Bind off the remaining 21 stitches. Sew the edge of the collar that includes the final bind-off row to the neck edge of the garment, matching the final bind-off stitches with the back neck.

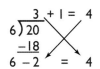

Use the shaping formula to determine an even distribution of bind-offs. In this example, bind off 3 stitches 4 times and bind off 4 stitches 2 times.

HORIZONTAL SHAWL COLLAR WITH BUTTONBANDS

It's a simple matter to add buttonbands (one for buttons and the other for buttonholes) to a shawl collar worked horizontally. In this case, the right and left halves of the collar are worked end to end in a single piece that includes buttonholes on the right body half and buttons on the left body half. As with other types of shawl collars, the measurements are based on the neck shaping on the garment fronts and back. This type of collar begins with stitches cast on to represent the combined length of the left front, back neck, and right front edges. Stitches are bound off when the bands reach the desired width, and then the shawl portion is shaped over the remaining center stitches.

Our example horizontal shawl collar with buttonbands is worked for a neck that measures 7" (18 cm) wide with a V-neck 7" (18 cm) deep. The fronts measure 11" (28 cm) to the base of the V-neck shaping and the shaping ends 1" (2.5 cm) before the shoulder. The collar measures 5½" (14 cm) high at the maximum length at the back neck.

The Flame Stitch cardigan, first published in the Spring/Summer 2005 issue of *Vogue Knitting*, is an example of a horizontal shawl collar with buttonbands.

Photo: Marco Zambelli

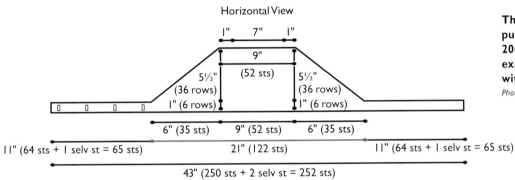

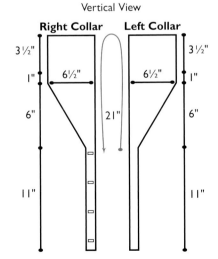

Schematic of the sample horizontal shawl collar with buttonbands as it is constructed both horizontally and vertically.

5.79 stitches and 6.66 rows = 1" (2.5 cm), averaged (see page 69)

KEY MEASUREMENTS

Neck width: 7" (18 cm)

Neck depth: 7" (18 cm)

Length of V shaping: 6" (15 cm)

Length of work-even portion of neckline: 1" (2.5 cm)

Buttonband width: 1" (2.5 cm)

Buttonband length: 11" (28 cm)

Collar length above bands: 5½" (14 cm)

Width of final bind-off: (right neck work-even length + back neck width + left neck work-even length) 1" (2.5 cm) + 7" (18 cm) + 1" (2.5 cm) = 9" (23 cm)

Width of horizontal collar shaping: (right collar shaping length + final bind-off width + left collar shaping length) 6" (15 cm) + 9" (23 cm) + 6" (15 cm) = 21" (53.5 cm)

Total width of bands plus collar: (right band length + right side neck length + back neck width + left side neck length + left band length) 11" (28 cm) + 7" (18 cm) + 7" (18 cm) + 7" (18 cm) + 11" (28 cm) = 43" (109 cm)

Conversion of Measurements to Numbers of Stitches and Rows

WIDTHS

Number of stitches to cast on ([total length × stitch gauge] + 2 selvedge stitches)
[43" × 5.79 stitches/inch] + 2 selvedge stitches = 250.97 stitches; round up to next even number = 252 stitches

Number of stitches in band ([length × stitch gauge] + 1 selvedge stitch)
[11" (28 cm) × 5.79 stitches/inch] + 1 selvedge stitch = 64.69 stitches; round up to nearest number = 65 stitches

Number of stitches in horizontal collar shaping (width × stitch gauge)
21" (53.5 cm) × 5.79 stitches/inch = 121.59 stitches; round up to nearest even number = 122 stitches

Number of stitches along each V shaping (length × stitch gauge)
6" (18 cm) × 5.79 stitches/inch = 34.74 stitches; round up to nearest odd number = 35 stitches

Number of stitches along bind-off edge (width × stitch gauge)
9" (23 cm) × 5.79 stitches/inch = 52.11 stitches; round down to nearest even number = 52 stitches

LENGTHS

Number of rows in bands (length × row gauge)
1" (2.5 cm) × 6.66 rows/inch = 6.66 rows; round down to nearest even number = 6 rows

Number of rows in collar shaping (length × row gauge)
5½" (14 cm) × 6.66 rows/inch = 36.63 rows; round down to nearest even number = 36 rows

Schematic of a typical cardigan body with V-neck shaping.

Step 1: Cast On Stitches

To begin, cast on for the entire length from the base of the right front, around the back neck and down to the base of the left front.

For our sample collar, cast on 252 stitches (62 repeats of the 4-stitch pattern + 2 balancing stitches + 2 selvedge stitches).

Step 2: Shape the Collar

The shaping is worked in two sections. In the first section, work for the desired band length, then bind off the band stitches, leaving just the collar stitches. In the second section, shape the collar by working evenly spaced decreases over the desired length, then bind off all of the remaining stitches.

Section 1: Buttonbands

For our example, the bands are worked over 6 rows. To conceal the buttonholes in the ribbing pattern, work four evenly spaced 3-row buttonholes (see page 272) on the 4th, 5th, and 6th rows. There are 64 stitches between the selvedge and neckline. Work the first buttonhole on the 3rd stitch in from the selvedge, leaving 61 stitches. The last stitch won't be included in the buttonholes, so work the remaining 3 buttonholes over the remaining 60 stitches, or at 20-stitch intervals: on the 3rd, 23rd, 43rd, and 63rd stitches from the selvedge.

Begin by working 3 rows in k2, p2 ribbing, beginning and ending each row with a selvedge stitch that is knitted every row. Then work the four 3-row buttonholes on the next 3 rows as described on page 272. On the next row, bind off the first 65 stitches in pattern for the left buttonband, work in rib as established across 122 stitches for the collar, then bind off the remaining 65 stitches for the right buttonband—122 collar stitches remain.

Section 2: Shape Shawl Collar

Rejoin yarn to the remaining 122 stitches and bind off 70 stitches to achieve the 52 stitches desired in the final bind off. For symmetrical shaping, bind off 35 stitches at each side

> 122 initial collar stitches – 52 final bind-off stitches = 70 stitches to bind off; 35 stitches at each side

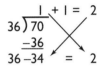

Use the shaping formula to determine an even distribution of bind-offs. In this example, bind off 1 stitch at the beginning of every row 2 times, then bind off 2 stitches at the beginning of every row 34 times.

We have 36 rows over which to work these bind-offs. Using the shaping formula, divide the 70 bind-offs by the 36 available rows to determine how to space the bind-offs evenly. The formula tells us to bind off 1 stitch at the beginning of every row 2 times and 2 stitches at the beginning of every row 34 times.

For our sample collar, bind off 1 stitch at the beginning of the next 2 rows, then bind off 2 stitches at the beginning of the next 34 rows—52 stitches remain.

Step 3: Bind Off Stitches and Finish

Bind off all stitches in pattern. Sew the bands and collar to the garment, beginning at the lower right front and ending at the lower left front and aligning the collar section with the V shaping.

LAPELS

Lapels impart a fine tailored look to a jacket. When associated with woven fabric, lapels tend to create sharp lines and crisp points. A softer version of these lines and points is produced with knitted fabric. From soft unshaped points that fold over at the neck of a casual pullover to highly structured extensions of collars on tailored jackets, lapels can be added to most types of garments.

CLASSIC LAPEL

A classic lapel is nothing more than a wide shawl collar without the shoulder-to-back neck section. When worked simultaneously with the garment fronts, lapels are created by converting to the collar pattern along the V shaping, much the same as the classic vertical shawl collar described on page 237. Lapels can also be knitted separately and sewn in place. Just as with a shawl collar, the lapel can be made wider at the outer edge for a more pronounced shaping.

The Bee Stitch Cardigan, first published in the Winter 2006/2007 issue of *Vogue Knitting*, is an example of a jacket with classic fold-back lapels.

Photo: Rose Callahan

 tip Plan for the back neck width to be close to the actual back neck measurement to support the low opening on the front and to help maintain crisp lines along the fold.

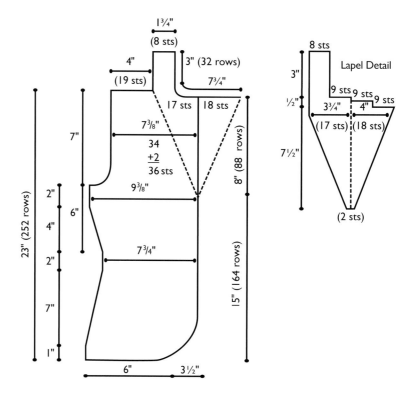

Schematic of the sample right front with classic fold-back lapels that are worked simultaneously with the body.

tip Our example lapels are for a jacket with a V-neck that measures 8" (20.5 cm) long. The lapels are worked simultaneously with the body and begin 1" (2.5 cm) below armhole in the work-even section of the bust. The fronts are worked even for ¼" (6 mm) after the center lapel bind-off.

Conversion of Measurements to Numbers of Stitches and Rows

WIDTHS

Number of stitches in bust width ([width × stitch gauge] + 2 selvedge stitches)

[9³/₈" (23.8 cm) × 4.6 stitches/inch] + 2 selvedge stitches = 45.125 stitches;

round down to nearest whole number = 45 stitches

Number of stitches in one-half cross-back width ([width × stitch gauge] + 2 selvedge stitches)

[7³/₈" (18.75 cm) × 4.6 stitches/inch] + 2 selvedge stitches = 35.9;

round up to nearest even number = 36 stitches

Number of stitches in shoulder ([width × stitch gauge] + 1 selvedge stitch)

[4" (10 cm) × 4.6 stitches/inch] + 1 selvedge stitch = 19.4 stitches;

round down to nearest whole number = 19 stitches

Number of stitches in outer lapel (width × stitch gauge)

4" (10 cm) × 4.6 stitches/inch = 18.4 stitches;

round down to nearest even number = 18 stitches

Number of stitches in V-neck (stitches in one-half cross-back − stitches in shoulder)

36 one-half cross-back stitches − 19 shoulder stitches = 17 stitches

Total number of stitches in lapel (stitches in outer lapel + stitches in V-neck)

18 outer lapel stitches + 17 inner lapel stitches = 35 stitches

Number of stitches in back collar (width × stitch gauge)

1¾" (4.5 cm) × 4.6 stitches/inch = 8.05 stitches;

round down to nearest number = 8 stitches

(2 selvedge stitches will be added to the back collar later)

Number of stitches in lapel bind-off (total lapel stitches − back collar stitches)

35 lapel stitches − 8 stitches = 27 stitches

LENGTHS

Number of rows in back collar (length × row gauge)

3" (7.5 cm) × 10.93 rows/inch = 32.79 rows;

round down to nearest even number = 32 rows

Number of rows in lapel (length × row gauge)

8" (20.5 cm) × 10.93 rows/inch = 87.44 rows;

round up to nearest even number = 88 rows

Number of rows in lapel set-up: 2 rows

Number of rows worked even after center lapel bind-off: (length × row gauge)

¼" (6 mm) × 10.93 rows/inch = 2.73 rows; round down to even number = 2 rows

Number of rows in center lapel bind-off (length × row gauge)

½" (1.3 cm) × 10.93 rows/inch = 5.46 rows; round up to nearest even number = 6 rows

Number of rows in lapel shaping (rows in lapel − bind-off rows − work-even rows at top − initial set-up rows)

88 total rows − 6 bind-off rows − 2 work-even rows at top − 2 rows in

initial set-up = 78 rows

GAUGE

Lapel: 4.6 stitches and 10.93 rows = 1" (2.5 cm)

KEY MEASUREMENTS

Bust width: 9³/₈" (23.8 cm)

One-half cross-back width: 7³/₈" (18.75 cm)

Shoulder width: 4" (10 cm)

V-neck shaping width: 3¾" (9.5 cm)

Inner lapel width: 3¾" (9.5 cm)

Outer lapel width: 4" (10 cm)

Width of back collar: 1¾" (4.5 cm)

Length of lapel: 8" (20.5 cm)

Length of work-even section after center lapel bind-off: ¼" (6 mm)

Length of back collar band: 3" (7.5 cm)

Length of center lapel bind-off: ½" (1.3 cm)

Step 1: Designate Stitches for Inner Lapel (V-neck shaping) and Outer Lapel

Designate the 2 center front stitches as the base of the lapel—1 stitch for the inner lapel (V-neck shaping) and 1 stitch for the outer lapel.

For our sample lapel, work this right-side row by working the 2 center front stitches in the lapel pattern instead of the body pattern. Then work 1 wrong-side row even—2 rows worked; 2 lapel stitches.

Step 2: Calculate Lapel Increases

The inner lapel matches the slope of the V-neckline shaping on the garment front as body stitches are converted to lapel stitches. The outer lapel increases 4" (10 cm) in width as stitches are increased along the length of the V-neckline shaping. Therefore, the shaping is calculated separately for each side although they will be worked simultaneously as the jacket front is knitted. Note that in this example, the armhole is shaped along the armhole edge at the same time as the lapels are shaped.

Section 1: Calculate Stitch Conversion for Inner Lapel (V-Neckline Shaping)
Along this edge, convert 16 body stitches into lapel stitches, from 1 inner lapel stitch at the base of the V to 17 inner lapel stitches at the shoulder.

17 inner lapel stitches at shoulder − 1 inner lapel stitch at base = 16 stitches to increase

We want to work these increases evenly spaced over 78 shaping rows. If we work all the increases on right-side rows, only 39 of these 78 rows will be available for inner lapel shaping. Using the shaping formula, divide the 39 available rows by 16 increases to determine how to space the increases evenly. The formula tells us to increase every 2nd right-side (i.e., every 4th) row 9 times and every 3rd right-side (i.e., every 6th) row 7 times. For truly even increases, alternate the two intervals.

For our sample lapel, increase 1 stitch at the inside edge (i.e., covert a body stitch to a collar stitch) [every 4th row, then every 6th row] 7 times, then every following 4th row 2 times—16 stitches converted over 78 rows. Then work even to the total length of the V-neckline, or until a total of 88 rows have been worked.

Section 2: Calculate Increases for Outer Lapel
Along the center front, or outer lapel edge, increase 17 stitches evenly spaced over the 78 shaping rows. Again, only 39 of these rows are available for increases. Using the shaping formula, divide the 39 available rows by 17 increases to determine how to space the increases evenly. The formula tells us to increase every 4th row 12 times and every 6th row 5 times. To make it easiest to keep track of the shaping intervals along the inner and outer lapel edges, distribute the outer lapel increases to coincide as much as possible with the inner lapel stitch conversions.

Use the shaping formula to determine an even distribution of converted stitches. In this example, convert 1 stitch every 2nd right-side (every 4th) row 9 times and 1 stitch every 3rd right-side (every 6th) row 7 times.

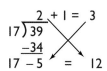

Use the shaping formula to determine an even distribution of increases. In this example, increase 1 stitch every 2nd right-side (every 4th) row 12 times and every 3rd right-side (every 6th) row 5 times.

For our sample lapel, at the same time as stitches are being converted to lapel stitches along the inner edge, increase 1 stitch at the outer edge [every 4th row, then every 6th row] 5 times, then increase 1 stitch every 4th row 7 times—17 outer lapel stitches increased over 78 rows; 35 lapel stitches total after all lapel stitches are converted or increased.

Section 3: Shape Upper Lapel and Back Collar

Shape the top of the lapel by using the sloped method (see page 77) to bind off 27 lapel stitches, beginning at the outer lapel edge, over ½" (1.3 cm), or 6 rows. Because bind-offs can only be worked at the beginning of rows, only 3 of these 6 rows will be available for shaping. Using the shaping formula, divide the 27 stitches to be bound off by 3 available bind-off rows. The formula tells us to bind off 9 stitches at the beginning of each of the 3 shaping rows—8 lapel stitches remain. Bind off the 19 shoulder stitches, then cast on 1 stitch on each side of the 8 remaining lapel stitches for selvedge stitches—10 lapel stitches. Work even on these remaining stitches for the length equal to half of the neck width.

For our sample lapel, use the sloped method to bind off 9 stitches at the outer lapel edge 3 times—8 stitches remain for back collar. Cast on 1 stitch at each edge for selvedge stitches, then work even on these 10 neckband stitches for 3" (7.5 cm), or 32 rows. Bind-off all stitches.

Step 3: Bind Off Stitches and Finish

Work the second lapel the same way, reversing all shaping. Sew the bind-off edges of the back collars together, then sew the selvedge edge of the collar to the back neck of the body.

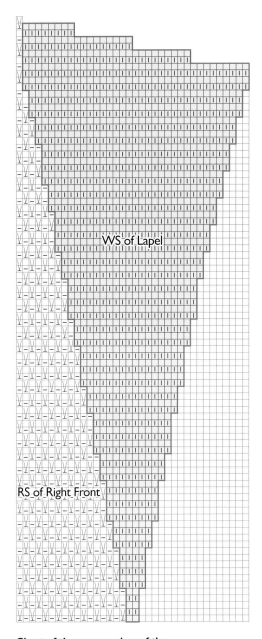

$$3 \overline{)\,27}^{\,9}$$

Use the shaping formula to determine an even distribution of bind-offs. In this example, bind off 9 stitches 3 times.

WS of Lapel

RS of Right Front

Chart of the reverse view of the right front lapel.

NOTCHED LAPEL

This type of lapel is similar to the classic lapel described on page 250, but it is worked independently and includes a separate collar that is sewn to the top of the lapels and across the back neck to create the classic notched look. The collar replaces the neckband on the classic lapel and functions as both the collar and the upper part of the lapel.

As with the separate shawl collar described on page 243, this lapel-and-collar combination involves matching the lapel length and width to the shape of the V-neck. It also involves planning the width of the collar to fit along ½" (1.3 cm) at the top of each side of the V-neck, then across the back neck.

Both edges of the lapel are shaped—the inner edge matches the V-neck shaping; the outer edge widens slightly to provide extra width when the lapel is turned back. When the lapel is knitted to the planned length, all but 1¼" (3.2 cm) of the stitches are bound off. The remaining stitches are shaped into a narrow wedge that fills in the gap between the top of the V-neck and the base of the collar. The wedge is shaped for about 1" (2.5 cm) with decreases on the side that will attach to the collar and increases on the side that will attach to the V-neck. Decreases then continue along the collar side while the side that will attach to the V-neck is worked even for about 1½" (3.8 cm). During this time, the wedge is decreased to 2 stitches, which will be used to seam one side of the wedge to the neckline and the other side to the collar. The collar is sewn to the ½" (1.3 cm) of neckline at each side between the lapel and the shoulder and across the back neck.

The collar is worked separately, and each edge is shaped with increases to match the decreases worked on the lapel wedge. The collar and lapel are sewn together along the wedge to create the characteristic notch, which typically falls about 3" (7.5 cm) below the shoulder seam. Begin by deciding on the width of the lapel to determine the number of stitches to increase at the outer edge and the number of stitches in the turn-back portion of the lapel, which, in turn, will determine the number of stitches to bind off at the top of the lapel before the wedge is shaped.

The Gray Time Dressing, first published in the Fall 1999 issue of *Knitter's Magazine,* is an example of a jacket with notched lapels.
Photo: Alexis Xenakis

The wrong side of the collar and lapel correspond to the right side of the garment.

In our example, the notched lapels are worked separately and seamed to the neckline of a jacket with a V-neck shaping that measures 10" (25.5 cm) long. The lapel is shaped on both the inner and outer edges. On the inner edge (the part attached to the neckline), 3¾" (9.5 cm) of width is added over 8" (20.5) of length. On the outer edge (the turn-back part), 1" (2.5 cm) of width is added over 7" (18 cm) of length. The turn-back bind-off row is worked 2½" (6.5 cm) below the end of the lapel. The lapels fit along 9½" (24 cm) of the total 10" (25.5 cm) V length. The edge of the collar fits along the remaining ½" (1.3 cm), and the wedge at the top of the lapel is shaped over 2½" (6.5 cm). The collar is 5" (12.5 cm) deep. The bottom 2½" (6.5 cm) is shaped with increases to match the decreases along the side wedge of the lapel.

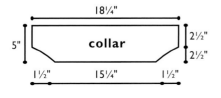

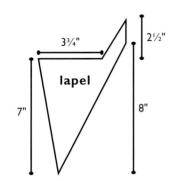

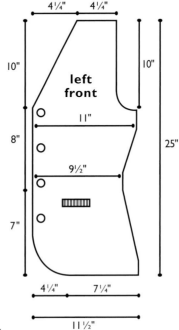

Schematic of the sample jacket front, collar, and lapel.

Conversion of Measurements to Number of Stitches and Rows

LAPEL WIDTHS

Number of stitches in lapel cast-on (1 lapel stitch at center + 1 selvedge stitch at each side)
Note: All increases will be made inside the selvedge stitches on each side

    1 lapel stitch + 2 selvedge stitches = 3 stitches

Number of stitches increased along outer lapel shaping (width × stitch gauge)

    1" (2.5 cm) × 5.25 stitches/inch = 5.25 stitches;

        round down to nearest whole number = 5 stitches

Number of stitches increased along inner lapel shaping (width × stitch gauge)

    3¾" (9.5 cm) × 5.25 stitches/inch = 19.68 stitches;

        round up to nearest even number = 20 stitches

Number of stitches at top of inner lapel shaping (cast-on stitches + increased stitches)

    3 cast-on stitches (1 center stitch + 2 selvedge stitches) + 20 increased stitches

    = 23 stitches

Number of stitches in lapel top bind-off (width × stitch gauge)

3½" (9 cm) × 5.25 stitches/inch = 18.37 stitches;
round down to even number so that we can decrease to 2 stitches = 18 stitches
(17 lapel stitches + 1 selvedge stitch)

Number of stitches in lapel/collar "wedge" (width × stitch gauge)

1¼" (3.2 cm) × 5.25 stitches/inch = 6.56 stitches. Note: There are 7 stitches on
every right-side (increase) row and 6 stitches on every wrong-side (decrease) row.
This number fluctuates as the inner lapel wedge increases to follow the V shaping
while the outer edge decreases for the collar attachment.

COLLAR WIDTHS

Number of stitches at collar cast-on (width × stitch gauge + 2 selvedge stitches)

15¼" (38.5 cm) × 5.25 stitches/inch + 2 selvedge stitches = 82 stitches

Number of stitches at collar above side increases (width × stitch gauge + 2 selvedge stitches)

18¼" (46.5 cm) × 5.25 stitches/inch + 2 selvedge stitches = 97.81 stitches;
round up to even number = 98 stitches

Number of stitches increased in collar (same number as bound off at the top side edge of lapel)

16 stitches; 8 stitches at each side (inside the selvedge stitches)

LAPEL LENGTHS

Number of rows in V-neck (length × row gauge)

10" (25.5 cm) × 7.10 rows/inch = 71 rows; round up to even number = 72 rows

Number of rows in lapel (length × row gauge)

9½" (24 cm) × 7.10 rows/inch = 67.45 rows;
round up to nearest even number = 68 rows

Number of rows in inner lapel shaping (length × row gauge)

8" (20.5 cm) × 7.10 rows/inch = 56.8 rows; round down to even number = 56 rows

Number of rows in outer lapel (length × row gauge)

7" (18 cm) × 7.10 rows/inch = 49.7 rows; round down to odd number = 49 rows

Number of rows in lapel "wedge" (length × row gauge)

2½" (6.5 cm) × 7.10 rows/inch = 17.75 rows; round up to even number = 18 rows

COLLAR LENGTHS

Number of rows in collar (length × row gauge)

5" (12.5 cm) × 7.10 rows/inch = 35.5 rows; round up to even number = 36 rows

Number of rows for collar increases (length × row gauge)

2½" (6.5 cm) × 7.10 rows/inch = 17.75 rows; round up to even number = 18 rows

Step 1: Cast On for Lapel

For our sample lapel, cast on 3 stitches (1 inner lapel stitch at center and 1 selvedge
stitch at each side).

Step 2: Shape Lapel

The inner lapel edge (the edge that will be sewn to the garment) increases 4¼" (11 cm) to match the slope of the V-neckline shaping on the garment front. The outer edge of the lapel (the edge that will be folded back) increases 1" (2.5 cm) to provide extra width to the turn-back section. Therefore, the shaping is calculated separately for each side although they will be worked simultaneously as the lapel is knitted.

Section 1: Calculate Increases for Inner Lapel (V-Neckline Shaping)

Along this edge, increase 20 stitches, from 3 stitches at the cast-on edge to a total of 23 stitches along this side. These increases are evenly spaced over 8" (20.5 cm), or 56 rows. Because all of the increases are worked on right-side rows, only 28 of these 56 rows are available for inner lapel shaping. Using the shaping formula, divide the 28 available rows by 20 increases to determine how to space these increases evenly. The formula tells us to increase every right-side (i.e., every 2nd) row 12 times and every 2nd right-side (i.e., every 4th) row 8 times. For truly even increases, alternate the two intervals.

For our sample lapel, increase 1 stitch at the inside edge [every 2nd row, then every 4th row] 8 times, then every 2nd row 4 times—20 stitches increased over 56 rows. Work this edge even to the total length of the lapel, or until a total of 68 rows have been worked.

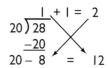

Use the shaping formula to determine an even distribution of increases along the inner collar. In this example, increase every 2nd right-side (every 4th) row 8 times and every right-side (every 2nd) row 12 times.

Section 2: Calculate Increases for Outer Lapel and "Wedge"

Along the outer lapel edge, 5 stitches are increased over the 49 shaping rows. The last 1" (2.5 cm), or 7 rows, of this section is worked even, leaving 42 rows over which to work the increases. All the increases are worked on right-side rows, so only 21 of the 42 rows are available for shaping the outer lapel. Using the shaping formula, divide the 21 available rows by 5 increases to determine an even spacing. The formula tells us to increase every 4th right-side (i.e., every 8th) row 4 times and every 5th right-side (i.e., every 10th) row 1 time. Work the single longer (10-row) interval first, then work the four shorter (8-row) intervals. To work the increases on right-side rows, work the first increase on the 11th row and the final increase on the 43rd row. Work all of the increases inside the selvedge stitch.

Use the shaping formula to determine an even distribution of increases. In this example, increase every 4th right-side row (every 8th row) 4 times and every 5th right-side row (every 10th row) 1 time.

After this edge has been worked for 49 rows, bind off 18 stitches (on the 50th row) for the turn-back edge. Then, shape the wedge by decreasing 1 stitch at the outer edge every right-side row until 2 stitches remain (1 lapel stitch + 1 selvedge stitch).

For our sample lapel, at the same time as increases are worked along the inner lapel, increase 1 stitch at the outer lapel edge on the 11th row, then every following 8th row 4 times, then work even until the edge measures 7" (18 cm), or 49 rows have been worked. On the next row, bind off 18 stitches for the turn-back edge. Shape the wedge by binding off 1 stitch at the outer edge every other row until 2 stitches remain, then bind off the final 2 stitches.

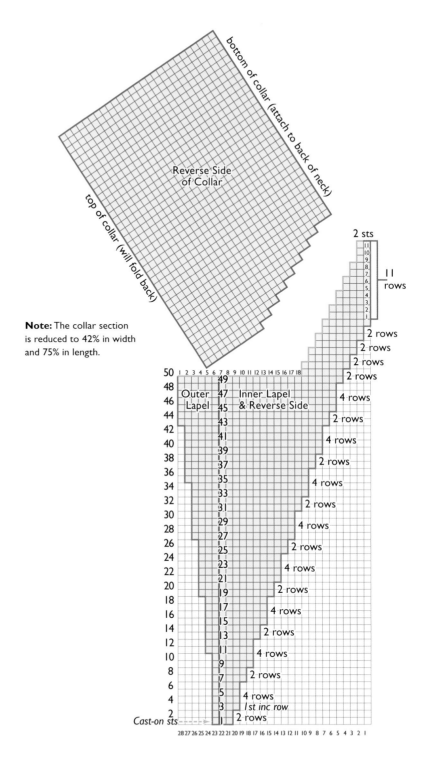

Note: The collar section is reduced to 42% in width and 75% in length.

Plot of the lapel and collar shaping showing how the pieces fit together.

Step 3: Cast On for Collar Section

For our sample collar/lapel, cast on 82 stitches.

Step 4: Shape Collar

Shape the sides of the collar to fit the lapel notches by working 2 rows even, then increasing (inside the selvedge stitches) the same number of stitches over the same number of rows as decreases were worked for the outer lapel "wedge" so that the two pieces will fit together perfectly. For our example, increase a total of 16 stitches, or 8 stitches, at each side, adding 1 stitch at each end of every other row 8 times to a total of 98 stitches. Work even until the piece measures 5" (12.5 cm), or a total of 36 rows have been worked, then bind off all stitches.

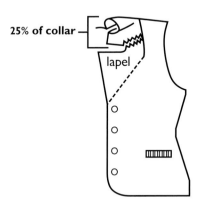

25% of collar

lapel

Sew the shaped edge of each side of the collar to the corresponding edge of each lapel.

Step 5: Finishing

The final step is to join the lapel to the neckline of the body, then join the shaped edges at the bottom of the collar to the lapel wedges, then join the collar to the last ½" (1.3 cm) of the side of the V-neckline and across the back neck.

For our sample lapel/collar, seam the shoulders of the jacket. Sew the lapels along the edge of the V-neckline. Match the shaped bottom edges of the collar to each lapel wedge and baste them together. Baste the collar along the last ½" (1.3 cm) at the top of the neckline at each side, then across the back neck. Sew the basted pieces together.

tip

A backstitch seam (see page 270) gives a professional look to the lapel-to-collar join. However, use a whipstitch (see page 266) along the collar-to-neckline join to avoid an overly obvious seam.

chapter eleven

Finishing Techniques

For a clean, professional look, the way you finish a garment is as important as the way you knit it. In general, finishing involves blocking the individual pieces, then joining them together, either by knitting or by sewing with a tapestry needle. First, the shoulders are seamed. Next, the neckline is finished with a neckband or collar (including front bands for a cardigan). Then, the sleeves are inserted into the armholes, and finally, the sleeve and side seams are joined. There are many ways to join the pieces; I've listed my favorites here.

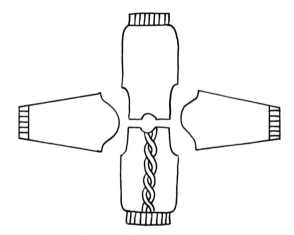

Unseamed pieces of a classic set-in sleeve pullover.

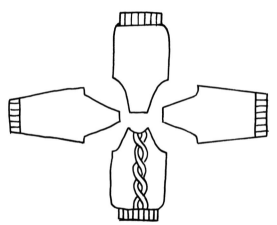

Unseamed pieces of a classic raglan pullover.

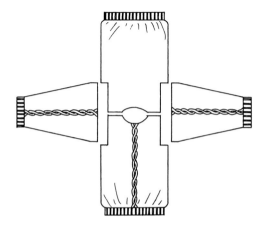

Unseamed pieces of a modified drop-shoulder pullover.

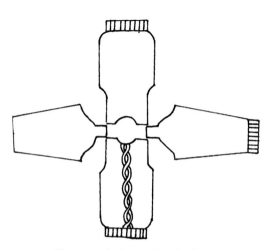

Unseamed pieces of a classic saddle-shoulder pullover.

BLOCKING

Blocking involves applying water or steam to "set" each knitted garment piece to a specific size and/or shape. The method to use depends on the fiber content of the yarn—check for guidelines on the ball band. In general, wool and other natural fibers can be safely blocked with heat or steam, but synthetics, novelties, or hairy yarns such as angora or mohair should be only slightly dampened and allowed to air-dry.

For professional results, place the knitted pieces right side down on a rigid padded surface. Although an ironing board can be used for small pieces, a blocking board with a covered surface featuring length and width lines is a worthwhile investment. Pat or pin the pieces to the desired length and width dimensions (follow the lines on the blocking board to ensure straight edges), stretching out or easing in the fabric as necessary.

To steam-block, hold the iron gently above the pieces and allow the steam to penetrate the fabric. If desired, place a pressing cloth over wool or cotton fabrics and move the iron gently across the surface. Do not block or press ribbing or any heavily textured areas—ribbing will lose its elasticity and high-relief textures will flatten. Remove the pins after the pieces have completely air-dried.

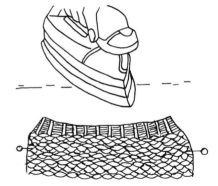

To steam-block, pin the pieces right side down on a flat surface, hold a steam iron above the pieces and allow the steam to penetrate the fabric.

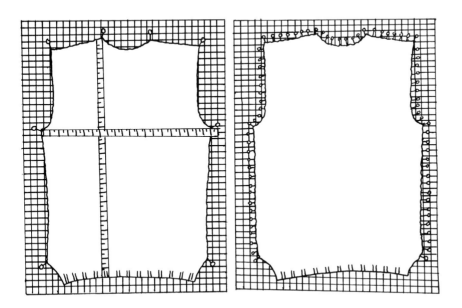

For best results, use a blocking board that has a 1" (2.5 cm) grid printed on the surface.

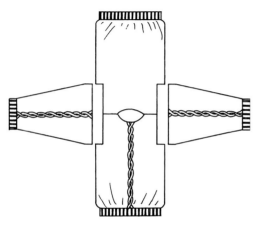

Most sweater types involve
one seam at each shoulder.

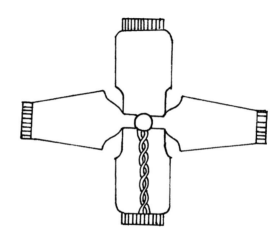

Saddle-shoulder sweaters have
two seams at each shoulder.

Knit stitches form a series of Vs.

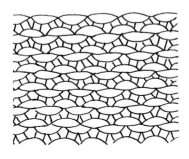

Purl stitches form alternating upward-
facing and downward-facing bumps.

SHOULDER SEAMS

Garment assembly begins with the shoulder seams. The key to seaming a garment is to make it appear as if the garment is seamless. To do this, it is important to recognize complete knit stitches, complete purl stitches, and the spaces between them. A knit stitch has two sides and looks like the letter V on the right side of the work. If the V appears upside down, you're looking at the left side of one stitch and the right side of the adjacent stitch, not the two halves of the same stitch.

Purl stitches also form Vs, but the structure looks like little "bumps." The bumps are actually the interlocking arches of the knit stitches as they appear on the reverse side. A series of purl stitches form alternating upward-facing and downward-facing bumps. When the rows of stitches on the wrong side are gently pulled apart, the Vs are visible in the background.

To clearly understand the structure of a purl stitch, place your tapestry needle under both sides of a knit stitch, then turn the work to the wrong side. The needle will cross the purl stitch. The top of each purl stitch forms an arch with two reverse arch bumps on each side. The reverse arches at each side are the backs of the "between-the-stitch" reverse Vs that form the sides of knit stitches. They appear a little lower than the center arch. The purl stitch is the highest bump that faces downward, while the sides form arches that face upward. The bump at the base of the purl stitch is the top arch of the stitch below.

The spaces between either knit or purl stitches, when gently pulled apart, resemble ladders with horizontal rungs between the individual stitches.

 tip   There are two categories of techniques used to sew knitted pieces together: "weaving" techniques and "sewing" techniques. Weaving techniques are unique to knits and are worked with the right sides of the garment facing outward. Sewing techniques are used for woven as well as knitted fabrics and are worked with the pieces held inside out.

THREE-NEEDLE BIND-OFF

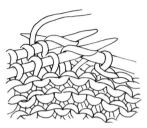

Figure 1

Although called a bind-off, this technique is used to join, or seam, two groups of live stitches (stitches that are still on the needles) and eliminates the bulk of a bind-off edge in the seam. This technique is ideal for joining stitches along shoulder seams. It offers the best properties of both the grafting (weaving) and seaming techniques without the associated drawbacks of either. Because the shoulder seam has to carry the weight of the garment, grafting does not always produce a strong enough seam. With the three-needle bind-off, the front and back stitches are first knitted together, then bound off to produce a stable seam without the bulk of the bind-off edges.

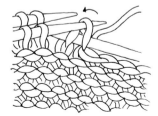

Figure 2

 tip   Seams that are worked on live stitches have less bulk than seams worked on bind-off edges.

To begin, there must be the same number of stitches on each needle. Hold the two needles parallel so that the right sides of the knitting face together.

Step 1: Using a third needle, knit the first stitch on each needle as if to k2tog, inserting the third needle into each stitch individually.

Step 2: *Knit the next stitch on each needle together in the same way (Figure 1)—2 stitches on the third needle.

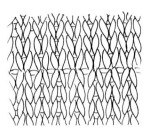

Figure 3

Step 3: Use the tip of one of the other needles to lift the first stitch on the third needle over the second stitch and off the needle (Figure 2)—1 stitch remains on the third needle.

Repeat Steps 2 and 3 until all stitches have been bound off (Figure 3).

HORIZONTAL-TO-HORIZONTAL SEAM

To begin, position the two pieces so that the bound-off edges abut and the right sides are facing up. Work from right to left and in the row of stitches just above the bind-off edge of the upper piece and below the bind-off edge of the lower piece. Begin at the top by bringing the threaded needle under the first full stitch (V) on the top (just above the bind-off edge), then bring the needle under the reverse V on the bottom just under the bind-off edge. Continue as follows:

Step 1: Under the next stitch (V) on the top piece.

Step 2: Under the next reversed V on the bottom piece (this V will appear upside down).

Repeat Steps 1 and 2, replicating the flow of a row of stitches and adjusting the tension on the seaming yarn after every 5 stitches to secure the seam.

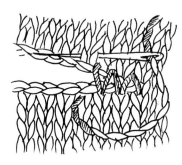

A horizontal-to-horizontal seam is used to join the bound-off edges of two pieces that have the same number of stitches (such as shoulders). Because the stitches run horizontally across the width of the fabric, this seam joins stitches to stitches. It is worked with yarn to match the garment threaded on a tapestry needle.

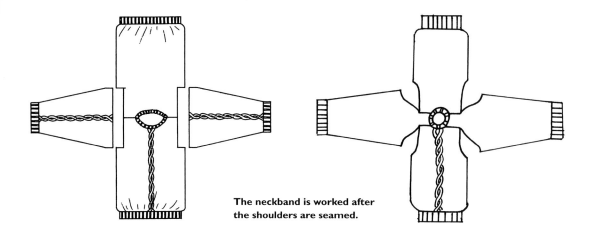

The neckband is worked after the shoulders are seamed.

NECKLINES

The neckline is typically finished right after the shoulders are seamed. Either stitches are picked up and knitted around the neck opening and the edging is worked directly from the picked-up stitches, or a collar is worked separately and sewn in place with whipstitches. For a cardigan, the front bands are typically worked at this point as well.

PICK UP AND KNIT

"Pick up and knit" is a most misunderstood term in knitting in that it implies two separate actions, when in truth, a single action is involved. The purpose is to add stitches to an existing piece of knitting. The pick-up row acts as a kind of cast-on from which to begin the added knitting. When done properly the picked-up stitches flow beautifully from the original knitting.

To pick up and knit stitches along a neckline edge, you'll combine techniques for picking up along vertical, horizontal, and sloped edges as described below.

 tip Holes are less likely to form if all of the stitches are picked up from bind-off or selvedge edges. Holes are more likely to form if some of the stitches are picked up and others are worked from stitches that were placed on holders.

For an even distribution of stitches, first divide the neckline in half by placing a marker at the center back and center front. For a round neck, place additional markers on each side halfway between the center back and center front markers to divide the neckline into quarters. For a V-neck, place additional markers at each edge of the back neck, as well as halfway between each back neck edge and the center front. Pick up half of the desired neckline stitches between the center back to the center front marker and pick up the remaining half of the stitches between the center front marker and the center back marker, making sure that the same number of stitches is picked up between the secondary markers on each side.

To begin, use a crochet hook to pull a loop through both legs of the edge stitch for the first stitch. Place the loop on the crochet hook onto a knitting needle, then use the knitting needle to pick up the remaining stitches as instructed.

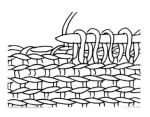

Use a crochet hook to pull a loop through both legs of the edge stitch.

Pick Up and Knit Along a Vertical Edge

With the right side facing, hold the piece so that the selvedge is at the top. Holding the working yarn behind the knitted piece, work from right to left between the first and second stitch of each row as follows:

Step 1: Insert the needle from front to back between the ladders that join the first and second stitches.

Step 2: Wrap the yarn around needle knitwise and pull a loop through to the front—1 stitch picked up.

Repeat Steps 1 and 2, always working between the first and second stitch, for the desired number of stitches.

Pick up between the two edge stitches along vertical edges.

Pick Up and Knit Along a Horizontal Edge

With the right side facing, hold the working yarn behind the knitted piece. Working from right to left in the row below the bind-off (or cast-on) edge, work as follows:

Step 1: Insert needle from front to back into the center V of a stitch.

Step 2: Wrap the yarn around the needle knitwise and pull a loop through to the front—1 stitch picked up.

Repeat Steps 1 and 2, always working in the center of each V, for the desired number of stitches.

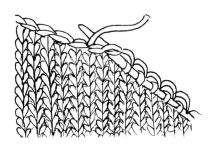

Pick up into the V below the bind-off (or cast-on) edge.

Pick up and Knit Along a Sloped Edge

When working along sloped edges, some stitches will be picked up in the center of existing stitches and others will be picked up between existing stitches. Picking up and knitting stitches along curved edges can require some trial and error to prevent holes from forming.

A round neckline includes horizontal, sloped, and vertical components.

A V-neckline includes sloped and vertical components.

PICK UP AND PURL

There are times when you may want to pick up stitches from the purl side of the existing knitting. With the wrong side facing and holding the piece so that the bind-off or selvedge edge is at the top, hold the working yarn in front and work from right to left as follows:

Step 1: Insert needle from back to front into the center of an existing stitch (for a horizontal edge) or between two stitches (for a vertical edge).

Step 2: Wrap the yarn around the needle purlwise and pull a loop through to the back—1 stitch picked up.

Repeat Steps 1 and 2 for the desired number of stitches.

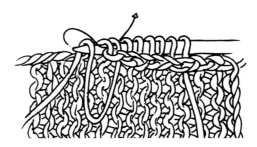

With the wrong side facing and holding the yarn in front, bring the needle from back to front, wrap the yarn around the needle purlwise, then pull the loop through to the back.

Horizontal whipstitch seam.

WHIPSTITCH SEAM

Collars (as well as hem facings and buttonbands) are typically attached using a whipstitch, which forms a tidy join without bulk. A whipstitch can be worked either vertically or horizontally. Begin by pinning or basting the pieces together, matching the widths and lengths as necessary. With the right side facing, and working close to the edges, bring the threaded needle down into the edge of one piece and up through the other piece directly opposite, then pull the working yarn to close the seam. Space the stitches fairly close to one another and maintain an even tension as you work.

Vertical whipstitch seam.

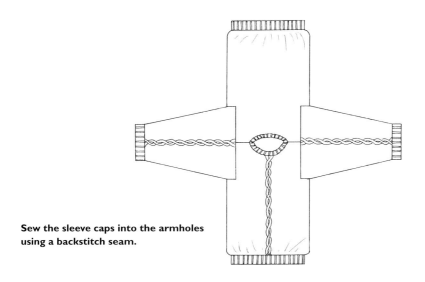

Sew the sleeve caps into the armholes
using a backstitch seam.

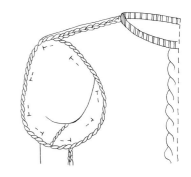

Pin the sleeve cap into the
armhole, easing the fit.

ARMHOLE SEAMS

Because they add weight and bulk, it's best to sew the armhole seams after the neck and
front edges have been finished. To begin, pin the right side of the sleeve cap to the right
side of the armhole, allowing the weight of the garment to pull against itself and stretch
the armhole slightly for a snug fit. With contrasting yarn, baste the pieces together.

BACKSTITCH SEAM

In addition to withstanding the stress of armholes, backstitch seams are commonly
used to add stability to openwork stitch patterns such as lace, or to create crisp,
sturdy seams in heavy garments such as coats. When worked at an even tension with
a small seam allowance, backstitch seams can give a professional finish to a garment.
A backstitch is worked from the wrong side with yarn to match the garment threaded
on a tapestry needle.

To begin, following the bumps of the purl stitches as a guide (look for the arch at the
top of the purl stitches), encircle the first stitch two times to secure the beginning of
the seam, then encircle each stitch by moving ahead two stitches, then back one stitch
as described below.

Horizontal to Horizontal

Use this method to join two horizontal (bind-off or cast-on) edges. Working from
right to left in the stitches directly below the bind-off row, bring the threaded
tapestry needle through the two pieces as follows:

Step 1: Up through the center of the second stitch.

Step 2: Down through the center of the first stitch.

Step 3: Up through the center of the third stitch.

Step 4: Down through the center of the second stitch.

Repeat these 4 steps to the end of the seam.

**Work just below the bind-off
row on both pieces.**

HORIZONTAL-TO-VERTICAL SEAM

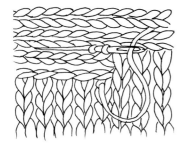

Work just below the bind-off row on the horizontal piece and inside the selvedge stitch on the vertical piece.

Use this method to join a horizontal (bind-off or cast-on) edge of one piece to a vertical (selvedge) edge of another piece, as when joining the bind-off edge of a sleeve into an armhole of a drop-shoulder silhouette. Position the two pieces so that the vertical edge of one piece abuts the horizontal edge of the other and the right sides are facing up. Half of this seam is worked as a horizontal-to-horizontal seam (bringing the needle under both halves of a stitch) and half is worked as a vertical-to-vertical seam (bringing the needle under the "rungs" of the ladders that define rows; see page 262).

Because this type of seam joins stitches to rows and because knitted stitches tend to be wider than they are tall (there are more rows to 1" [2.5 cm] than there are stitches), you cannot simply join one row of the armhole to every stitch of the sleeve. Instead, you must alternate between joining 2 rows and 1 row for every stitch as you go across the seam. You can remain vigilant with your eyes to determine when to join 2 rows and when to join 1 row, or you can use the shaping formula to determine the sequence.

To begin, count the number of rows in the armhole and count the number of stitches in the sleeve cap. For example, let's say we have a drop-shoulder armhole knitted at a gauge of 5 stitches and 7 rows to the inch and a sleeve cap that measures 14" (35.5 cm) across and will fit into an armhole that measures 14" (35.5 cm) around. We will therefore join 70 stitches (14 × 5) to 98 rows (14 × 7). Note that there are 28 more rows than stitches in the armhole.

$$\begin{array}{r} 98 \text{ rows} \\ - \ 70 \text{ stitches} \\ \hline 28 \text{ rows} \end{array}$$

$$28\overline{)70} \quad \begin{array}{l} 2 \\ -56 \end{array} \quad +1 = 3$$

$$28 - 14 \ = \ 14$$

Use the shaping formula to determine the ratio of pick-ups for rows and stitches.

Use the shaping formula to divide the 70 stitches by the 28 additional rows to determine how often to join an extra row when seaming. The diagonal relationship between the quotient (2) and the expanded remainder (14) tells us to join an extra row to every 2nd stitch 14 times. The diagonal relationship between the expanded quotient (3) and the remainder (14) tells us to also join an extra row to every 3rd stitch 14 times. For a truly even distribution, alternate the two intervals: *join 1 stitch to 1 row, then join 1 stitch to 2 rows, then [join 1 stitch to 1 row] 2 times, then join 1 stitch to 2 rows; repeat from * 13 more times.

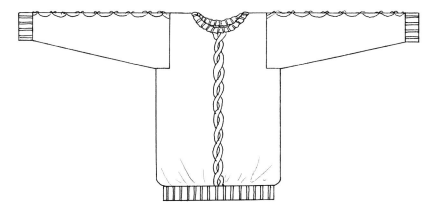

Sew the sleeve and side seams last.

SLEEVE AND SIDE SEAMS

Sew the sleeve and side seams as a single continuous seam.

VERTICAL-TO-VERTICAL SEAM (MATTRESS STITCH)

This type of seam is used along vertical (i.e., selvedge) edges, such as the side seams of sweaters and skirts, when there is the same number of rows on each piece. It is worked in the ladders between the selvedge stitch and the adjacent stitch on each piece with yarn to match the garment threaded on a tapestry needle.

Begin by working a figure eight at the base of the seam.

Position the two pieces so that the selvedge edges abut and right sides are facing up. To begin, join the yarn to the lower edge of one piece, then join the lower edges of the two pieces together by bringing the needle from back to front between the first two stitches in the first row on the left-hand piece, then from back to front between the first two stitches in the first row on the right-hand piece, then again from back to front between the first two stitches on the left-hand piece, following a figure-eight path. Continue as described below for stockinette or reverse stockinette stitch.

Stockinette Stitch

Step 1: Bring the tapestry needle under the ladder between the first and second stitch of the next row on the left side.

Step 2: Bring the needle under the ladder between the first and second stitch of the next row on the right side.

Repeat Steps 1 and 2 until all rows have been seamed.

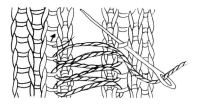

Work into the ladders between the edge stitches for stockinette stitch.

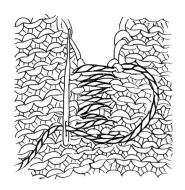

Work into the purl bumps of the edge stitches for reverse stockinette stitch.

Reverse Stockinette Stitch

Step 1: Bring the tapestry needle up through the down-facing purl bump (the head of the stitch) between the first and second stitch of the next row on the right-hand side.

Step 2: Bring the needle up through the up-facing purl bump between the first and second stitch of the next row on the left-hand side.

Repeat Steps 1 and 2 until all rows have been seamed.

VERTICAL BACKSTITCH SEAM

This seam is worked from bottom to top in the stitch above or below the up-facing purl bumps inside the selvedge edge. Begin by bringing the threaded needle up between the edge and the first row (or second row for fine yarns), then encircle the edge two times to secure the two pieces as described for backstitch seams on page 267.

Step 1: Bring the needle up through the space directly below the purl-stitch arch on the next row (or two rows away for fine yarns).

Step 2: Bring the needle down through the space directly above the same purl-stitch arch to encircle the stitch.

Step 3: Bring the needle up through the stitch directly below the purl-stitch arch one (or two) rows away.

Step 4: Bring the needle down through the stitch directly above the same purl-stitch arch.

Repeat Steps 1 to 4, alternately working below and above the downward-facing purl-stitch arches to the end of the seam.

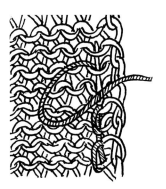

Front view

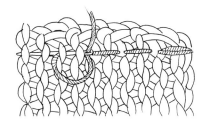

Side view

BUTTONHOLES

For the best results, practice buttonholes on both the right side and wrong side of a swatch worked in the desired pattern stitch. Depending on the stitch pattern, a buttonhole might look best when worked on a wrong-side row.

Figure 1

HORIZONTAL ONE-ROW BUTTONHOLE

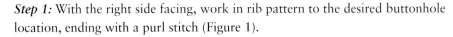

This technique produces a firm buttonhole in a single row. This type of buttonhole appears balanced at each edge and does not require reinforcing. Be sure to slip all stitches purlwise except the final stitch and be careful not to pull the working yarn too tightly when using the cable method to cast on stitches. The illustrations here are for working in k1, p1 ribbing.

Figure 2

Step 1: With the right side facing, work in rib pattern to the desired buttonhole location, ending with a purl stitch (Figure 1).

Step 2: If not working in ribbing, bring the working yarn to the front, slip 1 stitch, bring the yarn to the back, and let it hang free for the next three steps. If working in k1, p1 ribbing, plan to end with a purl stitch so that the yarn is already in front.

Step 3: Slip the next stitch, then bind off the first slipped stitch by lifting it up and over the second stitch and off the needle (Figure 2).

Step 4: Bind off 3 more stitches in the same manner—4 stitches bound off.

Figure 3

Step 5: Slip the first stitch on the right-hand needle back to the left-hand needle (Figure 3).

Step 6: Turn the work so the wrong side is facing, pick up the working yarn and pull on it to prevent a gap from forming at the beginning edge of the buttonhole, insert the right needle between the first two stitches on the left needle (Figure 4), then use the cable method (see box below) to cast on 5 stitches (1 more stitch than was bound off), bringing the yarn to the front between the needles before placing the 5th stitch on the left-hand needle.

Figure 4

Step 7: Turn the work so the right side is facing and slip the first stitch on the left-hand needle knitwise onto the right-hand needle, then lift the last (extra) cast-on stitch over the slipped stitch and off the needle (Figure 5).

Step 8: Return the last (slipped) stitch back onto the left-hand needle—1 buttonhole completed.

Figure 5

CABLE CAST-ON

*Insert the right needle tip between the first two stitches on the left needle, wrap yarn around the needle, and pull the loop through to the front, then place the loop on the tip of the left needle, without twisting the loop. Repeat from * for the desired number of stitches.

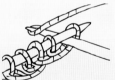

tip To rip out the bind-off stitches in a one-row buttonhole, lift the stitches over one another instead of pulling on the yarn as usual.

EYELET BUTTONHOLE

This is the simplest way to make a small, unobtrusive buttonhole that requires no reinforcing.

Step 1: With the right side facing, work to the buttonhole position (typically the center stitch of a buttonhole band).

Step 2: Bring the yarn forward, make a yarnover (yo), then knit the next 2 stitches together (k2tog), then work to the end of the row or to the next buttonhole if there are multiple buttonholes in the same row.

Step 3: Work the next row as usual, working the yarnover as a regular stitch.

An eyelet buttonhole produces a round hole that is unobtrusive and strong.

 tip When working eyelet buttonholes on k1, p1 ribbing, begin the buttonhole after a knit stitch (yarnover and work the purl stitch together with the next knit stitch as k2tog) so that the knit ribs remain unbroken.

VERTICAL THREE-ROW BUTTONHOLE

This technique produces a nearly invisible buttonhole in k1, p1 ribbing so that the buttonhole recedes along with the purl stitches in the rib. This buttonhole is worked during three consecutive rows as follows:

Row 1: With the right side facing, work in k1, p1 ribbing as established to 1 stitch before the desired buttonhole position, ending with a knit stitch, [yarnover] 2 times, k2tog, work in rib to end of row.

Row 2: Work to the double yarnover of the previous row, knit the first loop of the double yarnover and drop the second loop off the needle.

Row 3: Work in rib as established to the hole formed by the double yarnover, purl into the center of the hole, then drop the stitch on the needle above the hole off the needle—1 buttonhole completed.

A vertical three-row buttonhole produces a vertical gap that is one stitch wide and three rows long.

ZIPPERS

Zippers make for clean closures without interrupting stitch patterns. Take time to baste the zipper in place and sew carefully to prevent puckers.

Step 1: Pin the zipper in place.

Step 2: With contrasting thread and a sharp-point sewing needle, baste the zipper in place, being careful not to stretch the knitting.

Step 3: Try on the garment to ensure that the zipper lies flat. Adjust as necessary.

Step 4: With the right side facing and doubled matching thread, use small backstitches (see page 270) to sew the selvedge edges of the knitting close to the zipper teeth.

Step 5: With the wrong side facing and doubled matching thread, use whipstitches (see page 266) to sew the edges of zipper tape to the knitting, being careful that stitches do not show on the right side of the knitting.

Sew zippers in place by hand.

Twist Flowers Pullover

project

This pullover is an example of a classic silhouette worked in an allover stitch pattern. It features straight shoulders, a separate cowl collar, and tapered sleeves with set-in caps. The high round neck on the body is finished with a crocheted edging.

FINISHED SIZE

34¼ (42½, 50½)" (87 [108, 128.5] cm) bust circumference.
To fit bust measurements about 31–33 (34–40, 42–48)" (78.5–84 [86.5–101.5, 106.5–122] cm). Sweater shown measures 42½" (108 cm).

YARN

Worsted weight (#4 Medium).
Shown here: Jade Sapphire 100% Cashmere 6 Ply (100% cashmere; 150 yd [137 m]/55 g): #87 Purple Rain, 14 (16, 18) skeins.

NEEDLES

Size U.S. 9 (5.5 mm): straight and 16" (40 cm) circular (cir). Adjust needle sizes if necessary to obtain the correct gauge.

NOTIONS

Stitch holders or waste yarn; tapestry needle; size E/4 (3.5 mm) crochet hook.

SWATCH SIZE

51 stitches = 9" (23 cm) wide and 40 rows = 6¾" (17 cm) long in twist flowers pattern from chart.

GAUGE

5.67 stitches and 5.93 rows = 1" (2.5 cm) in twist flowers pattern from chart;
5.30 stitches and 6.66 rounds = 1" (2.5 cm) in Wrap 3, P3 pattern for cowl collar.

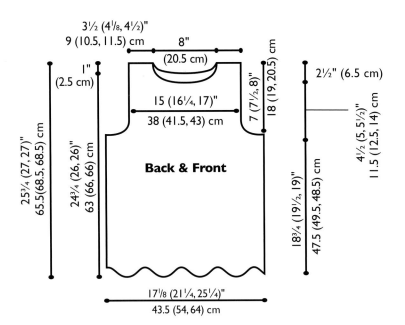

Back & Front

3½ (4⅛, 4½)"
9 (10.5, 11.5) cm

1" (2.5 cm)

8" (20.5 cm)

15 (16¼, 17)"
38 (41.5, 43) cm

7 (7½, 8)"
18 (19, 20.5) cm

25¾ (27, 27)"
65.5 (68.5, 68.5) cm

24¾ (26, 26)"
63 (66, 66) cm

18¾ (19½, 19)"
47.5 (49.5, 48.5) cm

2½" (6.5 cm)

4½ (5, 5½)"
11.5 (12.5, 14) cm

17⅛ (21¼, 25¼)"
43.5 (54, 64) cm

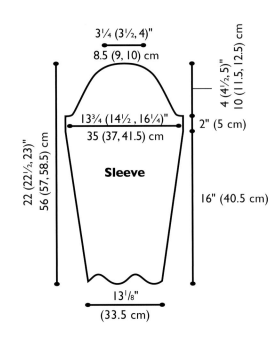

Sleeve

3¼ (3½, 4)"
8.5 (9, 10) cm

13¾ (14½, 16¼)"
35 (37, 41.5) cm

4 (4½, 5)"
10 (11.5, 12.5) cm

2" (5 cm)

22 (22½, 23)"
56 (57, 58.5) cm

16" (40.5 cm)

13⅛"
(33.5 cm)

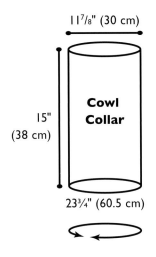

Cowl Collar

11⅞" (30 cm)

15" (38 cm)

23¾" (60.5 cm)

STITCH GUIDE

Wrap 3 (worked over 3 sts)

On RS rows, use the tip of the right-hand needle to lift the 3rd st on left-hand needle up and over the first 2 sts (do not drop the rem 2 sts off the needle). Then work the rem 2 sts on left-handled needle as k1, yo, k1. On WS rows, work the 3 sts of the wrap as p3 when you come to them. When working in rnds, work the 3 sts of the wrap as k3 when you come to them on the foll rnd.

Wrap 3, P3 Pattern (multiple of 6 sts)

Rnds 1 and 2: *K3, p3; rep from *.
Rnd 3: *Wrap 3, p3; rep from *.
Rnd 4: Rep Rnd 1.
Rep Rnds 1–4 for patt.

Picot Crochet (multiple of 2 sts + 1)

*Work 1 slip st in the next single crochet (sc), chain 4, skip 1 sc; rep from *, ending with 1 slip st in the last sc.

Twist Flowers

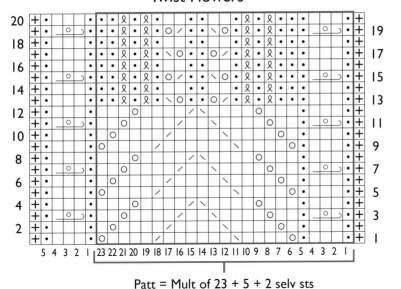

Patt = Mult of 23 + 5 + 2 selv sts
20-row repeat

	Key
☐	K on RS; P on WS
•	P on RS; K on WS
○	Yarnover
ℛ	Twist st
╱	K2tog on RS; P2tog on WS
╲	Ssk on RS; ssp or P2tog tbl on WS
+	Selvedge st
⊂○⊃	W3 (wrap 3) RS lift 3rd st on LHN backward over the first 2 sts, k1, yo, k1. On next WSR—Purl the 3 sts.
☐	Pattern repeat

CROCHET STITCHES

Crochet chain (ch)

Make a slipknot and place it on the hook. *Wrap the yarn counterclockwise around the hook (Figure 1) and pull it through the loop on the hook (Figure 2). Repeat from * for the desired number of chain stitches.

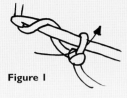

Figure 1

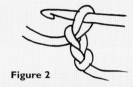

Figure 2

Single crochet (sc)

Working from right to left, insert hook from front to back into a stitch, grab the yarn, and draw through a loop. *Insert the hook through the next stitch (Figure 1), wrap the yarn around the hook; and pull a second loop through to the front. Wrap the yarn around the hook and pull a loop through both loops on the hook (Figure 2). Repeat from * for the desired number of stitches.

Figure 1

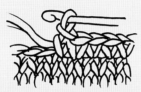

Figure 2

Slip-stitch crochet (sl st)

Working from right to left, insert hook from front to back into a stitch, grab the yarn to make a loop (Figure 1), and pull loop through to the front. *Insert the hook through the next stitch, grab the yarn to make a loop (Figure 2), and pull the new loop through the stitch, then through the loop already on the hook—1 stitch remains on hook. Repeat from * for the desired number of stitches.

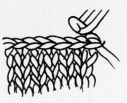

Figure 1

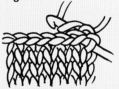

Figure 2

FRONT

With straight needles, CO 99 (122, 145) sts. Establish patt from Row 1 of Twist Flowers chart as foll: K1 (selvedge st, see Notes), work the 23-st patt rep a total of 4 (5, 6) times, work 5 rem sts from chart, k1 (selvedge st). Cont in established patt, work Rows 2–20 once, rep the entire 20-row chart 4 more times, then work Row 1 to Row 10 (16, 12) once more—110 (116, 112) total rows completed; piece should measure 18¾ (19½, 19)" (47.5 [49.5, 48.5] cm) from CO.

SHAPE ARMHOLES

Keeping in patt and using the sloped bind-off technique (see page 77), BO 2 (4, 4) sts at the beg of next 4 (2, 4) rows, then BO 0 (3, 3) sts at beg of foll 0 (2, 6) rows, then BO 0 (2, 2) sts at beg of next 0 (4, 4) rows, then BO 1 st at the beg of the foll 4 (6, 4) rows—87 (94, 99) sts rem. Work 18 (16, 14) more rows even in patt—26 (30, 32) total armhole rows completed; armholes measure about 4½ (5, 5½)" (11.5 [12.5, 14] cm); piece should measure 23¼ (24½, 24½)" (59 [62, 62] cm) from CO.

SHAPE NECK

(RS) Cont in patt, work 36 (39, 42) sts, join a second ball of yarn and, using the sloped bind-off technique, BO center 15 (16, 15) sts, work to end—36 (39, 42) sts rem each side. Working each side separately, at each neck edge BO 5 sts once, then BO 4 sts once, then BO 3 sts once, then BO 2 sts once, then BO 1 st once—21 (24, 27) sts rem at each side; 11 rows total in neck shaping. Beg and end with a WS row, work 4 rows even on right-hand side and work 3 rows even on left-hand side—42 (44, 48) total armhole rows completed; 152 (160, 160) total rows completed from CO; armholes measure about 7 (7½, 8)" (18 [19, 20.5] cm); piece should measure about 25¾ (27, 27)" (65.5 [68.5, 68.5] cm) from CO. Place sts on separate holders or waste yarn.

BACK

Work as for front until armhole shaping has been completed—87 (94, 99) sts rem. Work 28 (24, 24) more rows even in patt—36 (38, 42) total armhole rows completed; armholes measure about 6 (6½, 7)" (15 [16.5, 18] cm); piece should measure 24¾ (26, 26)" (63 [66, 66] cm) from CO.

SHAPE NECK

(RS) Cont in patt, work 32 (35, 38) sts, join a second ball of yarn and using the sloped bind-off method, BO center 23 (24, 23) sts, work to end—32 (35, 38) sts rem each side. Working each side separately, at each neck edge BO 6 sts once, then BO 5 sts once—21 (24, 27) sts rem at each side. Work 2 rows even on right-hand side and work 1 row even on left-hand side—42 (44, 48) total armhole rows completed; 152 (160, 160) total rows completed from CO; piece measures same as front. Place sts on separate holders or waste yarn.

SLEEVES

With straight needles, CO 76 sts for all sizes. Establish patt from Row 1 of Twist Flowers chart as foll: K1 (selvedge st), work the 23-st patt rep a total of 3 times, work 5 rem sts from chart, k1 (selvedge st). Cont in established patt and *at the same time* inc 1 st at each end of needle inside selvedge sts every 47 (23, 10) rows 2 (2, 5) times, then every 0 (24, 11) rows 0 (2, 4) times, working new sts in rev St st (purl on RS; knit on WS)—80 (84, 94) sts; 94 total sleeve rows completed; piece measures about 16" (40.5 cm) from CO. Work even in patt until 106 rows have been completed, ending with Row 6—piece should measure 18" (45.5 cm) from CO for all sizes.

SHAPE CAP

Using the sloped bind-off method, BO 4 sts at beg of next 4 rows, then BO 3 sts at beg of the foll 4 (2, 6) rows—52 (62, 60) sts rem. Cont as indicated for your size.

Size 34¼" (87 cm) Only

BO 2 sts at beg of next 4 rows, then BO 1 st at beg of the foll 2 rows, then BO 2 sts at beg of the foll 6 rows—30 sts rem.

Size 42½" (108 cm) Only

[BO 2 sts at beg of next 4 rows, then BO 1 st at beg of the foll 2 rows] 3 times—32 sts rem.

Size 50½" (128.5 cm) Only

BO 2 sts at beg of next 4 rows, then [BO 1 st at beg of next 2 rows, then BO 2 sts at beg of the foll 2 rows] 3 times—34 sts rem.

All Sizes

BO 3 sts at beg of next 4 rows—18 (20, 22) sts rem. BO all sts.

COWL COLLAR

With cir needle, CO 126 sts for all sizes. Place marker (pm) and join for working in rnds, being careful not to twist sts. Work in Wrap 3, P3 patt (see Stitch Guide) for 100 rnds—25 reps of 4-rnd patt completed; piece should measure 15" (38 cm) from CO. BO all sts.

FINISHING

Block pieces to measurements (see Notes on page 261). Place 21 (24, 27) held right front shoulder sts on one needle and the corresponding 21 (24, 27) held right back shoulder sts on another needle. Hold needles parallel with RS touching and WS facing out, and use tip of cir needle and the three-needle bind-off method (see page 263) to join shoulder sts; BO ridge will be on WS of garment. Rep for left shoulder sts. With yarn threaded on a tapestry needle, sew side seams.

NECK AND COWL COLLAR EDGING

Join yarn to one shoulder seam and use crochet hook to work 1 row of single crochet (sc) around neck opening, then work 1 row of picot crochet (see Stitch Guide) around neck opening. Fasten off last st. Work 1 row of sc, followed by 1 row of picot crochet around the CO and BO edges of cowl collar in the same manner.

With yarn threaded on a tapestry needle, sew sleeve seams. Sew sleeve caps into armholes. Weave in loose ends.

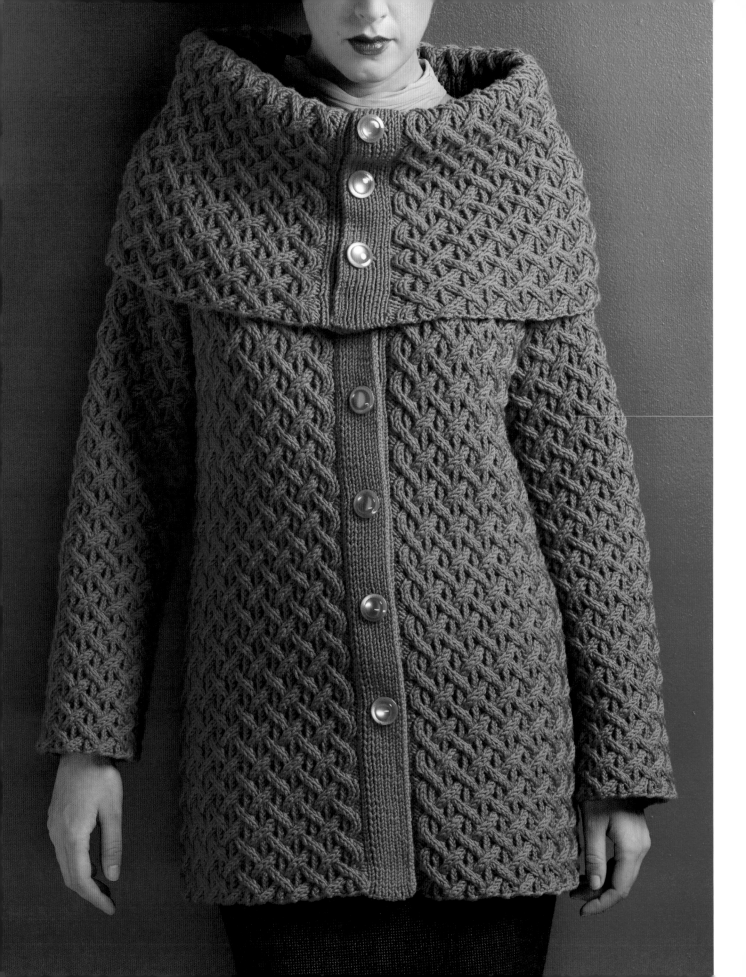

Cabled Coat with Cape Collar

This coat is an example of a drop-shoulder cardigan that is worked in one piece from the lower body to the armholes; the fronts and back are worked separately to the shoulders. It is worked in an allover cable pattern and features straight shoulders, a round neck, and tapered sleeves. The front bands and oversized collar are worked separately and sewn in place.

FINISHED SIZE

44½ (50)" (113 [127] cm) chest circumference, buttoned, including 1½" (3.8 cm) front band. To fit bust measurements about 34–41 (41–46)" (86.5–104 [104–117] cm). Coat shown measures 44½" (113 cm).

YARN

Worsted weight (#4 Medium).

Shown here: Trendsetter Merino 8-Ply (100% merino; 100 yd [91 m]/50 g): #222 turquoise, 35 (38) balls.

NEEDLES

One 40" (100 cm) circular needle (cir) each in sizes U.S. 9 (5.5 mm), 8 (5 mm), and 7 (4.5 mm). One 32" (80 cm) cir each in sizes U.S. 6 (4 mm), 5 (3.75 mm), 4 (3.5 mm), and 3 (3.25 mm). Adjust needle size if necessary to obtain the correct gauge.

NOTIONS

Cable needle (cn); tapestry needle; stitch holders or waste yarn; sewing pins; removable markers or safety pins; ten 1" (2.5 cm) buttons.

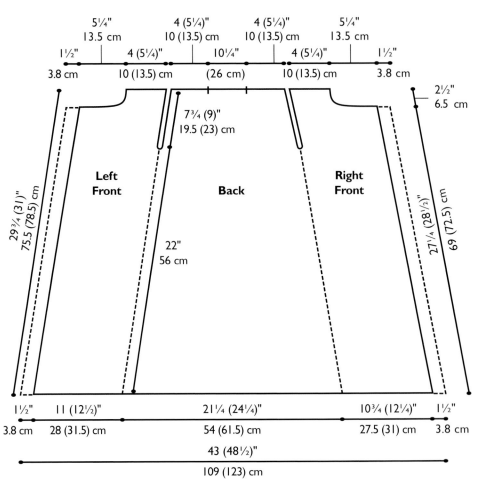

5¼"
13.5 cm

4 (5¼)"
10 (13.5) cm

4 (5¼)"
10 (13.5) cm

5¼"
13.5 cm

1½"
3.8 cm

4 (5¼)"
10 (13.5) cm

10¼"
(26 cm)

4 (5¼)"
10 (13.5) cm

1½"
3.8 cm

2½"
6.5 cm

7¾ (9)"
19.5 (23) cm

Left Front

Back

Right Front

29¾ (31)"
75.5 (78.5) cm

27¼ (28½)"
69 (72.5) cm

22"
56 cm

1½"
3.8 cm

11 (12½)"
28 (31.5) cm

21¼ (24¼)"
54 (61.5) cm

10¾ (12¼)"
27.5 (31) cm

1½"
3.8 cm

43 (48½)"
109 (123) cm

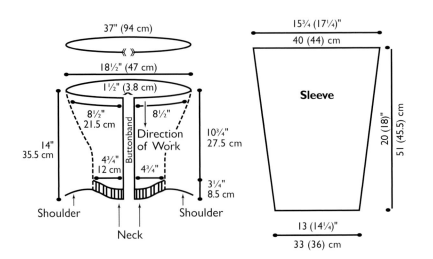

37" (94 cm)

18½" (47 cm)

1½" (3.8 cm)

8½"
21.5 cm

8½"

Buttonband

Direction of Work

10¾"
27.5 cm

14"
35.5 cm

4¾"
12 cm

4¾"

3¼"
8.5 cm

Shoulder

Neck

Shoulder

15¾ (17¼)"
40 (44) cm

Sleeve

20 (18)"
51 (45.5) cm

13 (14¼)"
33 (36) cm

Crosses & Twists
(mult of 10 + 11 + 2 selv sts)
8-row repeat + 1 foundation row (0)

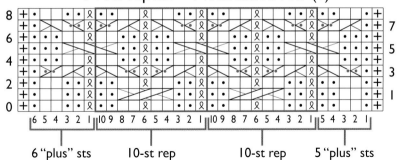

6 "plus" sts   10-st rep   10-st rep   5 "plus" sts

	K on RS; P on WS
•	P on WS; K on WS
Ջ	Twist st
	C5B: Slip 3 sts to cn, hold back, k2, k3 from cn
	C5F: Slip 2 sts to cn, hold front, k3, k2 from cn
	T4B: Slip 2 sts to cn, hold back, k2, p2 from cn
	T4F: Slip 2 sts to cn, hold front, p2, k2 from cn
+	Selvedge st
	Pattern repeat

SWATCH SIZES

51 stitches and 40 rows = 7¼" (18.5 cm) wide and 6½" (16.5 cm) long in crosses & twists pattern from chart on size 9 (5.5 mm) needle.

51 stitches and 32 rows = 6¼" (16 cm) wide and 5" (12.5 cm) long in crosses & twists pattern from chart on size 8 (5 mm) needle.

51 stitches and 32 rows = 6" (15 cm) wide and 4¼" (11 cm) long in crosses & twists pattern from chart on size 7 (4.5 mm) needle.

13 stitches and 50 rows = 1½" (3.8 cm) wide (unstretched) and 6¼" (16 cm) long in rib pattern for front bands on size 3 (3.25 mm) needle.

GAUGE

All gauges are in crosses & twists pattern from chart.

7.03 sts and 6.15 rows = 1" (2.5 cm) on size 9 (5.5 mm) needles.

8.16 sts and 6.4 rows = 1" (2.5 cm) size 8 (5 mm) needles.

8.5 sts and 7.52 rows = 1" (2.5 cm) on size 7 (4.5 mm) needles.

Notes

- Review dropped-shoulder construction on page 94 and cardigans worked in one piece on page 148.

- The body is worked in one piece from the cast-on edge to the armholes, then divided for working the fronts and back separately to the shoulders. The upper body is worked on smaller needles than the lower body.

- Knit the first and last stitch of every row for a garter-stitch selvedge unless otherwise indicated.

- Use the sloped method of binding off (see page 77) to shape the neckline and avoid "stair steps" along the bind-off edge.

BODY

With size 9 (5.5mm) cir needle, CO 303 (343) sts. Work the WS set-up row of the Crosses & Twists chart as foll: K1 (selvedge st, see Notes), work 6 "plus" sts once, work the 10-st patt rep a total of 29 (33) times, work 5 "plus" sts once, k1 (selvedge st). Cont in established patt, rep Rows 1–8 of chart *only* (do not rep the set-up row) 17 times, ending with Row 8—piece should measure about 22" (56 cm) from CO; 137 total chart rows completed (seventeen 8-row repeats), including set-up row.

DIVIDE FOR ARMHOLES

Change to size 8 (5mm) needle.

Next row: (RS; Row 1) Keeping in patt, work 76 (86) sts for right front (1 selvedge st, 5 "plus" sts, 7 [8] reps of 10-st pattern), and place the sts just worked onto a waste-yarn holder.

Work across next 150 (170) sts for back (15 [17] reps of 10-st patt) as foll: k1f&b or p1f&b in the first st of the first patt rep as necessary to maintain pattern, work 15 (17) patt reps, then work last st of final rep as k1f&b or p1f&b as necessary to maintain patt—152 (172) back sts. Sl rem 77 (87) sts for left front (7 [8] reps of 10-st pattern, 6 "plus" sts, 1 selvedge st) onto a waste-yarn holder.

BACK

Working inc'd sts at each side in garter st for selvedge sts, cont in established patt on 152 (172) back sts for 47 (55) more rows, ending with Row 8—48 (56) total armhole rows including dividing row.

Next row: (RS; Row 1) Work 34 (44) sts in patt for right back shoulder, BO the next 84 sts for back neck, work rem sts to end for left back shoulder—34 (44) sts rem for each shoulder; 49 (57) armhole rows completed; armholes should measure 7¾ (9)" (19.5 [23] cm).

Place shoulder sts on holders or waste yarn.

RIGHT FRONT

Temporarily place the 76 (86) held right front sts onto size 3 (3.25 mm) needle. Rejoin yarn with WS facing.

Next row: (WS; Row 2) Using size 8 (5 mm) needle, work first st as k1f&b or p1f&b as necessary to maintain patt, work in patt to end—77 (87) sts.

Cont with size 8 (5 mm) needle and working inc'd st in garter st for selvedge st, work 30 (38) more rows in patt, ending with Row 8—32 (40) total armhole rows including dividing row; armhole should measure 5 (6¼)" (12.5 [16] cm).

SHAPE NECK

Cont in patt and using the sloped bind-off method (see page 77), at neck edge (beg of RS rows) BO 12 sts once, then BO 8 sts once, then BO 6 sts once, then BO 5 sts 2 times, then BO 4 sts once, then BO 3 sts once, ending with RS Row 5—34 (44) shoulder sts rem; 43 sts total BO over 13 rows. Work 4 rows even in patt, ending with Row 1—49 (57) armhole rows completed; armhole should measure 7¾ (9)" (19.5 [23] cm). Place right shoulder sts on holder or waste yarn.

LEFT FRONT

Temporarily place 77 (87) held left front sts onto size 3 (3.25 mm) needle. Rejoin yarn with RS facing.

Next row: (RS; Row 1) Using size 8 (5 mm) needle, k1f&b or p1f&b as necessary to maintain patt, work in patt to end—78 (88) sts.

Cont with size 8 (5 mm) needle and working inc'd st in garter st for selvedge st, work 32 (40) more rows in patt, ending with Row 1—33 (41) total armhole rows; armhole should measure about 5¼ (6½)" (13.5 [16.5] cm).

SHAPE NECK

Cont in patt and using the sloped bind-off method, at neck edge (beg of WS rows) BO 13 sts once, then BO 8 sts once, then BO 6 sts once, then BO 5 sts 2 times, then BO 4 sts once, then BO 3 sts once, ending with WS Row 6—34 (44) shoulder sts rem; 44 sts total BO over 13 rows. Work 3 rows even in patt, ending with Row 1—49 (57) armhole rows completed; armhole should measure 7¾ (9)" (19.5 [23] cm). Place left shoulder sts on holder or waste yarn.

SLEEVES

With size 7 (4.5 mm) cir needle, CO 113 (123) sts. Do not join. Work the WS set-up row of the Crosses & Twists chart as foll: K1 (selvedge st), work 6 "plus" sts once, work the 10-st patt rep a total of 10 (11) times, work 5 "plus" sts once, k1 (selvedge st). Cont in established patt, rep Rows 1–8 of chart until piece measures 6" (15 cm) from CO. Change to size 8 (5 mm) cir needle and cont in patt until piece measures 13 (12)" (33 [30.5] cm) from CO. Change to size 9 (5.5 mm) cir needle and cont in patt until piece measures about 20 (18)" (51 [45.5] cm) from CO, ending with Row 1 or Row 5. BO all sts. **Note:** If you reach the desired length and the last row is either Row 4 or Row 8, work one additional row to complete the cable crossing that will close the top of the diamond motifs (on Rows 1 and 5) for a neater edge.

COLLAR

Note: The collar is worked from the top edge down to the neckline; the arrow on the schematic shows the direction of knitting. With size 9 (5.5 mm) cir needle, CO 263 sts for both sizes. Work the WS set-up row of the Crosses & Twists chart as foll: K1 (selvedge st), work 6 "plus" sts once, work the 10-st patt rep at total of 25 times, work 5 "plus" sts once, k1 (selvedge st). Cont in established patt, rep Rows 1–8 of chart 3 times, ending with Row 8—piece should measure about 4" (10 cm) long from CO and 37" (94 cm) wide (spread sts across two cir needles to measure width); 25 total chart rows completed, including set-up row. Change to size 8 (5 mm) cir needle and work 26 rows even in patt, ending with Row 2—piece should measure 8" (20.5 cm) long from CO and 37" (92.5 cm) wide. Change to size 7 (4.5 mm) cir needle and work 20 rows even in patt, ending with Row 6—piece should measure 10¾" (27.5 cm) long from CO and 30¾" (78 cm) wide.

COLLAR NECKLINE SHAPING

Change to size 6 (4mm) cir needle and work Row 7 of patt.

Dec row: (WS Row 8 of patt) Dec 52 sts as foll: K1 (selvedge st), k1, p2, k2tog, p1tbl, *k2tog, p2, p1tbl, p2, k2tog, p1tbl; rep from * to last 6 sts, k2tog, p2, k1, k1 (selvedge st)—211 sts rem; 1 st dec'd in each set of "plus" sts; 2 sts dec'd in each of 25 patt reps.

Next row: (RS) Beg twisted rib patt and dec 2 sts as foll: K1, p2tog *k1tbl, p1; rep from * to last 4 sts, k1tbl, p2tog, k1—209 sts rem; piece measures about 11" (28 cm) from CO.

Cont in twisted rib patt as foll:

Row 1: (WS) K1, *k1, p1tbl; rep from * to last 2 sts, k2.

Row 2: (RS) K1, *p1, k1tbl; rep from * to last 2 sts, p1, k1.

Cont in twisted rib, reduce collar width to neckline width by changing needle sizes as foll: Work 1" (2.5cm) with size 6 (4 mm) cir needle, 1" (2.5 cm) with size 5 (3.75 mm) cir needle, ½" (1.3 cm) with size 4 (3.5 mm) cir needle, ½" (1.3 cm) with size 3 (3.25 mm) cir needle—3" (7.5 cm) worked in twisted rib pattern; piece should measure 14" (35.5 cm) long from CO and 22" (56 cm) wide. BO all sts in patt.

FINISHING

Block pieces to measurements (see page 261). Place 34 (44) held right front shoulder sts on one needle and the corresponding 34 (44) held right back shoulder sts on another needle. Hold needles parallel with RS touching and WS facing out and use size 7 (4.5 mm) needle and the three-needle bind-off method (see page 263) to join shoulder sts; BO ridge will be on WS of garment. Rep for left shoulder sts. Pin BO edge of collar to neck opening with RS of collar corresponding to WS of coat so RS of collar will show on the right side when collar is folded down. With yarn threaded on a tapestry needle, use a whipstitch (see page 266) to sew collar to neck opening.

LEFT FRONT BAND

Note: For left front band, the body section is a plain buttonband and the collar section contains buttonholes.

With size 3 (3.25 mm) needles, CO 15 sts.

Row 1: (RS) K1 (selvedge st), [p1, k1] 6 times, p1, k1 (selvedge st).

Row 2: (WS) K1, [k1, p1] 6 times, k2.

Rep Rows 1 and 2 until piece measures 27¼ (28½)" (69 [72.5] cm) from CO, ending with a WS row. With RS facing, place a removable marker or safety pin in the first st to mark position for seam between neck and collar. Cont in patt until piece measures 14" (35.5 cm) from marker and *at the same time* make a 5-st one-row buttonhole (see page 271) on the center 5 sts when the band measures from neck marker 2¼" (5.5 cm), 5" (12.5 cm), 7¾" (19.5 cm), and 10½" (26.5 cm)—4 buttonholes completed. Work even in rib patt until piece measures 3½" (9 cm) from last buttonhole, 14" (35.5 cm) from neck marker, and about 41¼ (42½)" (105 [108] cm) from CO. BO all sts.

RIGHT FRONT BAND

Note: For right front band, the body section contains buttonholes and the collar section is a plain buttonband.

Using removable markers or safety pins, mark positions for 6 buttonholes along right front edge, the lowest 6¼ (7¾)" (16 [19.5] cm) above CO edge, the highest ¾" (2 cm) below the start of neck shaping, and the rem 4 evenly spaced in between. With size 3 (3.25 mm) needle, CO 15 sts. Work Rows 1 and 2 of rib patt as for left front band and *at the same time* make a 5-st one-row buttonhole on the center 5 sts when the band reaches each marked buttonhole position. Baste or pin the band to the front as you work, review the spacing after the first 3 buttonholes, and adjust as necessary for the rem 3 buttonholes. After completing last buttonhole, work even in rib patt until piece measures 14¾" (37.5 cm) above top buttonhole, 14" (35.5 cm) above seam between neck and collar, and about 41¼ (42½)" (105 [108] cm) from CO. BO all sts.

With yarn threaded on a tapestry needle, sew bands to fronts with seam allowances on WS of garment for body sections and on RS of garment for collar sections so seams will not show on right side when collar is folded down. Sew buttons to RS of left front band opposite buttonholes on right body, then sew buttons to WS of right front band (RS of collar) opposite buttonholes on left collar. With yarn threaded on a tapestry needle, sew sleeve seams. Pin sleeves into armholes and baste in place. With yarn threaded on a tapestry needle and using a backstitch (see page 267), sew sleeves into armholes. Weave in loose ends.

Double Leaves & *project* Twists Duster

This dress-length wrap is an example of a cardigan with a double-taper silhouette that is worked in a lacy pattern that includes twisted and wrapped stitches. It features overlapping fronts, straight shoulders, V-neck shaping, and set-in sleeves with bell cuffs. The collar is worked separately and sewn in place; the front edges are finished with crochet.

FINISHED SIZE

39¾ (46¼)" (101 [117.5] cm) chest circumference, buttoned. To fit bust measurements about 32–35 (36–40)" (81.5–89 [91.5–101.5] cm). Duster shown measures 39¾" (101 cm).

YARN

Worsted weight (#4 Medium).
Shown here: ArtYarns Ultramerino 6 (100% merino; 274 yd [250 m]/100 g): #223 peach, 15 (17) balls.

NEEDLES

One 32" (80 cm) circular needle (cir) each in sizes U.S. 7 (4.5 mm), 6 (4 mm), 5 (3.75 mm), 4 (3.5 mm), and 3 (3.25 mm). Adjust needle size if necessary to obtain the correct gauge.

NOTIONS

Cable needle (cn); stitch holders or waste yarn; tapestry needle; size E/4 (3.5 mm) crochet hook; four shank buttons, one 1" (2.5 cm), one ⅞" (2.2 cm), and two ¾" (2 cm).

Double Leaves & Twists Duster

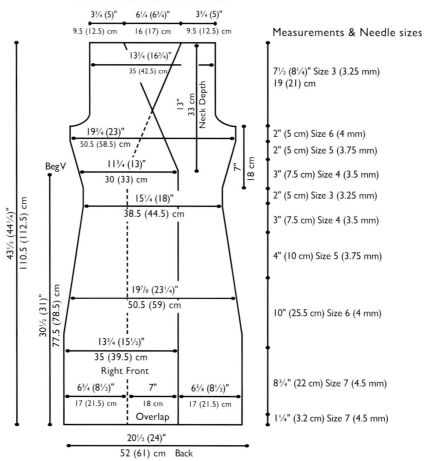

3¾ (5)"
9.5 (12.5) cm

6¼ (6¾)"
16 (17) cm

3¾ (5)"
9.5 (12.5) cm

13¾ (16¾)"
35 (42.5) cm

13"
33 cm Neck Depth

Measurements & Needle sizes

7½ (8¼)" Size 3 (3.25 mm)
19 (21) cm

19¾ (23)"
50.5 (58.5) cm

2" (5 cm) Size 6 (4 mm)

2" (5 cm) Size 5 (3.75 mm)

Beg V

11¾ (13)"
30 (33) cm

3" (7.5 cm) Size 4 (3.5 mm)

7"
18 cm

2" (5 cm) Size 3 (3.25 mm)

15¼ (18)"
38.5 (44.5) cm

3" (7.5 cm) Size 4 (3.5 mm)

4" (10 cm) Size 5 (3.75 mm)

43½ (44¼)"
110.5 (112.5) cm

30½ (31)"
77.5 (78.5) cm

19⅞ (23¼)"
50.5 (59) cm

10" (25.5 cm) Size 6 (4 mm)

13¾ (15½)"
35 (39.5) cm

Right Front

6¾ (8½)"
17 (21.5) cm

7"
18 cm

Overlap

6¾ (8½)"
17 (21.5) cm

8¾ (22 cm) Size 7 (4.5 mm)

1¼ (3.2 cm) Size 7 (4.5 mm)

20½ (24)"
52 (61) cm Back

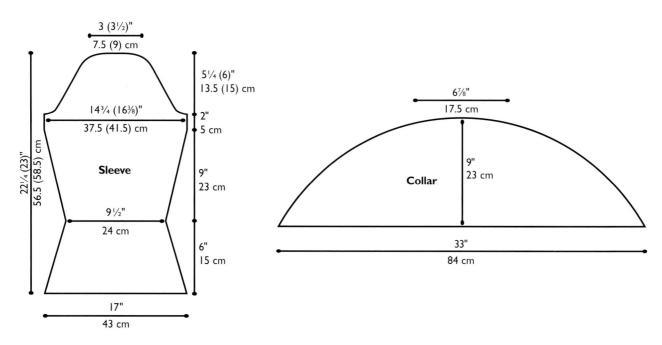

3 (3½)"
7.5 (9) cm

5¼ (6)"
13.5 (15) cm

14¾ (16⅜)"
37.5 (41.5) cm

2"
5 cm

22¼ (23)"
56.5 (58.5) cm

Sleeve

9"
23 cm

9½"
24 cm

6"
15 cm

17"
43 cm

6⅞"
17.5 cm

9"
23 cm

Collar

33"
84 cm

SWATCH SIZES

All swatches are worked in Double Leaves & Twist pattern from chart.

42 stitches and 43 rows = 6" (15 cm) on size 7 (4.5 mm) needle.

44 stitches and 48 rows = 6" (15 cm) on size 6 (4 mm) needle.

48 stitches and 50 rows = 6" (15 cm) on size 5 (3.75 mm) needle.

50 stitches and 50 rows = 6" (15 cm) on size 4 (3.5 mm) needle.

52 stitches and 52 rows = 6" (15 cm) on size 3 (3.25 mm) needle.

GAUGE

All gauges are in Double Leaves & Twist pattern from chart.

7 stitches and 7.16 rows = 1" (2.5 cm) on size 7 (4.5 mm) needle.

7.33 stitches and 8 rows = 1" (2.5 cm) on size 6 (4 mm) needle.

8 stitches and 8.33 rows = 1" (2.5 cm) on size 5 (3.75 mm) needle.

8.33 stitches and 8.33 rows = 1" (2.5 cm) on size 4 (3.5 mm) needle.

8.66 stitches and 8.66 rows = 1" (2.5 cm) on size 3 (3.25 mm) needle.

STITCH GUIDE

Twisted Ribbing (multiple of 3 sts + 5)

Row 1: (RS) K1 (selvedge st; knit every row), p1, k1 through back loop (k1tbl), *p2, k1tbl; rep from * to last 2 sts, p1, k1 (selvedge st; knit every row).

Row 2: (WS) K1 (selvedge st), k1, *p1 through back loop (p1tbl), k2; rep from * to last 3 sts, p1tbl, k1, k1 (selvedge st).

Rep Rows 1 and 2 for pattern.

Sssk

Sl 3 sts individually as if to knit, insert left-hand needle into the fronts of the 3 slipped sts, and knit them tog from this position—2 sts dec'd; dec slants to the left.

Picot Crocheted Edging

Work 1 sl in first st, *ch 4, skip 1 selvedge purl bump space, work 1 sl st in next purl bump space; rep from * to end. Fasten off last st.

4-Stitch Double Wrap (worked over 4 sts)

With RS facing, k1tbl, p2, k1tbl, then sl the 4 sts just worked onto cable needle (cn; Figure 1). With RS still facing, bring yarn to front between the cn and left-hand needle, then holding cn at front, wrap the sts twice (Figures 2 and 3)—4 sts on cn have been double-wrapped. Return the 4 sts on cn to right-hand needle (Figure 4) and cont in patt.

Figure 1

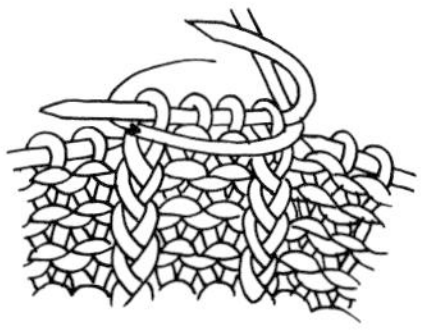

Figure 2

Figure 3

Figure 4

Notes

- Review cardigans with overlapping fronts (page 127), bell cuffs (page 206), vertical shawl collar (page 237), and V-neck shaping on pages 139 and 220.

- Knit the first and last stitch of every row for a garter-stitch selvedge unless otherwise indicated.

- The measurements on the schematic show the actual sizes of the pieces measured inside the selvedge stitches. The selvedge stitches are lost in the seams and do not count toward the finished bust sizes.

- Use the sloped method of binding off (see page 77) to shape the armholes, neckline, and sleeve cap to avoid "stair steps" along the bind-off edges.

Double Leaves & Twists Chart

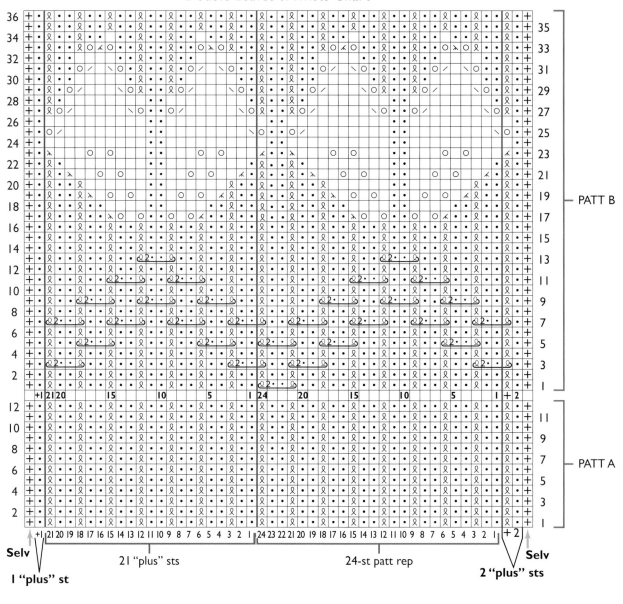

PATT B

PATT A

Selv

21 "plus" sts

24-st patt rep

Selv

1 "plus" st

2 "plus" sts

☐	K on RS; P on WS	
•	P on RS; K on WS	
○	Yarnover	
ℜ	K1tbl on RS; P1tbl on WS	
╱	K2tog	
╲	Ssk	
⁺	Selvedge st	
⌐	P2tog	
⚹	K3tog	
⅄	Sssk (see Stitch Guide)	
ℜ2·⚬	4-stitch double-wrap (see Stitch Guide)	
M	Make 1	
▨	No stitch	
☐	Pattern repeat	

Double Leaves & Twists Dec & Inc. Chart

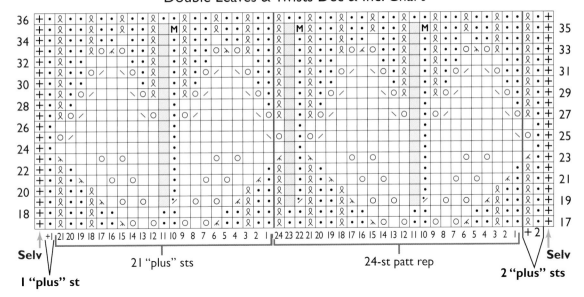

BACK

With size 7 (4.5 mm) needle, CO 146 (170) sts. Work in twisted rib patt (see Stitch Guide on page 293) for 12 rows—piece measures about 1¼" (3.2 cm). Establish patt from Row 1 of Double Leaves & Twist chart as foll: K1 (selvedge st; see Notes), work 2 "plus" sts once, work the 24-st patt rep a total of 5 (6) times, work 22 "plus" sts once, k1 (selvedge st). Cont in established patt, work Rows 2–36 of chart once, then work Rows 1–26 once more.

Note: For a neater join without the end-of-row eyelets on Row 25 abutting when the sides are seamed, on RS Row 23 work a single decrease on the last pattern repeat stitch of the row, then work the p1 and selvedge stitch. This will leave the last yarnover without a matching decrease. On Row 25, do not work the last yarnover; instead work k1tbl on the last pattern repeat stitch. The last k2tog will serve as the matching decrease for the last yarnover on Row 23. On Row 26, begin with the selvedge st and k1 "plus" stitch, then work p1tbl on the first pattern stitch.

When 62 chart rows have been completed and piece measures about 10" (25.5 cm) from CO, change to size 6 (4 mm) needle. Work Rows 27–36 of chart once, then work Rows 1–36 once, then work Rows 1–34 again—80 rows completed on size 6 (4 mm) needle; piece should measure 20" (51 cm) from CO. Change to size 5 (3.5 mm) needle. Work Rows 35–36 once, then work Rows 1–30 once—32 rows completed on size 5 (3.75 mm) needle; piece should measure 24" (61 cm) from CO. Change to size 4 (3.5 mm) needle. Work Rows 31–36 once, then work Rows 1–18 once—24 rows completed on size 4 (3.5 mm) needle; a total of five 36-row reps plus 18 rows have been worked (198 rows total); piece should measure 27" (68.5 cm) from CO. Change to size 3 (3.25 mm) needle.

Waist dec row: (RS; Row 19) Dec 1 st on the p2 sts between the two leaves at the end of each multiple (dec 2 sts per patt multiple and 1 st on the 22 ending "plus" sts) as shown on Double Leaves & Twist Dec/Inc chart as foll: P2tog on the 10th and 11th sts, then again on the 22nd and 23rd sts of the 5 (6) patt multiples and 1 st in the center p2tog of the "plus" sts to dec 11 (13) sts—135 (157) sts rem.

Work Rows 20–34 of chart once—16 rows completed on size 3 (3.25 mm) needle; piece should measure 29" (73.5 cm) from CO. Change to size 4 (3.5 mm) needle.

Inc row: (RS; Row 35) Beg increasing for bust by working a M1 inc on the p1 sts between the two leaves at the end of each multiple on patt sts 10 and 22 of the 5 (6) patt reps and on the 10th st of the "plus" sts to restore the st count to the 11 (13) p2 sts that were decreased in the waist shaping, as shown on the Double Leaves & Twist Dec/Inc chart—146 (170) sts.

Work Row 36 of chart once, then work Rows 1–22 of main chart once—24 rows completed on size 4 (3.5 mm) needle; piece measures about 32" (81.5 cm) from CO. Change to size 5 (3.75 mm) needle. Work Rows 23–36 once, then work Rows 1 and 2 once—16 rows completed on size 5 (3.75 mm) needle; piece should measure 34" (86.5 cm) from CO. Change to size 6 (4 mm) needle). Work Rows 3–18 once—16 rows completed on size 6 (4 mm) needle; piece should measure 36" (91.5 cm) from CO; 282 rows total: 270 chart rows and 12 rib rows.

SHAPE ARMHOLES

Change to size 3 (3.25 mm) needle. With RS facing and keeping in patt, use the sloped bind-off method (see page 77) to BO 4 sts at the beg of the next 2 rows, then BO 3 sts at the beg of the foll 2 rows, then BO 2 sts at the beg of the foll 2 rows, then BO 1 st at the beg of the foll 6 rows, ending with Row 30—24 sts dec'd; 122 (146) sts rem. Work Rows 31–36 once, then work Rows 1–36 once, then work Rows 1–10 (18) again—64 (72) rows completed on size 3 (3.25 mm) needle; armholes should measure 7½ (8¼)" (19 [21] cm); 346 (354) rows total; 334 (342) chart rows and 12 rib rows.

Next row: (RS) Keeping in patt, work 34 (44) sts for shoulder, BO center 54 (58) sts for back neck, work to end—34 (44) sts rem for each shoulder.

Place shoulder sts on separate on holders.

RIGHT FRONT

With size 7 (4.5mm) needle, CO 98 (110) sts. Work in twisted rib patt for 12 rows—piece measures about 1¼" (3.2 cm). Establish patt from Row 1 of Double Leaves & Twist chart for your size as foll:

Size 39¾" (101 cm) Only

K1 (selvedge st; see page 55), work 2 "plus" sts, work the 24-st patt rep 3 times, work 22 "plus" sts, k1 (selvedge st).

Size 46¼" (117.5 cm) Only

K1 (selvedge st; see page 55), work 2 "plus" sts, work 12 patt sts (sts 13 to 24), work the 24-st patt rep 3 times, work 22 "plus" sts, k1 (selvedge st).

Both Sizes

Cont as established, work Rows 2–36 of chart once, then work Rows 1–26 once more—62 chart rows completed; piece should measure 10" (25.5 cm) from CO.

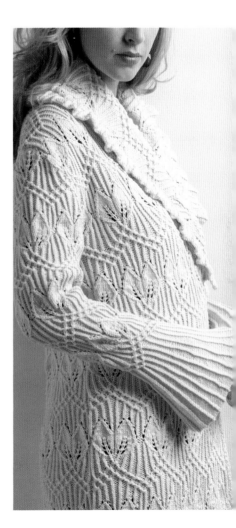

Note: Work the pattern last st on Rows 23 and 25 and the first pattern st on Row 26 as for the back.

Working patt rows as for back, work 80 rows on size 6 (4 mm) needle, 32 rows on size 5 (3.75 mm) needle, and 24 rows on size 4 (3.5 mm) needle—piece should measure 27" (68.5 cm) from CO. Change to size 3 (3.25 mm) needle.

Waist dec row: (RS; Row 19) Working in patt, dec 1 st by working p2tog in each of the p2 sts in the center of the leaves on the 10th and 11th sts, then near the end of the multiples on the 22nd and 23rd sts to dec 2 sts in each of the three 24-st patt reps, 1 st in the 22-st "plus" sts section, and 1 st in the 14-st partial patt section for the larger size. For the 14-st section at the beg of the larger size, the decs can only be worked on the 22nd and 23rd sts; on the "plus" sts for both sizes, the decs can only be worked at the beg of the multiple on the 10th and 11th sts—7 (8) sts dec'd; 91 (102) sts rem.

Cont to work as established for both sizes, work Rows 20–34 of chart once—16 rows completed on size 3 (3.25 mm) needle; piece should measure 29" (73.5 cm) from CO. Change to size 4 (3.5 mm) needle.

Inc row: (RS; Row 35) Working in patt, inc 2 sts by working M1 inc in each of the p1 sections that were dec'd for the waist to restore these sections back to p2—98 (110) sts.

Work Row 36 of chart once, then work Rows 1–10 (14) once—12 (16) rows completed on size 4 (3.5 mm) needle; piece should measure 30½ (31)" (77.5 [78.5] cm) from CO.

SHAPE V-NECK

Note: Neck shaping will still be in progress when armhole shaping is introduced; read the next sections all the way through before proceeding. For neck shaping, there are 108 (112) rows from the beg of the V shaping to the shoulder; the final 4 rows are worked even. The V is shaped over 104 (108) rows. When the V is shaped, we will work only at the neck edge; therefore, divide the row number in half.

Beg on next RS row, use the sloped bind-off method (see page 77) to BO 1 st at beg of next 52 (54) RS (neck edge) rows. *At the same time* cont to work even at the side edge except during armhole BO. Work as foll: Work Rows 11 (15)–22 once, dec 6 (4) sts foll the neck edge dec instructions (i.e., half the number of sts dec'd as rows worked)— 12 (8) rows worked; 6 (4) sts dec'd; 92 (106) sts rem; 24 rows completed on size 4 (3.5 mm) needle; 12 (8) rows from start of neck shaping; piece should measure 32" (81.5 cm) from CO. Change to size 5 (3.75 mm) needle. Cont neck shaping, work Rows 23–36 once, then work Rows 1 and 2 once—84 (98) sts; 16 rows completed on size 5 (3.75 mm) needle; piece should measure 34" (86.5 cm) from CO. Change to size 6 (4 mm) needle. Cont neck shaping, work Rows 3–18 once—76 (90) sts; 16 rows completed on size 6 (4 mm) needle; piece should measure 36" (91.5 cm) from CO; 282 rows total: 270 chart rows and 12 rib rows. Change to size 3 (3.25 mm) needle.

SHAPE ARMHOLE (CONT V-NECK SHAPING)

Keep in patt and cont neck decs and *at the same time* use the sloped bind-off method to shape the armhole as foll: BO 4 sts at the beg of the next WS row, then BO 3 sts at the beg of the foll WS row, then BO 2 sts at the beg of the foll WS row, then BO 1 st at the beg of the foll 3 WS rows, ending with Row 30—6 sts BO at neck and 12 sts BO at armhole; 58 (72) sts rem. Cont neck shaping, work Rows 31–36 once, then work Rows 1–36 once, then work Rows 1–6 (14) once more—24 (28) sts BO at neck; 34 (44) sts rem. Work 4 rows even as foll:

Size 39¾" (101 cm) Only
Work Rows 7–10.

Size 46¼" (117.5 cm) Only
Work Rows 15–18.

Both Sizes
A total of 64 (72) rows have been completed on size 3 (3.25 mm) needle; armhole measures about 7½ (8¼)" (19 [21] cm); 346 (354) rows total; 334 (342) chart rows and 12 rib rows. Place sts on holder.

LEFT FRONT

With size 7 (4.5mm) needle, CO 98 (110) sts. Work in twisted rib patt for 12 rows—piece measures about 1¼" (3.2 cm). Establish patt from Row 1 of Double Leaves & Twist chart as foll: K1 (selvedge st), work 2 "plus" sts once, work the 24-st patt rep a total of 3 (4) times, ending as foll.

Size 39¾" (101 cm) Only

End by working 22 "plus" sts, k1 (selvedge st).

Size 46¼" (117.5 cm) Only

End by working sts 1–10 of the 5th patt rep, k1.

Note: At the center front edge, the last wrapped sts will be patt sts 6–9.

Cont as established, work Rows 2–36 of chart once, then work Rows 1–26 once more—62 chart rows completed; piece should measure 10" (25.5 cm) from CO. Working patt rows while changing needles as for back, work 80 rows on size 6 (4 mm) needle, 32 rows on size 5 (3.75 mm) needle, and 24 rows on size 4 (3.5 mm) needle—piece should measure 27" (68.5 cm) from CO. Change to size 3 (3.25 mm) needle.

Waist dec row: (RS; Row 19) Work in patt, dec 2 sts by working p2tog on the 10th and 11th sts between the leaves and on the 22nd and 23rd sts in each of the 3 (4) complete patt reps, 1 st in 22-st "plus" sts section for the small size, and no sts in the 10-st partial patt section for larger size as shown on chart—91 (102) sts rem.

Note: For larger size, there will not be enough sts to work a dec inside the center front selvedge st; cont to work the first st in from the edge in rev St st as established.

Work Rows 20–34 of chart once—16 rows completed on size 3 (3.25 mm) needle; piece should measure 29" (73.5 cm) from CO. Change to size 4 (3.5 mm) needle.

Inc row: (RS; Row 35) Work in patt, inc 2 sts in each of the 3 (4) patt reps and 1 st in the "plus" sts of the smaller size by working M1 in each of the p1 sts that were dec'd at the waist to restore the sts to the beg st count—98 (110) sts.

Work Row 36 of chart once, then work Rows 1–10 (14) once—12 (16) rows completed on size 4 (3.5 mm) needle; piece should measure 30½" (31)" (77.5 [78.5] cm) from CO.

SHAPE NECK AND ARMHOLE

Note: This section is worked the same as the right front with the shaping rows reversed. See that section for a detailed description of the calculation techniques.

For neck shaping, beg on next WS row, use the sloped bind-off method to BO 1 st at beg of next 52 (54) WS rows. *At the same time* work Rows 11 (15) –22 once—92 (106) sts; 24 rows completed on size 4 (3.5 mm) needle; 12 (8) rows from start of neck shaping; piece should measure 32" (81.5 cm) from CO. Change to size 5 (3.75 mm) needle. Cont neck shaping, work Rows 23–36 once, then work Rows 1 and 2 once—84 (98) sts; 16 rows completed on size 5 (3.75 mm) needle; piece should measure 34" (86.5 cm) from CO. Change to size 6 (4 mm) needle. Cont neck shaping, work Rows 3–18 once—76 (90) sts; 16 rows completed on size 6 (4 mm) needle; piece should measure 36" (91.5 cm) from CO; 282 rows total: 270 chart rows and 12 rib rows. Change to size 3 (3.25 mm) needle.

SHAPE ARMHOLE (CONT V-NECK SHAPING)

Keeping in patt and cont neck decs, use the sloped bind-off method to BO 4 sts at the beg of the next RS row, then BO 3 sts at the beg of the foll RS row, then BO 2 sts at the beg of the foll RS row, then BO 1 st at the beg of the foll 3 RS rows, ending with Row 30—58 (72) sts rem. Cont neck shaping, work Rows 31–36 once, then work Rows 1–36 once, then work Rows 1–6 (14) once again—34 (44) sts rem.

Size 39¾" (101 cm) Only
Work Rows 7–10 once.

Size 46¼" (117.5 cm) Only
Work Rows 15–18 once.

Both Sizes
64 (72) rows completed on size 3 (3.25 mm) needle; armhole should measure 7½ (8¼)" (19 [21] cm); 346 (354) rows total; 334 (342) chart rows and 12 rib rows. Place sts on holder.

SLEEVES

With size 5 (3.75mm) needle, CO 120 sts.

BELL-CUFF SHAPING

Row 1: (RS) K1 (selvedge st), p1, k1tbl, *p4, k1tbl; rep from * 23 times to last 2 sts, p1, k1 (selvedge st).

Row 2: (WS) K2, *p1tbl, k4; rep from * to last 3 sts, p1tbl, k2.

Rows 3–8: Rep Rows 1 and 2 three more times.

Row 9: Dec 1 st in every other p4 section as foll: K1, p1, k1tbl, *p1, p2tog, p1, k1tbl, p4, k1tbl; rep from * to last 7 sts, p1, p2tog, p1, k1tbl, p1, k1—12 sts dec'd; 108 sts rem.

Row 10: K2, *p1tbl, k3, p1tbl, k4; rep from * to last 7 sts, p1tbl, k3, p1tbl, k2.

Row 11: K1, p1, k1tbl, *p3, k1tbl, p4, k1tbl; rep from * to last 6 sts, p3, k1tbl, p1, k1.

Rows 12–18: Rep Rows 10 and 11 three more times, then work Row 10 once more.

Row 19: Dec 1 st in every rem p4 section as foll: K1, p1, k1tbl, *p3, k1tbl, p1, p2tog, p1, k1tbl; rep from * to last 6 sts, p3, k1tbl, p1, k1—11 sts dec'd; 97 sts rem.

Row 20: K2, *p1tbl, k3; rep from * to last 3 sts, p1tbl, k2.

Row 21: K1, p1, *k1tbl, p3; rep from * to last 3 sts, k1tbl, p1, k1.

Rows 22–28: Rep Rows 20 and 21 three more times, then work Row 20 once more.

Row 29: Dec 1 st in every other p3 section as foll: K1, p1, k1tbl, *p2tog, p1, k1tbl, p3, k1tbl; rep from * to last 6 sts, p2tog, p1, k1tbl, p1, k1—12 sts dec'd; 85 sts rem.

Row 30: K2, *p1tbl, k2, p1tbl, k3; rep from * to last 6 sts, [p1tbl, k2] 2 times.

Row 31: K1, p1, *k1tbl, p2, k1tbl, p3; rep from * to last 6 sts, k1tbl, p2, k1tbl, p1, k1.

Rows 32–38: Rep Rows 30 and 31 three more times, then work Row 30 once more.

Row 39: Dec 1 st in every rem p3 section as foll: K1, p1, k1tbl, *p2, k1tbl, p2tog, p1, k1tbl; rep from * to last 5 sts, p2, k1tbl, p1, k1—11 sts dec'd; 74 sts rem.

Row 40: Beg working twisted rib patt as foll: K2, *p1tbl, k2; rep from * to end. Work 10 rows in twisted rib—50 rows total; piece measures about 6" (15 cm) from CO.

SHAPE SIDES

On Row 51, beg Double Leaves & Twists chart as foll.

Note: For sleeve, rep Rows 1–36 of Double Leaves chart for the center patt and the k1tbl, p2 twisted rib patt at the sides as the inc's are made. When the sleeves are seamed, the top will be in the double leaves patt and the under side will be in the twisted rib patt.

Establish patt from Row 1 of Double Leaves & Twist chart as foll: K1 (selvedge st), work 2 "plus" sts once, work the 24-st patt rep a total of 2 times, work 22 "plus" sts once, k1 (selvedge st). Cont in patt and *at the same time* beg on next RS row, inc 1 st at each end of needle inside selvedge sts every 4th row 14 (4) times, then every 5th (3rd) row 4 (20) times, working inc'd sts in twisted rib patt as they become available—18 (24) sts inc'd each side; 110 (122) sts total; 6 (8) reps of the 3-st twisted rib patt inc'd at each side; 80 rows of Double Leaves & Twist chart completed. Work even in patt for 16 more rows, ending with Row 24—96 chart rows completed, piece should measure 15" (38 cm) from CO and 9" (23 cm) from last row of cuff.

SHAPE CAP

Keeping in patt and using the sloped bind-off method, BO 4 sts at the beg of the next 2 rows, then BO 2 sts at the beg of the foll 6 (4) rows—90 (106) sts rem. [BO 1 st at the beg of the foll 2 rows, then BO 2 sts at the beg of the foll 2 rows] 8 (10) times—42 (46) sts rem. BO 4 sts at the beg of the next 4 rows—26 (30) sts rem. BO all sts.

COLLAR

With size 6 (4 mm) needle, CO 242 sts. CO will be the neck edge. Establish patt from Row 1 of Double Leaves & Twist chart as foll: K1 (selvedge st), work 2 "plus" sts once, work the 24-st patt rep a total of 9 times, work 22 "plus" sts once, k1 (selvedge st). Work Row 2 of patt. Starting on Row 3, use the sloped bind-off method to BO 1 st at beg of next 6 rows, then BO 2 sts at the beg of the foll 2 rows—232 sts rem. [BO 1 st at the beg of the foll 2 rows, then BO 2 sts at the beg of the foll 4 rows] 5 times—182 sts rem. BO 3 sts at the beg of the foll 4 rows, then BO 2 sts at the beg of the foll 4 rows—162 sts rem. BO 3 sts at the beg of the foll 2 rows, then BO 2 sts at the beg of the foll 4 rows, then BO 3 sts at the beg of the foll 2 rows—142 sts rem. BO 4 sts at the beg of the foll 6 rows, then BO 5 sts at the beg of the foll 4 rows—98 sts rem. BO 6 sts at the beg of the foll 8 rows—50 sts rem; piece should measure 9" (23 cm) from CO at center. BO all sts.

FINISHING

Block pieces to measurements (see Notes on page 293), taking care not to flatten collar ruffle. Place 34 (44) held right front shoulder sts on one needle and the corresponding 34 (44) held right back shoulder sts on another needle. Hold needles parallel with RS touching and WS facing out, and use tip of size 3 (3.25 mm) needle and the three-needle bind-off method (see page 263) to join shoulder sts; BO ridge will be on WS of garment. Rep for left shoulder sts.

OUTER COLLAR RUFFLE

With size 5 (3.75 mm) needle, CO 485 sts. Purl

Rows 1 and 3: (RS) K1 (selvedge st), p1, k1tbl, *   p1, k1 (selvedge st).

Rows 2 and 4: K2, *p1tbl, k5; rep from * to last 3 sts, p1tbl, k2.

Row 5: K1, p1, k1tbl, *p2tog, p1, p2tog, k1tbl; rep from * to last 2 sts, p1, k1—325 sts rem.

Rows 6 and 8: K2, *p1tbl, k3; rep from * to last 3 sts, p1tbl, k2.

Row 7: K1, p1, k1tbl, *p3, k1tbl; rep from * to last 2 sts, p1, k1.

Row 9: K1, p1, k1tbl, *p1, p2tog, k1tbl; rep from * to last 2 sts, p1, k1—245 sts rem.

Row 10: K2, *p1tbl, k2; rep from * to end.

BO all sts in patt on next RS row.

With yarn threaded on a tapestry needle, use a backstitch (see page 267) to sew BO edge of ruffle evenly along shaped BO edge of collar. With yarn threaded on a tapestry needle, use a whipstitch (see page 266) to sew CO edge of collar to neckline between starting points of V-neck shaping with RS of collar corresponding to WS of duster so RS of collar will show on the right side when collar is folded back.

BUTTON COVERS (MAKE 3)

Note: Make one button cover in each size; the second ¾" (2 cm) button is an inside button and is not covered.

Make a slipknot and place on crochet hook (see page 277 for crochet instructions). Ch 2, then work 8 sc in the slipknot.

Rnd 1: *2 sc in the next sc, 1 sc in the next sc; rep from *—12 sc.

Rnd 2: Work 1 sc in each sc around.

Rep Rnd 2 until cover extends a little bit beyond the edges of the chosen button when laid on top of it.

Dec rnd: *Skip 1 sc, 1 sc in the next sc; rep from *—6 sc.

If the cover has curled into a small pouch-shape with its WS facing out after working the dec rnd, turn it RS out again.

Insert the button, then work the dec rnd once more—3 sc rem. Join to first sc of dec rnd with a slip st, then fasten off last st. Thread starting tail on a tapestry needle, run the tail through the beginning 8 sc, drawstring-fashion, and pull snugly to close center hole. Cover two more buttons in different sizes in the same manner.

BUTTON BACKINGS (MAKE 4)

Make a slipknot and place on crochet hook. Work as for button covers until Rnd 2 has been completed—12 sc. Join to first sc of rnd with a slip stitch, and fasten off last st.

FRONT EDGE AND BUTTON LOOPS

With RS facing and crochet hook, join yarn to base of V-neck shaping on left front. Work picot crochet edging (see Stitch Guide on page 293) along left front to CO edge. Fasten off last st. With RS facing and crochet hook, join yarn to CO edge of right front and work picot crochet edging in the same manner along right front to base of V-neck shaping. With RS facing, rejoin yarn to beg of first picot on left front, ch 7 or 8 sts, join with a slip st to end of first picot. Test to make sure the button loop fits over the uncovered ¾" (2 cm) button, adjust if necessary, then fasten off. Mark positions for three button loops on right front edge, ¾" (2 cm), 2½" (6.5 cm), and 4¼" (11 cm) down from base of V-neck shaping, respectively. Apply three chained button loops in the same manner (about 10 to 15 ch sts, depending on button size) centered on marked positions to accommodate the smallest covered button in the highest position, the largest button in the lowest position, and the middle-size button in the center position. Test each loop to make sure it fits very closely around the button so the garment will stay snugly fastened.

Lay garment flat with right front overlapping left front and side selvedges aligned. Mark button positions on left front directly under the three right front button loops. Using two separated plies of yarn threaded on a tapestry needle, use a whipstitch to join button backing to the WS of left front underneath each marked button position. Sew three covered buttons to RS of left front with the smallest button on top, middle-size button in the center, and largest button on the bottom, sewing through both the garment and button backing layers. Mark button position on WS of right front aligned with the left front button loop. Whipstitch rem button backing to the WS of right front at marked position. Sew uncovered button to WS of right front, sewing through both garment and button backing.

With yarn threaded on a tapestry needle, sew the side seams. Sew the sleeve seams. Sew sleeve caps into armholes. Weave in loose ends.

Pea Coat

This cabled coat is an example of a double-taper body with a double-breasted front overlap. It features straight shoulders, V-neck shaping, and tapered sleeves with shaped turn-back cuffs and set-in caps. The cuffs, collar, and lapels are worked separately and sewn in place.

FINISHED SIZE

42 (46, 50)" (106.5 [117, 127] cm) chest circumference, buttoned. To fit bust measurements about 34–38 (38–42, 42–46)" (86.5–96.5 [96.5–106.5, 106.5–117] cm).
Coat shown measures 42" (106.5 cm).

YARN

Worsted weight (#4 Medium) for coat; DK weight (#3 Light) for button backs.

Shown here: Filatura Di Crosa Zara Plus (100% Extra Fine Merino; 77 yd [70 m]/50 g): #25 Crimson (MC), 28 (31, 34) balls.

Filatura Di Crosa Zara (100% Extra Fine Merino; 137 yd [125 m]/50 g): #1493 Crimson (CC), 1 ball (used for button backs).

NEEDLES

Body and sleeves—size U.S. 8 (5 mm): straight. **Cuffs**—size U.S. 9 (5.5 mm): straight. **Three-needle bind-off and I-cord edging**—size U.S. 7 (4.5 mm): 32" (80 cm) circular (cir). Adjust needle size if necessary to obtain the correct gauge.

NOTIONS

Cable needle (cn); stitch holders; tapestry needle; upholstery pins; sizes E/4 (3.5 mm) and G/7 (4.5 mm) crochet hooks; nine 1" (2.5 cm) buttons (one may be different to use for inner button).

GAUGE

All swatches are worked with smaller straight needles using pattern combinations as noted.

Collar:
5.6 sts and 6 rows = 1" (2.5 cm).

Body chart:
(This is the charted section of the front and back, excluding the twisted St st patt on each side) 42 center sts from chart (38 center sts in ribbon and latch motif, plus 2 rev St sts at each side) = 7½" (19 cm) wide; 96 sts of entire chart = 17" (43 cm) wide; 27 sts of left front side section measures 4¾" (12 cm) wide; 14 sts in the center of the ribbon and latch patt measure 2½" (6.5 cm) wide; 69 sts of the right front section measure about 12¼" (31 cm) wide; 34 rows = 6" (15 cm) long.

Sleeve, Cuff, and Collar chart:
36 sts = 6" (15 cm) wide; 34 rows = 6" (15 cm) long.

Twisted stockinette stitch:
36 sts = 8¼" (21.5 cm) wide; and 34 rows = 6" (15 cm) long.

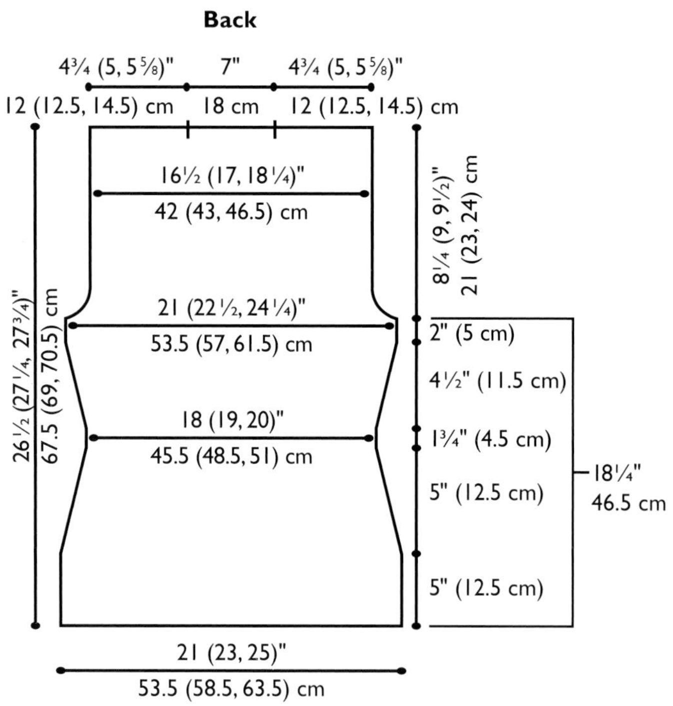
Back
4¾ (5, 5⅝)"
7"
4¾ (5, 5⅝)"
12 (12.5, 14.5) cm
18 cm
12 (12.5, 14.5) cm
16½ (17, 18¼)"
42 (43, 46.5) cm
21 (22½, 24¼)"
53.5 (57, 61.5) cm
18 (19, 20)"
45.5 (48.5, 51) cm
26½ (27¼, 27¾)"
67.5 (69, 70.5) cm
8¼ (9, 9½)"
21 (23, 24) cm
2" (5 cm)
4½" (11.5 cm)
1¾" (4.5 cm)
5" (12.5 cm)
5" (12.5 cm)
18¼"
46.5 cm
21 (23, 25)"
53.5 (58.5, 63.5) cm

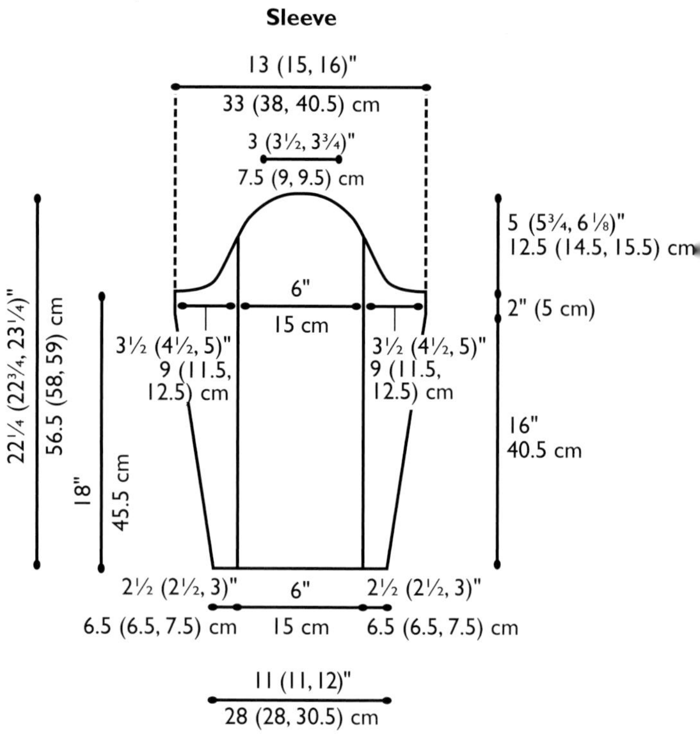
Sleeve
13 (15, 16)"
33 (38, 40.5) cm
3 (3½, 3¾)"
7.5 (9, 9.5) cm
5 (5¾, 6⅛)"
12.5 (14.5, 15.5) cm
6"
15 cm
2" (5 cm)
3½ (4½, 5)"
9 (11.5, 12.5) cm
3½ (4½, 5)"
9 (11.5, 12.5) cm
22¼ (22¾, 23¼)"
56.5 (58, 59) cm
18"
45.5 cm
16"
40.5 cm
2½ (2½, 3)"
6"
2½ (2½, 3)"
6.5 (6.5, 7.5) cm
15 cm
6.5 (6.5, 7.5) cm
11 (11, 12)"
28 (28, 30.5) cm

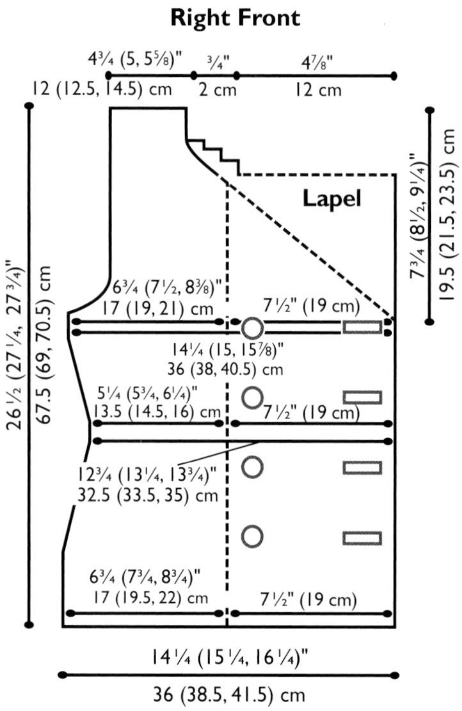
Right Front
4¾ (5, 5⅝)"
¾"
4⅞"
12 (12.5, 14.5) cm
2 cm
12 cm
Lapel
7¾ (8½, 9¼)"
19.5 (21.5, 23.5) cm
26½ (27¼, 27¾)"
67.5 (69, 70.5) cm
6¾ (7½, 8⅜)"
17 (19, 21) cm
7½" (19 cm)
14¼ (15, 15⅞)"
36 (38, 40.5) cm
5¼ (5¾, 6¼)"
13.5 (14.5, 16) cm
7½" (19 cm)
12¾ (13¼, 13¾)"
32.5 (33.5, 35) cm
6¾ (7¾, 8¾)"
17 (19.5, 22) cm
7½" (19 cm)
14¼ (15¼, 16¼)"
36 (38.5, 41.5) cm

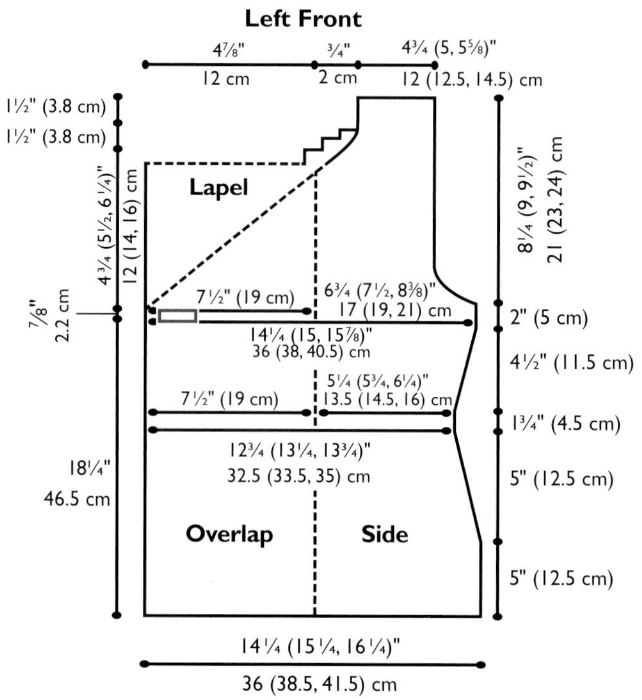
Left Front
4⅞"
¾"
4¾ (5, 5⅝)"
12 cm
2 cm
12 (12.5, 14.5) cm
1½" (3.8 cm)
1½" (3.8 cm)
Lapel
4¾ (5½, 6¼)"
12 (14, 16) cm
⅞"
2.2 cm
7½" (19 cm)
6¾ (7½, 8⅜)"
17 (19, 21) cm
14¼ (15, 15⅞)"
36 (38, 40.5) cm
7½" (19 cm)
5¼ (5¾, 6¼)"
13.5 (14.5, 16) cm
12¾ (13¼, 13¾)"
32.5 (33.5, 35) cm
18¼"
46.5 cm
Overlap
Side
8¼ (9, 9½)"
21 (23, 24) cm
2" (5 cm)
4½" (11.5 cm)
1¾" (4.5 cm)
5" (12.5 cm)
5" (12.5 cm)
14¼ (15¼, 16¼)"
36 (38.5, 41.5) cm

STITCH GUIDE

Twisted Stockinette

Row 1: (RS) Knit all sts through the back loop (tbl).

Row 2: (WS) Purl.

Repeat Rows 1 and 2 for pattern.

DBLT2B

RS rows: Sl 1 st onto cn and hold in back, k1tbl, k1tbl from cn.

WS rows: Sl 1 st onto cn and hold in back, p1tbl, p1tbl from cn.

DBLT2F

RS rows: Sl 1 st onto cn and hold in front, k1tbl, k1tbl from cn.

WS rows: Sl 1 st onto cn and hold in front, p1tbl, p1tbl from cn.

T2B

RS rows: Sl 1 st onto cn and hold in back, k1tbl, p1 from cn.

WS rows: Sl 1 st onto cn and hold in back, k1, p1tbl from cn.

T2F

RS rows: Sl 1 st onto cn and hold in front, p1, k1tbl from cn.

WS rows: Sl 1 st onto cn and hold in front, p1tbl, k1 from cn.

T3B

RS rows: Sl 1 st onto cn and hold in back, [k1tbl] 2 times, p1 from cn.

WS rows: Sl 2 sts onto cn and hold in back, k1, [p1tbl] 2 times from cn.

T3F

RS rows: Sl 2 sts onto cn and hold in front, p1, [k1tbl] 2 times from cn.

WS rows: Sl 1 st onto cn and hold in front, [p1tbl] 2 times, k1 from cn.

DBLT3B

WS rows: Sl 2 sts onto cn and hold in back, p1tbl, [p1tbl] 2 times from cn.

DBLT3F

WS rows: Sl 1 st onto cn and hold in front, [p1tbl] 2 times, p1tbl from cn.

DBLT4B

RS rows: Sl 2 sts onto cn and hold in back, [k1tbl] 2 times, [k1tbl] 2 times from cn.

DBLT4F

RS rows: Sl 2 sts onto cn and hold in front, [k1tbl] 2 times, [k1tbl] 2 times from cn.

Reverse Single Crochet (rev sc)

Working from left to right, insert crochet hook into work, wrap yarn over hook, and draw the yarn through, then wrap the yarn over the hook again and draw the yarn through both loops on the hook.

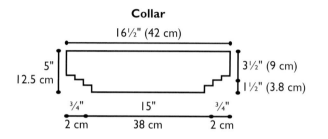

Collar

16½" (42 cm)

5"
12.5 cm

3½" (9 cm)

1½" (3.8 cm)

¾"
2 cm

15"
38 cm

¾"
2 cm

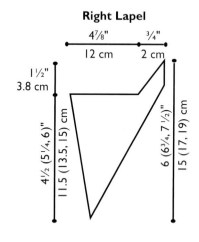

Right Lapel

4⅞"
12 cm

¾"
2 cm

1½"
3.8 cm

4½ (5¼, 6)"
11.5 (13.5, 15) cm

6 (6¾, 7½)"
15 (17, 19) cm

BACK

With MC and size 8 (5 mm) straight needles, CO 116 (124, 132) sts. Establish patt from Row 1 of Body chart (see page 312) as foll: K1 (selvedge st, see Notes), work 9 (13, 17) sts in twisted St st (see Stitch Guide), work center 96 sts in patt from chart, work 9 (13, 17) sts in twisted St st, k1 (selvedge st). Cont in established patt (see Notes) until piece measures 5" (12.5 cm) from CO, ending with a WS row.

HIP-TO-WAIST DECREASES

Cont in patt, dec 1 st at each side inside selvedge sts on next RS row, then every foll 4th (3rd, 2nd) row 3 (5, 3) times, then every foll 5th (4th, 3rd) row 3 (3, 7) times, ending with a WS row—102 (106, 110) sts rem; 7 (9, 11) sts removed from each side; 2 (4, 6) twisted St sts rem inside selvedge sts at each side; 28 rows in hip-to-waist dec section; piece measures about 10" (25.5 cm) from CO.

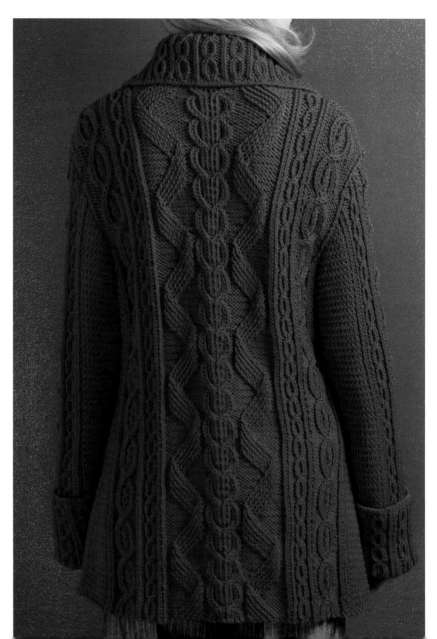

WAIST

Work 10 rows even in patt, ending with a WS row—piece should measure 11¾" (30 cm) from CO.

WAIST-TO-BUST INCREASES

Cont in patt, inc 1 st at each side inside selvedge sts on next RS row, then every foll 4th (3rd, 2nd) row 5 (3, 2) time(s), then every foll 5th (4th, 3rd) row 1 (4, 7) time(s), working inc'd sts in twisted St st and ending with a WS row—116 (122, 130) sts; 7 (8, 10) sts inc'd at each side; 9 (12, 16) twisted St sts inside selvedge sts at each side; 26 rows in waist-to-hip inc section; piece measures about 16¼" (41.5 cm) from CO. Work even in patt until piece measures 18¼" (46.5 cm) from CO, ending with Row 8 of chart—104 chart rows completed.

SHAPE ARMHOLES

Keeping in patt and using the sloped bind-off method (see page 77), BO 3 (4, 4) sts at the beg of next 2 (2, 2) rows, then BO 2 (3, 3) sts at beg of the foll 4 (2, 4) rows, then BO 1 (2, 2) st(s) at the beg of the foll 4 (4, 2) rows, then BO 0 (1, 1) st at the beg of the foll 0 (2, 2) rows. *At the same time* for size small only, on the last RS shaping row dec 1 st by working k2tog tbl on the first and last 2 Tw sts—20 (24, 26) sts dec'd; 96 (98, 104) sts rem.

Note: For the smallest size, the selvedge and 8 of 9 twisted St sts are dec'd on each side during the armhole shaping. On the last RS row, 1 twist st is also dec'd. After the armhole shaping, the selvedge is reestablished using the last twisted St st on each side. The st sequence for the rem 96 sts is as foll:

> selvedge st, p1, 1 Tw, 90 center chart sts, 1 Tw, p1, selvedge st.

Work even in patt until 46 (50, 54) armhole rows have been completed, ending with Row 6 (10, 14) of chart—armholes should measure 8¼ (9, 9½)" (21 [23, 24] cm); piece should measure 26½ (27¼, 27¾)" (67.5 [69, 70.5] cm from CO.

SHAPE SHOULDERS

Next row: (RS) Keeping in patt, work 29 (30, 33) sts for right back shoulder, BO center 38 sts for back neck, work in patt to end for left back shoulder—29 (30, 33) sts at each side. Place shoulder sts on separate holders.

Notes

- Review cardigans with overlapping fronts (see page 127), notched lapels (see page 254), and fold-back cuffs (see page 205).

- Knit the first and last stitch of every row for a garter-stitch selvedge stitch unless otherwise indicated.

- The measurements on the schematic show the actual sizes of the pieces for blocking purposes and include the selvedge stitches. However, the selvedges stitches, which are lost in the seams, do not count toward the finished bust sizes.

- Use the sloped method of binding off (see page 77) to shape the armholes, neckline, and sleeve cap to avoid "stair steps" along the bind-off edges.

- The left and right fronts contain a different number of stitches because each front has a different pattern arrangement. Because of the respective pattern gauges, the two fronts still have about the same measurements.

- The three-stitch one-row buttonholes are worked on wrong-side rows of the right front in a reverse stockinette background section of the chart so that the buttonhole stitches can be worked as knit stitches according to the instructions on page 271.

- There are only four buttonholes on the right front that correspond to the four functional buttons on the left front to keep the coat closed. The remaining four buttons shown on the right front are decorative buttons sewn directly to the right side of the front.

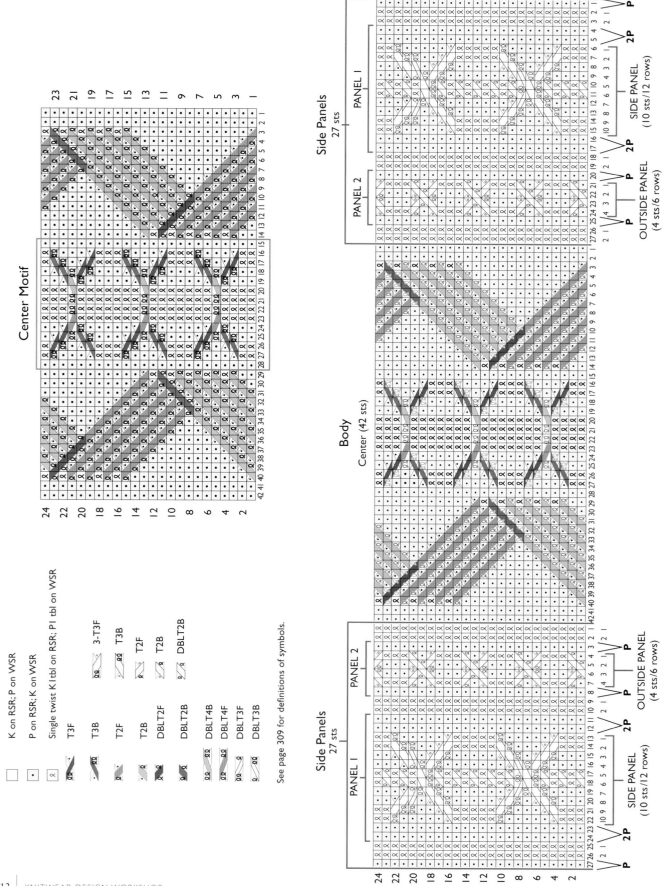

Center Motif

Body
Center (42 sts)

Side Panels
27 sts

PANEL 1

SIDE PANEL
(10 sts/12 rows)

OUTSIDE PANEL
(4 sts/6 rows)

PANEL 2

2P

P

Side Panels
27 sts

PANEL 1

PANEL 2

SIDE PANEL
(10 sts/12 rows)

OUTSIDE PANEL
(4 sts/6 rows)

2P

P

▢	K on RSR; P on WSR
•	P on RSR; K on WSR
✕	Single twist K1tbl on RSR; P1 tbl on WSR

T3F	3-T3F
T3B	T3B
T2F	T2F
T2B	T2B
DBLT2F	DBLT2B

| DBLT4B |
| DBLT4F |
| DBLT3F |
| DBLT3B |

See page 309 for definitions of symbols.

LEFT FRONT

Note: Although the left front is the same width as the right front, there is a 5-st difference in the stitch count for all sizes due to the different mixture of patt sts.

With MC and size 8 (5 mm) straight needles, CO 75 (79, 83) sts. Establish patt from Row 1 of Body chart as foll: K1 (selvedge st), work 9 (13, 17) sts in twisted St st, then work sts 1–27 of right-hand Side Panel, p1, work 11 sts in twisted St st, then work sts 15–28 (14 sts) of center section of chart, 11 sts in twisted St st, k1 (selvedge). Cont in established patt until piece measures 5" (12.5 cm) from CO, ending with a WS row.

HIP-TO-WAIST DECREASES

Cont in patt, dec 1 st at side edge (beg of RS rows; end of WS rows) inside selvedge st on next RS row, then every foll 4th (3rd, 2nd) row 3 (5, 3) times, then every foll 5th (4th, 3rd) row 3 (3, 7) times, ending with a WS row—68 (70, 72) sts rem; 7 (9, 11) sts removed at side; 2 (4, 6) twisted St sts rem inside selvedge at side; 28 rows in hip-to-waist dec section; piece should measure about 10" (25.5 cm) from CO.

WAIST

Work 10 rows even in patt, ending with a WS row—piece should measure 11¾" (30 cm) from CO.

WAIST-TO-BUST INCREASES

Cont in patt, inc 1 st at side edge inside selvedge at side edge on next RS row, then every foll 4th (3rd, 2nd) row 5 (3, 2) times, then every foll 5th (4th, 3rd) row 1 (4, 7) time(s), working inc'd sts in twisted St st and ending with a WS row—75 (78, 82) sts; 7 (8, 10) sts inc'd at side; 9 (12, 16) twisted St sts inside selvedge st at side; 26 rows in waist-to-bust inc section; piece should measure 16¼" (41.5 cm) from CO. Cont even in patt until piece measures about 18" (45.5 cm), ending with Row 6 of chart—102 chart rows completed.

Next row: (RS) Work in patt to last 8 sts, work a three-stitch one-row buttonhole (see page 271) over next 3 sts for inner buttonhole to support the front overlap, work in patt to end.

Work 1 WS row even, ending with Row 8 of chart—104 chart rows completed; piece should measure 18¼" (46.5 cm) from CO.

SHAPE ARMHOLE AND V-NECK

Note: Neck and armhole shaping are worked at the same time; read the next sections all the way through before proceeding.

For armhole shaping, use the sloped bind-off method to BO 3 (4, 4) sts at the beg of the next RS row, then BO 2 (3, 3) sts at beg of the foll 2 (1, 2) RS row(s), then

BO 1 (2, 2) st(s) at the beg of the foll 2 (2, 1) RS row(s), then BO 0 (1, 1) st at the beg of the foll 0 (1, 1) RS row. *For size Small only,* on the last RS BO row, work k2tog tbl on the first 2 Tw sts—10 (12, 13) sts removed at armhole edge.

Note: For the smallest size, there is a single dec (k2tog tbl) on the first 2 twist sts beside the p1 on the last armhole dec row. When looking at the armhole edge on a RS row, the rem twisted St st is converted to a selvedge st. The st just inside the selvedge st at the armhole is a purl st and the 3rd st is a single column of k1tbl as for the back.

At the same time, beg on the 2nd WS row of armhole shaping (the 108th row) use the sloped bind-off method to shape neck as foll.

Size 42" (106.5 cm) Only
[BO 2 sts at the beg of the next 2 WS rows (neck edge), then BO 1 st at the beg of the foll (3rd) WS row] 4 times, then BO 2 sts at the beg of the next 8 WS rows—36 sts dec'd; 29 shoulder sts rem.

Size 45" (114.5 cm) Only
[BO 2 sts at the beg of the next 2 WS rows (neck edge), then BO 1 st at the beg of the foll (3rd) WS row] 7 times, then BO 1 st at the beg of the foll WS row—36 sts dec'd; 30 shoulder sts rem.

Size 48½" (123 cm) Only
[BO 2 sts at the beg of the next 2 WS rows (neck edge), then BO 1 st at the beg of the foll (3rd) WS row] 6 times, then BO 1 st at the beg of the foll 6 WS rows—36 sts dec'd; 33 shoulder sts rem.

All Sizes
Work even in patt until 46 (50, 54) armhole rows have been completed, ending with Row 6 (10, 14) of chart—armhole should measure 8¼ (9, 9½)" (21 [23, 24] cm); piece should measure 26½ (27¼, 27¾)" (67.5 [69, 70.5] cm) from CO. Work 1 more RS row to end with same patt row as back. Place sts on holder.

RIGHT FRONT

With MC and size 8 (5 mm) straight needles, CO 80 (84, 88) sts (see Notes on page 311). Establish patt from Row 1 of Body chart as foll: k1 (selvedge st), work the 42 center sts of the Body chart, then work sts 1–27 of the left-hand Side Panel, work 9 (13, 17) sts in twisted St st, k1 (selvedge st). Cont in patt, work Rows 2–24 of chart once, then work Rows 1–7 once more. Work a three-stitch one-row buttonhole beg on the 4th purl st (chart st 6) after the 24-st center motif (chart sts 33 to 10) on the next row (Row 8 of chart and 32nd row from CO; see Notes on page 311). Cont in established patt until piece measures 5" (12.5 cm) from CO, ending with a WS row.

HIP-TO-WAIST DECREASES

Note: The next three buttonholes are worked at the same time as the garment is shaped; read the next sections all the way through before proceeding.

For buttonholes, work a three-stitch one-row buttonhole in the same location as the first buttonhole the next 3 times you work Row 8 of chart (the 56th, 80th, and 104th rows from CO). *At the same time* dec 1 st at side edge (end of RS rows; beg of WS rows) beg inside selvedge st on next RS row, then every foll 4th (3rd, 2nd) row 3 (5, 3) times, then every foll 5th (4th, 3rd) row 3 (3, 7) times, ending with a WS row—73 (75, 77) sts rem; 7 (9, 11) sts removed at side; 2 (4, 6) twisted St sts rem inside selvedge at side; 28 rows in hip-to-waist dec section; piece should measure about 10" (25.5 cm) from CO.

WAIST

Work 10 rows even in patt, ending with a WS row—piece should measure 11¾" (30 cm) from CO.

WAIST-TO-BUST INCREASES

Cont in patt, inc 1 st at side edge inside selvedge st on next RS row, then every foll 4th (3rd, 2nd) row 5 (3, 2) times, then every foll 5th (4th, 3rd) row 1 (4, 7) time(s), working inc'd sts in twisted St st and ending with a WS row—80 (83, 87) sts; 7 (8, 10) sts inc'd at side; 9 (12, 16) twisted St sts inside selvedge st at side; 26 rows in waist-to-hip inc section; piece measures about 16¼" (41.5 cm) from CO. Cont even in patt until piece measures 18¼" (46.5 cm) from CO, ending with Row 8 of chart—104 chart rows completed.

SHAPE ARMHOLE AND V-NECK

Note: As for left front, neck and armhole shaping are worked at the same time; read the next sections all the way through before proceeding.

Work 1 RS row even. For armhole shaping, use the sloped bind-off method to BO 3 (4, 4) sts at the beg of next WS row, then BO 2 (3, 3) sts at beg of the foll 2 (1, 2) WS row(s), then BO 1 (2, 2) st(s) at the beg of the foll 2 (2, 1) WS row(s), then BO 0 (1, 1) st at the beg of the foll 0 (1, 1) WS row. For size Small only, on the last WS BO row work p2tog tbl on the first 2 Tw sts—10 (12, 13) sts removed at armhole edge.

Note: For the smallest size, there is a single dec worked as p2tog tbl on the first 2 Tw sts beside the p1 on the last armhole dec row. When looking at the armhole edge on a RS row, the rem twisted St st is converted to a selvedge st. The st just inside the selvedge st at the armhole is 1 purl st and the 3rd st is a single column of k1tbl as for the back.

At the same time beg on the 2nd RS armhole row (the 107th row), use the sloped bind-off method to shape neck as foll.

Size 42" (106.5 cm) Only
BO 1 st at the beg of next RS row (neck edge), then BO 2 sts at the beg of the next 20 RS rows—41 sts dec'd; 29 shoulder sts rem.

Size 45" (114.5 cm) Only
[BO 2 sts at the beg of the next 2 RS rows, then BO 1 st at the beg of the foll (3rd) RS row] 3 times, then BO 2 sts at the beg of the foll 13 RS rows—41 sts dec'd; 30 shoulder sts rem.

Size 48½" (123 cm) Only
[BO 2 sts at the beg of the next 2 RS rows, then BO 1 st at the beg of the foll (3rd) RS row] 7 times, then BO 2 sts at the beg of the foll 3 RS rows—41 sts dec'd; 33 shoulder sts rem.

All Sizes
Work even in patt until 45 (49, 53) armhole rows have been completed, ending with Row 5 (9, 13) of chart—armhole should measure 8¼ (9, 9½)" (21 [23, 24] cm); piece should measure 26½ (27¼, 27¾)" (67.5 [69, 70.5] cm) from CO. Work 2 more rows to end with same patt row as back. Place sts on holder.

SLEEVES

With MC and size 8 (5 mm) straight needles, CO 58 (58, 66) sts. Establish patt from Row 1 of Sleeve, Cuff, and Collar chart as foll: K1 (selvedge st), work 10 (10, 14) sts in twisted St st, work the 36-st section for center sleeve in patt from chart, work 10 (10, 14) sts in twisted St st, k1 (selvedge st). Work 1 WS row even. Cont in patt and *at the same time* inc 1 st at each side inside selvedge sts on the next RS row, then every 18th (10th, 13th) row 2 (6, 3) times, then every foll 17th (9th, 12th) row 3 (3, 4) times, working inc'd sts in twisted St st and ending with Row 6 of chart—70 (78, 82) sts; 6 (10, 8) sts inc'd at each side; 16 (20, 22) twisted St sts inside selvedge sts at each side; 90 chart rows completed; piece measures about 15¾ " (40 cm) from CO. Work even in patt for 12 more rows, ending with Row 6 of the patt rep (Row 18 of chart)—102 rows completed; piece should measure 18" (45.5 cm) from CO.

Sleeve Center, Cuff, and Collar

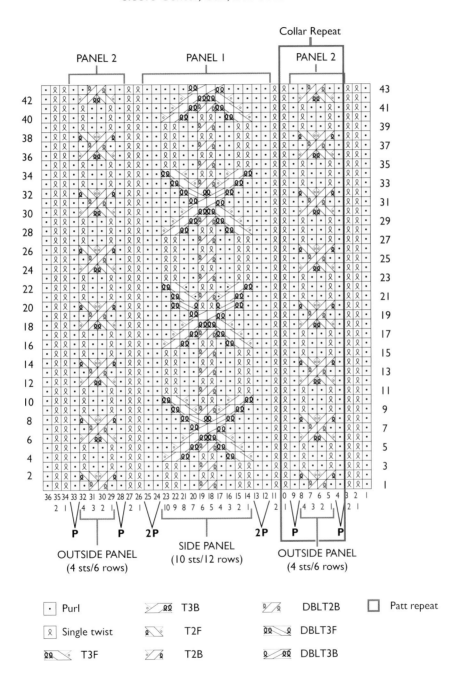

Purl	T3B	DBLT2B	Patt repeat
Single twist	T2F	DBLT3F	
T3F	T2B	DBLT3B	

See page 309 for definitions of symbols.

SHAPE CAP

Keeping in patt and using the sloped bind-off method, BO 3 (4, 4) sts at beg of next 4 (2, 2) rows, then BO 2 (3, 3) sts at the beg of the foll 2 (2, 4) rows—54 (64, 62) sts rem. [BO 2 sts at the beg of the next 2 rows, then BO 1 st at the beg of the foll 2 rows] 3 (4, 2) times—36 (40, 50) sts rem. BO 1 st at beg of foll 6 (8, 16) rows, then BO 3 sts at the beg of the foll 4 rows—18 (20, 22) sts rem; 28 (32, 34) total sleeve cap rows. BO all rem sts.

CUFFS

With MC and smaller straight needles, CO 64 (64, 72) sts. Establish patt from Row 1 of Sleeve, Cuff, and Collar chart as foll: Work 14 (14, 18) sts on right-hand side as: K1 (selvedge st), p2 (2, 6), work 2 twist sts (k1tbl), p2, 2 twist sts, p1, work sts 5–8 (4 sts) of Panel 2, work center cuff according to entire 36-st chart, work 14 (14, 18) sts on left-hand side as: sts 5–8 (4 sts) of Panel 2, p1, 2 twist sts, p2, 2 twist sts, p2 (2, 6), k1 (selvedge st). Work even in patt for 5 more rows, ending with Row 6 of chart. Change to size 9 (5.5 mm) straight needles. Work 18 more rows in patt, ending with Row 12 of chart—24 rows completed; piece should measure 4¼" (11 cm). BO all sts.

LAPELS

Note: RS of lapels corresponds to WS of body so the RS of the lapels will show on the front side when the lapels are folded back.

RIGHT LAPEL

With MC and size 8 (5 mm) straight needles, CO 2 sts. Work 2 rows even in St st, ending with a WS row.

Note: When shaping lapel, work the shaping inside the selvedge sts. Work the last st of every RS row and first st of every WS row in garter st; if there are not enough sts to work a complete cable crossing, work the sts as twist sts or rev St sts instead as required to maintain patt. Work in patt from Right Lapel chart for your size, working new sts into chart patt as shown by outline as foll.

Size 42" (106.5 cm) Only

Following the Right Lapel (Small) chart, work as foll: CO 2 sts at beg of next RS row, CO 3 sts at beg of foll RS row, [CO 2 sts at beg of next 2 RS rows, then CO 3 sts at beg of foll RS row] 3 times, then CO 2 sts at beg of foll RS row, ending with Row 25 of chart—30 sts. BO 27 sts at beg of Row 26 of chart—3 sts rem; piece measures about 4½" (11.5 cm) from CO, measured straight up along unshaped selvedge. Using the sloped BO method on the left-hand side, cont to inc on the right-hand side as foll: inc 1 st at beg of next 3 RS rows and dec 1 st at beg of next 4 WS rows, ending with Row 34 of chart—2 sts rem. Work 1 RS row even—35 rows completed from CO; piece should measure 6" (15 cm). BO all sts on next WS row.

Size 45" (114.5 cm) Only

Following Right Lapel (Medium) chart, work as foll: CO 2 sts at beg of next 14 RS rows, ending with Row 29 of chart—30 sts. BO 27 sts at beg of Row 30 of chart—3 sts rem; piece measures about 5¼" (13.5 cm) from CO, measured straight up along unshaped selvedge. Using the sloped BO method on the left-hand side, cont to inc on the right-hand side as foll: inc 1 st at beg of next 3 RS rows and dec 1 st at beg of next 4 WS rows, ending with Row 38 of chart—2 sts rem. Work 1 RS row even—39 rows completed from CO; piece should measure 6¾" (17 cm). BO all sts on next WS row.

Size 48½" (123 cm) Only

Following Right Lapel (Large) chart, work as foll: CO 2 sts at beg of next 12 RS rows, then CO 1 st at beg of next 4 RS rows, ending with Row 33 of chart—30 sts. BO 27 sts at beg of Row 34 of chart—3 sts rem; piece measures about 6" (15 cm) from CO, measured straight up along unshaped selvedge. Using the sloped BO method on the left-hand side, cont to inc on the right-hand side as foll: inc 1 st at beg of next 3 RS rows and dec 1 st at beg of next 4 WS rows, ending with Row 42 of chart—2 sts rem. Work 1 RS row even—43 rows completed from CO; piece should measure 7½" (19 cm). BO all sts on next WS row.

Right Lapel (Medium)

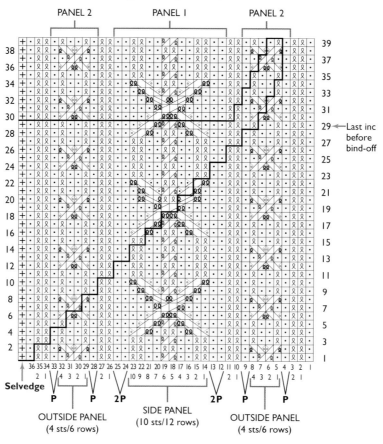

PANEL 2　　PANEL 1　　PANEL 2

29 ← Last inc before bind-off

Selvedge

P　　P　　2P　　2P　　P　　P

OUTSIDE PANEL
(4 sts/6 rows)

SIDE PANEL
(10 sts/12 rows)

OUTSIDE PANEL
(4 sts/6 rows)

Right Lapel (Small)

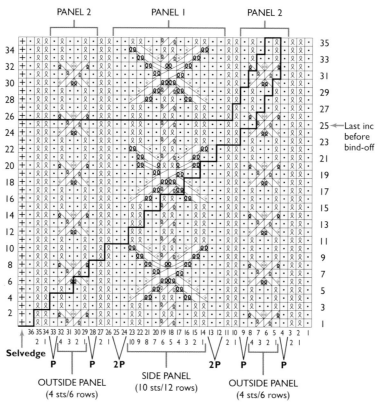

PANEL 2　　PANEL 1　　PANEL 2

25 ← Last inc before bind-off

Selvedge

P　　P　　2P　　2P　　P　　P

OUTSIDE PANEL
(4 sts/6 rows)

SIDE PANEL
(10 sts/12 rows)

OUTSIDE PANEL
(4 sts/6 rows)

Right Lapel (Large)

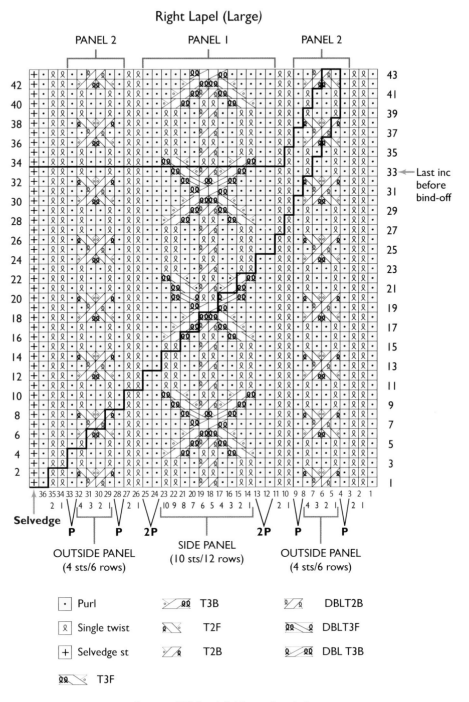

PANEL 2 PANEL 1 PANEL 2

← Last inc before bind-off

Selvedge

P P 2P 2P P P

OUTSIDE PANEL
(4 sts/6 rows)

SIDE PANEL
(10 sts/12 rows)

OUTSIDE PANEL
(4 sts/6 rows)

·	Purl		T3B		DBLT2B
ℓ	Single twist		T2F		DBLT3F
+	Selvedge st		T2B		DBL T3B
	T3F				

See page 309 for definitions of symbols.

LEFT LAPEL

With MC and size 8 (5 mm) straight needles, CO 2 sts. Work 2 rows even in St st, ending with a WS row. Work as for right lapel for your size, reversing the shaping.

Note: As for right lapel, work the first st of every RS row and last st of every WS row in garter st; if there are not enough sts to work a complete cable crossing, work the sts as twisted knit sts or rev St st instead, as required to maintain patt.

COLLAR

Note: RS of collar corresponds to WS of body so the RS of the collar will show on the outside when the collar is folded back.

With MC and size 8 (5 mm) straight needles, CO 86 sts. Establish patt from Row 1 of Sleeve, Cuff, and Collar chart as foll: Work the last 4 sts of the pattern repeat box once, rep the 7-st patt 11 times, then work the first 5 sts of the next patt rep box once. Cont in patt, inc 1 st at each side (inside selvedge sts) on the next 4 RS rows, working new sts in patt as shown, and ending with Row 10 of chart—94 sts (13 reps of 7 + 1 "plus" st + 2 selvedge sts). Work even through Row 30 of chart—piece should measure 5" (12.5 cm). BO all sts.

FINISHING

Block pieces to measurements (see page 261). Place 29 (30, 33) held right front shoulder sts on one needle and the corresponding 29 (30, 33) right back shoulder sts on another needle. Holding needles parallel with RS touching and WS facing out, use MC and tip of cir needle in smallest size and the three-needle bind-off method (see page 263) to join shoulder sts; BO ridge will be on WS of garment. Rep for left shoulder sts. With MC threaded on a tapestry needle, sew side seams. Baste the shaped edge of each lapel along V-neck edge, making sure that RS of each lapel is on the WS of the coat. With MC, use a whipstitch (see page 266) to sew lapels to neck edge. Pin collar to neck edge with RS of collar on WS of coat, matching the 4 inc'd sts at each side of collar to 4 dec'd sts along inner edges of lapels. With MC, use a whipstitch to

SLEEVES AND CUFFS

Hold cuff and sleeve with CO edges tog and RS of cuff touching WS of sleeve. With MC threaded on a tapestry needle, use a whipstitch to sew sleeve to cuff along CO edges. Seam cuffs with RS of cuffs facing, then seam sleeves with RS of sleeves facing. With size G/7 (4.5 mm) crochet hook, work 1 row of rev sc (see Stitch Guide on page 309) around BO edge of each cuff. With MC threaded on a tapestry needle, sew sleeves into armholes. Fold up cuffs.

BUTTON BACKINGS (MAKE 9)

With CC, make a slipknot and place on size E/4 (3.5 mm) crochet hook. Ch 2 (see page 277 for crochet instructions), then work 8 sc in the slipknot.

Rnd 1: *2 sc in the next sc, 1 sc in the next sc; rep from *—12 sc.

Rnd 2: Work 1 sc in each sc around.

Join to first sc of rnd with a slip st, then fasten off last st. Thread starting tail on a tapestry needle, run the tail through the beginning 8 sc drawstring-fashion, and pull snugly to close center hole. Make seven more button backings in the same manner. For the 9th backing, work Rnd 2 twice before fastening off to make a slightly larger backing for inner button.

BUTTONS

Lay garment flat with right front overlapping left front and side folds aligned with side seams. Mark button positions on RS of left front directly under the four right front buttonholes. Using three separated plies of CC threaded on a tapestry needle, whipstitch a button backing to the WS of left front underneath each marked button position. Sew four buttons to left front, sewing through both the garment and button backing layers. Mark positions for four decorative buttons on RS of right front as shown in photograph. Whipstitch a button backing to the WS of right front underneath each marked button position, then sew the bottom three decorative buttons to right front, sewing through all layers. Place larger button backing on top of the highest regular-size backing and whipstitch tog with CC. Sew the top decorative button to the RS of right front and the inner button to the WS of right front at top marked position, sewing through garment and both button backing layers.

LEFT FRONT, COLLAR, AND LAPEL EDGING

With MC, size G/7 (4.5 mm) crochet hook, and RS facing, join yarn to lower corner of left front. With RS still facing, work 1 row of rev sc along edge of left front, left lapel, collar, and right lapel, ending at base of right lapel. Fasten off last st.

RIGHT FRONT I-CORD EDGING

With MC, size 7 (4.5 mm) cir needle, and WS of coat facing, pick up and purl (see page 266) 66 sts along 104 rows of right front (52 spaces between selvedge purl bumps) from base of right lapel to CO edge as foll: [Pick up 1 st in each of next 3 spaces between selvedge purl bumps, then pick up 2 sts in next purl-bump space] 12 times, then [pick up 1 st in next purl-bump space, then pick up 2 sts in next purl-bump space] 2 times—66 sts. Turn piece so RS is facing and use the cable method (see page 271) to CO 3 sts—69 sts total. Work attached I-cord as foll: (RS) *K2, sl last I-cord st knitwise with yarn in back, knit next picked-up st, pass slipped I-cord st over (1 picked-up st joined), return 3 sts on right-hand needle to left-hand needle, and bring yarn around behind the piece into position to work another RS row; rep from * until all picked-up sts have been joined—3 I-cord sts rem. Break yarn and draw through rem sts to fasten off. Stretch a few inches of I-cord gently sideways to maximize its width, fold stretched section to WS to cover selvedge sts and pick-up welt, and pin in place. Cont in this manner until entire length of I-cord has been pinned. With MC threaded on a tapestry needle, whipstitch I-cord to first column of sts inside front selvedge sts on WS.

Weave in loose ends.

Appendix

ABBREVIATIONS

beg(s)	begin(s); beginning
BO	bind off
CC	contrasting color
cm	centimeter(s)
cn	cable needle
CO	cast on
cont	continue(s); continuing
dec(s)	decrease(s); decreasing
dpn	double-pointed needles
foll	follow(s); following
g	gram(s)
inc(s)	increase(s); increasing
k	knit
k1f&b	knit into the front and back of same stitch
kwise	knitwise; as if to knit
m	marker(s)
MC	main color
mm	millimeter(s)
M1	make one (increase)
p	purl
p1f&b	purl into front and back of same stitch
patt(s)	pattern(s)
psso	pass slipped stitch over
pwise	purlwise; as if to purl
rem	remain(s); remaining
rep	repeat(s); repeating
rev St st	reverse stockinette stitch

rnd(s)	round(s)
RS	right side
sl	slip
sl st	slip st (slip 1 stitch purlwise unless otherwise indicated)
ssk	slip 2 stitches knitwise, one at a time, from the left needle to right needle, insert left needle tip through both front loops and knit together from this position (1 stitch decrease)
st(s)	stitch(es)
St st	stockinette stitch
tbl	through back loop
tog	together
WS	wrong side
wyb	with yarn in back
wyf	with yarn in front
yd	yard(s)
yo	yarnover
*	repeat starting point
* *	repeat all instructions between asterisks
( )	alternate measurements and/or instructions
[ ]	work instructions as a group a specified number of times

(For examples of this process, visit www.shirleypaden.com)

☐ **The idea: Draw a sketch that captures the design details**

☐ **The fabric: Select the stitch pattern and the yarn**
- Chart stitch pattern to understand its construction elements before making the swatch.
- Swatch with several different yarns and needle sizes.
- Block and take a gauge of the chosen swatch.

☐ **Essential measurements and numbers**
- Determine actual body measurements.
- Determine garment and sleeve measurements and gauge: widths with ease and lengths.
- Determine number of stitches to cast on.
- Determine shaping schedules for body and sleeve.

☐ **Draw a schematic with width and length measurements**

☐ **List swatch measurements, row and stitch gauge, needle size, and conversion of width and length measurements to number of stitches and rows**

☐ **Draw a working schematic with widths and lengths translated to numbers of stitches and rows**
- Record all of the stitch and row numbers for each section beneath every measurement.
- Use as math check.
- Any extra stitches or rows, including selvedge stitches or back neck shaping rows should be included.
- Include all bind-off stitches for the neck and armholes.

☐ **Center the pattern**
- Plan what stitches will run along the side edges and how the pattern will flow around the garment when it is seamed.
- Determine where the pattern will break at the armholes and flow along the armhole edge.
- Determine where the pattern will end at the base of the neck and at the shoulders.
- Determine how the top pattern rows on the front and back will look when they come together as the shoulders are seamed.
- If these alter garment length and width (row and stitch numbers); adjust schematics accordingly.

☐ **Prepare a worksheet: Include all of the instructions, charts, and calculations**
- Calculate yarn requirements.
- Chart the body and sleeve to visualize the pattern flow, including border, armhole, neck, shoulder, and sleeve taper and cap shaping.
- Work through how the garment will be finished.
- Add new information to the working schematic as necessary.

☐ **Write the formal pattern**
- Write the knitting instructions, omitting all the calculations.

STANDARD MEASUREMENTS AND SIZING

From the Craft Yarn Council of America (craftyarncouncil.com)

BABY

BABY'S SIZE		3 months	6 months	12 months	18 months	24 months
Chest	inch	16	17	18	19	20
	cm	40.5	43	45.5	48	51
Center Back Neck to Cuff	inch	10½	11½	12½	14	18
	cm	26.5	29	31.5	35.5	45.5
Back Waist Length	inch	6	7	7½	8	8½
	cm	15	18	19	20.5	21.5
Cross Back (shoulder to shoulder)	inch	7¼	7¾	8¼	8½	8¾
	cm	18.5	19.5	21	21.5	22
Sleeve Length to Underarm	inch	6	6½	7½	8	8½
	cm	15	16.5	19	20.5	21.5
Upper Arm	inch	5½	6	6½	7	7½
	cm	14	15	16.5	18	19
Armhole Depth	inch	3¼	3½	3¾	4	4¼
	cm	8.5	9	9.5	10	11
Waist	inch	18	19	20	20½	21
	cm	45.5	48	51	52	53.5
Hips	inch	19	20	20	21	22
	cm	48	51	51	53.5	56

CHILD'S SIZE		2	4	6	8	10	12	14	16
Chest	inch	21	23	25	26½	28	30	31½	32½
	cm	53.5	58.5	63.5	67.5	71	76	80	82.5
Center Back Neck to Cuff	inch	18	19½	20½	22	24	26	27	28
	cm	45.5	49.5	52	56	61	66	68.5	71
Back Waist Length	inch	8½	9½	10½	12½	14	15	15½	16
	cm	21.5	24	26.5	31.5	35.5	38	39.5	40.5
Cross Back (shoulder to Shoulder)	inch	9¼	9¾	10¼	10¾	11¼	12	12¼	13
	cm	23.5	25	26	27.5	28.5	30.5	31	33
Sleeve Length to Underarm	inch	8⅛	10½	11½	12½	13½	15	16	16½
	cm	21.5	26.5	29	31.5	34.5	38	40.5	42
Upper Arm	inch	7	7½	8	8½	8¾	9	9¼	9½
	cm	18	19	20.5	21.5	22	23	23.5	24
Armhole Depth	inch	4¼	4¾	5	5½	6	6½	7	7½
	cm	11	12	12.5	14	15	16.5	18	19
Waist	inch	21	21½	22½	23½	24½	25	26½	27½
	cm	53.5	54.5	57	59.5	62	63.5	67.5	70
Hips	inch	22	23½	25	28	29½	31½	33	35½
	cm	56	59.5	63.5	71	75	80	84	90

WOMAN'S SIZE		X-Small	Small	Medium	Large	1X	2X	3X	4X	5X
Bust	inch	28–30	32–34	36–38	40–42	44–46	48–50	52–54	56–58	60–62
	cm	71–76	81.5–86.5	91.5–96.5	101.5–106.5	112–117	122–127	132–137	142–147.5	152.5–157.5
Center Back Neck to Cuff	inch	27–27½	28–28½	29–29½	30–30½	31–31½	31½–32	32½–33	32½–33	33–33½
	cm	68.5–70	71–72.5	73.5–75	76–77.5	78.5–80	80–81.5	82.5–84	82.5–84	84–85
Back Waist Length	inch	16½	17	17¼	17½	17¾	18	18	18½	18½
	cm	42	43	44	44.5	45	45.5	45.5	47	47
Cross Back (shoulder to shoulder)	inch	14–14½	14½–15	16–16½	17–17½	17½	18	18	18½	18½
	cm	35.5–37	37–38	40.5–42	43–44.5	44.5	45.5	45.5	47	47
Sleeve Length to Underarm	inch	16½	17	17	17½	17½	18	18	18½	18½
	cm	42	43	43	44.5	44.5	45.5	45.5	47	47
Upper Arm	inch	9¾	10¼	11	12	13½	15½	17	18½	19½
	cm	25	26	28	30.5	34.5	39.5	43	47	49.5
Armhole Depth	inch	6–6½	6½–7	7–7½	7½–8	8–8½	8½–9	9–9½	9½–10	10–10½
	cm	15–16.5	16.5–18	18–19	19–20.5	20.5–21.5	21.5–23	23–24	24–25.5	25.5–26.5
Waist	inch	23–24	25–26½	28–30	32–34	36–38	40–42	44–45	46–47	49–50
	cm	58.5–61	63.5–67.5	71–76	81.5–86.5	91.5–96.5	101.5–106.5	112–114.5	117–119.5	124.5–127
Hips	inch	33–34	35–36	38–40	42–44	46–48	52–53	54–55	56–57	61–62
	cm	84–86.5	89–91.5	96.5–101.5	106.5–112	117–122	132–134.5	137–139.5	142–145	155–157.5

MAN

MAN'S SIZE		Small	Medium	Large	X-Large	XX-Large
Chest	inch	34–36	38–40	42–44	46–48	50–52
	cm	86.5–91.5	96.5–101.5	106.5–112	117–122	127–132
Center Back Neck to Cuff	inch	32–32½	33–33½	34–34½	35–35½	36–36½
	cm	81.5–82.5	83.5–85	86.5–87.5	89–90	91.5–92.5
Back Hip Length	inch	25–25½	26½–26¾	27–27½	27½–27¾	28–28½
	cm	63.5–65	67.5–68	68.5–70	70–70.5	71–72.5
Cross Back (shoulder to shoulder)	inch	15½–16	16½–17	17½–18	18–18½	18½–19
	cm	139.5–40.5	42–43	44.5–45.5	45.5–47	47–48.5
Sleeve Length to Underarm	inch	18	18½	19½	20	20½
	cm	45.5	47	49.5	51	52
Upper Arm	inch	12	13	15	16	17
	cm	30.5	33	38	40.5	43
Armhole Depth	inch	8½–9	9–9½	9½–10	10–10½	10½–11
	cm	21.5–23	23–24	24–25.5	25.5–26.5	26.5–28
Waist	inch	28–30	32–34	36–38	42–44	46–48
	cm	71–76	81.5–86.5	91.5–96.5	106.5–112	117–122
Hips	inch	35–37	39–41	43–45	47–49	51–53
	cm	89–94	99–104	109–114.5	119.5–124.5	129.5–134.5

VARIATIONS ON THE SHAPING FORMULA

The shaping Formula used throughout this book is based on Cheryl Brunette's original "More or Less Right" Formula from her first *Sweater 101* booklet. I have applied this technique to a broad range of garment construction calculations: to calculate sleeve increases, front border pick-ups, single/double tapered bodies, raglan shaping, V-neck shaping, buttonhole placements, etc. I have also created variations to accommodate special situations such as increasing/decreasing only on right-side rows or wrong-side rows.

$$
\begin{array}{l}
\overset{D}{\textcircled{5}} + 1 = \textcircled{6}\,^E \\
A\ 15\overline{)85}\ _F \\
\underline{-75} \\
15 - \textcircled{10} \quad = \quad \textcircled{5}\,_C \\
_B
\end{array}
$$

A = Divisor / # of stitches to be inc or dec

B = Remainder / # of repeats

C = Expanded Remainder / # of repeats

D = Quotient / St to inc or dec

E = Expanded Quotient / st to inc or dec

F = Dividend / # of current stitches

BASIC SHAPING FORMULA

In the basic formula, you divide the number of stitches to be increased or decreased into the number of stitches that are currently on your needles. In Cheryl Brunette's original example, there are 85 stitches on the needles after the border has been completed. The written pattern says to increase 15 stitches evenly across the next row to account for the gauge difference in the body stitch pattern. In this case, divide the number of stitches needed (15), into the number of stitches on the needles (85). The diagonal relationships between the quotient (5) and expanded remainder (5) and between the expanded quotient (6) and the remainder (10) tell how to space these 15 increases evenly.

The quotient and the expanded quotient represent the numbers of stitches that are worked before making the increases or decreases.

The remainder and the expanded remainder represent the numbers of times the increase or decrease interval will be worked.

Step One: Subtract the remainder (B) from the divisor (A) to give what I call the expanded remainder (C).

Step Two: Add 1 to the quotient (D) to give the expanded quotient (E).

Step Three: Circle the quotient and the expanded quotient (shown in red). These represent the numbers of stitches that are worked before making the increases or decreases.

Step Four: Circle the remainder and the expanded remainder (shown in green). These represent the numbers of times the increases or decreases will be worked.

Step Five: Draw a diagonal line from the quotient (D) to the expanded remainder (C) [5 → 5] and another diagonal line from the expanded quotient (E) to the remainder (B) [6 → 10].

Step Six: Follow the arrows to determine the number of times to work each interval.

Increases

Note: If working running-thread make-one (M1) increases, increase after the last stitch in the interval; if working lifted (k1f&b) increases, increase in the last stitch of the interval.

The line 5 → 5 tells us to increase 1 stitch either on or after every 5th stitch 5 times.

The line 6 → 10 tells us to increase 1 stitch either on or after every 6th stitch 10 times.

Decreases

Note: Decreases are worked on the last two stitches in the interval.

The line 5 → 5 tells us to decrease 1 stitch every 5th stitch (i.e., k3, k2tog) 5 times.

The line 6 → 10 tells us to decrease 1 stitch every 6th stitch (i.e., k4, k2tog) 10 times.

 MATH CHECK!

Check your math to make certain that the correct number of stitches will be added to or subtracted from the number of stitches on the needles. When checking the math, align the equations for the two intervals so that the quotient (5) is directly above the expanded quotient (6). The sum of the remainder (10) and the expanded remainder (5) should equal the divisor (15). The sum of the products of the two equations should equal the dividend (85)

$$(5) + 1 = (6)$$
$$15 \overline{)85}$$
$$-75$$
$$15 - (10) = (5)$$

MATH CHECK
$$(5) \times (5) = 25$$
$$(6) \times (10) = 60$$
$$15 / 85$$

ADJUSTED SHAPING FORMULA

The basic shaping formula always places the final increase or decrease on the last stitch of the row. To center all of the increases or decreases across the row so that there are about the same number of stitches before the first increase/decrease as there are after the last increase/decrease, split one of the intervals represented by either quotient between the beginning and the end of the row.

It's an easy matter to make these adjustments right on the shaping formula. First, divide the quotient or expanded quotient in half (as evenly as possible for odd numbers) to determine the number of stitches worked before the first interval and after the last interval. Then subtract 1 from the expanded remainder or remainder to account for the interval that was split between the two ends of the needle.

If the quotient or expanded quotient that we are dividing is an even number, there will be the same number of stitches at the beginning as the end.

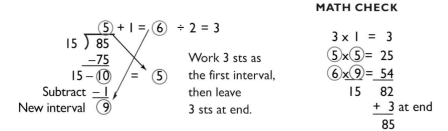

If the quotient or expanded quotient that we are dividing is an odd number (5 in this example), there will be one more stitch at the beginning than at the end.

With the standard formula, instructions for working increases in the example below would be: Increase 1 stitch on or after every 5th stitch 5 times, then on or after every 6th stitch 10 times. Here, to balance the ends, instead of working the last increase on the last stitch, divide the first interval by two (as evenly as possible) and work half of those stitches before the first increase and the other half after the last increase. Because 5 in our example does not divide evenly in half, work 3 stitches of this interval at the beginning and 2 stitches at the end. In this case, the first increase is worked on or after the 3rd stitch, then additional increases are worked on or after the 5th stitch 4 times and the 6th stitch 10 times, ending with 3 stitches before the end of the row. Knit these stitches to finish the row.

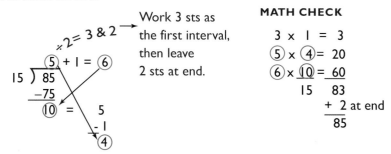

CALCULATIONS THAT HAVE NO REMAINDER

Sometimes, there will be no remainder in the shaping formula, such as when dividing 11 increases/ decreases into 44 stitches or rows.

$$11 \overline{)\, 44}^{\,4}$$

When there is no remainder in the shaping formula, simply work the number of stitches in the divisor (11) the number of times given in the quotient (4).

Width Calculations

Width calculations involve working with stitches.

> Increase 1 st either on (knit in the stitch below) or after (M1) every 4th stitch 11 times.
>
> Decrease by working [k2, k2tog (the 3rd and 4th stitches)] 11 times.

Length Calculations

Length calculations involve working with rows.

> Increase 1 stitch at each end of the needle every 4th row 11 times.
>
> Decrease 1 stitch at the each end of the needle every 4th row 11 times.

CALCULATIONS THAT HAVE ALMOST NO REMAINDER

When the quotient and remainder differ by just 1, the remainder is close enough to the quotient that the formula is sufficiently balanced without any adjustment. In these cases, you can choose whether to follow the instructions for the basic formula or the adjusted formula.

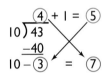

BASIC FORMULA

MATH CHECK

④ × ⑦ = 28
⑤ × ③ = 15
⎯⎯⎯⎯⎯⎯
10 / 43

The decreases begin after working 2 sts and end on the last stitch.
[k2, k2tog] 7x, then [k3, k2tog] 3x.

ADJUSTED FORMULA

$$\begin{array}{r} ④ \\ ⑩\overline{)\,43} \\ -40 \\ \hline 3 \end{array}$$

MATH CHECK

④ × ⑩ = 40
+3 remaining
⎯⎯⎯⎯⎯⎯
43

The number of stitches left at the beginning and end are not exact, but are balanced.
[k2, k2tog] 10x, end k3.

USING THE SHAPING FORMULA FOR CALCULATIONS INVOLVING LENGTHS

When calculating shaping intervals along lengths (rows), the dividend represents the number of rows over which the shaping is to occur and the divisor represents the number of stitches to be increased or decreased. The basic formula will automatically place the final increase/decrease on the final row of the shaping. This formula works beautifully when paired increases/decreases are desired, such as when shaping sleeves, necklines, or raglans, or tapering the body from hip to waist and from waist to bust in double-taper silhouettes.

For example, let's say that there are 50 stitches at the top of the cuff and you must increase 50 stitches (25 stitches on each side) over the next 110 rows to taper a sleeve. The diagonal relationships in the shaping formula on page 336 tells us to increase 1 stitch at each end of the needle every 4th row 15 times, then on every 5th row 10 times for a total of 50 stitches increased over 110 rows.

Step One: Determine the number of stitches to be increased/decreased (50).

Step Two: Divide this number of stitches by 2 to account for balanced increases/ decreases that are worked on each end of the needle (25).

Step Three: Determine the number of rows over which the shaping is to be worked (110).

Step Four: Use the shaping formula to divide the number of increase/decrease rows (25) into the number of rows over which the shaping is to be worked (110).

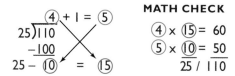

In this example, the taper begins at the end of the first interval (on the 4th row) and ends on the last shaping row. There are cases, such as when working hips-to-waist shaping, when you will want the taper to begin on the very first row instead of at the end of the first interval. In this case, subtract the first shaping row, along with its increases/decreases, from the row and stitch count and insert the revised numbers into a modified formula.

For example, let's say that there are 98 stitches at the hips and you must decrease 14 stitches (7 stitches at each side) to 84 stitches at the waist over the next 49 rows. To start the taper on the first row, decrease 1 stitch at each end of the needle on the first row, then use the shaping formula to determine the distribution of the remaining 6 decreases over 48 rows.

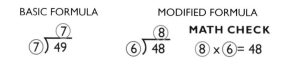

EXPANDED SHAPING FORMULA

In some situations, you will want to work all of the decreases/increases just on right-side or just on wrong-side rows. When shaping a V-neckline with bind-offs, for example, the decreases may all be worked on wrong-side rows for the left-hand side of the neck and all on right-side rows for the right-hand side of the neck. When shaping a raglan, for another example, you may want all of the shaping to occur on right-side rows. Because the expanded quotient is derived by adding 1 to the quotient in the basic formula, some intervals will involve even numbers and some will involve odd numbers, which would put the shaping on both right-side and wrong-side rows.

For example, to decrease 15 stitches over 85 rows, the first interval of shaping every 5th row 5 times would necessitate working the 2nd and 4th shaping rows on wrong-side (WS) rows.

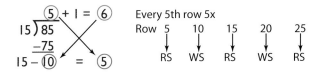

To limit the shaping to right-side (or wrong-side) rows only, you can simply divide the number of rows (the dividend) in half before working the basic shaping formula, then remember that each interval specified by the quotient or expanded quotient represents right-side rows only. Therefore, you would actually knit twice the number of rows specified. This is how the single-sided formula has been used throughout this book.

If, however, you want to track the calculations and represent the formula in a way that shows exactly how all the components are worked, adjustments can be made right on the shaping formula in a version I call the expanded formula. The expanded formula is based on working 2-row pairs and will always place the shaping in increments of even-numbered rows.

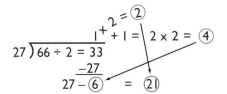

BASIC FORMULA

MATH CHECK

Decrease 1 stitch every right-side (every 2nd) row 21 times, then every 2nd right-side (every 4th) row 6 times.

EXPANDED FORMULA

MATH CHECK

Decrease 1 stitch every 2nd row 21 times, then every 4th row 6 times.

To work the expanded shaping formula, first divide the number of rows (the dividend) by 2 to acknowledge that the increases/decreases are worked every other row. Because the quotient and the expanded quotient represent the rows on which to work the increase/decrease, simply multiply each by 2 to know how many rows to actually knit between increase/decrease rows.

DETERMINING DISTRIBUTION OF DOUBLE INCREASES/DECREASES

Up to this point, the basic formula has been used to increase just 1 stitch in each interval. But there are circumstances when you will need to increase/decrease more stitches than there are shaping rows available to perform those actions. In these scenarios, double (2-stitch) increases/decreases will need to be worked as well as single (1-stitch) increases/decreases. The shaping formula can be used to calculate an even distribution of these double increases/decreases.

For example, let's say you are shaping the V-neckline on a cardigan and need to decrease 46 stitches over 68 rows and that you want to work the decreases on right-side rows only. Therefore, there are only 34 right-side rows available for working the 46 decreases. You would therefore need to work double decreases on some of the 34 rows in order to decrease the necessary 46 stitches.

Step One: Subtract the number of stitches to increase/decrease (46) from the number of available shaping rows (34) to determine the number of rows that will require double increases/decreases (12).

Step Two: Subtract the number of double-decrease rows (12) from the number of shaping rows (34) to determine the number of rows that will require single increases/decreases (22).

Step Three: Use the shaping formula to divide the number of double-decrease rows (12) into the number of shaping rows (34) to determine an even distribution of double-decrease rows. In this example, decrease 2 stitches on every 2nd decrease row 2 times, then decrease 2 stitches on every 3rd decrease row 10 times. The other 22 shaping rows will involve single increases or decreases.

$$12\overline{)34} \quad \begin{array}{c} ②+1=③ \\ \underline{-24} \\ 12-⑩ = ② \end{array}$$

MATH CHECK

$$② \times ② = 4$$
$$③ \times ⑩ = 30$$
$$12 / 34$$

OTHER APPLICATIONS

PICKING UP STITCHES

There are occasions when you will want to pick up stitches along a knitted edge where the gauge needed for the pick-up stitches will be different from the gauge of the knitted section. Use the shaping formula to calculate an even rate of pick-ups.

Step One: Determine the stitch count for the length based on the gauge of the pick-up pattern, then determine the number of rows in the section where stitches will be picked up.

Step Two: Subtract the smaller number from the larger to determine the number of rows to skip along the knitted edge or extra stitches to squeeze in while picking up.

Step Three: Divide the larger number by the number of rows to skip or squeeze in stitches and use the diagonal relationships in the shaping formula to determine an even placement of the skips or squeezes.

For example, let's say we want to pick up 105 ribbing stitches along a stockinette piece that is 120 rows long. In this example, we will skip a total of 15 rows along the length of the pick up. Use the shaping formula to determine the distribution of the rows to be skipped. In this case, skip every 8th row 15 times.

$$15\overline{)120} \quad \begin{array}{c} 8 \\ \underline{-120} \\ 0 \end{array}$$

To avoid placing the first skip at the very bottom and skipping the last row, divide one interval in half and, in this case, position the first skipped row on the fourth row: Pick up 1 stitch in every row for 3 rows, skip 1 row, [pick up 1 stitch every row for 7 rows, skip 1 row] 14 times, pick up 1 stitch on the next row, skip 1 row, pick up 1 stitch in the final 2 rows.

BUTTONHOLE PLACEMENT

You can also use the shaping formula to plan for an even distribution of buttonholes when picking up stitches to work a horizontal buttonhole band. For example, let's say that we want to work 6 buttonholes along a band that measures 15" (38 cm) and that we want to place the bottom buttonhole $^5\!/_8$" (1.5 cm) above the bottom edge and the top button $^5\!/_8$" (1.5 cm) below the neck edge. For this example, our gauge is 6 stitches and 8 rows per inch (2.5 cm) on the body and 7 stitches and 9 rows per inch (2.5 cm) on the band.

Step One: Determine the total length of the buttonhole band by subtracting the neck depth from the total length of the garment. Multiply the band length by the stitch gauge to determine the number of stitches in the band.

    15" (38 cm) × 7 stitches/inch = 105 stitches in band

Step Two: Determine how far above the bottom of the sweater and how far below the top of the neck you want the first and last buttonholes placed, then subtract this length from the total length of the band. Multiply these lengths by the pick-up stitch gauge to calculate how many of the band stitches will fall below the first buttonhole and above the last buttonhole. (This example is for vertical buttonholes; the formula can also be used for horizontal buttonholes or vertically knitted bands.)

    $^5\!/_8$" (1.5 cm) × 7 stitches/inch = 4.375; round up to whole number = 5 stitches

Step Three: Subtract the number of stitches below the first buttonhole and above the last buttonhole from the total number of stitches in the band to determine the number of stitches in the buttonhole placement area. (Note: You already know that the first buttonhole will be worked after the 5th stitch.)

    105 stitches in band − 5 stitches below first buttonhole − 5 stitches above last buttonhole = 95 stitches in button placement area

Step Four: Use the shaping formula to divide the number of rows in the buttonhole placement area (95) by the number of remaining buttonholes (5). In this example, place the first buttonhole on the 5th stitch, then place the remaining five buttonholes on every 19th stitch.

$$\begin{array}{r} 19 \\ 5\overline{)\,95} \\ -95 \\ \hline 0 \end{array}$$

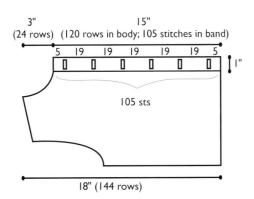

Use the shaping formula to determine pick-up stitches for a front band and button placement on a cardigan.

BIBLIOGRAPHY

Brunette, Cheryl. *Sweater 101*: How to Plan Sweaters that Fit . . . & Organize Your Knitting life at the Same Time.* Poughkeepsie, New York: Patternworks, 1991.

Cook, James Gordon. *Handbook of Textile Fibres: Natural Fibres.* 5th ed. Vol. 1. Durham, England: Merrow Publishing, 1984.

———. *Handbook of Textile Fibres: Man-Made Fibres.* 5th ed. Vol. 2. New York: Hyperion Books, 1984.

Duncan, Ida Riley. *The Complete Book of Progressive Knitting.* New York: Liveright, 1966.

Eichenseer, Erika. *Omas Strickgeheimnisse: 200 bezaubernde Muster.* Germany: Rosenheimer: Rosenheim, 2000.

Elalouf, Sion. *The Knitting Architect.* Knitting Fever, 1982.

Ellen, Alison. *The Handknitter's Design Book.* Newton Abbot, Devon: David & Charles, 1992.

Erickson, Mary Anne, and Eve Cohen. *Knitting by Design: A Step-by-Step Guide to Designing and Knitting Your Own Clothes.* Toronto: Bantam Books, 1986.

Fee, Jacqueline. *The Sweater Workshop.* Loveland, Colorado: Interweave, 1983.

Harmony Guide to Knitting Stitches. Vol. 1. London: Lyric Books, 1986.

Harmony Guide to Knitting Stitches. Vol. 2. London: Lyric Books, 1987.

Harmony Guide to Knitting Stitches. Vol. 3. London: Lyric Books, 1990.

The Harmony Guide to Aran Knitting. New York: Lyric Books, 1991.

The Harmony Guide to Knitting Techniques. London: Lyric Books, 1990.

Hiatt, June Hemmons. *Principles of Knitting: Methods and Techniques of Hand Knitting.* New York: Simon and Schuster, 1989.

Klopper, Gisela. *Beautiful Knitting Patterns.* New York: Sterling, 2005.

Michelson, Carmen, and Mary Ann Davis. *Knitter's Guide to Sweater Design.* Loveland, Colorado: Interweave, 1989.

Newton, Deborah. *Designing Knitwear.* Newtown, Connecticut: Taunton, 1992.

Pizzuto, Joseph James, Allen C. Cohen, and Art Price. *Fabric Science.* 4th ed. New York: Fairchild, 1980.

Righetti, Maggie. *Sweater Design in Plain English.* New York: St. Martin's Press, 1990.

Robinson, Debby. *The Encyclopedia of Knitting Techniques.* New York: Gallery Books, 1989.

Shida, Hitomi. *Knitting Patterns Book 250.* Tokyo: Nihonbogusha: Nihon Vogue, 2005.

Stanley, Montse. *Handknitter's Handbook.* Newton Abbot, Devon: David & Charles, distributed in the United States by Sterling Pub. Co., 1986.

Stewart, Evelyn Stiles. *The Right Way to Knit Book 2.* Columbus, Ohio: Knit Services, 1969.

Thomas, Mary. *Mary Thomas's Knitting Book.* New York: Dover Publications, 1972.

Thomas, Mary. *Mary Thomas's Book of Knitting Patterns.* New York: Dover Publications, 1972.

Vogue Knitting The Ultimate Knitting Book. New York: Pantheon Books, 1989.

Walker, Barbara G. *A Treasury of Knitting Patterns.* New York: Charles Scribner's Sons, 1968.

Walker, Barbara G. *A Second Treasury of Knitting Patterns.* New York: Charles Scribner's Sons, 1970.

SOURCES FOR SUPPLIES

YARNS

Artyarns (wholesale only; see website for retail locations)
39 Westmoreland Ave.
White Plains, NY 10606
artyarns.com

Jade Sapphire Exotic Fibres (wholesale only; see website for retail locations)
West Nyack, NY 10994
jadesapphire.com

Knit One Crochet Too (wholesale only; see website for retail locations)
91 Tandberg Tr., Unit 6
Windham, ME 04062
knitonecrochettoo.com

Tahki/Stacy Charles Inc.
70-30 80th St., Bldg. 36
Ridgewood, NY 11385
tahkistacycharles.com

Trendsetter Yarns, intl. (wholesale only; see website for retail locations)
16745 Saticoy St., Ste. 101
Van Nuys, CA 91406
trendsetteryarns.com

BUTTONS

M&J Trimming (buttons for Cable Coat)
1008 6th Ave. at 38th St.
New York, NY 10018
(Blue Coat buttons)

Tender Buttons (buttons for Pea Coat and Duster)
143 E. 62nd St.
New York, NY 10065

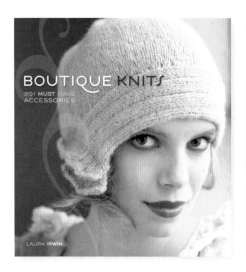

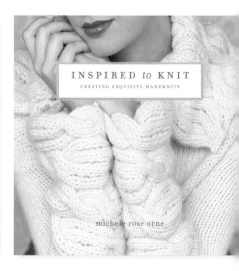